Hymn and Scripture
Selection Guide

Hymn and Scripture Selection Guide

A Cross-Reference Tool for Worship Leaders

(Revised and Expanded)

Donald A. Spencer

BAKER BOOK HOUSE
Grand Rapids, Michigan 49516

Published by Baker Book House Company
P.O. Box 6287, Grand Rapids, MI 49516-6287

ISBN: 0-8010-8339-7

Printed in the United States of America

With Love and Gratitude
To
My wife, Barbara,
our children, Todd, Amy, and Stephanie,
and to my parents, Mr. and Mrs. Amos Spencer

Contents

Introduction

Who Can Use this Book?

Pastors
Ministers of Music
Students of Hymnology
Leaders of Church-Related Organizations
Anyone finding value in correlated use of hymns and Scripture

For Pastors

An example: Pastor Smith is preparing his sermon for Sunday morning. He has selected Scripture and given the sermon a title. As he continues to develop the sermon, he must take time to prepare the entire service. As he begins, the immediate question surfaces: "Which hymns would be most suitable?" Pastor Smith is aware that many members of his church have probably learned as many Biblical truths through singing as through his sermons. If he can find the right hymns to go with his sermon emphasis he will strengthen the service. He turns to his copy of *Hymn and Scripture Selection Guide* and finds several suitable hymns he will use. Two of the hymns correlating with his sermon are not found in his church's hymnal. The poetic text of one of these hymns will be a meaningful addition to his sermon.

For Ministers of Music

An example: Mrs. Johnson's pastor has just given her the sermon topic and text for Sunday. It is her responsibility to "put the rest of the service together." She must also finalize plans for a special hymn service to be held Sunday evening. She turns to her *Hymn and Scripture Selection Guide*. In the first section she finds two hymns for Sunday morning that will correlate with the pastor's sermon emphasis. She then turns to the second section. She wants the special Sunday evening service to be more than just a "fun time of singing." She locates various Scripture passages she can use with many of the hymns to make the entire service a more spiritual experience.

Others

An example: John and Susan are hosting a Bible study group in their home. After some time around the piano singing some "old favorites," John asks the group to sing two specific songs, chosen by using his *Hymn and Scripture Selection Guide*. He leads the group in talking about the two hymns and moves into the correlating Bible study passage for the evening.

In each of these examples, the leaders sought to make worship and Bible study more meaningful by correlating the use of hymns and Scripture. *Hymn and Scripture Selection Guide* was the tool they needed to accomplish this task with minimal research.

Hymn and Scripture Selection Guide was originally published in 1977 by Judson Press. Since that time new hymnals have emerged with new hymns. Therefore, a revision was in order, omitting 43 hymns from the 1977 edition and adding 95 hymns.

The decision of how many hymns and which ones should be included has been made by examining over 20 denominational and interdenominational hymnals published in recent years. A custom computer program was used to rank each hymn. More weight was given to those in more recently published hymnals and to those in the most widely circulated hymnals. The result is the 432 hymns you find in this book. It is likely that more than half of the hymns in this book will be found in almost any major evangelical hymnal, making this book an invaluable tool.

Hymns with Scripture References

The first section of *Hymn and Scripture Selection Guide* presents the 432 hymns in alphabetical order. The related Scripture passages, taken from the Old and New Testaments as commonly in use by American Protestant denominations, are listed under each hymn. Passages that are directly related to a hymn, such as paraphrases and direct quotations, are in boldface type. Under the title of each hymn in italics there are topical headings and summary phrases intended to show the relationship between the hymn and the Scripture passage.

For practical purposes, the number of references is limited. In almost every case, many Scripture passages of marginal correspondence that could be listed for a hymn have been omitted. The effort of this work is to provide an adequate number of references for each hymn and for each stanza where appropriate. The user of this book may want to write in the margins additional Scripture references, notes, references to poems, comments, or similar information that one has found useful with a particular hymn.

Scripture with Hymn References

The second section of this book is a listing of **14,137** Scripture passages in their order as found in the Bible. Under each of these are hymns or stanzas of hymns that are, or could be, appropriate to that passage. The number of that hymn in *Hymn and Scripture Selection Guide* is listed along with the hymn title in an abbreviated form. Some references apply to particular stanzas or phrases and many Scripture passages may relate to multiple topics. Therefore, all hymns and Scripture references should be verified for compatibility with the desired emphasis.

Hymnals vary; therefore, if a stanza reference is given and the relationship is not apparent, the other stanzas of the hymn should be examined. Since stanzas used vary from hymnal to hymnal, one may need to check the hymn in part one of the book to determine exactly which stanza was referenced. The advantages of modern computer technology have been utilized in compiling this section of *Hymn and Scripture Selection Guide*. The 1977 edition depended on a number of manual techniques, continually re-compiling and transferring references. All references in the 1977 edition have been reviewed for accuracy. A computer program specifically written for compiling this book has greatly increased the accuracy and comprehensive nature of this section.

Topical Index

New to this edition of *Hymn and Scripture Selection Guide* is a topical index. Included are 2,562 topical references. The addition of this section will make this book an even more valuable tool for worship planning.

* * *

The author is grateful for suggestions of the publisher and of those having reviewed the 1977 edition. These suggestions have resulted in various enhancements, including:

In part one, when Scripture references are included for specific stanzas, those stanzas are identified by key words.

In part two, hymn references include an abbreviated hymn title, making this book more "user friendly."

A topical index has been added as part three.

Throughout the almost eight years spent in compiling the original edition of *Hymn and Scripture Selection Guide*, it was my prayer that it would be an effective tool in making congregational singing and worship more meaningful. I am grateful that many have affirmed its usefulness and have encouraged this revision. I pray it will be a valuable tool as users continue their efforts in meaningful correlation of hymns and Scripture.

"I will sing with the spirit, and I will sing with the understanding also" (1 Cor. 14:15, KJV).

Donald A. Spencer

Hymns with Scripture References

1. A Charge to Keep I Have

Charles Wesley, 1762

*An expression of commitment to a victorious
life and to serve God faithfully*

Deut. 10:12; John 12:26; Eph. 2:10; 4:1; 1 Peter
4:10–11

St. 1 (A charge . . .) John 15:8; 1 Cor. 6:20

St. 2 (To serve . . .) Eph. 5:17

St. 3 (Arm me . . .) Rom. 14:12; 2 Cor. 5:9–10

St. 4 (Help me . . .) Eph. 6:10; Phil. 3:14

2. A Child of the King

Harriett E. Buell, 1877

Relationship with God expressed as adoption

Rom. 8:14–17; John 1:12; Gal. 4:1–7; Eph. 1:5;
1 John 3:1–2

St. 1 (My Father is rich . . .) Ps. 104:24

St. 2 (My Father's own Son . . .) Phil. 2:5–11

St. 3 (I once was an . . .) Ps. 51:5

St. 4 (A tent or a cottage . . .) 2 Cor. 5:1

3. A Mighty Fortress Is Our God

Martin Luther, 1529

*Expression of dependence and confidence in
God as Divine helper; God as our refuge and
strength*

Psalm 46

Deut. 33:27; 2 Sam. 22:2–4; Pss. 59:16–17; 73:26;
91:2; 94:22; 118:6, 8; Isa. 26:4; 40:28–29; Heb.
2:14–17; 6:13–19; 13:6

A Pilgrim Was I and A-wandering, see
"Surely Goodness and Mercy"

A Ruler Once Came to Jesus By Night, see
"Ye Must Be Born Again"

4. A Shelter in the Time of Storm

Vernon J. Charlesworth;
adapted by Ira D. Sankey, 1885

Testimony of faith and dependence on our Lord

1 Sam. 2:2; Pss. 62:7; 94:22; Isa. 32:2

A Wonderful Savior Is Jesus My Lord, see
"He Hideth My Soul"

5. Abide with Me

Henry F. Lyte, 1847

*Evening; peace and comfort; God's presence in
life and death*

Pss. 23:4; 92:2; 139:7–12; 145:18; Matt. 28:20; Luke
24:29; 1 John 3:24

6. According to Thy Gracious Word

James Montgomery, 1825

Remembrance of the Lord's Supper

Luke 22:19–20

Matt. 26:26–29; John 6:53–58; 1 Cor. 11:23–28

**Ah, Dearest Jesus, How Hast Thou
Offended?,** see "Ah, Holy Jesus, How Hast
Thou Offended?"

7. Ah, Holy Jesus, How Hast Thou
Offended?

Johann Heermann, c. 1630

*Incarnation; Jesus' suffering and death for our
sin*

Isa. 53; John 10:11; 19:17–30; Rom. 5:6–11; Gal.
3:13; 1 Peter 3:18

Alas! And Did My Savior Bleed?, see "At the
Cross"

8. Alas! And Did My Savior Bleed?

Isaac Watts, 1707

*Atonement; death of Christ for my sins; salva-
tion*

Isa. 53; John 19:17–18; Rom. 5:6–11; 2 Cor. 1:5;
Eph. 1:7; 2:13; Col. 1:20–22; Heb. 9:12–26; 1 John
1:7; 4:19

9. All Creatures of Our God and King
St. Francis of Assisi, 1225
Praise and adoration to God as creator
Pss. 145:10–13; 148
Pss. 96:1–6; 117; 150:6; Rom. 11:36; Rev. 4:11

10. All for Jesus   Mary D. James, 1889
Expression of total and complete consecration
Matt. 22:37; Rom. 6:13; 12:1–2; 2 Cor. 5:15

11. All Glory, Laud and Honor
Theodulph of Orleans, c. 800
Palm Sunday; praise to Christ as King
Mark 11:1–10: John 12:1–13

12. All Hail the Power of Jesus' Name
E. Perronet, 1780
and J. Rippon, 1787
Worship of Christ as Lord and King; name of Christ
Zech. 14:9; Phil. 2:9–11; Col. 1:15–19; Rev. 5:13;
11:15
St. 1 (All hail the power . . .) Ps. 148:2; Rev.
5:11–13; 7:11–12
St. 2 (Ye chosen seed of . . .) Deut. 7:6–9; Eph.
1:4–6; 1 Peter 2:9; Rev. 17:14
St. 3 (Let every kindred . . .) Ps. 145:21

13. All My Heart This Night Rejoices
Paul Gerhardt, 1653
Trans. Catherine Winkworth, 1858
Expression of joy and worship at Christmas
Luke 1:14; 2:8–10; 2:11

All My Heart Today Rejoices, see "All My
Heart This Night Rejoices"

All My Life Long I Had Panted, see "Satisfied"

14. All People That On Earth Do Dwell
William Kethe, 1561
*Joyful praise and adoration for the loving care
and guidance of an omnipotent God*
Psalm 100
1 Chron. 16:23–36; Pss. 2:11; 67:3; 150:6; Jer.
33:11
St. 1 (All people . . .) Ps. 100:1–2

St. 2 (Know that . . .) Ps. 100:3
St. 3 (O enter . . .) Ps. 100:4
St. 4 (For why? . . .) Ps. 100:5

All Praise to Him Who Reigns Above, see
"Blessed Be the Name"

15. All Praise to Thee, My God, This Night
Bishop Thomas Ken, 1674
*Evening; praise for day and prayer for peaceful
night's rest enabling service for God*
Pss. 4:8; 42:8; 63:6; 92:1–2; Prov. 3:24; Luke 24:29;
1 Thess. 4:14

16. All That Thrills My Soul Is Jesus
Thoro Harris, 1931
*Testimony of the love, grace, and redemption
that is ours through Jesus Christ*
John 15:9–11; Rom. 6:8–11; Gal. 2:20; Col. 3:11
St. 2 (Love of Christ so . . .) Rom. 5:15; Eph.
3:18–19
St. 3 (What a wonderful . . .) Isa. 1:18
St. 4 (Ev'ry need His hand . . .) Phil. 4:19
St. 5 (By the crystal . . .) Isa. 35:10; Rev.
5:11–13; 22:1

17. All the Way My Savior Leads Me
Fanny J. Crosby, 1875
*Assurance and trust in Jesus' guidance and
leadership in life*
Pss. 32:8; 48:14; John 10:3–5; 12:26; 14:18, 27; 2
Cor. 3:5; 12:9
St. 2 (. . . Cheers each winding . . .) John 4:14;
6:32–35; 1 Cor. 10:4
St. 3 (. . . Oh, the fullness of . . .) Isa. 35:10;
John 14:1–3; Heb. 4:9

18. All Things Are Thine
John Greenleaf Whittier, 1872
Stewardship; church dedication
1 Chron. 29:14
Gen. 28:22; Lev. 27:30–33; 2 Chron. 2:4; Hag. 2:8;
Mal. 3:8–10; 1 Cor. 16:2

19. All Things Bright and Beautiful
Cecil F. Alexander, 1848
Praise for the beauty and blessings of God's creation
Pss. 104:24; 136:3–9; John 1:3; Rom. 1:20; Heb.
11:3; Rev. 4:11

All to Jesus I Surrender, see "I Surrender All"

Almighty Father, Strong to Save, see "Eternal Father, Strong to Save"

20. Am I a Soldier of the Cross?
Isaac Watts, 1724

Expression of commitment to endure and be good soldiers of Jesus Christ
2 Tim. 2:3–4
> 1 Cor. 16:13; Eph. 6:10–20; Phil. 1:27–30; 1 Tim. 6:12

21. Amazing Grace
John Newton, 1779
St. 5, John Rees, 1859

Testimony of God's infinite grace
> John 1:16–17; Rom. 5:20–21; 1 Cor. 15:10; 2 Cor. 12:9; Eph. 1:6–7; 2:4–9; Titus 2:11; 3:3–7

Last st. (When we've been there . . .) Ps. 145:1–2

22. America the Beautiful
Katharine Lee Bates, 1893

Prayer expressing desire for God's grace and blessing on America
> 2 Chron. 7:14; Ps. 33:12; Prov. 14:34

23. And Can It Be That I Should Gain?
Charles Wesley, 1738

Expression of wonder and confidence in God's love and his gift of salvation
> Pss. 13:5; 86:13; John 3:16–17; Rom. 5:8; Eph. 2:4–9

24. Angels, from the Realms of Glory
James Montgomery, 1816

Birth of Jesus . . . angels, shepherds and wise men came to worship the newborn king

St. 1 (Angels, from . . .) Luke 2:10–14; Heb. 1:6

St. 2 (Shepherds, in . . .) Matt. 1:23; Luke 2:8–20; John 1:9

St. 3 (Sages, leave . . .) Matt. 2:1–12

St. 4 (Saints, before . . .) Mal. 3:1

25. Angels We Have Heard on High
Traditional French Carol

Birth of Jesus . . . angels and shepherds
> Luke 2:7–20
> Refrain Luke 2:14

26. "Are Ye Able," Said the Master
Earl Marlatt, 1925

Expression of complete consecration
> Matt. 20:22; Mark 8:34; Luke 14:27; John 12:26

St. 2 (. . . to remember . . .) Luke 23:39–43

27. Are You Washed in the Blood?
Elisha A. Hoffman, 1878

Through God's grace we are cleansed by the blood of the Lamb
> Ps. 51:2, 7; Isa. 1:18; Eph. 1:6–8; Titus 3:5–7; Heb. 9:14; 1 Peter 1:18–19; 1 John 1:7–9; Rev. 7:14

St. 2 (Are you walking daily . . .) Eph. 5:2

St. 3 (When the Bridegroom . . .) Matt. 25:1–3

St. 4 (Lay aside the garments . . .) Gen. 35:2; Zech. 13:1

28. Are You (Art Thou) Weary, Heavy Laden?
John M. Neale, 1862

Based on an early Greek hymn
Rest and guidance sought from Jesus
Matt. 11:28–30
> Exod. 33:13–14; Ps. 55:22; Isa. 14:3; Heb. 4:1–11

St. 2 (Has he marks to lead . . .) John 20:25–27

St. 3 (Is there a diadem . . .) Matt. 27:29

Art Thou Weary, Art Thou Languid?, see "Are You (Art Thou) Weary, Heavy Laden?"

29. As with Gladness Men of Old
William C. Dix, 1860

Christmas; prayer that we may be led to Christ just as the wise men
> Matt. 2:1–12

30. Ask Ye What Great Thing I Know
Johann C. Schwedler, 1741

Faith; praise of Christ, the crucified
1 Cor. 2:2
> Mark 5:19; John 3:14–17; Acts 2:36; 1 Cor. 1:31; Gal. 2:20; 6:14; 1 Peter 3:15

31. At Calvary
William R. Newell, 1895

Testimony of God's love and grace through Christ's suffering and death on the cross; atonement; salvation
> Luke 23:33; Rom. 5:6–11; 1 Cor. 1:18; Eph. 2:13–18; 1 John 4:10; Rev. 1:5–6

32. At the Cross
Isaac Watts, 1707
Refrain: Ralph Hudson, 1885

Cross of Jesus; atonement; death of Christ for my sins; salvation
> Isa. 53; John 19:17–18; Rom. 5:6–11; 1 Cor. 1:18; Gal. 6:14; Eph. 1:7; 2:13; Heb. 9:12–26; 1 Tim. 1:15; 1 John 1:7; 4:19

33. At the Name of Jesus
Caroline M. Noel, 1870

Name of Jesus; humanity and Lordship of Christ; expression of submission to Christ
Phil. 2:9–11
> Ps. 72:19; Matt. 1:21; Acts 4:12

St. 1 (At the name of . . .) John 1:1; Phil. 2:10–11

St. 2 (At His voice . . .) Gen. 1:1; John 1:1–3

St. 3 (Humbled for a . . .) Rom. 8:3; Phil. 2:7–8

St. 4 (In your hearts . . .) Heb. 2:10; James 1:12

St. 5 (Brothers, this . . .) Luke 21:27

34. Awake, My Soul, and With the Sun
Thomas Ken, 1694

Morning; facing a new day renewed
> Pss. 5:3; 61:8; 92:1–2; 108:2–3; Rom. 13:11–12

35. Awake, My Soul, Stretch Every Nerve
Philip Doddridge, 1755

God calls us to run the race and receive our reward
Heb. 12:1–2
> 1 Cor. 9:24; Phil. 2:16; 3:12–14

36. Away in a Manger
Anonymous, c. 1885

Birth of Christ; God's care of children
> Mark 10:13–16; Luke 2:7, 12, 16; Eph. 5:1

Battle Hymn of the Republic, see "Mine Eyes Have Seen the Glory"

Be Not Dismayed Whate'er Betide, see "God Will Take Care of You"

37. Be Still, My Soul
Katharina A. von Schlegel, 1752

Expression of quiet confidence in God's providential care, guidance, and leadership
Ps. 46:10
> Pss. 27; 37:3–5; 118:8; Prov. 3:5; Isa. 30:15

St. 2 (. . . thy God doth . . .) Ps. 107:28–30; Mark 4:37–41; Heb. 10:34

St. 3 (. . . the hour is . . .) Rev. 7:17; 21:4

38. Be Thou My Vision
Ancient Irish hymn
Trans. Mary E. Byrne, 1905

Testimony of God's care, guidance, supremacy, and example; unity with God
> Prov. 29:18; Matt. 5:48; 19:21; 1 Cor. 8:6; Eph. 5:1; Phil. 3:7, 12; Heb. 7:26; 1 Peter 2:21; 1 John 5:20

St. 2 (Be Thou my wisdom . . .) John 1:12; 14:20

St. 3 (Riches I heed not . . .) Matt. 6:19–21

39. Because He Lives
Gloria and William Gaither, 1971

Testimony that "Life is worth the living" because Jesus lives
John 14:19
> Rom. 6:9–11; 1 Cor. 15:55–57; Heb. 7:24–25

40. Begin, My Tongue, Some Heavenly Theme
Isaac Watts, 1707

Acknowledging an omnipotent God's boundless love, mercy, and faithfulness
> 1 Chron. 16:8; Pss. 26:7; 35:28; 40:10–11; 86:8; 89:1; 145; Isa. 25:1

St. 4 (O might I hear . . .) Matt. 25:21

41. Beneath the Cross of Jesus
Elizabeth C. Clephane, 1872

We take our stand beneath Jesus' cross and express those things we feel when thinking of the cross
> Isa. 32:2; Luke 9:23; 1 Cor. 1:17–18; Gal. 6:14

42. Blessed Assurance
Fanny J. Crosby, 1873

Testimony; joy of the new life in Christ; submission to God
> Ps. 40:3; Isa. 12:2; Rom. 8:16–17; 15:13; Titus 2:13; 3:5–7; Heb. 13:12–15; 1 Peter 1:7–9; Rev. 1:5–6

43. Blessed Be the Name
William H. Clark, 19th century
Refrain, Ralph Hudson, 1887

Praise to Christ as Savior; name of Christ; reign of Christ
> Ps. 7:17; Matt. 12:21; Acts 4:12; Phil. 2:9–11; Heb. 1:3–4; Rev. 5:12

St. 1 (All praise to Him . . .) 1 John 4:14; Rev. 11:15

St. 2 (His name above all . . .) Mark 16:19; Acts 5:31

St. 3 (Redeemer, Savior . . .) John 3:16–17; Rev. 1:5–6

St. 4 (His Name shall be . . .) Isa. 9:6

44. Blessed Jesus, at Thy Word
Tobias Clausnitzer, 1671
Trans. C. Winkworth, 1858
Through Jesus and with the aid of the Holy Spirit, we approach God in worship
Ps. 96:8–9; Luke 11:28; John 4:23–24; Heb. 13:15–16

St. 2 (All our knowledge . . .) 1 Cor. 2:10; Eph. 2:18

St. 3 (Glorious Lord, Thy . . .) 2 Sam. 22:29; Ps. 34:15

45. Blessed Redeemer
Avis B. Christiansen, 1920
Expression of love and praise as one recalls Jesus' love, suffering, and death
Luke 23:12–46; 1 Cor. 15:3; 2 Cor. 5:15; 1 Peter 3:18

St. 2 (Father, forgive them . . .) Luke 23:33–34

46. Blest Be the Tie That Binds
John Fawcett, 1782
Mutual concern and fellowship of Christians
Ps. 133:1; John 13:34–35; Rom. 12:5; 15:1–2; Gal. 3:28; 6:2; 1 Peter 3:8

47. Bread of the World in Mercy Broken
Reginald Heber, 1827
Prayer expressing desire for God's grace as we contemplate the meaning of the Lord's Supper
John 6:51
Matt. 26:26–28; John 6:58; 1 Cor. 11:23–26

48. Break Thou the Bread of Life
Mary A. Lathbury, 1877
The nourishing of our spiritual lives by God's Word is compared to Jesus' feeding of the multitude; prayer that God's Spirit will help us to understand the truth of the Scripture
Deut. 8:3; Jer. 15:16; Matt. 4:4; 14:15–21; Luke 24:32, 45; John 6:35

St. 1 (Break Thou the bread . . .) John 5:39

St. 2 (Bless Thou the truth . . .) Ps. 119:44–45; John 8:32

St. 3 (Thou art the bread of . . .) John 17:17; 2 Tim. 3:15–16

St. 4 (O send Thy Spirit . . .) 1 Cor. 2:10–13; 2 Peter 1:20–21

49. Breathe on Me, Breath of God
Edwin Hatch, 1878
Prayer for the Holy Spirit's indwelling so God's will might prevail in our lives
John 20:22
Ezek. 36:27; Matt. 3:11; Rom. 8:9–11; 2 Cor. 3:17–18; Gal. 5:5, 17–18, 22–25; 1 John 4:13

50. Brethren, We Have Met to Worship
George Atkins, 1825
A call to fellow Christians to worship
Pss. 29:2; 95:6–7; 122:1; John 4:23–24; 6:58

Last st. (Let us love our . . .) Luke 22:30; 1 John 3:11; Rev. 2:17

51. Brightest and Best of the Sons of the Morning
Reginald Heber, 1811
Christmas; the star leads to the true light; like the wise men, we praise him and offer our gifts
Matt. 2:1–12; Rev. 22:16

52. Built on the Rock
Nikolai F. S. Grundtvig, 1837
Trans. Carl Doving, 1909
Christ as foundation of the church and present in its worship; our bodies are the temple of Christ
Matt. 16:15–18; 18:20; Acts 7:48–50; 2 Cor. 6:16; Eph. 1:22–23; 2:19–22; Col. 1:18

Calling Today, see "Jesus Is Tenderly Calling"

53. Children of the Heavenly Father
Caroline Sandell Berg, 1855
Trans. Ernest W. Olson, 1925
God's guidance and care of his children
Pss. 97:10; 103:13, 17; 2 Tim. 4:18; 1 Peter 5:10

St. 1 (Children of the . . .) Prov. 14:26; Gal. 3:26

St. 2 (God His own doth . . .) Gen. 50:21; Acts 2:25; 2 Thess. 3:3

St. 3 (Neither life nor . . .) John 10:28; Rom. 8:38–39

St. 4 (Though he giveth . . .) Job 1:21; Ps. 37:28; 1 Thess. 5:23

54. Christ Arose
Robert Lowry, 1874
Easter; resurrection of Christ; praise for Christ's victory over death and the grave

Acts 13:29–30; 1 Cor. 15:4, 20–23

St. 1 and 2 Matt. 27:57–66; Mark 15:46–47

St. 3 and Refrain Matt. 28:1–9; Mark 16:1–6; Rom. 6:9; 14:9

55. Christ for the World We Sing
Samuel Wolcott, 1869

World missions; based on theme: 'Christ for the world and the world for Christ'

Pss. 40:3; 67:2; 96:2–3; Mark 13:10; 16:15; Luke 24:47; Rom. 10:12–15; 1 Peter 4:10–11; 1 John 5:4–5

St. 4 (. . . with joyful song . . .) Isa. 51:11

Christ Has for Sin Atonement Made, see "What a Wonderful Savior"

56. Christ Is Made the Sure Foundation
7th Century, Latin Hymn
Trans. John M. Neale, 1851

The church's foundation is Jesus Christ

Ps. 118:21–23; 1 Cor. 3:11; Eph. 1:22–23; 2:20–22; Col. 1:18; 2 Tim. 2:19

57. Christ Is the World's True Light
George W. Briggs, 1931

Christ is the light of the world, including all nations; world unity in Christ

John 1:4–5, 9; 8:12; 1 Cor. 8:6; 12:13; Col. 3:11

St. 1 (Christ is the world's . . .) John 12:46; Heb. 2:10, 14–15

St. 2 (In Christ all races . . .) Joel 3:10; Gal. 3:26–29

St. 3 (One Lord, in one great . . .) John 10:16; Rev. 11:15

58. Christ Receiveth Sinful Men
Erdmann Neumeister, 1718

By grace, we are cleansed and made acceptable to God through Christ

Isa. 55:7; Mic. 7:18–19; Luke 15:2; Acts 10:43; Eph. 1:6–8; 1 Tim. 1:14–15; Titus 2:11; 3:5–7

St. 2 (Come, and He will give . . .) Matt. 11:28–29

St. 3 (Now my heart condemns . . .) Rom. 6:14; 8:1; Heb. 9:14

St. 4 (Christ receiveth sinful . . .) John 6:37

Christ Returneth, see "It May Be at Morn"

59. Christ the Lord Is Risen Today
Charles Wesley, 1739

Praise for the resurrection of Christ

Matt. 28:1–9; Acts 2:24–32; Rom. 6:9–10; 1 Cor. 15:20–23, 54–57

60. Christ, Whose Glory Fills the Skies
Charles Wesley, 1740

Christ as the light of life for the Christian in a world of darkness; worship; morning

Isa. 9:2; Mal. 4:2; John 1:4–9; 8:12; 12:46; 2 Cor. 4:6; 1 Thess. 5:4–5; Rev. 21:23

61. Close to Thee
Fanny J. Crosby, 1874

Expression of desire to stay close to God in one's Christian walk

Ps. 23; Acts 17:27–28; James 4:8

62. Come, Christians, Join to Sing
Christian Henry Bateman, 1843

A call to joyful and eternal praise of Christ, the King

Pss. 67:3; 95:1–3; 145:1–3; Col. 3:16; Heb. 13:15; 1 Peter 2:9

St. 1 (Come, Christians . . .) Ps. 150:6

St. 2 (Come, lift your . . .) John 15:13

St. 3 (Praise yet our . . .) Rev. 5:11–13

Come, Every Soul by Sin Oppressed, see "Only Trust Him"

63. Come, Holy Ghost, Our Souls Inspire
Rabanus Maurus, 9th Century
Trans. John Cosin, 1627

Prayer for the presence, power, and leadership of the Holy Spirit

Ezek. 36:27; Matt. 3:11; Luke 11:13; John 14:16; Acts 2:38; Rom. 5:5; 8:11–16; 1 Cor. 6:19; Eph. 3:16

Come, Holy Ghost, Creator Blest, see "Come, Holy Ghost, Our Souls Inspire"

64. Come, Holy Spirit, Dove Divine
Adoniram Judson, 1832

Prayer for the Holy Spirit's presence in baptism

Luke 3:21–22; Rom. 6:3–4; Col. 2:12

65. Come, Holy Spirit, Heavenly Dove
Isaac Watts, 1707

Prayer for Holy Spirit to kindle true love in our hearts

John 6:63; Rom. 5:5; 8:9–11; Gal. 5:22

St. 2 (In vain we . . .) Amos 5:23

Come, O Creator Spirit, Come, see "Come, Holy Ghost, Our Souls Inspire"

66. Come, Thou Almighty King

Anonymous, c. 1757

Prayer for divine presence in worship; praise to an omnipotent God, the Word Incarnate, and the Holy Spirit that is present in us; Trinity

Ps. 47:6–7; John 4:23–24; 2 Cor. 13:14; 1 John 5:7

St. 1 (Come, Thou Almighty . . .) 1 Chron. 29:10–13; Ps. 51:15

St. 2 (Come, Thou Incarnate . . .) John 1:14; Eph. 6:17

St. 3 (Come, holy Comforter . . .) John 14:16–18, 26; Rom. 15:13

St. 4 (To Thee, great One . . .) 1 John 5:7

67. Come, Thou Fount of Every Blessing

Robert Robinson, 1758

Praise for God's grace and blessing; salvation

Pss. 68:19; 107:8; Eph. 1:3; James 1:17

St. 1 (Come, Thou fount . . .) Ps. 66:2

St. 2 (Here I raise . . .) 1 Sam. 7:12; Ps. 56:13; Eph. 1:6–8

St. 3 (O to grace how . . .) Ps. 84:2; Jer. 3:22; 2 Cor. 1:22

68. Come, Thou Long–Expected Jesus

Charles Wesley, 1744

Jesus' birth; coming of long-desired Messiah; prayer for Christ's rule in our hearts

Isa. 9:6–7; Mal. 3:1; Matt. 1:22–23; Mark 1:1–3; Luke 1:32–35; 2:1–7

69. Come, We That Love the Lord

Isaac Watts, 1707

Songs of praise of saints marching to Zion, the beautiful city of God

Pss. 9:11; 50:2; 149:1–2; Isa. 35:10; Heb. 12:22; Rev. 14:1–3; 21:2

70. Come, Ye Disconsolate

St. 1, 2—Thomas Moore, 1824

St. 3—Thomas Hastings, 1831

Invitation to prayer for God's healing of all sorrows and sin's guilt

Ps. 34:18–19; 2 Cor. 1:3–7; 12:9; Heb. 4:16

St. 1 (Come, ye disconsolate . . .) Exod. 25:17–22

St. 2 (Joy of the desolate . . .) John 14:16–18, 26–27

St. 3 (Here see the Bread of . . .) John 6:32–35; Rev. 7:17; 22:1

71. Come, Ye Faithful, Raise the Strain

John of Damascus, 8th century

Trans. John M. Neale, 1859

Call to praise and rejoicing at Jesus' resurrection

Mark 16:6; Acts 2:24–32; 1 Cor. 15:20–22; 1 Peter 1:3

72. Come, Ye Sinners, Poor and Needy

Joseph Hart, 1759

Invitation to accept Christ as Savior

Matt. 5:6; 11:28; Mark 10:16; John 6:37; Rev. 22:17

St. 2 (Come, ye thirsty . . .) John 4:14

73. Come, Ye Thankful People, Come

Henry Alford, 1844

Harvesttime compared to spiritual harvest; thanksgiving at harvesttime; parable of wheat and tares

Matt. 13:24–30; 36–43

Heb. 13:15; Rev. 14:15

74. Count Your Blessings

Johnson Oatman, Jr. 1897

In discouragement, conflict and burdens, we should view these in light of the ways God has blessed and promises to continue blessing us

Pss. 40:5; 68:19; 103:1–4; James 1:17

St. 1 (When upon life . . .) Ps. 42:5; Isa. 54:11

St. 2 (Are you ever . . .) Ps. 55:22; 1 Peter 4:13; 5:7

St. 3 (When you look . . .) Prov. 22:2; Matt. 6:19–21; Acts 20:33

St. 4 (So amid the . . .) Isa. 41:13

Creator Spirit, By Whose Aid, see "Come, Holy Ghost, Our Souls Inspire"

75. Crown Him with Many Crowns

Matthew Bridges, 1851

St. 6—Godfrey Thring, 1874

We acknowledge Christ as Lord and King; each "crown" represents an aspect of Christ

Matt. 25:31; Luke 1:32–33; Rom. 14:9; Heb. 2:7–10; 12:2; Rev. 19:12

St. 1 (. . . with many crowns . . .) 1 Peter 3:22; Rev. 5:11–14; 11:15

St. 2 (. . . the Son of God . . .) Heb. 4:15; 1 John 4:15

St. 3 (. . . the Lord of Love . . .) John 20:20; 1 John 3:16a

St. 4 (. . . the Lord of Peace . . .) Isa. 9:6–7; John 14:27; 16:33

St. 5 (. . . the Lord of Years . . .) Ps. 102:24–25; Col. 1:16–17

St. 6 (. . . the Lord of Life . . .) John 1:4; 11:25–26; Rom. 6:8–11

76. Day by Day
Caroline Sandell Berg, 1865
Trans. A. L. Skoog

We look to God for strength and help in each day of our lives

Deut. 33:25; Ps. 55:22; Isa. 26:3; 40:29; 41:10; John 14:27; 2 Cor. 1:3–5; Heb. 4:16; 1 Peter 5:7

77. Day Is Dying in the West
Mary A. Lathbury, 1877

Evening; expression of man's closeness to God and nature

Pss. 4:8; 19:1–2; 104:23–24; Luke 24:29
Refrain Ps. 69:34; Isa. 6:3

78. Dear Lord and Father of Mankind
John G. Whittier, 1872

Expression of quiet confidence in God's leadership

Ps. 4:4; Isa. 26:3; 30:15; Hab. 2:20; Rom. 8:6; 1 John 1:9

St. 1 (Dear Lord and Father . . .) Ps. 25:11; Mark 5:15; Eph. 4:23

St. 2 (In simple trust like . . .) Matt. 4:18–22; Luke 9:23

St. 3 (O sabbath rest by . . .) Luke 6:12

St. 4 (Drop Thy still dews . . .) John 16:33; 2 Thess. 3:16

St. 5 (Breathe through the . . .) 1 Kings 19:9–13

79. Depth of Mercy! Can There Be?
Charles Wesley, 1740

When I repent, God's great mercy, love, and grace triumph over my sin

Ps. 86:5; Isa. 44:22; 55:7; Mic. 7:18–19; Luke 18:13; Rom. 2:4; Eph. 2:4–5; 1 Tim. 1:14–15

80. Down at the Cross
Elisha A. Hoffman, 1878

Testimony of salvation through the cross and blood of Christ; name of Christ

Ps. 79:9; Zech. 13:1; John 19:17–18; Acts 4:12; Rom. 5:6–11; Eph. 2:13; Col. 1:20–23; Titus 2:14; 3:5–6; 1 Peter 2:24; Rev. 1:5–6

Draw Me Nearer, see "I Am Thine, O Lord"

Dying with Jesus, By Death Reckoned Mine, see "Moment by Moment"

Encamped Along the Hills of Light, see "Faith Is the Victory"

81. Eternal Father, Strong to Save
William Whiting, 1860

Prayer for God's protection and guidance for those on sea, land, and air; trinity

Ps. 95:3–6

St. 1 (Eternal Father . . .) Pss. 89:9; 107:23–32

St. 2 (O Christ, the Lord . . .) Matt. 8:23–27

St. 3 (O Spirit, whom the . . .) Gen. 1:1–2, 20; Isa. 40:31

St. 4 (O Trinity of love . . .) Ps. 107:31

82. Face to Face   Carrie E. Breck, 1898

Anticipation of heaven and seeing Christ face to face

1 Cor. 13:12

John 17:24; 2 Cor. 3:18; 5:8; 1 Thess. 4:13–17; 1 John 3:2; Rev. 22:4

St. 3 (What rejoicing in . . .) Isa. 40:4

83. Fairest Lord Jesus
Anonymous, 1677; Trans. 1873

Expression of simple praise and adoration of Christ; Jesus as fairer, brighter, and purer than all God's creation

Ps. 45:2; 1 Cor. 1:31; Phil. 2:9–11; 1 Tim. 6:16; Heb. 13:8

St. 1 (Fairest Lord Jesus! . . .) John 5:23; 1 Thess. 2:19–20

St. 2 (Fair are the meadows . . .) 1 John 3:3

St. 3 (Fair is the sunshine . . .) John 8:12; Heb. 1:3; Rev. 22:16

84. Faith Is the Victory
John H. Yates, 1891

*Faith is the victory that overcomes the world;
Christian warfare*
> Gal. 2:20; Eph. 6:10–18; 2 Tim. 2:3–4; 1 John
> 5:4–5; Jude 1:3

85. Faith of Our Fathers
Frederick W. Faber, 1849
*Christian heritage; we sing of the faith of our
forefathers*
Jude 1:1
> Pss. 22:4–5; 78:1–7; 145:4; Matt. 24:14; Col. 1:12

Far Away in the Depths of My Spirit, see
"Wonderful Peace"

86. Fight the Good Fight
John S. B. Monsell, 1863
*Christ is our guide and strength as we "fight the
fight" in running our course in life*
1 Tim. 6:12
> Rom. 8:37; 1 Cor. 15:57–58; Phil. 1:27–30; 3:14; 2
> Tim. 2:3–4; Heb. 10:23
> St. 1 (Fight the good fight . . .) Phil. 4:13; 1 Tim.
> 6:12; Rev. 2:10
> St. 2 (Run the straight race . . .) John 14:6; Phil.
> 3:14; Heb. 12:1
> St. 3 (Cast care aside, lean . . .) Prov. 3:5; 1 Peter
> 5:7
> St. 4 (Faint not nor fear . . .) John 20:31; Gal.
> 6:9; Col. 3:11

Fill Me Now, see "Hover O'er Me, Holy Spirit"

87. Footsteps of Jesus
Mary B. C. Slade, 1871
*Testimony expressing commitment to follow
Jesus*
> Luke 5:11; 9:57–62; John 10:4; 1 Peter 2:21
> St. 2 (Tho' they lead o'er . . .) John 9:1–11
> St. 3 (If they lead thro' . . .) Prov. 29:7
> St. 4 (Then at last, when . . .) Rev. 7:17

88. For All the Saints
William W. How, 1864
*Anticipation of joining all the saints of the past
in heaven*
> Acts 20:32; 1 Thess. 4:13–17; Heb. 4:9; 11:13–16; 1
> Peter 1:3–5; Rev. 14:13

89. For the Beauty of the Earth
Folliott S. Pierpoint, 1864

*Hymn of grateful praise for common blessings
of life*
> Pss. 68:19; 104:24; 107:21–22; Eph. 5:20; James
> 1:17; Rev. 14:7

90. Forth in Thy Name, O Lord, I Go
Charles Wesley, 1749
*Prayer for faithfulness in daily service and an
awareness of the presence of Christ; promise of
heaven for those who run the course in true service*
Ps. 71:16
> Luke 17:10; John 12:26; Col. 1:10; 3:17, 24

91. Free From the Law
Phillip P. Bliss, 1873
*Testimony of salvation through grace, not by
works of the law*
> Rom. 6:23; 8:2; 10:4; Heb. 10:10
> St. 1 (Free from the law . . .) John 8:36; Gal.
> 2:16; 3:13
> St. 2 (Now are we free . . .) Matt. 11:28; Rom.
> 8:1–3
> St. 3 (Children of God . . .) John 5:24; Rom.
> 8:15–17; Jude 24

92. From All That Dwell Below the Skies
Isaac Watts, 1719
*Worldwide and eternal praise to God as creator
and redeemer*
Ps. 117 paraphrase
> Pss. 67:3; 145:21; 148:5; 150:6; 1 Peter 2:9; Rev.
> 15:4

93. From Every Stormy Wind that Blows
Hugh Stowell, 1828
*We look to God and his mercy seat for help in
trouble*
> Exod. 25:17–22; Ps. 107:29; Isa. 25:4; 41:10; Lam.
> 3:22–23; 2 Cor. 1:3–5; Heb. 4:16
> St. 2 (There is a place where . . .) Isa. 61:3
> Last St. (Ah, there on eagle . . .) Isa. 40:31

94. From Heaven Above to Earth I Come
Martin Luther, 1535
Trans. Catherine Winkworth, 1855
Christmas; birth of Jesus
> Luke 1:30–33; 2:7–14; John 1:14

95. Gentle Mary Laid Her Child
Joseph S. Cook, 1919

Christmas; birth of Christ
Luke 2:7
Matt. 2:1–12; Luke 2:7–20; Gal. 4:4–5

96. Give to the Winds Thy Fears
Paul Gerhardt, 1653
Trans. John Wesley, 1739
Expression of trust in God in all of life and its
problems
Pss. 23:4; 34:4; 37:5; 56:3–4; Isa. 41:10; John 14:27;
2 Cor. 1:3–5; 1 Peter 5:7

97. Glorious Things of Thee Are Spoken
John Newton, 1779
Zion; God's eternal presence in the world and
church
Pss. 9:11; 87:3; Isa. 4:5; 33:20–21

St. 1 (Glorious things . . .) Pss. 48:1–2; 87:3;
Matt. 7:24–25; 16:18

St. 2 (See the streams . . .) Exod. 17:1–6; John
4:10–14

St. 3 (Round each habitation . . .) Exod.
13:21–22; 33:14; Num. 9:15

Glory to His Name, see "Down at the Cross"

98. Go, Tell It on the Mountain
Traditional Spiritual
Birth of Jesus; Christmas
Luke 2:8–20

99. Go to Dark Gethsemane
James Montgomery, 1820
We learn from Christ's experiences of prayer,
cross bearing, death, and resurrection
Phil. 3:10–11; 1 Peter 2:21

St. 1 (Go to dark . . .) Matt. 26:36–45; Luke
22:39–46

St. 2 (Follow to the . . .) John 18:28–40;
19:1–16; 2 Cor. 1:5

St. 3 (Calv'ry's . . .) John 19:16–30

St. 4 (Early hasten . . .) John 20:1–18

100. God Be with You
Jeremiah E. Rankin, 1880
Benediction; prayer for God's presence and care
Ps. 73:23–24; Acts 20:32; Rom. 15:33

St. 1 (. . . By his counsels . . .) Ps. 95:7; Isa.
40:11

St. 2 (. . . 'Neath his wings . . .) Deut. 8:3; Pss.
17:8; 36:7

St. 3 (. . . When life's perils . . .) Nah. 1:7

101. God Himself Is with Us
Gerhard Tersteegen, 1729
Awe in presence of God in worship
Gen. 28:15–17; Pss. 33:8; 89:7; 96:9; Hab. 2:20;
John 4:24; Acts 17:27

102. God Is My Strong Salvation
James Montgomery, 1827
God as our salvation, light, and strength
Ps. 27:1–3
Exod. 15:2; 2 Sam. 22:29; Pss. 29:11; 37:39; Isa.
12:2; 26:3; Eph. 6:10–13; 2 Thess. 3:3

103. God Moves in a Mysterious Way
William Cowper, 1773
We express trust and confidence in God's care
and guidance in spite of our failure to under-
stand his way and methods
Rom. 11:33–34
2 Sam. 22:7–20; Ps. 77:19; Prov. 3:5; Eccles. 3:11;
Jer. 17:7; Dan. 4:35; Mark 4:11

God of All Ages, see "God of Our Fathers"

104. God of Grace and God of Glory
Harry Fosdick, 1930
Prayer for wisdom and courage for daily living
from a God of grace and glory
Deut. 31:6; Ps. 84:11–12; 2 Cor. 1:12; 10:4; Eph.
6:10–17; Phil. 4:13; 2 Tim. 1:7; Heb. 4:16; 13:6;
James 1:5

105. God of Our Fathers
Daniel Roberts, 1876
Prayer for national care and guidance from
God in the future as in the past
Exod. 3:14–15; 1 Kings 8:57; Pss. 46:7; 78:4; 145:4;
Isa. 25:1; 63:16; Jer. 32:17–20; Dan. 4:3; 1 Tim.
2:1–2

God Sent His Son, see "Because He Lives"

106. God, That Madest Earth and Heaven
Reginald Heber and
Frederick L. Hosmer, 1827
Evening; prayer for God's presence and guid-
ance

Pss. 3:5; 42:8; 91:11; 104:23; 139:17–18; Prov. 3:24; Luke 24:29; 1 Thess. 5:9–10

107. God the Almighty One
Henry F. Chorley, 1842
John Ellerton, 1870
Prayer for peace to an Almighty God of mercy and righteousness in spite of man's failures and rebellion

Pss. 103:9–17; 116:5; Isa. 32:17; Dan. 9:3–19; Mic. 7:18; John 14:27

St. 1 (God the Omnipotent . . .) Job 37:2–5; Ps. 103:13

St. 2 (God the All merciful . . .) Pss. 6:1; 69:16; James 1:21

St. 3 (God the All righteous . . .) Pss. 119:142; 145:17–20; Luke 21:33

God, Who Made the Earth and Heaven, see "God, That Madest Earth and Heaven"

108. God Who Touchest Earth with Beauty
Mary S. Edgar, 1925
Prayer for renewal, purity, joy, strength, and righteousness; Christian living

Eccles. 3:11; Ezek. 36:25–27; Matt. 5:8; John 3:6; 2 Cor. 5:17; Eph. 4:22–24; Phil. 4:8

109. God Will Take Care of You
Civilla D. Martin, 1904
Expression of dependence on God's providential care

Deut. 31:8; Pss. 55:22; 57:1; 91:11; 121; Isa. 41:10; Luke 12:6–7; Phil. 4:19; 1 Peter 5:7

Good Christian Friends, Rejoice, see "Good Christian Men, Rejoice"

110. Good Christian Men, Rejoice
Anonymous, 14th Century
Trans. John M. Neale, 1853
Call to praise and rejoicing for Jesus' birth; Christmas

Matt. 2:10; Luke 2:10–20

111. Good Christian Men, Rejoice and Sing
Cyril A. Alington, 1925
Call to praise for Jesus' resurrection and victory over death

Luke 24:1–8; Acts 2:2

112. Grace Greater Than Our Sin
Julia H. Johnston, 1911
Testimony of God's great grace that pardons and cleanses our sins

Ps. 51:1–3, 7; Isa. 1:18; Rom. 3:24–26; 5:20; 6:14; Eph. 1:6–8; 2:4–9; Titus 3:5–7

113. Great God, We Sing That Mighty Hand
Philip Doddridge, 1755
New Year; God's support, guardian care, and hope in the future

Pss. 65:11; 89:13; 102:24; Prov. 4:10; Acts 26:22; 1 Peter 5:6

114. Great Is Thy Faithfulness
Thomas O. Chisholm, 1923
Testimony of God's great faithfulness, love, and mercy

Lam. 3:22–23; James 1:17

Deut. 7:9; Pss. 9:10; 36:5–7; 100:5; 102:25–27; Isa. 25:1; Luke 1:68–73; 1 Cor. 1:9

115. Guide Me, O Thou Great Jehovah
William Williams, 1745
Prayer for God's presence, guidance, and care

Pss. 23; 28:7; 48:14; 73:24; Phil. 4:19

St. 1 (Guide me, O . . .) Exod. 16:4, 18; Deut. 9:29

St. 2 (Open now the . . .) Exod. 13:21–22; 2 Sam. 22:2

St. 3 (When I tread . . .) Josh 3:17; Ps. 27:4–6; Rev. 1:18; 7:9–17

116. Hail the Day That Sees Him Rise
Charles Wesley, 1739
Praise for Jesus' ascension and eternal reign

Ps. 24:7; Acts 1:9–11; Heb. 9:24

117. Hail, Thou Once Despised Jesus
Attr. to John Bakewell, 1757
Alt. by Martin Madan, 1760
Praise for atonement, intercession, and forgiveness through Christ

Isa. 53:3–6; Luke 24:26; Gal. 3:13; Phil. 2:8–11; Heb. 2:9–10; 12:2; 1 Peter 1:18–19; Rev. 1:5–6

St. 1 (Hail, Thou once . . .) 1 Peter 2:24

St. 2 (Paschal Lamb, by . . .) Isa. 53:7; John 1:29; Eph. 1:7

St. 3 (Jesus, hail! . . .) Rom. 8:34; Heb. 7:25–26; 9:24

St. 4 (Worship, honor . . .) Rev. 5:9–13; 7:9–10

118. Hail to the Lord's Anointed
James Montgomery, 1821

Advent; praise at the coming of Christ

Ps. 72; Isa. 9:2, 6–7; Jer. 23:5–6; Matt. 11:3; Matt. 21:9; Luke 1:31–33; John 1:29; Acts 10:38

Hallelujah, What a Savior, see "Jesus, What a Friend for Sinners" and "Man of Sorrows, What a Name"

119. Happy the Home When God Is There
Henry Ware, Jr., 1846

Unity and happiness in the Christian home

Josh. 24:15; Matt. 12:25; Mark 10:7–9; Eph. 5:21–33; 6:1–4; Col. 3:18–21; 1 Tim. 5:8

120. Hark! The Herald Angels Sing
Charles Wesley, 1739

Praise at the birth of Jesus and for the purpose of Christ's coming to earth

Isa. 9:6; Luke 2:13–14; Gal. 4:4–6; Heb. 1:6

St. 1 (Hark! the herald . . .) Luke 2:11, 13–14

St. 2 (Christ, by highest . . .) Isa. 7:14; Matt. 1:21–23; John 1:14

St. 3 (Hail the heav'n . . .) Mal. 4:2; Luke 1:77–79

121. Hark, the Voice of Jesus Calling
Daniel March, 1868

Expression of commitment to serve God by doing our part to the best of our ability

Isa. 6:8

Matt. 9:37–38; 25:34–40; Luke 10:2; John 12:26; Col. 3:24

122. Have Thine Own Way, Lord
Adelaide A. Pollard, 1902

Personal expression of submission to the will of God

Deut. 26:16; Ps. 40:8; Rom. 6:13; 12:1–2; Heb. 13:21

St. 1 (. . . Thou art the potter . . .) Isa. 64:8; Jer. 18:3–6

St. 2 (. . . Search me and try me . . .) Pss. 51:7; 139:23

St. 3 (. . . Wounded and weary . . .) Pss. 62:11–12; 109:22

St. 4 (. . . Hold o'er my being . . .) Ezek. 36:27; Rom. 8:9–10

Have You Been to Jesus?, see "Are You Washed in the Blood?"

123. He Hideth My Soul
Fanny J. Crosby, 1890

Expression of confidence in God's care and in Jesus as Savior

Exod. 33:22; Ps. 5:11; Isa. 32:2; 1 John 4:14

St. 1 and Refrain Pss. 63:1; 91:1; 1 Cor. 10:4; 1 Tim. 1:15

St. 2 (. . . He taketh my burden away . . .) Ps. 55:22; 2 Cor. 12:9

St. 3 (With numberless blessings . . .) Ps. 68:19; Eph. 1:3

St. 4 (When clothed in his brightness . . .) Heb. 9:28; Rev. 3:5

124. He Keeps Me Singing
Luther B. Bridgers, 1910

The presence of Christ in our lives gives us a song in our heart

Isa. 41:10; John 15:11; Gal. 2:20

St. 1 (There's within my heart . . .) John 14:27; Eph 5:19

St. 2 (All my life was wrecked . . .) 2 Cor. 5:17

St. 3 (Feasting on the riches . . .) Ps. 63:7; 2 Tim. 2:1

St. 4 (Tho' sometimes He leads . . .) John 16:33

St. 5 (Soon He's coming back . . .) Luke 21:27; Col. 3:4; 1 Thess. 4:17

Refrain John 14:13; Phil. 2:9

125. He Leadeth Me
Joseph H. Gilmore, 1862

Expression of confidence in God's guidance and care in our lives and in death

Pss. 23; 48:14; 73:23–24; 139:1–12; Isa. 41:13; 48:17

He Lifted Me, see "In Loving Kindness Jesus Came"

126. He Lives
Alfred H. Ackley, 1933

Testimony: Christ lives today! Easter

Job 19:25; John 14:19; Rom. 6:4–11; Gal. 2:20; Phil. 3:10; 1 Peter 1:3; Rev. 1:18

St. 2 (In all the world . . .) Titus 2:13; James 5:8

St. 3 (Rejoice, rejoice . . .) John 16:22; Phil. 3:1

Refrain Eph. 3:17

127. He the Pearly Gates Will Open
Frederick A. Blom
Trans. Nathaniel Carlson
Testimony of Jesus' love and our anticipation of eternal life in heaven
John 15:9; Rom. 5:8; Rev. 22:14

128. He Who Would Valiant Be
John Bunyan, 1684
We follow Christ and depend on him in our Christian pilgrimage
Josh. 23:6; 1 Chron. 22:13; Ps. 60:12; 1 Cor. 15:58; 2 Cor. 10:4; 1 Tim. 6:12; 1 John 5:4

129. Heaven Came Down and Glory Filled My Soul
John W. Peterson, 1961
Testimony expressing the joy of salvation
2 Cor. 5:17; Eph. 1:7; 1 Tim. 1:15; 1 Peter 1:3
St. 1 (O what a wonderful . . .) John 8:12; 12:46; 2 Cor. 4:6
St. 2 (Born of the Spirit . . .) Acts 13:39; Rom. 5:1; 8:11
St. 3 (Now I've a hope . . .) John 14:2; 2 Cor. 5:1

130. Heavenly Sunlight
Henry J. Zelley, 1899
Testimony; Jesus is our light; we walk in his light
Isa. 9:2; John 1:4–5; 8:12; 12:46; Rom. 13:12; Eph. 5:8; Rev. 21:23–24

131. Here, O My Lord, I See Thee Face to Face
Horatius Bonar, 1855
Lord's Supper; Communion
Matt. 26:26–29; 1 Cor. 10:16–22; 11:23–26; 2 Cor. 4:18

132. Higher Ground
Johnson Oatman, Jr., 1898
Testimony of desire and effort to press on to new heights in Christian experience
1 Cor. 9:24; Phil. 3:12–14; Col. 3:1–2; Heb. 12:1–2

133. Holy Bible, Book Divine
John Burton, Sr., 1803
The value and importance of God's Word in our lives
Pss. 19:7–11; 119:9–11, 105; Rom. 15:4; 2 Tim. 3:15–16

Holy God, Thy Name We Bless, see "Holy God, We Praise Thy Name"

134. Holy God, We Praise Thy Name
Attr. to Ignaz Franz, 1774
Trans. Clarence Walworth, 1853
All earth and heaven throughout the ages give praise to God
Pss. 30:4; 99:9; 145:21; Isa. 6:3; 1 Peter 2:9; Rev. 15:4
St. 1 (Holy God, we praise Thy . . .) Heb. 1:8
St. 2 (Hark, the loud celestial . . .) Rev. 4:8–11
St. 3 (Lo! the apostolic train . . .) Ps. 145:4; Eph. 2:19–20
St. 4 (Holy Father, Holy Son . . .) 1 John 5:7

Holy Spirit, Breathe on Me, see "Breathe on Me, Breath of God"

135. Holy Spirit, Light Divine
Andrew Reed, 1817
Prayer for Holy Spirit's light, cleansing, joy, and complete control of our hearts
John 14:16; Rom. 8:9–11; 14:17; 1 Cor. 6:19; 12:7
St. 1 (. . . light divine . . .) Eph. 5:8–9
St. 2 (. . . power divine . . .) Luke 24:49; Titus 3:5
St. 3 (. . . joy divine . . .) Acts 13:52; Rom. 14:17
St. 4 (. . . all divine . . .) John 14:17

136. Holy Spirit, Truth Divine
Samuel Longfellow, 1864
Holy Spirit as divine truth, love, power, right, peace, and joy
1 Cor. 6:19; Gal. 5:22–23; Eph. 3:16; 2 Tim. 1:7; 1 John 2:20
St. 1 (. . . truth . . .) John 14:16–17; 16:13
St. 2 (. . . love . . .) John 13:35; Rom. 5:5
St. 3 (. . . power . . .) Luke 24:49; Acts 1:8
St. 4 (. . . right . . .) Rom. 8:1–4; 2 Cor. 3:17
St. 5 (. . . peace . . .) John 16:33; Rom. 8:6
St. 6 (. . . joy . . .) John 15:11; Acts 13:52; Rom. 14:17

137. Holy, Holy, Holy
Reginald Heber, 1826
Praise and adoration to a God of power, perfection, and holiness
Exod. 15:11; Deut. 32:3–4; Pss. 30:4; 113:3; 145:8–21; 148; Isa. 6:3; 1 John 5:7; Rev. 4:8–11

Holy, Holy, Holy, Lord God of Hosts, see "Day is Dying in the West"

138. Hope of the World
Georgia E. Harkness, 1954

Christ as the only hope for a lost world; world-wide missions

1 Cor. 3:11; 15:57; Col. 1:27; 1 Peter 1:3

St. 1 (. . . Thou Christ of great . . .) Matt. 9:36

St. 2 (. . . God's gift from high . . .) John 6:35; 2 Cor. 9:15

139. Hosanna, Loud Hosanna
Jeannette Threlfall, 1873

Palm Sunday; Christ's triumphal entry

Matt. 21:1–11; Mark 11:9–10; John 12:12–13

140. Hover O'er Me, Holy Spirit
Elwood R. Stokes, 1879

Prayer expressing desire for filling of the Holy Spirit

John 14:16–17; 1 Cor. 3:16; Eph. 5:18; 1 John 4:13

How Can I Say Thanks, see "My Tribute"

141. How Firm a Foundation
From Rippon's "A Selection of Hymns," 1787

Our foundation is faith in God's Word, presence, and his promises to us

Deut. 7:9; 31:6; Ps. 46:1; Isa. 28:16; Rom. 8:35–39; 1 Cor. 3:11; Heb. 13:5–6

St. 1 (How firm a foundation . . .) Luke 21:33

St. 2 (Fear not, I am with . . .) Isa. 41:10

St. 3 (When through the deep . . .) Ps. 18:6; Isa. 43:2

St. 4 (When through fiery . . .) Zech. 13:9; 1 Peter 1:7

St. 5 (The soul that on Jesus . . .) Acts 2:27; 1 Cor. 1:9

How Great Our Joy, see "While By the Sheep"

142. How Great Thou Art
Carl Boberg, 1886
Trans. Stuart K. Hine, 1949

Expression of praise and awe for God's power as seen in creation and redemption

Deut. 3:24; Pss. 48:1; 145:3

St. 1 and 2   Pss. 8:1, 3; 19:1

St. 3 (And when I think . . .) John 3:17; Rom. 8:3

St. 4 (When Christ shall . . .) John 14:3; Col. 3:4; 1 Thess. 4:16–17

143. How Sweet the Name of Jesus Sounds
John Newton, 1779

Expression of adoration, love, and praise for Jesus and all that his name represents

Ps. 8:9; John 20:31; Acts 4:12; Phil. 2:9–11

144. I Am His and He Is Mine
George W. Robinson, 1890

Expression of the believer's joy in an eternal relationship with Jesus

Jer. 31:3; Rom. 5:9–11; 6:4–11; 8:38–39; 14:8; Gal. 2:20; 1 John 4:13

I Am So Glad That Our Father in Heaven, see "Jesus Loves Even Me"

145. I Am Thine, O Lord
Fanny J. Crosby, 1875

Expression of desire to be closer to Christ, his love, and his will

Pss. 16:11; 73:28; John 15:4–5; Rom. 12:1–2; 14:8; 1 Cor. 7:22–24; Eph. 2:13; Heb. 10:22

St. 2 (Consecrate me now . . .) Rom. 7:6; Heb. 12:28

St. 3 (O, the pure delight . . .) Phil. 4:6

St. 4 (There are depths of . . .) Heb. 4:9; 1 Peter 4:13

146. I Am Trusting Thee, Lord Jesus
Frances R. Havergal, 1874

Expression of eternal trust in Jesus for salvation, guidance, and power

Ps. 37:3–5; Prov. 3:5; Isa. 26:3–4; Jer. 17:7; John 14:1; Gal. 2:20; 1 Peter 5:7

I Am Weak, But Thou Art Strong, see "Just a Closer Walk with Thee"

I Can Hear My Savior Calling, see "Where He Leads Me"

I Come to the Garden Alone, see "In the Garden"

147. I Gave My Life for Thee
Frances R. Havergal, 1858

Christ suffered and gave his life for me, therefore, I am indebted to him
> Ps. 116:12; Matt. 20:28; Rom. 12:1–2; 1 Cor. 6:20; 2 Cor. 5:15; Gal. 2:20; Eph. 2:1–8; Titus 2:14; 1 John 3:16

I Have a Song I Love to Sing, see "Since I Have Been Redeemed"

148. I Have Decided to Follow Jesus
Source unknown
Expression of commitment to follow only Jesus
Matt. 8:19; 16:24; John 12:26; 1 Peter 2:21

I Have Found a Friend in Jesus, see "The Lily of the Valley"

I Hear the Savior Say, see "Jesus Paid it All"

149. I Hear Thy Welcome Voice
Lewis Hartsough, 1872
Acceptance of Christ as Savior
Ps. 51:7; John 7:37; 14:6; Heb. 10:19–23; Rev. 22:17

I Heard an Old, Old Story, see "Victory in Jesus"

150. I Heard the Bells on Christmas Day
Henry W. Longfellow, 1863
Reminder of the Christmas message of "Peace on earth, good will to men!"
Micah 5:5; Luke 2:14

151. I Heard the Voice of Jesus Say
Horatius Bonar, 1846
We hear Jesus call us to find in him rest, living water, and the light of life
John 10:27; Rev. 3:20
St. 1 (. . . Come unto Me and rest . . .) Matt. 11:28–30
St. 2 (. . . Behold, I freely give . . .) John 4:10–14; Rev. 22:17
St. 3 (. . . I am this dark world's . . .) John 8:12; Eph. 5:8

I Know Not Why God's Wondrous Grace, see "I Know Whom I Have Believed"

152. I Know That My Redeemer Lives
Charles Wesley, 1742

Praise and expression of assurance that Jesus is alive
> Job 19:25; Mark 16:6; John 11:25–26; Acts 2:31–32; Rom. 6:9; 1 Cor. 15:20–22; 2 Tim. 1:10; Heb. 7:25; 1 Peter 1:3–5; Rev. 1:18

153. I Know That My Redeemer Liveth
Jessie B. Pounds, 1893
Resurrection; eternal life; return of Christ
Job 19:25–27
John 2:22; Rom. 6:9; 1 Peter 1:3–5; Rev. 1:18
St. 1 (. . . that my Redeemer . . .) John 10:28; 1 John 2:25; 5:11
St. 2 (. . . His promise never . . .) Ps. 119:89; Luke 21:33; 1 John 3:2
St. 3 (. . . my mansion He . . .) John 14:2–3; Col. 3:4

154. I Know Whom I Have Believed
Daniel W. Whittle, 1883
In the midst of many things about God that are a mystery to us, we cling to our faith and commitment
2 Tim. 1:12
John 3:16–17; 1 Cor. 1:30–31; Eph. 1:3–10
St. 1 (. . . why God's wondrous grace . . .) 2 Cor. 8:9; Gal. 4:4–5
St. 2 (. . . how this saving faith . . .) John 20:31; Gal. 3:22
St. 3 (. . . how the Spirit moves . . .) John 16:7–14
St. 4 (. . . when my Lord may come . . .) Mark 13:35; 1 Thess. 4:16–17

155. I Lay My Sins on Jesus
Horatius Bonar, 1843
We bring our sins and needs to Jesus and express our desire to be like him
Isa. 53:5–6; Col. 2:13; 1 Tim. 2:5
St. 1 (I lay my sins . . .) Ps. 51:2–3, 7; Isa. 1:18; John 1:29
St. 2 (I lay my wants . . .) Luke 6:17–19; 2 Cor. 9:8; 1 Peter 5:7
St. 3 (I long to be . . .) Matt. 11:29; John 13:15; Phil. 2:5–7

156. I Love Thy Kingdom, Lord
Timothy Dwight, 1800
Expression of praise and thanks to God for the church; importance of the church
Pss. 26:8; 137:5–6; Matt. 16:15–18; 1 Tim. 3:15

157. I Love to Tell the Story
Catherine Hankey, 1866

Expression of joy in telling of Jesus' love; witnessing; testimony
>Ps. 66:16; Isa. 63:7; John 3:16–17; Acts 1:8; 1 Peter 3:15; 1 John 4:14

I Must Needs Go Home By the Way of the Cross, see "The Way of the Cross Leads Home"

158. I Must Tell Jesus
Elisha A. Hoffman, 1894

Testimony that Jesus can help in all life's problems
>Pss. 34:19; 55:22; Isa. 41:10; Matt. 11:28–30; John 16:33; Phil. 4:6; Heb. 2:18; 1 Peter 5:7

159. I Need Thee Every Hour
Annie S. Hawks, 1872

Expression of dependence on God's help and companionship
>Pss. 40:17; 73:28; 86:1–10; Isa. 55:6; Acts 17:27–28; Heb. 4:16

St. 1 (. . . most gracious Lord . . .) Isa. 26:3; John 16:33

St. 2 (. . . stay Thou near by . . .) 1 Cor. 10:13; Heb. 2:18

I Serve a Risen Savior, see "He Lives"

160. I Sing the Almighty Power of God
Isaac Watts, 1715

We sing of the power of the God of creation
>1 Chron. 29:11–13; Neh. 9:6; Pss. 33:6–9; 95:3–6; 104:24; Acts 4:24; Rev. 4:11

161. I Sought the Lord
Anonymous, Pilgrim Hymnal, 1904

Testimony of God's love in reaching out to us
>Jer. 29:13; Luke 19:10; Acts 17:27

St. 2 (Thou didst reach forth . . .) Matt. 14:28–33

162. I Stand Amazed in the Presence
Charles H. Gabriel, 1905

Atonement; expression of love and praise for Christ's love, death, and suffering for our salvation
>John 3:16–17; 15:13; Eph. 2:4–7; Titus 3:3–6; 1 John 4:9–10

St. 1 (I stand amazed . . .) Luke 9:43

St. 2 (For me it was . . .) Luke 22:41–44

St. 3 (In pity angels . . .) Luke 22:43

St. 4 (He took my sins . . .) Isa. 53:4–6; Luke 23:33; 1 Peter 2:24

St. 5 (When with the . . .) Isa. 35:10; 1 Peter 4:13; Rev. 22:4

163. I Surrender All
Judson W. VanDeVenter, 1896

Expression of complete submission to God
>Matt. 22:37; John 15:4–5; Rom. 6:13; 12:1–2; 1 Cor. 6:19–20; Eph. 3:16–17; 2 Tim. 1:7

I Was Sinking Deep in Sin, see "Love Lifted Me"

164. I Will Sing of My Redeemer
Philip P. Bliss, 1876

A song of testimony and praise for the redemption that is ours through Christ; atonement; gospel
>Ps. 89:1; Isa. 53:4–6; 2 Cor. 2:14; Gal. 2:20; Eph. 1:7; 2:4–6; 1 John 4:9–10

St. 1 (. . . And His wondrous love . . .) John 8:36; Gal. 3:13

St. 2 (. . . How my lost estate to . . .) Matt. 20:28; Rom. 5:8

St. 3 (. . . His triumphant power . . .) Rom. 6:9–11; 1 Cor. 15:54–57

St. 4 (. . . And His heav'nly love . . .) John 5:24; Rom. 6:23

Refrain Col. 1:14; 1 Peter 1:18–19

165. I Will Sing the Wondrous Story
Francis H. Rowley, 1886

Song of testimony of the salvation that is ours through Christ; atonement; gospel
>Ps. 89:1; Isa. 35:10; Rom. 5:8; Col. 1:11–14; 1 Peter 2:24–25; 1 John 4:9–10

St. 1 (I will sing the wondrous . . .) Luke 23:33; Phil. 2:6–8

St. 2 (I was lost, but Jesus . . .) Isa. 53:6; Matt. 18:11–14

St. 3 (I was bruised, but Jesus . . .) Ps. 147:3; Luke 4:18; 7:21–22

St. 4 (Days of darkness still . . .) John 8:12; 12:46; 1 Peter 5:7

St. 5 (He will keep me till the . . .) Ps. 23:6; Rom. 14:8

Refrain Eph. 2:19; Rev. 22:1–5

166. I Would Be True
Howard A. Walter, 1907

Commitment to be true to the ways and teachings of Jesus

Acts 11:23; 1 Cor. 16:13–14; Eph. 4:1–3; 1 Tim. 4:12; 1 Peter 3:8

167. If Thou but Suffer God to Guide Thee
Georg Neumark, 1640

Trans. Catherine Winkworth, 1863

God's eternal, providential care and guidance for those who trust in him

Deut. 31:8; Pss. 9:10; 25:4–10; 118:14; Prov. 3:5–6; Isa. 58:11; Phil. 4:19

If Thou But Trust in God to Guide Thee, see "If Thou But Suffer God to Guide Thee"

If You Are Tired of the Load of Your Sin, see "Let Jesus Come Into Your Heart"

If You Will Only Let God Guide You, see "If Thou But Suffer God to Guide Thee"

168. I'll Go Where You Want Me To Go
Mary Brown, St. 1, 19th cent.

Charles E. Prior, St. 2 and 3

Commitment to serve God in whatever way he leads

Isa. 6:8; Jer. 1:7–8; Matt. 9:37–38; Matt. 28:19–20

169. I'll Live for Him
Ralph E. Hudson, 1882

Expression of commitment to life in Christ, who died for me

Matt. 22:37; Acts 17:28; Rom. 6:6–18; 1 Cor. 6:20; 2 Cor. 5:15; Gal. 2:20; Titus 2:14

I'm Pressing on the Upward Way, see "Higher Ground"

170. Immortal, Invisible, God Only Wise
Walter C. Smith, 1867

Praise to an almighty God; God as light that reveals but obscures its source

1 Tim. 1:17; 6:13–16

Dan. 2:20–22; Rom. 1:20; James 1:17; 1 John 1:5; Rev. 1:8

St. 2 (Unresting, unhasting . . .) Pss. 9:7–8; 36:6

St. 3 (To all, life Thou . . .) Job 33:4; Ps. 36:9; Acts 17:28

St. 4 (Great Father of glory . . .) Ps. 72:19; Rev. 5:11–12

171. Immortal Love, Forever Full
John Greenleaf Whittier, 1866

The constancy of God's immortal love

Ps. 139:7–10; Jer. 31:3; Matt. 9:20–22; Rom. 8:38–39; Eph. 3:17–19

Last st. (O Lord and Master . . .) John 13:13–15

172. In Christ There Is No East or West
John Oxenham, 1908

Brotherhood; oneness of fellowship in Christ

Ps. 133:1; Rom. 12:5; 1 Cor. 12:12–13; Gal. 3:26–28; 5:13; Col. 3:11; 1 Peter 2:17

173. In Heavenly Love Abiding
Anna L. Waring, 1850

Expression of faith and assurance in God's love, guidance, and providential care

Deut. 31:8; Pss. 23; 95:7; 125:2; John 15:10; Jude 21

174. In Loving Kindness Jesus Came
Charles H. Gabriel, 1905

Testimony: Jesus came to redeem my soul from sin's darkness

Ps. 40:2; John 3:16–17; Eph. 1:3–8; 2:4–6; Col. 1:12–14; 1 Tim. 1:15; Titus 2:14; 1 Peter 2:24–25

In the Cross, see "Jesus, Keep Me Near the Cross"

175. In the Cross of Christ I Glory
John Bowring, 1825

Testimony of allegiance to the cross of Christ and what it represents

Gal. 6:14

John 19:17–18; 1 Cor. 1:17–18; Eph. 2:13–16; 1 Peter 2:24

176. In the Garden
C. Austin Miles, 1912

Expression of sharing in Mary Magdalene's experience of meeting Jesus on Easter morning

John 20:10–18

177. In the Hour of Trial
James Montgomery, 1834

Expression of desire for Jesus' closeness and help in time of trial and temptation
Deut. 4:30–31; Ps. 55:22; John 16:33
St. 1 (In the hour of . . .) Matt. 10:33; Mark 14:66–72
St. 2 (With forbidden . . .) Matt. 26:36–45; Luke 23:33
St. 3 (Should Thy mercy . . .) Pss. 34:19; 116:3–7; Rom. 8:28

178. Infant Holy, Infant Lowly
Traditional Polish Carol
Trans. Edith M. G. Reed, 1921
Setting of Jesus' birth recalled; Christmas
Luke 2:1–20

Is Your Life a Channel of Blessing?, see "Make Me a Blessing"

179. It Came Upon a Midnight Clear
Edmund H. Sears, 1849
Birth of Jesus; angels' song
Luke 2:9–14
Matt. 25:31; Heb. 1:6

180. It Is Well with My Soul
Horatio G. Spafford, 1873
Expression of faith regardless of life's conditions
Ps. 103:1–4; Rom. 8:28; 15:13; 2 Cor. 5:7; Gal. 2:20; 2 Tim. 1:12; Heb. 10:22
St. 2 (Though Satan should . . .) Eph. 6:16; Heb. 2:14; 1 John 3:8
St. 3 (My sin—O the bliss . . .) 1 Cor. 15:3; 2 Cor. 5:21
St. 4 (And, Lord, haste the . . .) Matt. 24:30–31; 1 Cor. 15:53

181. It May Be at Morn
H. L. Turner, 1878
Anticipation of Christ's second coming and our eternal life with him
Matt. 24:30–31, 36, 42–44; 25:13; Luke 12:35–40; Heb. 10:37; Rev. 22:20
St. 2 (It may be at midday . . .) Matt. 24:27
St. 3 (While hosts cry . . .) Matt. 16:27; 25:31
St. 4 (O joy! O delight! . . .) Isa. 35:10; Rev. 21:4
Refrain 1 Thess. 2:19–20; 2 Thess. 1:10

It May Not Be on the Mountain's Height, see "I'll Go Where You Want"

It Only Takes a Spark, see "Pass It On"

182. I've Found a Friend
James G. Small, 1863
Love of Jesus; Jesus as friend; expression of close relationship with Jesus
Jer. 31:3; John 15:13–15; Rom. 8:35–39; Gal. 2:20; 1 John 4:19

I've Wandered Far Away From God, see "Lord, I'm Coming Home"

183. Jerusalem, My Happy Home
Joseph Bromehead, 1795
Immortal life; heaven anticipated and viewed as the New Jerusalem
Rev. 21:2, 4
Ps. 122:2; Isa. 35:10; 65:17–19; 2 Cor. 5:8; Heb. 11:16; 12:22; Rev. 21; 22:4

184. Jerusalem, the Golden
Bernard of Cluny, 12th Century
Trans. John M. Neale, 1851
Expression of anticipation and desire for heaven, the New Jerusalem
Isa. 35:10; 65:17–19; Jer. 3:17; Heb. 11:16; 12:22; Rev. 7:9–17; 21
St. 1 Josh. 5:6; 1 Cor. 2:9; 2 Cor. 3:18

185. Jesus Calls Us, O'er the Tumult
Cecil F. Alexander, 1852
Jesus calls us to follow him and love him more than anything else
Matt. 4:18–20; 10:37–38; 16:24; Luke 5:32; John 10:3–5, 27; 12:26; 21:15–17; 2 Tim. 1:9

186. Jesus Christ Is Risen Today
14th century, anonymous
Christ endured the cross to redeem us and is now alive and reigns as Lord and King
Matt. 28:1–9; Luke 24:46–48; Rom. 6:9–10; 1 Cor. 15:12–20; Heb. 12:2

187. Jesus, I My Cross Have Taken
Henry F. Lyte, 1824
Expression of total commitment to Jesus' challenge to take up our cross and follow him; Christian life

Matt. 16:24–25; Mark 10:28; Luke 9:23–24; Rom.
12:1–2; 2 Cor. 4:10–11; 1 Peter 2:21–25

188. Jesus Is All the World to Me
Will L. Thompson, 1904
*Testimony that Jesus is my friend and the one
on whom I can place complete dependence*
John 15:14–15
John 6:35; 8:12; Eph. 6:10; Phil. 4:13
St. 2 (. . . my friend in trials . . .) 2 Cor. 1:5
St. 3 (. . . and true to Him I'll . . .) Mark 8:34; 2
Tim. 2:12–13
St. 4 (. . . I want no better . . .) John 10:27–28;
1 John 2:25

Jesus Is Calling, see "Jesus Is Tenderly
Calling"

189. Jesus Is Coming Again
John W. Peterson, 1957
Anticipation of Jesus' return
Matt. 25:13; 26:64; Acts 1:11; Heb. 10:37; Rev. 1:7

Jesus Is Coming to Earth Again, see "What If
It Were Today?"

190. Jesus Is Tenderly Calling Thee Home
Fanny J. Crosby, 1883
The call or invitation of Jesus
Matt. 11:28–29; 25:34; Luke 5:32; John 10:3–5; 1
Thess. 5:24; 2 Thess. 2:14; Heb. 3:15; Rev. 3:20;
22:17

191. Jesus, Keep Me Near the Cross
Fanny J. Crosby, 1869
*Cross of Jesus; consecration and devotion; hope
and aspiration*
Zech. 13:1; John 19:17–30; 1 Cor. 1:17–18; Gal.
6:14; Col. 1:20–23; 1 Peter 2:24; Jude 21

192. Jesus, Lover of My Soul
Charles Wesley, 1740
*Love of Christ; Christ is our all, our refuge and
our Savior*
Eph. 3:6–19
Ps. 37:19; Acts 2:25; Rom. 8:35–39; 2 Cor. 1:5; 12:9
St. 3 (Thou, O Christ . . .) Ps. 147:3; Luke
7:21–22; 1 John 1:7–10
St. 4 (Plenteous grace . . .) Zech 13:1; Rom.
5:20–21; Eph. 1:7

193. Jesus Loves Even Me
Philip P. Bliss
*Testimony and expression of joy in the confi-
dence of Jesus' love*
John 15:13; Rom. 8:35–39; Eph. 3:16–19; 5:1–2

194. Jesus Loves Me
Anna B. Warner, 1859
Expression of confidence in Jesus' love
John 15:13; Rom. 8:35–39; Eph. 3:16–19; 5:1–2; 1
John 3:16

Jesus, My Lord Will Love Me Forever, see
"Now I Belong to Jesus"

195. Jesus Paid it All
Elvina M. Hall, 1865
*God's grace and cleansing are complete
through Jesus; salvation is by grace and not by
our own merit*
Isa. 53:4–5; Rom. 3:24–26; 5:6; 2 Cor. 5:21; Eph.
1:7–9; Titus 2:14; 3:5–6; 1 Peter 2:22–25
St. 1 (I hear the Savior say . . .) 2 Cor. 12:9–10
St. 2 (Lord, now indeed I find . . .) Matt. 8:2–3
St. 3 (For nothing good have I . . .) Isa. 1:18
St. 4 (And when before the . . .) Rev. 7:14–15

196. Jesus, Priceless Treasure
Johann Franck, 1650
Trans. Catherine Winkworth, 1863
*Expression of confidence in the complete suffi-
ciency of Christ*
John 15:15; Rom. 8:38–39; Col. 1:17–18

Jesus Saves, see "We Have Heard the Joyful
Sound"

197. Jesus Savior, Pilot Me
Edward Hopper, 1871
*Prayer for Jesus' guidance in life as a pilot
guides a ship at sea*
Pss. 89:9; 107:28–30; Matt. 8:23–27; Mark 4:39;
James 1:6

198. Jesus Shall Reign
Isaac Watts, 1719
*Worldwide missions; reign and kingdom of
Christ*
Ps. 72
Ps. 67; Luke 1:32–33; 1 Cor. 15:23–28; Phil.
2:9–11; Heb. 1:8; Rev. 11:15

199. Jesus, Still Lead On

Nikolaus von Zinzendorf, 1721
Trans. Jane L. Borthwick, 1846

*Prayer for Jesus' leadership throughout our
lives and to heaven*

Ps. 73:24; Rom. 8:18; Heb. 4:9; James 1:12; Jude 21

200. Jesus, the Very Thought of
Thee Bernard of Clairvaux, 12th Century
Trans. Edward Caswall, 1849

*Praise and love for Christ; name of Christ; joy;
devotion; salvation*

Luke 1:47; John 16:33; Acts 2:28

St. 1 (Jesus, the very thought . . .) 1 Cor. 13:12;
Eph. 3:17

St. 2 (Nor voice can sing, nor . . .) Ps. 66:2; Acts
4:12

St. 3 (O Hope of every contrite . . .) Pss. 34:18;
51:17; Rom. 15:13

St. 4 (But what to those who . . .) John 15:9;
Rom. 8:35–39

201. Jesus, Thou Joy of Loving
Hearts

Bernard of Clairvaux, 12th century
Trans. Ray Palmer, 1858

*Expression of praise, devotion, joy, prayer, and
aspiration*

Ps. 107:9; Luke 1:47; John 4:14; 14:1; 15:10–11;
Eph. 3:17–19

St. 1 (Jesus, Thou joy of . . .) John 6:35; Rev.
7:17

St. 2 (Thy truth unchanged . . .) Ps. 100:5; Heb.
13:8

Last St. (O Jesus, ever with . . .) Matt. 28:20;
John 1:4–9; Col. 1:13

202. Jesus, Thy Blood and
Righteousness   Zinzendorf, 1739
Trans. John Wesley, 1740

Atonement; blood of Jesus; salvation

Isa. 53:5; Rom. 3:24–25; 5:8–11; Eph. 1:7; Col.
1:20–22; 1 Tim. 2:5–6; 1 Peter 1:18–19; 1 John
2:1–2

203. Jesus, Thy Boundless Love to
Me   Paul Gerhardt, 1653
Trans. John Wesley, 1738

*Expression of commitment to a Christ of per-
fect and limitless love that overcomes all situa-
tions in life*

Jer. 31:3; John 15:4, 9–10; Rom. 8:35–39; Gal. 2:20;
Eph. 2:4–5; 3:17–19

204. Jesus, What a Friend for
Sinners   J. Wilbur Chapman, 1910

*Expression of commitment to Jesus as friend,
our strength, comfort, guide, and our all*

John 15:13–15; Eph. 3:19; Rom. 6:11; 8:35–39

St. 1 (. . . what a Friend . . .) 1 Tim. 1:15

St. 2 (. . . what a Strength . . .) 2 Cor. 12:9; Phil.
4:13

St. 3 (. . . what a Help in . . .) John 14:18; 2 Cor.
1:5

St. 4 (. . . what a Guide . . .) Ps. 107:28–30; Matt.
8:23–27

St. 5 (. . . do now receive . . .) Song of Songs
2:16; John 1:12; 17:10

205. Joy to the World Isaac Watts, 1719

*Birth of Jesus; praise for God's redemption;
Christmas*

Ps. 98; Luke 2:11

Matt. 1:18–23; Luke 1:46–55,68–69; Gal. 4:4–5

206. Joyful, Joyful, We Adore Thee

Henry van Dyke, 1907

*Praise and adoration of a God of majesty and
power; joy of living in God's world*

1 Chron. 16:23–33; Pss. 32:11; 98; Hab. 3:18–19; 1
John 1:5–7

St. 1 (Joyful, Joyful . . .) Isa. 9:2; 60:19; John
12:36, 46; James 1:17

St. 2 (All Thy works . . .) Ps. 19:1; 104:24;
145:10; 148

St. 3 (Thou art giving . . .) Ps. 103:3–5; 1 Cor.
8:6; 1 John 4:13

St. 4 (Mortals join . . .) Job 38:7; 1 Cor. 15:57

207. Just a Closer Walk with Thee

Anonymous

*Prayer for strength and guidance from Christ
in the Christian walk*

2 Sam. 22:33; Ps. 73:26; Isa. 41:10; 2 Cor. 12:9; 13:4

208. Just As I Am, Without One
Plea   Charlotte Elliott, 1834

*All barriers are broken down as we come to
Jesus for cleansing and pardon*

Ps. 51:1–2; Isa. 55:7; John 6:37; 2 Cor. 7:5; Eph. 2:13–14; Titus 3:5–6; 1 John 1:9; Rev. 22:17

209. Just When I Need Him
William C. Poole, 1907

Testimony that Jesus is always close to us in our times of need

Pss. 46:1; 55:22; Matt. 11:28–30; Phil. 4:19; Heb. 13:5–6

King of My Life, I Crown Thee Now, see "Lead Me to Calvary"

210. Lead, Kindly Light
John H. Newman, 1833

Prayer for God's guidance, presence, comfort, and leadership; God as a light in a world of darkness

Deut. 31:8; Ps. 43:3; 2 Sam. 22:29; Isa. 42:16; John 8:12

211. Lead Me to Calvary
Jennie E. Hussey, 1921

Remembrance of God's love and the events of Gethsemane and Calvary

Luke 23:33; John 19:17; Heb. 12:2–3
St. 1 (King of my life . . .) Luke 24:46; John 19:2
St. 2 (Show me the tomb . . .) John 19:38–42
St. 3 (Let me, like Mary . . .) Luke 24:1–9
St. 4 (May I be willing . . .) Matt. 20:22; Luke 9:23

212. Lead On, O King Eternal
Ernest W. Shurtleff, 1887

Challenge to follow Christ in spiritual warfare

Isa. 48:17; Eph. 6:10–20; 1 Tim. 6:12; 2 Tim. 2:3–4; 4:7–8; Jude 3; Rev. 17:14
St. 1 (. . . the day of march . . .) 2 Cor. 12:9
St. 2 (. . . till sin's fierce . . .) 1 Cor. 15:56–58
St. 3 (. . . we follow, not . . .) Gal. 6:14; 2 Tim. 4:8; Rev. 2:10

213. Leaning on the Everlasting Arms
Elisha A. Hoffman, 1887

Fellowship with Jesus gives peace; Christ as our refuge on our pilgrimage in life

Deut. 33:27; Ps. 16:11; 118:6; Prov. 3:23; 1 Cor. 1:9

Lest I Forget Gethsemane, see "Lead Me to Calvary"

214. Let All Mortal Flesh Keep Silence
Liturgy of St. James, c. 5th century
Trans. Gerard Moultrie, 1864

God comes to earth . . . all earth and heaven give praise

Hab. 2:20; Zech. 2:13; Luke 1:76–79; John 1:4–5; Rev. 4:8–11

215. Let All the World in Every Corner Sing
George Herbert, 1633

Individuals, church, everyone, and everything praises God

1 Chron. 16:23–30; Pss. 47:6; 66:4; 67:3–5; 69:34; 150:6; Heb. 2:12; Rev. 5:13

216. Let Jesus Come Into Your Heart
Lelia N. Morris, 1898

Invitation to accept Jesus as Savior

Isa. 55:7; Acts 2:38; Rom. 10:10; 2 Cor. 5:17; 6:2; Heb. 10:22; Rev. 3:20

Let There Be Light, see "Thou Whose Almighty Word"

217. Let Us Break Bread Together
Traditional Spiritual

Expression of praise and a prayer for mercy upon observance of Lord's Supper

Matt. 26:26–29; John 6:53–58; 1 Cor. 11:23–38

218. Let Us with a Gladsome Mind
John Milton, 1623

Expression of praise to God for his eternal kindness and mercy

Ps. 136:1–2, 7, 25–26

Pss. 63:3; 100:5; 106:1; 107:8–9; 145:9; James 1:17

219. Lift High the Cross
G. W. Kitchin and M. R. Newbolt, 1916

A call to the church to proclaim the message of the cross and Jesus' suffering and death

John 12:32; 1 Cor. 1:18; Gal. 6:14; Heb. 12:2

220. Lift Up Your Heads, Ye Mighty Gates
George Weissel, 1642
Trans. Catherine Winkworth, 1855

Anticipation of Christ's coming; Advent

Ps. 24:7–10

Luke 21:28; 2 Cor. 4:6; James 5:8

221. Like a River Glorious
Frances R. Havergal, 1874
Testimony that one finds perfect peace in life when the heart is "stayed upon Jehovah"
Ps. 29:11; Isa. 26:3; 48:18; Nah. 1:7; John 14:27

222. Living for Jesus
Thomas O. Chisholm, 1917
In response to Christ's death for us, we commit ourselves to a life totally for him
Matt. 16:24–25; Mark 12:33; Luke 9:23–24; Acts 17:28; Rom. 6:13–18; 2 Cor. 5:15; Gal. 2:20; Col. 1:10
St. 2 (. . . who died in my place . . .) Luke 23:33; Rom. 12:1
St. 3 (. . . wherever I am, doing . . .) Luke 17:10; Phil. 1:29
St. 4 (. . . through earth's little . . .) Matt. 11:28–30; Luke 19:10

223. Lo, He Comes with Clouds Descending
Charles Wesley, 1758
Second coming and reign of Jesus
Dan. 7:13–14; Matt. 25:31–46; Mark 13:26–27; 14:62; Luke 21:27–28; Acts 1:11; 1 Thess. 4:16–17; Heb. 9:28; Rev. 1:7–8

224. Lo, How a Rose E'er Blooming
German Carol, c. 16th century
Christmas; birth of Jesus
Isa. 11:1; John 1:14

225. Look, Ye Saints! The Sight Is Glorious
Thomas Kelly, 1809
Praise to the eternal, victorious Christ as Savior, King, and Lord
Rev. 11:15
Matt. 25:31; Acts 2:36; Phil. 2:9–11; 1 Tim. 6:15–16; Heb. 2:7–10; 12:2; Rev. 5:11–12

226. Lord, Dismiss Us with Thy Blessing
John Fawcett, 1773
Prayer and thanks for God's joy, peace, blessings, and grace; benediction
Num. 6:24–26; Pss. 16:11; 67:1; Rom. 15:13; Eph. 6:23–24; 2 Thess. 3:16; Heb. 13:20–21; 2 Peter 1:2

227. Lord, I'm Coming Home
William J. Kirkpatrick, 1892
Confession of sin; expression of repentance and acceptance of Christ as Savior
Isa. 55:7; Luke 15:11–24; Acts 3:19

Lord Jesus, I Long to Be Perfectly Whole, see "Whiter Than Snow"

228. Lord Jesus, Think on Me
Synesius of Cyrene, c. 410
Trans. Allen W. Chatfield, 1876
Prayer that Jesus would remember me, cleanse me from my sin, and bring me to the eternal "rest"
Pss. 25:7; 40:17; 106:4; James 4:8

229. Lord, Speak to Me, That I May Speak
Frances R. Havergal, 1872
Prayer expressing desire to follow Jesus' example in service to him
Ps. 119:12–13; Isa. 6:8; Matt. 28:19–20; John 13:15; Acts 1:8; Rom. 12:1–2; 14:7; 2 Tim. 2:2, 24–25

230. Love Divine, All Loves Excelling
Charles Wesley, 1747
A prayer to a God of pure love, expressing desire for God's indwelling spirit; sanctification
John 14:21; Eph. 3:18–19; 1 John 3:1; 4:7–21
St. 1 (Love divine, all . . .) Pss. 86:15; 106:4; John 14:16–17
St. 2 (Breathe, O breathe . . .) John 20:22; Gal. 5:1; Heb. 4:3–11
St. 3 (Come, Almighty to . . .) Ps. 145:2; 1 Cor. 2:16–17; Rev. 7:15
St. 4 (Finish then Thy . . .) 2 Cor. 3:18; 5:17; 2 Peter 3:13–14

Love Divine, So Great and Wondrous, see "He the Pearly Gates Will Open"

231. Love Lifted Me
James Rowe, 1912
Testimony of Christ's love as experienced through salvation
Luke 8:22–25; John 3:16–17; 15:13; Gal. 2:20; Eph. 2:4–5; 1 John 4:9–10

Loved with Everlasting Love, see "I Am His and He Is Mine"

Low in the Grave He Lay, see "Christ Arose"

Macedonia, see "The Vision of a Dying World"

232. Majestic Sweetness Sits Enthroned   Samuel Stennett, 1787

Exaltation, reign and Lordship of Christ; eternal life; atonement; praise

Luke 22:69; John 17:1–5; Acts 2:24–43; 5:30–31; Rom. 14:9; 1 Cor. 15:22–28; Eph. 2:4–6; Col. 1:15–20; Heb. 1:3; 2:9; Rev. 5:12–13

233. Make Me a Blessing
Ira B. Wilson, 1909

Prayer that God will use me as an ambassador for Christ, telling others of his love for us and for them

Isa. 6:8; Matt. 4:19; 5:14–16; Luke 14:23; John 21:15–17; Acts 1:8; 22:15; Rom. 14:7; 2 Tim. 2:21

234. Make Me a Captive, Lord
George Matheson, 1890

A hymn acknowledging some of the seeming paradoxes of a life totally committed to God

Matt. 16:25; John 12:24–25; 2 Cor. 12:10

Make Me a Channel of Blessing, see "Make Me a Blessing"

235. "Man of Sorrows," What a Name   Philip P. Bliss, 1875

Christ as Savior; suffering and death of Christ; Easter

Isa. 53:3–6; Mark 10:45; Luke 1:47; Phil. 2:7–11; Heb. 12:2; 1 Peter 1:18–19; 1 John 4:14

St. 2 (Bearing shame . . .) John 19:1–3; Col. 1:20; Heb. 13:12

St. 3 (Guilty, vile . . .) John 1:29; 1 Peter 2:24

St. 4 (Lifted up was . . .) John 3:14; 19:30; Heb. 10:12

St. 5 (When He comes . . .) Isa. 35:10; John 14:2–3; Rev. 14:3

Marvelous Grace of Our Loving Lord, see "Grace Greater Than Our Sin"

Marvelous Message We Bring, see "Jesus Is Coming Again"

Master of Eager Youth, see "Shepherd of Tender (Eager) Youth"

236. May the Grace of Christ Our Savior   John Newton, 1779

Benediction prayer

Num. 6:24–26; Ps. 67:1; 2 Cor. 13:14; Eph. 4:1–7

237. Mine Eyes Have Seen the Glory
Julia W. Howe, 1862

An expression of patriotic emotion

Ps. 76:11–12; Isa. 42:12–13; Zech. 9:14; Rom. 8:37

238. Moment by Moment
Daniel W. Whittle, 1893

Testimony that I belong to Christ and am kept in his love; life in Christ

John 14:18–19; 16:33; 2 Cor. 1:5; 12:9–10; Gal. 2:19–20; Eph. 3:17; Col. 1:27; 2 Thess. 3:3; 1 Peter 1:5; 5:7

239. More About Jesus
Eliza E. Hewitt, 1887

Expression of desire to know more about Jesus, his word, and his will

Eph. 3:19; 4:13–15; Phil. 3:8–11; Col. 1:9; 3:2; 2 Peter 3:18

St. 2 (. . . let me learn . . .) John 14:26; 1 John 2:27

St. 3 (. . . in His Word . . .) John 5:39; 1 Peter 2:2

240. More Love to Thee, O Christ
Elizabeth Prentiss, 1856

Expression of desire to show more love to Christ

Deut. 6:5; Phil. 1:9; 2 Thess. 3:5; 1 John 4:19

241. Morning Has Broken
Eleanor Farjeon, 1931

An expression of praise for the morning and for a new day

Gen. 1:5; 1 Chron. 23:30; Pss. 57:8–11; 118:24

242. Must Jesus Bear the Cross Alone?   Thomas Shepherd, 1693

As God's servants, we bear our own crosses and persevere until we receive our reward in heaven

Mark 8:34–38; Luke 14:27; Phil. 3:10; Col. 3:24; Rev. 14:12–13

243. My Faith Has Found a Resting Place   Lidie H. Edmunds, 19th c.

Testimony that salvation comes only by the atoning death of Jesus

Rom. 5:1–11; Eph. 2:8; 2 Tim. 1:12; 1 Peter 2:24

St. 3 (My heart is leaning . . .) John 20:31

St. 4 (My great physician . . .) Luke 19:10

244. My Faith Looks Up to Thee
Ray Palmer, 1830

Expression of confidence in our faith in Christ and in forgiveness of sins

Jer. 33:8; Rom. 1:16–17; 5:1–2; Eph. 3:12; Heb. 12:2

St. 1 (My faith looks up . . .) John 1:29

St. 2 (May Thy rich grace . . .) 2 Cor. 4:16; 12:9; Titus 2:14

St. 3 (While life's dark . . .) Ps. 73:24; Isa. 60:20

My Father Is Rich in Houses and Lands, see "A Child of the King"

My Hope Is Built on Nothing Less, see "The Solid Rock"

245. My Jesus, I Love Thee
William R. Featherstone, 1862

Expression of love and gratitude for Jesus and what he has done for us

Matt. 22:37; 1 Peter 1:8; 1 John 4:19

St. 4 (In mansions of glory . . .) John 4:2–3

My Life, My Love I Give to Thee, see "I'll Live for Him"

My Savior's Love, see "I Stand Amazed in the Presence"

246. My Tribute   Andrae Crouch, 1971

Expression of praise and thanks for the salvation we have through Jesus

Ps. 72:18–19; Rom. 5:1–11; 1 Cor. 15:57; Titus 3:4–7; 1 Peter 1:3–8; Rev. 1:5b–6

Near the Cross, see "Jesus, Keep Me Near the Cross"

247. Near to the Heart of God
Cleland B. McAffee, 1901

Nearness to God, through Jesus, brings rest, comfort, joy, and peace

Exod. 33:13–14; Pss. 34:18; 73:28; Isa. 55:6; Matt. 11:28–30; Acts 17:27; Phil. 4:7; Heb. 4:16; James 4:8

248. Nearer, My God, to Thee
Sarah F. Adams, 1840

Prayer of devotion expressing desire for closer fellowship with God

Gen. 28:10–21; Pss. 16:8; 73:28; 145:18; Isa. 55:6; Acts 17:27

249. Nearer, Still Nearer
Lelia N. Morris, 1898

Prayer expressing desire for closeness to Christ

Pss. 19:13; 145:18; Eph. 2:13; Phil. 2:21; Heb. 10:22

St. 2 (. . . nothing I bring . . .) Ps. 51:17

250. No, Not One
Johnson Oatman, Jr., 1895

Testimony that Jesus is our friend, always near to help in all needs of life

Prov. 18:24; John 15:13–15; 1 Cor. 1:9

St. 1 (There's not a friend . . .) Ps. 103:3

St. 2 (No friend like Him . . .) Phil. 2:5–10

St. 3 (There's not an hour . . .) John 8:12

St. 4 (Did ever saint find . . .) John 6:37

St. 5 (Was e'er a gift like . . .) John 4:10; 2 Cor. 9:15

251. Nothing But the Blood
Robert Lowry, 1876

Atonement; only through the blood of Jesus do we find cleansing and pardon for sin

Isa. 1:18; Zech. 13:1; Rom. 3:24–25; Eph. 1:7; Col. 1:14; Heb. 9:14, 22; 1 Peter 1:18–19

252. Now I Belong to Jesus
Norman J. Clayton, 1943

Testimony of salvation and total commitment to Christ reflecting the Scripture, "Ye are not your own; for ye are bought with a price"

Rom. 1:6; 5:1–11; 8:35–39; 14:7–9; 1 Cor. 6:19–20; 15:56–57; Gal. 2:20; Titus 3:5–7

253. Now Thank We All Our God
Martin Rinkart, 1636
Trans. Catherine Winkworth, 1858

Expression of thanks to an omnipotent God for all his blessings

1 Chron. 16:8,34–36; 29:13; Pss. 68:19; 75:1; 1 Thess. 5:18; Heb. 13:15; Rev. 11:17

254. Now the Day Is Over
Sabine Baring–Gould, 1865

Evening prayer

Pss. 3:5; 4:8; 42:8; 63:6–8; 139:11–12; Prov. 3:24

O Beautiful for Spacious Skies, see "America the Beautiful"

255. O Breath of Life
Bessie P. Head (date unknown)
Expression of prayer for the Holy Spirit to bring revival
Pss. 51:10–12; 85:6; John 20:22

O Christian, Haste, Your Mission High, see "O Zion, Haste"

256. O Come, All Ye Faithful
Latin Hymn
Trans. Frederick Oakeley, 1841
Invitation to join in worship and praise at the birth of Jesus; Christmas
Luke 1:68–69; 2:1–20; John 1:14

257. O Come, O Come, Emmanuel
Latin Hymn
Trans. John M. Neale, 1851
Anticipation of Jesus coming to earth; Christmas; Advent
Isa. 7:14; Jer. 23:5–6; Matt. 1:21–23
St. 1 (. . . O come, Emmanuel . . .) Isa. 7:14
St. 2 (. . . Thou Rod of Jesse . . .) Isa. 11:1
St. 3 (. . . Thou Dayspring . . .) Luke 1:78; 2:32
St. 4 (. . . Thou Key of David . . .) Isa. 22:22; Rev. 3:7–8
St. 5 (. . . Desire of nations . . .) Hag. 2:7

258. O Could I Speak the Matchless Worth
Samuel Medley, 1789
Expression of testimony, praise, and adoration of Christ as Savior
Luke 1:32; John 5:32; 1 Cor. 1:31; Phil. 2:9–10; Heb. 1:1–4; 2:9–12; 2 Peter 3:18; Jude 24–25; Rev. 5:9–13

259. O Day of God, Draw Nigh
Robert B. Y. Scott, 1958
Expression of prayer for justice and peace
Ps. 105:7; Isa. 2:12–22; 30:18; 51:4–5

260. O Day of Rest and Gladness
Christopher Wordsworth, 1862
Praise on Lord's Day to the Trinity; Lord's Day as the day of creation of light, resurrection of Christ, and sending of Holy Spirit
Lev. 23:3; Ps. 118:24; Isa. 66:23
St. 1 (O day of rest . . .) Gen. 2:2–3; Isa. 6:3
St. 2 (On Thee, at the . . .) Gen. 1:3–5; Mark 16:2; John 20:19–22
Last st. (New graces . . .) Ps. 116:7; Heb. 4:9–11

261. O For a Closer Walk with God
William Cowper, 1769
Confession of sin; expression of repentance and desire to walk closer to God
Gen. 5:24; Pss. 34:18; 56:13; Prov. 4:18; Isa. 55:6–7; Mic. 6:8; Acts 17:27–30; Gal. 5:16; Eph. 5:8

262. O For a Heart to Praise My God
Charles Wesley, 1742
Expression of desire for a heart characterized by praise, holiness, humility, renewal, and love
Deut. 5:29; 1 Kings 8:61; Pss. 9:1; 51:10; Jer. 24:7; Heb. 10:22; James 4:8, 10

263. O For a Thousand Tongues to Sing
Charles Wesley, 1739
Praise to Christ as Savior and Lord; name of Jesus
1 Chron. 16:23–25; Pss. 96:1–4; 103:1–4; Isa. 12:4–5; 1 Cor. 1:31; Phil. 2:9–11
St. 1 (O for a thousand . . .) Pss. 35:28; 71:23
St. 2 (Jesus, the name . . .) Matt. 1:21; Acts 4:12
St. 3 (He breaks the . . .) Isa. 1:18; John 8:34–36; Rom. 3:24–25;
St. 4 (Hear Him ye deaf . . .) Matt. 11:5

264. O God of Love, O King of Peace
Henry W. Baker, 1861
Prayer expressing desire for God to bring peace on earth
Pss. 29:11; 46:9–11; Isa. 26:12; 1 Cor. 14:33

265. O God, Our Help in Ages Past
Isaac Watts, 1719
Prayer for God's presence and power in our lives and our nation
Ps. 90:1–5, 14
Pss. 33:20; 46:1; 48:14; 91:1–2; Isa. 26:4; Lam. 5:19; 2 Thess. 3:3

266. O Happy Day That Fixed My Choice
Philip Doddridge, 1755
Conversion described as a "choice, bond, great transaction, and rest for a long–divided heart"; joy in salvation

Ps. 32:11; Isa. 61:10; 2 Cor. 5:17; Gal. 2:20; Phil. 4:4; Titus 3:5–6

267. O, How I Love Jesus
Frederick Whitfield, 1855

Expression of love for God and Jesus

Ps. 66:2; Matt. 12:21; Acts 4:12; Phil. 2:9–11; Heb. 1:4; 1 Peter 1:8

St. 2 (. . . of a Savior's love . . .) Rom. 6:2–11; Eph. 2:13

St. 3 (. . . what my Father hath . . .) John 8:12; Col. 1:13

St. 4 (. . . of One whose loving . . .) Heb. 4:15–16; 1 Peter 5:7

Refrain 1 John 4:19

268. O Jesus, I Have Promised
J. E. Bode, 1868

Prayer of complete discipleship, looking to God for strength and guidance

Luke 9:23–24; John 12:26; 15:14; 21:15–17; Rom. 12:1–2, 11; Col. 3:24; 1 Tim. 1:12; Heb. 6:10–11; 12:1

269. O Jesus, Thou Art Standing
William W. How, 1867

Jesus stands, knocks, and pleads at the door of our hearts

Rev. 3:20

John 10:1–9; 14:6; Rev. 22:17

270. O Little Town of Bethlehem
Phillips Brooks, 1868

Jesus' birth in Bethlehem as prophesied; prayer that he would be born in me again

Micah 5:2

Matt. 1:18–23; 2:1–2; Luke 2:1–7, 11

O Lord my God, When I In Awesome Wonder, see "How Great Thou Art"

271. O Love How Deep, How Broad, How High
Latin Hymn, 15th century
Trans. Benjamin Webb, 1854

Testimony recalling the deep love of God as seen in all Jesus did in our behalf

John 3:16–17; Rom. 5:8; 2 Cor. 8:9; Phil. 2:6–11; 1 John 4:10

St. 2 Matt. 3:13–17; 4:1–11; Heb. 4:15

272. O Love, That Will Not Let Me Go
George Matheson, 1882

Testimony of one having experienced the fullness of God's love, light, and joy

Jer. 31:3; John 12:32; 15:9–11

St. 1 (O Love that . . .) Rom. 8:35–39; Eph. 3:17–19

St. 2 (O Light that . . .) 2 Sam. 22:29; Ps. 36:9; John 8:12

St. 3 (O Joy that . . .) Ps. 16:11; Rom. 15:13

St. 4 (O Cross that . . .) Gal. 6:14

273. O Master, Let Me Walk with Thee
Washington Gladden, 1879

Prayer expressing desire for companionship with the Master and aspiration to be more like Christ in character and service

Matt. 20:26–28; Luke 6:40; John 12:26; 13:13–14; Gal. 5:13; Eph. 2:10; Col. 1:10; 2 Thess. 2:17; Heb. 12:1; James 1:22; 1 John 2:6

274. O Perfect Love
Dorothy F. Gurney, 1883

Marriage; wedding prayer

Eph. 5:31

Gen. 2:18, 23–24; Mark 10:7–9; Eph. 5:21–33

275. O Sacred Head, Now Wounded
Bernard of Clairvaux
Trans. James W. Alexander, 1830

Prayer of thanks; expression of devotion to Christ for his suffering and death in our place

Isa. 53

Luke 24:26; Phil. 2:8; Heb. 2:9; 1 Peter 3:18

St. 1 (O Sacred head . . .) Isa. 53:3; Matt. 27:26–50; John 19:2

St. 2 (What Thou, my . . .) Isa. 53:5; John 10:11; Rom. 5:6–11

St. 3 (What language . . .) 1 Cor. 15:57

276. O Sing a Song of Bethlehem
Louis F. Benson, 1899

A hymn recalling Jesus' birth in Bethlehem, his life in Nazareth and Galilee, and his death on Calvary

Luke 2:4–20; John 7:41–42

St. 2 (. . . a song of Nazareth . . .) Matt. 2:23; Luke 2:51

St. 3 (. . . a song of Galilee . . .) Matt. 14:24–32

277. O Sons and Daughters
Jean Tisserand, 1490
Trans. John M. Neale, 1851
Jesus' resurrection; women and angels at empty tomb
Matt. 28:1–9; Luke 24:6; John 20:29; 2 Cor. 6:18; 1 Peter 1:3

O Soul, Are You Weary and Troubled, see "Turn Your Eyes Upon Jesus"

278. O Splendor of God's Glory Bright
St. Ambrose of Milan, c. 340
Praise; Christ addressed as light
Ps. 36:9; Isa. 60:19; John 1:1–9; 8:12; Heb. 1:3

O Spread the Tidings 'Round, see "The Comforter Has Come"

279. O That Will Be Glory For Me
Charles H. Gabriel, 1900
Testimony anticipating eternal life in heaven
John 14:2–4; Rom. 8:17–18; 1 Cor. 15:51–57; 2 Cor. 3:18; 5:8; Heb. 4:9–11; 1 John 2:25; 3:2; Rev. 14:13

280. O the Deep, Deep Love of Jesus
S. Trevor Francis, c. 1890
Affirmation that Jesus' love is eternal, unchangeable, and limitless
John 13:1; 15:9; Rom. 8:35–39; Gal. 2:20: Eph. 3:17–19

281. O to Be Like Thee!
Thomas O. Chisholm, 1897
Prayer expressing desire to be more like Jesus
John 13:15; Eph. 4:24; Phil. 2:5; 1 Peter 2:21

O What a Wonderful, Wonderful Day, see "Heaven Came Down and Glory Filled My Soul"

282. O Word of God Incarnate
William W. How, 1867
Incarnate Word; God's eternal word as guide in our life; church's role in transmitting the Word
Ps. 119:105, 130, 160; Isa. 40:8; Mark 13:31; John 1:1–5, 14; 5:39; Rom. 15:4; Col. 3:16; 2 Tim. 3:16–17; 2 Peter 1:19–21

283. O Worship the King
Robert Grant, 1833
Praise to an omnipotent God and an expression of trust in God's care
Ps. 104
Pss. 47:6–7; 59:16–17; 145:1–13; 1 Tim. 6:15–16
St. 1 (O worship the King . . .) 1 Chron. 29:11–13; Pss. 89:18; 104:1
St. 2 (O tell of his might . . .) Pss. 21:13; 104:1–4
St. 3 (Thy bountiful care . . .) Job 37:9–13; Ps. 104:5–28
St. 4 (Frail children of . . .) Pss. 13:5; 46:1; 56:3–4; Isa. 26:3–4

284. O Zion, Haste
Mary A. Thompson, 1868
A call to Christians to take the message of Christ to the world
Ps. 67:2; Isa. 52:7; 61:1; Luke 24:46–47; John 3:15–17; 17:18; Acts 1:8; Rom. 10:15
St. 1 (O Zion, haste . . .) Matt. 18:14; 2 Peter 3:9; 1 John 1:5
St. 2 (Behold how many . . .) Prov. 11:7
St. 3 (Proclaim to every . . .) Acts 17:28; 1 John 4:9–10

285. Of the Father's Love Begotten
Aurelius Prudentius, 4th cent.
Trans. John Neale, 1854
and H. W. Baker, 1859
Birth of Jesus; Christ, the first and last, existing eternally
John 1:14; Phil. 2:7–11; Heb. 13:8; 1 John 4:9; Rev. 1:8

On a Hill, Far Away, see "The Old Rugged Cross"

286. On Jordan's Stormy Banks I Stand
Samuel Stennett, 1787
Anticipation of heaven compared with Israel's anticipation of the promised land
Deut. 4:22; Isa. 35:10; John 14:1–3; 1 Cor. 2:9; Heb. 11:16; 1 John 2:25; 3:2; Rev. 14:13; 21:4

287. Once in Royal David's City
C. F. Alexander, 1848
Jesus' birth and childhood; Christmas; Jesus' humanity and example
Luke 2:4–7, 11–12, 40, 52; 2 Cor. 8:9

288. Once to Every Man and Nation
James Russell Lowell, 1845
A challenge to stand by Christian truth and principles in the face of evil
Deut. 30:15–19; Josh. 24:15; Ps. 84:10; Luke 16:13; Rom. 12:9, 21; 2 Cor. 13:7–8; 1 Thess. 5:21–22

289. One Day   J. Wilbur Chapman, 1910
Jesus' birth, life, death, resurrection, and second coming; atonement; salvation
John 3:13–17; Rom. 4:25; 5:6; 2 Cor. 9:15; Gal. 4:4–5; Phil. 2:5–11; 1 Tim. 3:16; Heb. 9:28; 12:2
St. 1 (. . . when heaven was . . .) Matt. 1:21–23; John 1:14; 1 John 2:6
St. 2 (. . . they led him up . . .) Isa. 53:3; Mark 15:15–39
St. 3 (. . . they left him . . .) Matt. 27:57–66; John 19:38–42
St. 4 (. . . the grave could . . .) John 20:1–18; Acts 2:24; Eph. 1:19–20
St. 5 (. . . the trumpet will . . .) Acts 1:11; 1 Thess. 4:15–17

290. Only Trust Him
John H. Stockton, 1869
Invitation to trust in Jesus' blood and word for salvation
Isa. 44:22; John 3:16–18; 5:24; Acts 10:43; 16:30–31; Rom. 3:22–28; Titus 3:5–6
St. 1 (Come, every soul . . .) Matt. 11:28; Heb. 4:3
St. 2 (For Jesus shed . . .) Isa. 1:18; Col. 1:14; 1 John 1:7
St. 3 (Yes, Jesus is the . . .) Jer. 17:7; John 14:6

291. Onward, Christian Soldiers
Sabine Baring–Gould, 1864
Call for church and individuals to follow Christ as soldiers in spiritual warfare
Matt. 16:18; 1 Cor. 15:57–58; 16:13; Eph. 6:10–20; 1 Tim. 6:12; 2 Tim. 2:3–4; 1 Peter 5:8–11
St. 1 (Onward, Christian soldiers . . .) Deut. 31:8; Matt. 23:8

292. Open My Eyes, That I May See
C. H. Scott, 1895
Prayer that our eyes and ears would be open to God's truth and will, and that our mouth would be open to share that truth with others
Ps. 40:8; Prov. 20:12; Ezek. 36:27; Matt. 13:16; Mark 8:18; Col. 1:9; 1 John 5:6

St. 1 (. . . eyes . . .) Ps. 119:18; John 8:32
St. 2 (. . . ears . . .) Prov. 4:20; 15:31; Matt. 11:15
St. 3 (. . . mouth . . .) Ps. 49:3; Rom. 5:5; Eph. 4:15

293. Open Now Thy Gates of Beauty   Benjamin Schmolck, 1732
Trans. Catherine Winkworth, 1863
Worship in God's presence
Gen. 28:16–17; Pss. 48:1–2; 50:2; 118:19–21

Our God, Our Help in Ages Past, see "O God, Our Help in Ages Past"

Our Great Savior, see "Jesus, What a Friend for Sinners"

Out in the Highways and Byways of Life, see "Make Me a Blessing"

294. Out of My Bondage, Sorrow and Night   W. T. Sleeper, 1887
Invitation to come to Jesus for freedom from bondage, victory, peace, and joy
Ps. 86:1–7; Isa. 25:4; 61:1; Matt. 11:28; John 6:37; Acts 16:30–31; Rom. 8:1–2; 1 Tim. 1:15; Rev. 3:20; 22:17

295. Pass It On   Kurt Kaiser, 1969
Testimony of the joy and responsibility we have to share God's love with the world
John 13:35; Acts 4:20; 1 John 4:11

296. Pass Me Not, O Gentle Savior
Fanny Crosby, 1868
Expression of desire for forgiveness, cleansing, and salvation
Ps. 34:18; John 6:37; 2 Peter 3:9; Rev. 22:17
St. 2 (Let me at Thy . . .) Mark 9:24
St. 3 (Trusting only . . .) Ps. 51:17
St. 4 (Thou the spring . . .) Acts 4:12

297. Peace, Perfect Peace
Edward H. Bickersteth, 1875
Jesus gives perfect peace in all challenges to our faith
Ps. 29:11; Isa. 25:8; 26:3; John 14:27; 16:33; Eph. 2:14–17; Phil. 4:7

298. Praise Him! Praise Him!
Fanny J. Crosby, 1869

Praise and adoration of Christ as Redeemer, Lord, and King
Pss. 71:23; 150:2; Col. 1:18–20; Heb. 1:3–8; Rev. 1:5–6; 5:11–14

St. 1 (. . . Sing, O earth . . .) Ps. 148:2; Isa. 40:11

St. 2 (. . . For our sins He . . .) Isa. 53; Hab. 3:18; Gal. 1:4–5

St. 3 (. . . Heav'nly portals . . .) Ps. 148:2; Matt. 25:31; Heb. 8:1

299. Praise, My Soul, the King of Heaven
Henry F. Lyte, 1834

Praise and adoration of the eternal, omnipotent God for his majesty, power, faithfulness, and mercy

Ps. 103 Paraphrase
1 Chron. 29:10–13; Pss. 47:6–7; 92:8; 1 Tim. 1:14–17

St. 1 (Praise, my soul, the . . .) Pss. 103:1–4; 145:13; Lam. 5:19

St. 2 (Praise Him for His . . .) Ps. 103:5–12

St. 3 (Fatherlike, He tends . . .) Ps. 103:13–18

St. 4 (Angels in the height . . .) Pss. 103:19–22; 148:1–2

300. Praise the Lord Who Reigns Above
Charles Wesley, 1743

Expression of praise to God

Ps. 150
1 Chron. 29:11–13; Pss. 47:7–8; 92:1–5; 105:2; 145:3

St. 2 (Celebrate . . .) Ps. 33:2; Eph. 5:19

St. 3 (Him, in whom . . .) Matt. 6:9–10; Acts 17:28

301. Praise the Lord! Ye Heavens Adore Him
Anonymous, c. 1800
St. 3—Edward Osler, 1836

Worship; praise and adoration to the omnipotent God of creation and salvation

Ps. 148 Paraphrase
1 Chron. 16:31; Neh. 9:6; Ps. 145:10–13, 21; Rev. 4:11; 5:11–14

302. Praise the Savior, Ye Who Know Him
Thomas Kelly, 1806

Expression of devotion, trust, and commitment to Jesus
Eph. 2:12; 2 Tim. 1:12; 1 John 4:15

St. 2 (Jesus is the name . . .) Acts 4:12; Eph. 6:10–17

St. 3 (Trust in Him, ye . . .) Rom. 8:37–39; Heb. 13:8

303. Praise to God, Immortal Praise
Anna L. Barbauld, 1772

Praise and thanksgiving for God's loving care and blessings
1 Chron. 16:34; Pss. 13:6; 67; 107:1; Heb. 13:15

304. Praise to the Lord, the Almighty
Joachim Neander, 1680
Trans. Catherine Winkworth, 1863

Praise to God, our creator, for his greatness, care, and guidance
1 Chron. 29:11; Job 22:26; Pss. 101:1–4; 145:10; Isa. 25:1; Rev. 19:6b–7a

St. 1 (. . . the Almighty, the . . .) Pss. 42:11; 103:1–4

St. 2 (. . . who o'er all things . . .) Pss. 36:7; 37:4–5; 93

St. 3 (. . . who doth prosper . . .) Pss. 103:2; 106:1

St. 4 (. . . O let all that is . . .) Pss. 103:1; 106:48

305. Prayer Is the Soul's Sincere Desire
James Montgomery, 1818

Prayer as the Christian's breath and an expression of the soul's feelings
Pss. 6:9; 130:2; Matt. 6:5–13; Rom. 8:26; 1 Cor. 14:15; Phil. 4:6; 1 John 5:14–15

Last stanza (O Thou by whom . . .) John 14:6

306. Precious Lord, Take My Hand
Thomas A. Dorsey, 1938

Prayer for God's guidance in life and to life everlasting
Pss. 16:8–11; 48:14; 139:24; Isa. 40:30–31; 41:13

307. Redeemed, How I Love to Proclaim It
Fanny J. Crosby, 1882

Expression of joy of one redeemed by the blood of Jesus
Pss. 66:16; 107:2; Rom. 3:24–26; 1 Cor. 1:30–31; Col. 1:12–14; 1 Peter 1:18–19; 1 John 3:1

St. 1 (Redeemed, how I love . . .) John 1:12; Gal. 4:4–7; Eph. 1:6–7

St. 2 (Redeemed, and so happy . .) John 16:22; 1 Peter 1:8

St. 3 (I think of my blessed . . .) Exod. 15:2

308. Rejoice, the Lord Is King
Charles Wesley, 1746

Expression of joy and praise to Christ as eternal king and victor over death; resurrection; Easter
Phil. 4:4

Ps. 145:1–2, 13; Zech. 14:9; Matt. 28:18; Luke 1:32–33, 47; 1 Tim. 1:17

St. 2 (Jesus the Savior reigns . . .) Heb. 1:3; 1 Peter 3:22

St. 3 (His kingdom cannot fail . . .) Rev. 1:18

St. 4 (Rejoice in glorious hope . . .) 1 Thess. 2:19

309. Rejoice, Ye Pure in Heart
Edward H. Plumptre, 1865

Admonition to people of all ages to rejoice, give thanks, and sing; processional

Pss. 5:11–12; 20:4–5; 32:11; 33:1; 147:1, 7; 148:12–13; 2 Cor. 2:14; Phil. 4:4; Col. 3:16; 1 Tim. 6:12

310. Rescue the Perishing
Fanny J. Crosby, 1869

Challenge to bring the gospel to every person; missions

Isa. 61:1; Mark 16:15–16; Luke 14:23; 19:10; Acts 26:18; 2 Peter 3:9

St. 1 (Rescue the perishing, care . . .) John 3:36; Acts 10:43

St. 2 (Though they are slighting . . .) Pss. 34:18; 51:17; 2 Peter 3:9

St. 3 (Down in the human heart . . .) 1 Cor. 10:13

St. 4 (Rescue the perishing, duty . . .) Matt. 7:14; John 20:21

311. Revive Us Again
William P. Mackay, 1863

Expression of praise and a prayer for spiritual renewal

Ps. 85:6; 1 Cor. 1:31; 15:57; 2 Cor. 4:16; 9:15; Rev. 5:12–13

St. 1 (. . . for the Son of Thy . . .) Heb. 10:12

St. 2 (. . . for Thy Spirit of . . .) John 1:4–5; 12:46; 2 Cor. 4:6

St. 3 (All glory and praise . . .) 1 Peter 1:19; Rev. 5:12

312. Ride On, Ride On in Majesty!
Henry H. Milman, 1827

Palm Sunday; Jesus' triumphal entry, suffering, and death

Zech. 9:9; Matt. 21:1–11; John 12:12–15

313. Rise Up, O Men of God!
William P. Merrill, 1911

Call to men to give their all to Christ and his church

John 12:26; 21:15–17; Rom. 12:10–11; Gal. 5:13; Eph. 6:7

St. 1 (. . . have done with lesser . . .) Deut. 11:13; Matt. 22:37

St. 2 (. . . His Kingdom tarries . . .) Heb. 10:37

St. 3 (. . . the church for you . . .) Acts 20:28

St. 4 (. . . lift high the cross . . .) Matt. 12:50; Gal. 6:14

Rise Up, O Saints of God, see "Rise Up, O Men of God"

314. Rock of Ages
Augustus M. Toplady, 1776

Jesus as the rock of our salvation and the only means of salvation

Exod. 33:22; Pss. 61:1–8; 78:35; John 19:34; Acts 4:12; Rom. 5:6–11; 1 Cor. 3:11; 10:4; Eph. 2:8–9, 13

315. Room at the Cross for You
Ira F. Stanphill, 1946

Cross of Jesus; invitation to accept Christ as Savior

Isa. 55:7; Matt. 18:14; John 3:16–17; 1 Cor. 1:18; Col. 1:20; 2 Peter 3:9; Rev. 22:17

316. Satisfied   Clara T. Williams, 1858

Testimony that Jesus satisfies one's spiritual thirst, hunger, and poverty

Ps. 107:8–9; Matt. 5:6; John 4:14; 6:35; Rev. 22:17

317. Saved! Saved! Saved!
Oswald J. Smith, 1918

Testimony of the salvation that is ours through Jesus' death

Ps. 66:16; 2 Cor. 9:15; Gal. 2:20; Eph. 1:7

St. 3 (When poor and needy . . .) Matt. 11:28

318. Savior, Again to Thy Dear Name   John Ellerton, 1866

Prayer for peace, protection, and comfort from an omnipresent God; benediction

Num. 6:24–26; Ps. 29:11; Isa. 26:3, 12–13; John 14:27; Rom. 15:13; Eph. 6:23–24; 2 Thess. 3:16

319. Savior, Like a Shepherd Lead Us
Attr. to Dorothy Thrupp, 1836

Prayer expressing desire for Jesus' care and guidance like a shepherd cares for his sheep
Pss. 23; 95:7; Isa. 40:11; John 10:3, 14–16, 27–28

St. 1 (Savior, like a shepherd . . .) Ps. 23:1–2; Ezek. 34:14–15

St. 2 (We are Thine, do Thou . . .) Pss. 4:1; 23:3; Matt. 18:12–14

St. 3 (Thou hast promised to . . .) Ps. 103:10–12; John 6:37; 8:36

St. 4 (Early let us seek Thy . . .) Prov. 8:17; Eph. 2:4

320. Savior, Teach Me Day by Day
Jane E. Leeson, 1842

Expression of desire to love, serve, and follow Christ because he first loved us
John 13:34; 14:23; 21:15–17; Eph. 3:17–19; 5:2; 1 Thess. 4:9; 1 John 3:16; 4:19

St. 2 (With a child's glad heart . . .) Eph. 5:1, 8

321. Savior, Thy Dying Love
Sylvanus D. Phelps, 1862

A Christian's response to the love shown by Jesus on the cross
Luke 10:27; Rom. 12:1; 2 Cor. 5:15; Eph. 5:2; 1 John 3:16–18; 4:19

St. 2 (At the blest mercy seat . . .) Matt. 16:24; Heb. 9:24

St. 3 (Give me a faithful heart . . .) 1 Sam. 16:7; John 13:15

St. 4 (All that I am and have . . .) Matt. 25:21

322. Send the Light!
Charles H. Gabriel, 1890

A call to worldwide missions
Luke 24:47; John 12:46; Acts 26:17–18; 2 Cor. 4:4–6

St. 2 (We have heard . . .) Acts 16:9–10

St. 4 (Let us not grow . . .) Gal. 6:9

323. Shall We Gather at the River
Robert Lowry, 1864

A hymn anticipating life in heaven: the throne of God, the heavenly river, and the gathering of the saints
Rev. 22:1

Heb. 11:16; Rev. 22:1–5

324. Shepherd of Tender (Eager) Youth
Clement of Alexandria, c. 200
Trans. H. M. Dexter, 1846

Expression of praise and a prayer for guidance by Christ as shepherd
Ps. 23; Ezek. 34:12–16; 1 Peter 2:24–25

St. 2 (Thou art our holy Lord . . .) Isa. 53:6; Gal. 3:13

St. 3 (Thou art the great high . . .) Heb. 7:25; 8:1

St. 4 (Ever be Thou our guide . . .) Ps. 23:3

325. Silent Night! Holy Night!
Joseph Mohr, 1818

Birth of Jesus; Christmas
Matt. 2:9–10; Luke 1:77–79; 2:7–20; John 1:4–5

Simply Trusting Every Day, see "Trusting Jesus"

326. Since I Have Been Redeemed
Edwin O. Excell, 1884

Joyful testimony of one who has been redeemed
Ps. 107:2; Isa. 35:10; Rom. 15:9; Eph. 1:6–7; Col. 1:12–14; Titus 2:14

St. 2 (. . . a Christ who satisfies . . .) Ps. 107:9; Phil. 2:13

St. 3 (. . . a witness bright and . . .) Ps. 34:4; 1 Peter 3:15

St. 4 (. . . a home prepared for me . . .) John 14:2; 2 Cor. 5:1

327. Since Jesus Came Into My Heart
Rufus H. McDaniel, 1914

Testimony of salvation; expression of joy; anticipation of heaven
Rom. 5:11; 10:9–10; 2 Cor. 5:17

St. 1 (What a wonderful . . .) John 12:46

St. 2 (I have ceased from . . .) Heb. 10:22; 1 Peter 2:25

St. 3 (There's a light in . . .) Ps. 23:4; Rev. 22:14

St. 4 (I shall go there . . .) Rev. 22:14

328. Sing Praise to God Who Reigns Above
Johann J. Schutz, 1675
Trans. Frances E. Cox, 1864

Praise to an omnipotent God of creation who is always nearby to guide

1 Chron. 16:25–36; Pss. 47:6–7; 59:16–17;
118:28–29; 146; Isa. 12:2–5; Heb. 13:15; 1 Peter 2:9

St. 2 (What God's almighty pow'r . . .) Ps. 121:4

St. 3 (The Lord is never far . . .) Pss. 139:7;
145:18

St. 4 (Thus, all my gladsome . . .) Ps. 35:9

Sing the Wondrous Love of Jesus, see "When
We All Get to Heaven"

Sing Them Over Again to Me, see "Wonderful
Words of Life"

329. Sing to the Lord of Harvest
John S. B. Monsell, 1866
Harvest hymn of praise and thanksgiving
Pss. 65:9–13; 67:6; 85:12; Matt. 9:37–38; Acts 14:17

Sinners Jesus Will Receive, see "Christ
Receiveth Sinful Men"

330. So Send I You
E. Margaret Clarkson, 1944
A call to missions and service
Isa. 6:8; Luke 4:18; John 20:21

331. Softly and Tenderly
Will L. Thompson, 1880
*Jesus calls, pleads, and waits for sinners and
promises mercy and pardon*
Isa. 55:7; Matt. 11:28; 1 Thess. 5:24; 1 John 1:9;
Rev. 3:20; 22:17

332. Soldiers of Christ, Arise
Charles Wesley, 1749
*Equipped with the proper spiritual armor, we
press on to victory in spiritual warfare and in
the Christian life*
1 Cor. 15:57–58; 2 Cor. 12:9; Eph. 6:10–18; 1 Tim.
6:12; 2 Tim. 2:3–4; 4:7–8; 1 John 4:4

Something for Jesus, see "Savior, Thy Dying
Love"

Something for Thee, see "Savior, Thy Dying
Love"

Sometimes I Feel Discouraged, see "There Is
a Balm in Gilead"

333. Spirit Divine, Attend Our Prayer
Andrew Reed, 1829
Prayer for presence of the Holy Spirit
Ezek. 36:27; Matt. 3:11; John 14:16–17; Acts 1:8;
4:31; 9:31; Rom. 8:9, 26; Gal. 5:25

Spirit Divine, Hear Our Prayer, see "Spirit
Divine, Attend Our Prayer"

334. Spirit of God, Descend Upon My Heart
George Croly, 1854
*Expression of prayer for the indwelling spirit of
God to take control of our lives and teach us to
love as God loves*
Deut. 6:5; Job 32:8; 33:4; Ps. 51:10–12; John 15:26;
Rom. 5:5; Gal. 5:25; Eph. 3:16–19; 2 Tim. 1:7

335. Spirit of the Living God
Daniel Iverson, 1926
*Prayer expressing desire for God's spirit to take
complete control of our lives*
Ezek. 36:26–27; Zech. 4:6; Luke 11:13; John 20:22;
Rom. 8:6–9; 1 Cor. 6:19–20; Gal. 5:16–25

336. Stand Up and Bless the Lord
James Montgomery, 1824
Call for eternal praise to an almighty God
1 Chron. 23:30; Neh. 9:5; Pss. 63:4; 103:1–2; 135:1

St. 1 (. . . Ye people of His . . .) Deut. 6:5; Ps.
51:15; 1 Peter 2:9

St. 2 (Though high above . . .) Pss. 2:11; 22:23;
Heb. 12:28

St. 3 (O for the living . . .) Ps. 51:15; Isa. 6:5–6;
Rom. 8:26

St. 4 (God is our strength . . .) Pss. 27:1;
103:3–4; Isa. 12:2

St. 5 (. . . the Lord your God . . .) 1 Chron.
16:36; Ps. 145:1–2

337. Stand Up, Stand Up for Jesus
George Duffield, 1858
*In Christ's strength, we engage in spiritual war-
fare, pressing on to final victory*
Rom. 8:37; 1 Cor. 15:55–58; 16:13; Eph. 6:10–20;
Phil. 1:27–30; 1 Tim. 6:12; 2 Tim. 2:3–4; 4:7–8;
Heb. 10:23

338. Standing on the Promises
R. Kelso Carter, 1886
*Expression of dependence on the promises of
God*

Acts 2:38–39; Rom. 4:20–21; 2 Cor. 1:20–22; Gal. 3:14–22, 29; Heb. 9:15; 10:23; James 1:12; 2 Peter 1:3–4; 1 John 2:25

339. Sun of My Soul, Thou Savior Dear
John Keble, 1820
Prayer for God's presence and light at evening and through the night
Pss. 4:6–8; 84:11; 139:11–12; Luke 24:49

340. Sunshine in My Soul
Eliza E. Hewitt, 1887
In Jesus' presence, there is light like sunshine and joy in our lives
Ps. 32:11; Isa. 35:10; John 1:4–9; 8:12; 15:11; 2 Cor. 4:6; Phil. 4:4

341. Surely Goodness and Mercy
John W. Peterson and Alfred B. Smith, 1958
Jesus as guardian and shepherd of our lives
Ps. 23
Exod. 15:13; Pss. 16:11; 48:14; 106:1
St. 1 (A pilgrim was I . . .) Rom. 2:4; 1 Peter 2:25
St. 2 (He restoreth my . . .) Pss. 23:3; 27:1; 37:23; 51:12; Isa. 40:31
St. 3 (When I walk . . .) Ps. 23:4; John 14:2
Refrain Ps. 23:6; Luke 14:15; Rev. 19:9

342. Sweet By and By
Sanford F. Bennett, 1868
Anticipation of eternal life in heaven
Ps. 23:6; Dan. 7:18; Heb. 13:14; Rev. 22:1–5

343. Sweet Hour of Prayer
William Walford, 1845
We take all of our cares and needs to God in prayer
Pss. 5:3; 6:9; 55:22; 65:2; Matt. 6:5–13; Acts 3:1; Phil. 4:6; 1 Peter 5:7
St. 3 (. . . from Mt. Pisgah . . .) Deut. 3:27

344. Sweet, Sweet Spirit
Doris Akers, 1965
Prayer for the presence of the Holy Spirit in worship
Ps. 133:1; Matt. 18:20; Gal. 5:25; Eph. 4:3

Sweetly, Lord, Have We Heard Thee Calling, see "Footsteps of Jesus"

345. Take My Life and Let It Be
Frances R. Havergal, 1874
Personal expression of complete consecration to God
1 Chron. 29:5; Matt. 22:37; Rom. 6:13; 12:1; 1 Cor. 6:19–20; 2 Tim. 2:20–21

346. Take the Name of Jesus with You
Lydia Baxter, 1870
The name of Jesus
Matt. 12:21; John 14:13–14; 20:31; Acts 4:12; Phil. 2:9–10; Col. 3:17; Heb. 13:15

347. Take Time to Be Holy
William D. Longstaff, 1882
Holiness and spiritual maturity require a close relationship with Jesus as Lord and Master of our lives
Lev. 20:7–8; 2 Cor. 7:1; Eph. 4:24; Heb. 12:14; 1 Peter 1:15–16
St. 1 (. . . speak oft with thy . . .) Matt. 4:4; John 15:4–5; Rom. 15:1
St. 2 (. . . the world rushes on . . .) Matt. 6:6; John 13:15; Phil. 2:5
St. 3 (. . . let Him be thy guide . . .) Pss. 48:14; 118:8; Prov. 3:5
St. 4 (. . . be calm in thy soul . . .) Ps. 143:10; John 16:13

Take Up Thy Cross and Follow Me, see "Wherever He Leads, I'll Go"

348. "Take Up Thy Cross," the Savior Said
Charles W. Everest, 1833
Discipleship; call of Christ to take up our crosses and follow him, knowing he will strengthen us
Matt. 16:24–27; Luke 9:57–62; John 12:26; 2 Cor. 12:9–10; 1 Peter 2:21

349. Teach Me Thy Way, O Lord
B. Mansell Ramsey, 1919
Expression of desire to know God's way in dealing with all circumstances of life
Pss. 25:4–5; 27:11; 37:23; 143:10; Hos. 14:9; Rom. 12:2
St. 1 (Teach me thy way . . .) 2 Cor. 5:7
St. 4 (Long as my life . . .) 2 Tim. 4:7–8

350. Tell Me the Old, Old Story
A. Catherine Hankey

Expression of desire to know the ageless story of Jesus, his love, and his care
>   Mark 5:19; Rom. 3:22–24; 2 Peter 3:18; 1 John 4:19

351. Tell Me the Story of Jesus
Fanny J. Crosby, 1880
Events in life of Jesus recalled: birth, temptation, humiliation, crucifixion, and resurrection
>   Matt. 20:28; Mark 8:31; Acts 10:38–41

St. 1 (Tell me the story of . . .) Luke 2:13–14

St. 2 (Fasting alone in the . . .) Isa. 53:3–4; Luke 4:1–14

St. 3 (Tell of the cross . . .) Mark 15:46; 16:6; John 19:17–18

352. Ten Thousand Times Ten Thousand
Henry Alford, 1867
Expression of anticipation and desire for heaven
>   Isa. 35:10; Dan. 7:10, 18; 1 Cor. 15:54–57; 2 Cor. 5:8; 1 Thess. 4:13–17; Jude 14; Rev. 5:11–12; 19:6

353. The Church's One Foundation
Samuel J. Stone, 1866
Christ as the creator and foundation of the church
>   Isa. 28:16; Matt. 16:15–18; Eph. 1:22–23; 2:19–22; Col. 1:18

St. 1 (The Church's one . . .) Acts 20:28; 1 Cor. 3:11

St. 2 (Elect from every . . .) Eph. 4:4–6; 1 Peter 1:2; 2:9

354. The Comforter Has Come
Frank Bottome, 1890
Expression of testimony and joy in the coming of the Holy Spirit
>   Matt. 3:11; John 14:16–17; 16:7–8; Rom. 5:5

The Cross Upon Which Jesus Died, see "Room at the Cross for You"

355. The Day of Resurrection
John of Damascus, 8th century
Trans. John M. Neale, 1862
Expression of joy and praise in celebration of the day of Jesus' resurrection
>   Matt. 28:1–9; Mark 16:6; Acts 2:24–28; 1 Cor. 15:57

St. 2 (Our hearts be pure . . .) Isa. 9:2

356. The Day Thou Gavest
John Ellerton, 1870
Praise and prayer continue day and night through the church eternally; evening
>   Ps. 113:2–3

>   Pss. 42:8; 92:1–2; Isa. 26:9; Eph. 3:21

Last stanza Ps. 145:13

357. The First Noel
English carol, 17th century
Christmas; visit to newborn Savior by shepherds and wise men
>   Matt. 2:1–12; Luke 2:8–20

Refrain Luke 1:33

358. The God of Abraham Praise
From a Hebrew Doxology, c. 1400
Trans. Thomas Olivers, 1770
Praise to the almighty, eternal God
>   Exod. 3:14; Pss. 22:23; 106:48; Isa. 6:3; Lam. 5:19; John 8:58; Heb. 6:13–20; Rev. 1:8; 11:17

359. The Great Physician
William Hunter, 1859
The name of Jesus; Jesus' compassion and care; forgiveness of sins
>   Ps. 103: 3; Matt. 1:21–23; 9:12; Acts 4:10–12; 10:43; 1 John 2:12

St. 1 (The great physician . . .) Matt. 4:23; Luke 7:20–22

St. 2 (Your many sins are . . .) Mark 2:5; John 3:3, 16; 2 Cor. 5:8

St. 3 (All glory to the . . .) Mark 16:16; John 20:31

Refrain Matt. 12:21; Phil. 2:9–11

360. The Head That Once Was Crowned
Thomas Kelly, 1820
Christ's victory over death; exaltation of Jesus
>   John 12:32; 16:19–22; 19:1–5; Acts 2:36; 5:30–31; Phil. 2:5–11; 1 Thess. 2:19–20; Heb. 2:7–9; 12:2

361. The Heavens Declare Thy Glory
Isaac Watts, 1719
God's Word is greater than all the creations of God found in nature
>   Pss. 19; 33:4; 119:89, 105; Rom. 15:4; 2 Tim. 3:16–17; Heb. 4:12; 1 Peter 1:24–25

362. The King of Love My Shepherd Is
Henry W. Baker, 1868

Testimony of Jesus' goodness and care as compared to that of a shepherd for his sheep
Ps. 23 Paraphrase
Ps. 95:7; Isa. 40:11; Ezek. 34:31; John 10:14–15, 27; 1 Peter 5:7

St. 1 (The King of love my . . .) Ps. 23:1; Phil. 4:19

St. 2 (Where streams of . . .) Ps. 23:2; Isa. 49:10; John 10:9

St. 3 (Perverse and foolish . . .) Ps. 23:3; Isa. 53:6; Luke 15:3–7

St. 4 (In death's dark vale . . .) Ps. 23:4; Heb. 2:14–15

St. 6 (And so through . . .) Pss. 23:6; 79:13; 84:2–4; 145:7

363. The King Shall Come When Morning Dawns   Early Greek Hymn
Trans. John Brownlie, 1907
Anticipation of Jesus' second coming; Jesus' second coming compared to the glory of his birth and his resurrection
Matt. 25:31; 26:64; Luke 21:27–28; Rev. 22:20

364. The Light of the World Is Jesus   Philip P. Bliss, 1875
Jesus is the light of life and the light of the world
Isa. 60:1–3; John 1:4–9; 8:12; 12:46; Eph. 5:8–14; 1 John 1:5–7; Rev. 21:23–24; 22:5

365. The Lily of the Valley
Charles W. Fry, 1881
Jesus is our friend and is present in all the needs of life
Ps. 94:19; Song of Songs 2:1; 5:10; John 14:18; Rom. 8:35–39; 2 Cor. 1:3–7; Heb. 4:15–16; 13:5–6; 1 Peter 5:7; Rev. 22:16

St. 1 (I have found a friend . . .) Ps. 55:22; 1 John 1:9

St. 2 (He all my grief has . . .) Heb. 2:18

St. 3 (He will never, never . . .) Deut. 8:3; 1 Thess. 4:17

The Lord Is My Shepherd, see "The Lord's My Shepherd"

366. The Lord's My Shepherd
Scottish Psalter, 1650
An expression of confidence in God's protection and care

Ps. 23 Paraphrase
Ps. 95:7; Isa. 40:11; Ezek. 34:31; John 10:14–15, 27; 1 Peter 5:7

The Lord's Our Rock, In Him We Hide, see "A Shelter in the Time of Storm"

367. The Old Rugged Cross
George Bennard, 1913
Testimony expressing love for the cross of Jesus and what it means
John 19:17–18; Rom. 5:6–11; 1 Cor. 1:17–18; Gal. 6:14; Phil. 2:8; Col. 2:13–15; Heb. 12:2; 1 Peter 2:24

368. The Savior Is Waiting
Ralph Carmichael, 1958
Invitation of Christ to accept him as Savior
Acts 2:21; Rom. 10:9–10; Heb. 3:15; Rev. 3:20; 22:17

St. 2 (If you'll take one step . . .) John 12:46

369. The Solid Rock   Edward Mote, 1834
Testimony that our hope of salvation lies in Jesus' blood, righteousness, unchanging grace, oath, and covenant
John 14:6; Acts 4:12; Rom. 5:1–5; 1 Cor. 3:11; 1 Tim. 2:5; Heb. 6:17–19; 1 Peter 1:3; 3:15

St. 4 (When He shall come . . .) 1 Thess. 4:16–17

370. The Son of God Goes Forth to War   Reginald Heber, 1827
We join the martyrs of the past in following Christ as the leader in spiritual warfare
Eph. 6:10–20; Phil. 1:27–30; 1 Tim. 6:12; 2 Tim. 2:3–4; 4:7–8; 1 Peter 5:8–9; 1 John 5:4–5; Jude 3; Rev. 17:14

St. 1 (The Son of God goes . . .) Mark 10:38; Luke 9:23

St. 2 (The martyr first . . .) Acts 7:54–60

371. The Spacious Firmament
Joseph Addison, 1712
Praise for the majesty and power of God as seen in his creation
Gen. 1:1–19; Pss. 19:1–6; 102:25; 148:1–6; Isa. 40:26; Jer. 10:12–13; Rom. 1:20; Heb. 11:3

372. The Strife Is O'er
Latin Hymn, 1695
Trans. Francis Pott, 1861

Praise for Jesus' resurrection and victory over death
> Luke 24:1–7; Rom. 6:9–10; 1 Cor. 15:54–57; Col. 2:15; Rev. 19:1–2

373. The Vision of a Dying World
Anne Ortlund, 1966
Expression of prayer that God would arouse and empower the church for worldwide missions and evangelism
> Mark 16:15; Luke 10:2; John 4:35; Acts 16:9–10; Rom. 10:14–15

374. The Way of the Cross Leads Home
Jessie B. Pounds, 1906
Testimony that our only way to eternal life is by the cross of Jesus
> Matt. 16:24; 1 Cor. 1:18; 3:11; 2 Cor. 5:1; Col. 1:19–22; 1 Tim. 2:5–6a

The Whole World Was Lost, see "The Light of the World is Jesus"

375. There Is a Balm in Gilead
Traditional Spiritual
Spiritual offering peace, comfort, and encouragement
Jer. 8:22
> Pss. 42:5, 11; 43:5; Jer. 46:11; 51:8; Luke 4:18
> St. 1 (Sometimes I feel . . .) Deut. 31:6–8; Josh. 1:9; Ps. 51:12; Lam 5:21; Hab. 3:2

376. There Is a Fountain
William Cowper, 1771
We acknowledge the atonement for our sins through Jesus' death
Zech. 13:1
> Ps. 36:9; Matt. 26:28; John 19:34; Rom. 5:6–11; Eph. 1:7; 2:13; Titus 2:14; Heb. 9:14; 1 Peter 1:18–19; 1 John 1:7
> St. 2 (The dying thief . . .) Luke 23:39–43

377. There Is a Green Hill Far Away
Cecil F. Alexander, 1848
Jesus' suffering and death for our sins; atonement
> John 19:17–18; Rom. 5:6–11; Eph. 2:13–18; 5:2; Col. 1:20–22; 1 Thess. 5:9–10; 1 Tim. 2:5–6; Titus 2:14; Heb. 13:12; 1 Peter 2:24; 3:18; 1 John 4:19

There Is a Name I Love to Hear, see "O, How I Love Jesus"

There Is a Place of Quiet Rest, see "Near to the Heart of God"

378. There Is Power in the Blood
Lewis E. Jones, 1899
The blood of Christ has power to cleanse and pardon from sin
> Ps. 51:2, 7; Isa. 1:18; Rom. 3:24–25; Eph. 1:7–8; 2:13; Heb. 9:14; 1 Peter 1:18–19

There Is Sunshine in My Soul Today, see "Sunshine in My Soul"

379. There Shall Be Showers of Blessing
Daniel W. Whittle, 1883
Affirmation of the promise of times of spiritual blessing and renewal
Ezek. 34:26
> Pss. 51:12; 85:6; Hos. 6:3

There's a Call Comes Ringing, see "Send the Light"

There's a Land That Is Fairer Than Day, see "Sweet By and By"

380. There's a Song in the Air
Josiah G. Holland, 1871
Praise expressed at the birth of Jesus
> Matt. 2:2, 10; Luke 1:68–69; 2:7–20, 29–32

There's a Sweet, Sweet Spirit in This Place, see "Sweet, Sweet Spirit"

381. There's a Wideness in God's Mercy
Frederick W. Faber, 1854
God's boundless love and mercy to mankind
> Pss. 36:5; 86:5–7, 15; 103:8–13; Lam. 3:21–26; John 3:16; Rom. 8:35–39; Eph. 1:6–8; 2:4–7; 1 John 1:7–9

There's Not a Friend Like the Lowly Jesus, see "No, Not One"

There's Within My Heart a Melody, see "He Keeps Me Singing"

382. Thine Is the Glory
Edmond L. Budry, 1884
Jesus resurrection and victory over death
> Matt. 6:13; Luke 24:1–8; Acts 2:24

St. 1 (Thine is the glory . . .) Matt. 28:2
St. 2 (Lo! Jesus meets us . . .) 1 Cor. 15:55–57
St. 3 (No more we doubt . . .) Rom. 8:37

383. This Is My Father's World
Maltbie D. Babcock, 1901
God's majesty, power, love, care, and guidance is revealed in nature and in Jesus
Pss. 8; 24:1; 145:10–13; Rev. 4:11
St. 3 (. . . O let me ne'er forget . . .) John 16:33; Rom. 16:20

384. This Is the Day the Lord Hath Made
Isaac Watts, 1719
Celebration of the day of resurrection
Ps. 118:24; Matt. 12:8; Mark 16:1–8; John 20:1–20; Rom. 6:9–10

385. Thou Art the Way: to Thee Alone
George W. Doane, 1824
Jesus as the way, the truth, and the life; Christ as the only way to God
John 14:6
John 5:24; 10:9–10; Rom. 5:1–2
St. 1 (. . . the Way, to Thee . . .) Eph. 2:18; 1 Tim. 2:5
St. 2 (. . . the Truth, Thy . . .) John 8:32; 16:13; 17:19
St. 3 (. . . the Life, the . . .) John 11:25; 2 Tim. 1:10; 1 John 5:12

386. Thou Didst Leave Thy Throne
Emily E. S. Elliott, 1864
Jesus' humble birth, life, and ministry; invitation; Christmas
Matt. 8:20; Luke 2:1–7; John 1:11; 2 Cor. 8:9; Phil. 2:5–11; Heb. 1:2–8; 4:7

Thou My Everlasting Portion, see "Close to Thee"

387. Thou, Whose Almighty Word
John Marriott, 1813
Prayer of desire for light expressed to God as three in one; Trinity
Gen. 1:2–4; Isa. 60:1–3; Mal. 4:2; John 8:12; 2 Cor. 4:6; 1 John 1:5

388. 'Tis Midnight and on Olive's Brow
William B. Tappan, 1822
Jesus' prayer and suffering at Gethsemane

Matt. 26:36–45; Luke 22:39–44; John 18:1

389. 'Tis So Sweet To Trust in Jesus
Louisa M. R. Stead, 1882
Expression of complete trust in Jesus for salvation and a full life
Ps. 37:5; John 5:24; 6:68; 20:29–31; Acts 10:43; Rom. 1:16–17; 5:1–2; Eph. 2:12–13
St. 4 (I'm so glad . . .) Matt. 28:20

390. To God Be the Glory
Fanny J. Crosby, 1875
Praise to God for all that He has done for us through Jesus
Pss. 72:18–19; 126:3; John 3:16–17; Rom. 5:1–2, 11; 1 Cor. 6:20; Gal. 1:3–5; Eph. 5:19–20; 1 Tim. 1:14–17; 1 Peter 1:3–8; 1 John 4:14; Rev. 1:5–6

Trust and Obey, see "When We Walk with the Lord"

391. Trusting Jesus
Edgar P. Stites, 1876
Expression of simple, uncomplicated trust in Jesus
Pss. 37:3–5; 56:3–4; Prov. 3:5–6; 2 Cor. 3:4–5; Eph. 6:16; 1 John 5:4–5

392. Turn Your Eyes Upon Jesus
Helen H. Lemmel, 1922
Invitation and call of Jesus to accept him as Savior
Isa. 45:22; 2 Cor. 4:6; 1 John 5:12; Rev. 22:17
St. 1 (O soul, are you weary . . .) John 10:10; 12:46
St. 2 (Through death into life . . .) Rom. 8:37; Gal. 5:24; 1 Peter 2:24

393. Under His Wings
William O. Cushing, c. 1896
Affirmation of God's care and protection
Pss. 27:5; 36:7; 91:1–4; 2 Thess. 3:3
St. 2 (. . . what a refuge . . .) Matt. 11:28; 2 Cor. 1:5

Up Calvary's Mountain, see "Blessed Redeemer"

Up From the Grave He Arose, see "Christ Arose"

394. Victory in Jesus
Eugene M. Bartlett, Sr., 1939
Testimony of a life that is eternally victorious through Jesus
1 Cor. 15:57
> Acts 4:12; Rom. 8:37; Titus 3:4–6; 1 Peter 2:24; 1 John 5:4
>
> St. 1 (. . . an old, old story . . .) Isa. 53:5; Matt. 20:28; Acts 3:19
>
> St. 2 (. . . about His healing . . .) Ps. 34:18; Matt. 4:23–24; 15:30
>
> St. 3 (. . . about a mansion . . .) John 14:2; Rev. 5:11–12; 21:21; 22:1
>
> Refrain 1 Cor. 6:20

Walking in Sunlight All of My Journey, see "Heavenly Sunlight"

395. Watchman, Tell Us of the Night
John Bowring, 1825
Anticipation of a new day in Christ
Isa. 21:11–12
> Isa. 60:1–3; Rom. 13:12; 2 Peter 1:19

396. We Are God's People
Bryan Jeffery Leech, 1976
Testimony of the relationship we have with fellow believers because of our relationship with God
> Ps. 100:3; 2 Cor. 6:16; Eph. 2:19–22; 1 Peter 2:9
>
> St. 1 (. . . God's people, the . . .) 1 Peter 2:6–9
>
> St. 2 (. . . God's loved ones . . .) 1 John 4:19
>
> St. 3 (. . . the body of which . . .) John 14:23; Rom. 5:4–8; 1 Cor. 12:27
>
> St. 4 (. . . a temple, the . . .) 1 Cor. 3:16

397. We Gather Together
Netherlands Folk Song
Trans. Theodore Baker, 1894
Hymn of petition and thanks to God as defender and guide
> Deut. 31:8; Pss. 5:11; 32:8; Acts 14:22; Rom. 8:31
>
> St. 1 (We gather together . . .) Pss. 67:1; 94:12; 119:134; Heb. 12:5–7
>
> St. 2 (Beside us to guide . . .) Pss. 48:14; 145:13
>
> St. 3 (We all do extol . . .) John 16:33

398. We Give Thee but Thine Own
William W. How, 1858

Expression of commitment to Christian stewardship
> Gen. 28:22; Deut. 16:17; 1 Chron. 29:14; Prov. 3:9; Hag. 2:8; Mal. 3:8–10; 1 Cor. 16:2; 2 Cor. 9:7

399. We Have Heard the Joyful Sound
Priscilla J. Owens, 1882
We are commanded to spread the gospel to every land by song and spoken word
> Ps. 67:2; 96:2–3; Isa. 52:7; Mark 16:15; Luke 24:47; John 3:17; Acts 1:8; 4:12; Rom. 1:16; 10:13–15

400. We Plow the Fields and Scatter
Matthias Claudius, 1782
Trans. Jane M. Campbell, 1861
Expression of thanks and acknowlegement that all good gifts come from God
> Gen. 1:11–18; 2:4–5; Job 5:10; Ps. 65:9–11; Isa. 55:10; Acts 14:17; James 1:17

We Praise Thee, O God, see "Revive Us Again"

401. We Praise Thee, O God, Our Redeemer
Julia C. Cory, 1902
Praise for God's loving care, guidance and for the redemption He provides
Luke 1:68
> 1 Chron. 16:23–36; Pss. 95:1–6; 111:1; Heb. 13:15
>
> St. 1 (We praise Thee, O God . . .) Ps. 103:1–2; Isa. 47:4
>
> St. 2 (We worship Thee, God . . .) Ps. 16:8; 46:7
>
> St. 3 (With voices united our . . .) Ps. 67:5; 145:1–2

We Sing the Almighty Power of God, see "I Sing the Almighty Power of God"

402. We Three Kings
John H. Hopkins, 1857
Visit of wise men to infant Jesus; Christmas
> Matt. 2:1–11

403. We Would See Jesus; Lo! His Star Is Shining
J. Edgar Park, 1913
Birth, life, and ministry of Jesus; discipleship
> Matt. 2:2; John 12:21; Heb. 2:9
>
> St. 1 (. . . lo! His star is . . .) Matt. 2:1–2, 9–11; Luke 2:7, 13–14
>
> St. 2 (. . . Mary's son most . . .) Luke 2:52; John 1:4–5; 14:6
>
> St. 3 (. . . on the mountain . . .) Matt. 5:1–12

Last st. (. . . in the early . . .) Matt. 16:24–26; John 10:4; 12:26

We're Marching to Zion, see "Come, We That Love the Lord"

404. We've a Story to Tell to the Nations   H. Ernest Nichol, 1896

Missions; reminder that we have a Savior to share around the world
> Pss. 67:2; 96:2–3; Isa. 9:2; 52:7; Matt. 24:14; 28:19–20; Luke 24:47; John 12:46; Acts 1:8; 26:17–18

St. 3 (We've a message to give . . .) John 3:16–17; 1 John 4:10

405. Welcome, Happy Morning!
Venantius H. C. Fortunatus, 6th century
Trans. John Ellerton, 1868

Jesus' resurrection and victory over death and hell
> Matt. 28:1–9; 1 Cor. 15:20; Rev. 1:18

406. Were You There?
Traditional Spiritual

Remembrance of Jesus' crucifixion, burial, and resurrection
> Mark 15:15–47; John 19:16–18, 38–42

What a Fellowship, What a Joy Divine, see "Leaning on the Everlasting Arms"

407. What a Friend We Have in Jesus   Joseph M. Scriven, 1855

We take all needs of life to God in prayer
> Ps. 6:9; 55:22; 57:1; John 15:13–16; Phil. 4:6; 1 Thess. 5:17; 1 Peter 5:7; 1 John 5:14–15

What a Wonderful Change in My Life, see "Since Jesus Came Into My Heart"

408. What a Wonderful Savior
Elisha A. Hoffman, 1891

Testimony of the salvation that is ours through the blood of Jesus
> Isa. 53:4–12; Rom. 5:6–11; 1 Cor. 15:57; Eph. 1:7; Titus 2:14; 1 Peter 1:18–19; 1 John 1:7–9; 4:14

St. 1 (Christ has for sin . . .) 1 Cor. 6:20

St. 2 (I praise Him for . . .) Eph. 2:13

What Can Wash Away My Sin?, see "Nothing But the Blood"

409. What Child Is This?
William C. Dix, 1865

Birth of Jesus; Christmas
> Matt. 2:1–12; Luke 2:6–20

410. What If It Were Today?
Lelia N. Morris, 1912

Anticipation of the return and future reign of Christ
> Matt. 25:13; Mark 13:32–37; Luke 12:35–40; Acts 1:9–11; Titus 2:13; 2 Peter 3:3–14

St. 1 (Jesus is coming . . .) John 14:3; Heb. 9:28

St. 2 (Satan's dominion . . .) Rom. 16:20; 1 Thess. 4:16–17

St. 3 (Faithful and true . . .) Luke 18:8; 2 Peter 3:14; 1 John 2:28

Refrain 1 Thess. 2:19–20; 1 Tim. 6:15

411. What Wondrous Love Is This?
American Folk Hymn

We sing of God and his great love expressed to us in Jesus Christ
> John 15:13; Rom. 5:8; Gal. 3:13; Eph. 3:17–19; 1 John 3:1, 16; 4:19; Rev. 7:9–10

When All My Labors and Trials Are O'er, see "O That Will Be Glory For Me"

412. When All Thy Mercies, O My God   Joseph Addison, 1712

Testimony about the wonderful mercies and goodness of God
> 1 Chron. 16:34; Pss. 31:7; 63:3; 86:5, 15; 89:1; 103:2–4; Luke 1:50

413. When I Survey the Wondrous Cross   Isaac Watts, 1707

We look at the cross and Jesus' suffering and death in our behalf
> John 19:17–18; 1 Cor. 1:18; 2:2; Gal. 6:14; Phil. 2:8

St. 1 (When I Survey . . .) Phil. 3:7–8

St. 2 (Forbid it, Lord . . .) 1 Cor. 1:31; 1 John 2:15–16

St. 3 (See, from His . . .) Matt. 27:29; John 19:34

St. 4 (Were the whole . . .) John 15:13

414. When in Our Music God Is Glorified   Fred Pratt Green, 1971

A testimony and reminder concerning the correct use of music in worship
2 Chron. 5:13–14; Pss. 33:1–3; 66:2; 71:22–23; 92:1–4; 95:1–2; Mark 14:26; Col. 3:16

415. When Morning Gilds the Skies
Anonymous, German, 1828
Trans. Edward Caswall, 1854

A morning song of worship and praise
1 Chron. 23:30; Pss. 5:3; 30:4–5; 59:16–17; 108:1–4; 150:6; John 5:23; Phil. 2:9–11; Heb. 13:15; Rev. 5:12

When Peace Like a River, see "It Is Well with My Soul"

416. When the Roll Is Called Up Yonder   James M. Black, 1893

Expression of joyful anticipation of eternal life in heaven
John 14:2–3; 1 Cor. 15:52; Col. 3:4; 1 Thess. 4:16–17

St. 3 (let us labor for . . .) 1 Cor. 15:58; Heb. 4:9–11

When the Trumpet of the Lord Shall Sound, see "When the Roll Is Called Up Yonder"

When Upon Life's Billows, see "Count Your Blessings"

417. When We All Get to Heaven
Eliza E. Hewitt, 1898

Anticipation of heaven and eternal life with Christ
Isa. 35:10; John 14:2–3; Acts 20:32; Rom. 8:17–18; 1 Cor. 15:54–57; 2 Cor. 5:8; 1 Thess. 4:17; 1 John 2:25; Rev. 14:13

St. 3 (Let us then be true . . .) 1 Peter 4:13
St. 4 (Onward to the prize . . .) Phil. 3:14; Rev. 21:21

418. When We Walk with the Lord
John H. Sammis, 1887

Expression of trust, commitment to obey God, and a testimony of the joy that follows
Exod. 19:5; Deut. 5:33; Pss. 4:5; 37:3–5; 143:8–10; John 14:12, 23; 2 Cor. 5:7; Col. 2:6–7; 1 John 2:6

419. Where Cross the Crowded Ways   Frank M. North, 1903

Prayer regarding social concerns and service
Ps. 86:15; Zech. 7:9; Matt. 9:36; John 13:34–35; Eph. 6:6; 1 John 3:17

420. Where He Leads Me
E. W. Blandy, 1890

Jesus calls us to follow him and promises to go with us
Matt. 8:19; 16:24–25; 20:22; Luke 9:23; John 10:27; 12:26; 2 Cor. 1:5

421. Wherever He Leads, I'll Go
B. B. McKinney, 1937

Expression of complete submission to Jesus as Lord and Master of our lives
Mark 8:34–35; Luke 9:23; John 12:26; 1 Peter 2:21

St. 2 (He drew me closer . . .) Rom. 12:2
St. 4 (My heart, my life . . .) Matt. 22:37; John 13:13

422. While By the Sheep
Traditional German carol

Joy and praise expressed for the birth of Jesus
Isa. 12:3; Luke 2:4–20

St. 2 (There shall be born . . .) Matt. 2:6

While Shepherds Kept Their Watching, see "Go, Tell It on the Mountain"

423. While Shepherds Watched Their Flocks   Nahum Tate, 1700

Visit of shepherds to baby Jesus; Christmas
Luke 2:8–14

424. Whiter Than Snow
James L. Nicholson, 1872

The blood of Jesus cleanses and gives one a new heart
Ps. 51:2, 7; Isa. 1:18; Rom. 3:24–25; 1 Cor. 6:11; 2 Cor. 5:17; Heb. 9:14; 1 John 1:7–9

St. 2 (. . . look down from Your throne . . .) Rom. 12:1–2
St. 3 (. . . for this I most humbly . . .) Zech. 13:1
St. 4 (. . . You see that I patiently . . .) 1 Chron. 28:9; Ps. 51:10

Who Can Cheer the Heart Like Jesus, see "All That Thrills My Soul Is Jesus"

425. Who Is He in Yonder Stall?

Benjamin R. Hanby, 1866

Series of questions about Jesus' life and ministry; Affirmation that Jesus is Lord and King of Glory

Phil. 2:6–11; Rev. 17:14b

St. 1 (. . . in yonder stall . . .) Luke 2:6–18; 4:1–2

St. 2 (. . . the people bless . . .) Luke 4:22; Acts 10:38

St. 3 (. . . that stands and . . .) John 12:9

St. 4 (Lo! at midnight . . .) Mark 14:32–34; 15:22–24

St. 5 (. . . that from the . . .) Matt. 28:18; Rom. 1:4; 14:9

426. Who Is on the Lord's Side?

Frances R. Havergal, 1877

Commitment to follow Christ in spiritual warfare

Exod. 32:26; Josh. 24:15; Eph. 6:10–20; 1 Tim. 6:12; 2 Tim. 2:1–4

Whosoever Heareth, see "Whosoever Will"

427. Whosoever Will   Philip P. Bliss, 1870

Universal invitation of the gospel
Rev. 22:17

Luke 11:10; John 3:15–17; Acts 2:21; 10:34, 43; Rom. 10:11–13

428. Wonderful Grace of Jesus

Haldor Lillenas, 1918

Testimony and praise for the love and grace of Jesus experienced by a believer

John 1:16–17; 8:32–36; Rom. 5:15–21; 2 Cor. 8:9; Eph. 2:4–9

429. Wonderful Peace

W. D. Cornell, 19th c.

Testimony about the peace and comfort found through life in Christ

Ps. 29:11; Isa. 26:3; John 14:27; Phil. 4:7; 2 Thess. 3:16

430. Wonderful Words of Life

Philip P. Bliss, 1874

Jesus has the words of life

Ps. 119:11, 172; Matt. 4:4; John 5:24; 6:63, 68; 20:31; Col. 3:16

Would You Be Free From the Burden of Sin?, see "There is Power in the Blood"

431. Ye Must Be Born Again

William T. Sleeper, 1877

Necessity of the new birth for salvation
John 3:1–7

Rom. 6:4; 2 Cor. 5:17; 1 Peter 1:23; 1 John 5:1

432. Ye Servants of God

Charles Wesley, 1744

Eternal praise to the Lord of power, majesty, and of our salvation
Rev. 7:9–12

Deut. 32:3; Pss. 96:1–10; 103:19–22; Isa. 12:1–6; Phil. 2:9–11; 1 Tim. 6:15–16; Jude 24–25; Rev. 5:9–14

Years I Spent in Vanity and Pride, see "At Calvary"

You Servants of God, see "Ye Servants of God"

Scripture with
Hymn References

Old Testament

400	We Plow the Fields

GENESIS 9:8–17

369–St. 2	The Solid Rock

GENESIS 9:13–17

338	Standing on the Promises

GENESIS 12:1–3

74	Count Your Blessings
105	God of Our Fathers
233	Make Me a Blessing
358	The God of Abraham Praise

GENESIS 12:7

286	On Jordan's Stormy Banks I Stand

GENESIS 13:8

172	In Christ There Is No East
206–St. 3	Joyful, Joyful, We Adore Thee

GENESIS 13:15

286	On Jordan's Stormy Banks I Stand

GENESIS 14:18–19

299	Praise, My Soul, the King

GENESIS 15:1

265	O God, Our Help in Ages Past
304	Praise to the Lord, the Almighty

GENESIS 15:1–21

358	The God of Abraham Praise

GENESIS 15:6

161	I Sought the Lord
167	If Thou But Suffer God to Guide
418	When We Walk with the Lord

GENESIS 17:1

66–St. 1	Come, Thou Almighty King
261	O For a Closer Walk with God
418	When We Walk with the Lord

GENESIS 17:1–8

358	The God of Abraham Praise

GENESIS 17:8

286	On Jordan's Stormy Banks I Stand

GENESIS 17:13

369–St. 3	The Solid Rock

GENESIS 18:19

119	Happy the Home When God Is There

GENESIS 18:25

107–St. 3	God the Almighty One

GENESIS 21:33

299	Praise, My Soul, the King
358	The God of Abraham Praise

GENESIS 22:18

418	When We Walk with the Lord

GENESIS 24:26–27

358	The God of Abraham Praise

GENESIS 24:35

74–St. 3	Count Your Blessings

GENESIS 24:48

358	The God of Abraham Praise

GENESIS 26:3

338	Standing on the Promises

GENESIS 26:24

141	How Firm a Foundation
358	The God of Abraham Praise

GENESIS 28:10–21

248	Nearer, My God, to Thee

GENESIS 28:13

105	God of Our Fathers

GENESIS 28:15

3	A Mighty Fortress Is Our God
5	Abide with Me
74–St. 4	Count Your Blessings
97–St. 3	Glorious Things of Thee
100	God Be with You
109	God Will Take Care of You
114	Great Is Thy Faithfulness
115	Guide Me, O Thou Great Jehovah
141	How Firm a Foundation
159	I Need Thee Every Hour
207	Just a Closer Walk with Thee
265	O God, Our Help in Ages Past

GENESIS 28:16–17

101	God Himself Is with Us
293	Open Now Thy Gates of Beauty

GENESIS 28:20–21

53	Children of the Heavenly Father
115	Guide Me, O Thou Great Jehovah

GENESIS 28:22

18	All Things Are Thine
398	We Give Thee but Thine Own

GENESIS 31:3

141	How Firm a Foundation

GENESIS 31:8

109	God Will Take Care of You

GENESIS 31:13

248–St. 4	Nearer, My God, to Thee

GENESIS 35:1–3

248	Nearer, My God, to Thee

GENESIS 35:2

27–St. 4	Are You Washed in the Blood?
261	O For a Closer Walk with God

GENESIS 35:15

248–St. 4	Nearer, My God, to Thee

GENESIS 39:5

74	Count Your Blessings

GENESIS 47:9

128	He Who Would Valiant Be

GENESIS 48:15–16

105	God of Our Fathers

GENESIS 49:10

75–St. 4	Crown Him with Many Crowns

GENESIS 49:18

102	God Is My Strong Salvation

GENESIS 49:25–26

67	Come, Thou Fount
74	Count Your Blessings
123–St. 3	He Hideth My Soul
397	We Gather Together

GENESIS 50:24

286	On Jordan's Stormy Banks I Stand

EXODUS 2:24

358	The God of Abraham Praise

EXODUS 3:5–6

358	The God of Abraham Praise

EXODUS 3:7

177	In the Hour of Trial
419	Where Cross the Crowded Ways

EXODUS 3:12

141	How Firm a Foundation
265	O God, Our Help in Ages Past

EXODUS 3:14–15

105	God of Our Fathers
299	Praise, My Soul, the King
358	The God of Abraham Praise

EXODUS 4:12

292–St. 3	Open My Eyes

EXODUS 4:31

101	God Himself Is with Us

EXODUS 6:2–3

66–St. 1	Come, Thou Almighty King
105	God of Our Fathers

EXODUS 6:6–7

53	Children of the Heavenly Father

EXODUS 6:8

286	On Jordan's Stormy Banks I Stand

EXODUS 9:27

107–St. 3	God the Almighty One

EXODUS 13:21–22

76	Day by Day
97–St. 3	Glorious Things of Thee
115–St. 2	Guide Me, O Thou Great Jehovah
125	He Leadeth Me
210	Lead, Kindly Light

EXODUS 14:14

397–St. 3	We Gather Together

EXODUS 14:27–31

115–St. 2	Guide Me, O Thou Great Jehovah

EXODUS 15:2

3	A Mighty Fortress Is Our God
67	Come, Thou Fount
102	God Is My Strong Salvation
105	God of Our Fathers
124	He Keeps Me Singing
141	How Firm a Foundation
206	Joyful, Joyful, We Adore Thee
307–St. 3	Redeemed, How I Love to Proclaim
326	Since I Have Been Redeemed

EXODUS 15:3

212	Lead On, O King Eternal

EXODUS 15:11

66–St. 1	Come, Thou Almighty King
134	Holy God, We Praise Thy Name
137	Holy, Holy, Holy
170	Immortal, Invisible
358	The God of Abraham Praise

EXODUS 15:13

115	Guide Me, O Thou Great Jehovah
125	He Leadeth Me
167	If Thou But Suffer God to Guide
173–St. 2	In Heavenly Love Abiding
341	Surely Goodness and Mercy
397–St. 2	We Gather Together

EXODUS 15:18

66–St. 1	Come, Thou Almighty King
304	Praise to the Lord, the Almighty
308	Rejoice, the Lord Is King
358	The God of Abraham Praise

EXODUS 15:26

418	When We Walk with the Lord

EXODUS 16:4–18

50	Brethren, We Have Met to Worship
53–St. 2	Children of the Heavenly Father
97–St. 3	Glorious Things of Thee
115–St. 1	Guide Me, O Thou Great Jehovah
365–St. 3	The Lily of the Valley

EXODUS 16:7

34	Awake, My Soul, and With the Sun
60	Christ Whose Glory Fills
241	Morning Has Broken

EXODUS 16:15

100–St. 2	God Be with You

EXODUS 16:23–30

260	O Day of Rest and Gladness

EXODUS 16:35

100–St. 2	God Be with You
365–St. 3	The Lily of the Valley

EXODUS 17:1–6

97–St. 2	Glorious Things of Thee
314	Rock of Ages

EXODUS 17:7

101	God Himself Is with Us

EXODUS 18:11

283	O Worship the King
300	Praise the Lord Who Reigns Above

EXODUS 19:4

93–Last St.	From Every Stormy Wind
109	God Will Take Care of You
393	Under His Wings

EXODUS 19:5

166	I Would Be True
418	When We Walk with the Lord

EXODUS 19:6

347	Take Time to Be Holy

EXODUS 19:16

107–St. 1	God the Almighty One

EXODUS 20:3–5

185	Jesus Calls Us
261	O For a Closer Walk with God

EXODUS 20:8–11

260	O Day of Rest and Gladness

EXODUS 20:11

160	I Sing the Almighty Power of God
371	The Spacious Firmament

EXODUS 20:12

119	Happy the Home When God Is There

EXODUS 20:18

107–St. 1	God the Almighty One

EXODUS 22:29

398	We Give Thee but Thine Own

EXODUS 23:12

260	O Day of Rest and Gladness

EXODUS 23:16

73	Come, Ye Thankful People, Come

EXODUS 23:20

115	Guide Me, O Thou Great Jehovah

EXODUS 23:24–25

261	O For a Closer Walk with God

EXODUS 23:27

397–St. 3	We Gather Together

EXODUS 24:8

27	Are You Washed in the Blood?

EXODUS 25:17–22

70–St. 1	Come, Ye Disconsolate
93	From Every Stormy Wind

EXODUS 25:22

247	Near to the Heart of God

EXODUS 26:34

70–St. 1	Come, Ye Disconsolate
93	From Every Stormy Wind

EXODUS 29:45–46

141	How Firm a Foundation
265	O God, Our Help in Ages Past

EXODUS 30:6

70–St. 1	Come, Ye Disconsolate
93	From Every Stormy Wind

EXODUS 31:12–17

260	O Day of Rest and Gladness

EXODUS 32:1–8

67–St. 3	Come, Thou Fount
261–St. 3	O For a Closer Walk with God

EXODUS 32:16

282	O Word of God Incarnate

EXODUS 32:26–29

122	Have Thine Own Way, Lord
212	Lead On, O King Eternal
288	Once to Every Man and Nation
321–St. 4	Savior, Thy Dying Love

345	Take My Life and Let It Be
426	Who Is on the Lord's Side?

EXODUS 33:13–14

3	A Mighty Fortress Is Our God
28	Are You (Art Thou) Weary?
58–St. 2	Christ Receiveth Sinful Men
76	Day by Day
97–St. 3	Glorious Things of Thee
100	God Be with You
101	God Himself Is with Us
115	Guide Me, O Thou Great Jehovah
141	How Firm a Foundation
151–St. 1	I Heard the Voice of Jesus Say
247	Near to the Heart of God
265	O God, Our Help in Ages Past

EXODUS 33:20

170	Immortal, Invisible

EXODUS 33:22

109	God Will Take Care of You
123	He Hideth My Soul
314	Rock of Ages

EXODUS 34:6–7

79	Depth of Mercy! Can There Be?
218	Let Us with a Gladsome Mind
381	There's a Wideness
412	When All Thy Mercies, O My God

EXODUS 34:7

424	Whiter Than Snow

EXODUS 34:8

101	God Himself Is with Us

EXODUS 34:9

78	Dear Lord and Father of Mankind
79	Depth of Mercy! Can There Be?
208	Just As I Am, Without One Plea
261	O For a Closer Walk with God
319	Savior, Like a Shepherd Lead Us
331–St. 4	Softly and Tenderly
424	Whiter Than Snow

EXODUS 34:12–14

261–St. 3	O For a Closer Walk with God
424–St. 1	Whiter Than Snow

EXODUS 34:14

283	O Worship the King

EXODUS 34:17
261–St. 3   O For a Closer Walk with God

EXODUS 34:21
260   O Day of Rest and Gladness

EXODUS 35:2–3
260   O Day of Rest and Gladness

LEVITICUS 8:35
1   A Charge to Keep I Have

LEVITICUS 10:3
283   O Worship the King

LEVITICUS 10:10
108   God Who Touchest Earth

LEVITICUS 11:44
345.   Take My Life and Let It Be

LEVITICUS 11:45
108   God Who Touchest Earth
347   Take Time to Be Holy

LEVITICUS 16:2
70–St. 1   Come, Ye Disconsolate

LEVITICUS 16:31
260   O Day of Rest and Gladness

LEVITICUS 17:11
8   Alas! And Did My Savior Bleed?
27   Are You Washed in the Blood?
43–St. 3   Blessed Be the Name
80   Down at the Cross
117   Hail, Thou Once Despised Jesus
202   Jesus, Thy Blood and Righteousness
235   "Man of Sorrows," What a Name
251   Nothing But the Blood
263–St. 3   O For a Thousand Tongues to Sing
267–St. 2   O, How I Love Jesus
298–St. 2   Praise Him! Praise Him!
376   There Is a Fountain
378   There Is Power in the Blood
408   What a Wonderful Savior

LEVITICUS 18:4–5
418   When We Walk with the Lord

LEVITICUS 19:2
134   Holy God, We Praise Thy Name

137   Holy, Holy, Holy
347   Take Time to Be Holy

LEVITICUS 19:2–3
262   O For a Heart to Praise My God

LEVITICUS 19:3
260   O Day of Rest and Gladness

LEVITICUS 19:30
101   God Himself Is with Us
260   O Day of Rest and Gladness

LEVITICUS 20:7–8
347   Take Time to Be Holy

LEVITICUS 20:24
286   On Jordan's Stormy Banks I Stand

LEVITICUS 20:26
262   O For a Heart to Praise My God

LEVITICUS 22:32
347   Take Time to Be Holy

LEVITICUS 22:32–33
134   Holy God, We Praise Thy Name
137   Holy, Holy, Holy

LEVITICUS 23:1–3
260   O Day of Rest and Gladness

LEVITICUS 23:32
260   O Day of Rest and Gladness

LEVITICUS 26:1
261   O For a Closer Walk with God

LEVITICUS 26:2
260   O Day of Rest and Gladness

LEVITICUS 26:4–5
329   Sing to the Lord of Harvest

LEVITICUS 26:6
15   All Praise to Thee, My God
102   God Is My Strong Salvation
221   Like a River Glorious
264   O God of Love, O King of Peace
429   Wonderful Peace

LEVITICUS 26:12
97–St. 3   Glorious Things of Thee

100	God Be with You
261	O For a Closer Walk with God
336	Stand Up and Bless the Lord
396	We Are God's People

LEVITICUS 26:40

261	O For a Closer Walk with God

LEVITICUS 26:45

105	God of Our Fathers

LEVITICUS 27:30–33

18	All Things Are Thine
398	We Give Thee but Thine Own

NUMBERS 6:24–26

100	God Be with You
226	Lord, Dismiss Us
236	May the Grace of Christ
318	Savior, Again to Thy Dear Name

NUMBERS 6:26

78	Dear Lord and Father of Mankind
429	Wonderful Peace

NUMBERS 7:89

70–St. 1	Come, Ye Disconsolate
93	From Every Stormy Wind

NUMBERS 9:15–23

97–St. 3	Glorious Things of Thee
115	Guide Me, O Thou Great Jehovah

NUMBERS 10:34–35

115–St. 2	Guide Me, O Thou Great Jehovah

NUMBERS 11:7–9

100–St. 2	God Be with You

NUMBERS 11:9

365–St. 3	The Lily of the Valley

NUMBERS 11:11

123–St. 2	He Hideth My Soul

NUMBERS 11:14

207	Just a Closer Walk with Thee

NUMBERS 11:25

63	Come, Holy Ghost
335	Spirit of the Living God

NUMBERS 12:3

166–St. 2	I Would Be True

NUMBERS 14:8

286	On Jordan's Stormy Banks I Stand

NUMBERS 14:11

79	Depth of Mercy! Can There Be?

NUMBERS 14:17–19

70	Come, Ye Disconsolate
79	Depth of Mercy! Can There Be?
208	Just As I Am, Without One Plea
249	Nearer, Still Nearer
296	Pass Me Not, O Gentle Savior
319–St. 3	Savior, Like a Shepherd Lead Us
381	There's a Wideness
412	When All Thy Mercies, O My God

NUMBERS 15:39–41

122	Have Thine Own Way, Lord
163	I Surrender All
345	Take My Life and Let It Be
347	Take Time to Be Holy
418	When We Walk with the Lord

NUMBERS 18:20

18	All Things Are Thine

NUMBERS 18:21–24

18	All Things Are Thine

NUMBERS 20:2–13

115–St. 2	Guide Me, O Thou Great Jehovah

NUMBERS 21:20

343–St. 3	Sweet Hour of Prayer

NUMBERS 22:38

292–St. 3	Open My Eyes
418	When We Walk with the Lord

NUMBERS 23:12

292–St. 3	Open My Eyes

NUMBERS 23:14

343–St. 3	Sweet Hour of Prayer

NUMBERS 23:19

338	Standing on the Promises

NUMBERS 23:21

| 299 | Praise, My Soul, the King |

NUMBERS 23:26

| 292–St. 3 | Open My Eyes |
| 418 | When We Walk with the Lord |

NUMBERS 24:4

| 292 | Open My Eyes |

NUMBERS 24:16

| 292 | Open My Eyes |

NUMBERS 27:16–17

| 165–St. 2 | I Will Sing the Wondrous Story |

NUMBERS 32:12

| 345 | Take My Life and Let It Be |

NUMBERS 32:23

| 1–St. 3 | A Charge to Keep I Have |

NUMBERS 35:34

| 101 | God Himself Is with Us |

DEUTERONOMY 1:11

| 338 | Standing on the Promises |

DEUTERONOMY 1:30

| 3 | A Mighty Fortress Is Our God |
| 397–St. 3 | We Gather Together |

DEUTERONOMY 1:31

53	Children of the Heavenly Father
109	God Will Take Care of You
115	Guide Me, O Thou Great Jehovah
173	In Heavenly Love Abiding
393	Under His Wings

DEUTERONOMY 1:33

| 115–St. 2 | Guide Me, O Thou Great Jehovah |

DEUTERONOMY 2:7

53	Children of the Heavenly Father
109	God Will Take Care of You
115	Guide Me, O Thou Great Jehovah
173	In Heavenly Love Abiding
393	Under His Wings

DEUTERONOMY 3:22

| 102 | God Is My Strong Salvation |
| 397–St. 3 | We Gather Together |

DEUTERONOMY 3:23–25

| 286 | On Jordan's Stormy Banks I Stand |

DEUTERONOMY 3:24

142	How Great Thou Art
160	I Sing the Almighty Power of God
283	O Worship the King
300	Praise the Lord Who Reigns Above
328	Sing Praise to God Who Reigns

DEUTERONOMY 3:27

| 343–St. 3 | Sweet Hour of Prayer |

DEUTERONOMY 4:5–9

| 133 | Holy Bible, Book Divine |
| 361 | The Heavens Declare Thy Glory |

DEUTERONOMY 4:6–9

| 105 | God of Our Fathers |

DEUTERONOMY 4:7–8

| 22 | America the Beautiful |

DEUTERONOMY 4:14

| 133 | Holy Bible, Book Divine |

DEUTERONOMY 4:22

| 286 | On Jordan's Stormy Banks I Stand |

DEUTERONOMY 4:23

| 261 | O For a Closer Walk with God |

DEUTERONOMY 4:29

70	Come, Ye Disconsolate
261	O For a Closer Walk with God
424–St. 4	Whiter Than Snow

DEUTERONOMY 4:30–31

| 177 | In the Hour of Trial |

DEUTERONOMY 4:31

79	Depth of Mercy! Can There Be?
114	Great Is Thy Faithfulness
412	When All Thy Mercies, O My God

DEUTERONOMY 4:37

| 105 | God of Our Fathers |
| 358 | The God of Abraham Praise |

DEUTERONOMY 4:39

| 9 | All Creatures of Our God |
| 66 | Come, Thou Almighty King |

160	I Sing the Almighty Power of God
283	O Worship the King
299	Praise, My Soul, the King
301	Praise the Lord! Ye Heavens
328	Sing Praise to God Who Reigns

DEUTERONOMY 4:40

1	A Charge to Keep I Have
418	When We Walk with the Lord

DEUTERONOMY 5:7–8

262	O For a Heart to Praise My God

DEUTERONOMY 5:12–15

260	O Day of Rest and Gladness

DEUTERONOMY 5:16

119	Happy the Home When God Is There

DEUTERONOMY 5:24

142	How Great Thou Art

DEUTERONOMY 5:29–33

122	Have Thine Own Way, Lord
262	O For a Heart to Praise My God
345	Take My Life and Let It Be
418	When We Walk with the Lord

DEUTERONOMY 6:1–3

418	When We Walk with the Lord

DEUTERONOMY 6:4

137	Holy, Holy, Holy
253–St. 3	Now Thank We All Our God

DEUTERONOMY 6:5

222	Living for Jesus
231–St. 2	Love Lifted Me
240	More Love to Thee, O Christ
245	My Jesus, I Love Thee
262	O For a Heart to Praise My God
313–St. 1	Rise Up, O Men of God
334	Spirit of God, Descend
336–St. 1	Stand Up and Bless the Lord
345	Take My Life and Let It Be
421–St. 4	Wherever He Leads, I'll Go

DEUTERONOMY 6:6

430	Wonderful Words of Life

DEUTERONOMY 6:6–7

229	Lord, Speak to Me

DEUTERONOMY 6:7

119	Happy the Home When God Is There

DEUTERONOMY 6:10

286	On Jordan's Stormy Banks I Stand

DEUTERONOMY 6:13–14

358	The God of Abraham Praise

DEUTERONOMY 6:17

18	All Things Are Thine
321	Savior, Thy Dying Love

DEUTERONOMY 6:17–18

1	A Charge to Keep I Have
418	When We Walk with the Lord

DEUTERONOMY 6:24

53–St. 4	Children of the Heavenly Father

DEUTERONOMY 6:25

418	When We Walk with the Lord

DEUTERONOMY 7:6–9

12–St. 2	All Hail the Power of Jesus' Name
396	We Are God's People

DEUTERONOMY 7:8–9

114	Great Is Thy Faithfulness
319	Savior, Like a Shepherd Lead Us

DEUTERONOMY 7:9

105	God of Our Fathers
141	How Firm a Foundation
299	Praise, My Soul, the King

DEUTERONOMY 7:12

122	Have Thine Own Way, Lord

DEUTERONOMY 7:21

101	God Himself Is with Us

DEUTERONOMY 7:25

261	O For a Closer Walk with God

DEUTERONOMY 8:2

17	All the Way My Savior Leads Me
115	Guide Me, O Thou Great Jehovah
125	He Leadeth Me
166	I Would Be True

DEUTERONOMY 8:3

48	Break Thou the Bread
50	Brethren, We Have Met to Worship
100–St. 2	God Be with You
133	Holy Bible, Book Divine
282	O Word of God Incarnate
316	Satisfied
347–St. 1	Take Time to Be Holy
361	The Heavens Declare Thy Glory
365–St. 3	The Lily of the Valley
430	Wonderful Words of Life

DEUTERONOMY 8:5

| 397–St. 1 | We Gather Together |

DEUTERONOMY 8:6

| 261 | O For a Closer Walk with God |
| 418 | When We Walk with the Lord |

DEUTERONOMY 8:9–20

| 67 | Come, Thou Fount |

DEUTERONOMY 8:10

74	Count Your Blessings
89	For the Beauty of the Earth
253	Now Thank We All Our God

DEUTERONOMY 8:15–16

| 115 | Guide Me, O Thou Great Jehovah |

DEUTERONOMY 8:16

| 50 | Brethren, We Have Met to Worship |

DEUTERONOMY 8:19

| 261 | O For a Closer Walk with God |

DEUTERONOMY 9:7

| 79 | Depth of Mercy! Can There Be? |

DEUTERONOMY 9:24

| 79 | Depth of Mercy! Can There Be? |

DEUTERONOMY 9:29

| 115–St. 1 | Guide Me, O Thou Great Jehovah |

DEUTERONOMY 10:12–13

1	A Charge to Keep I Have
222	Living for Jesus
231–St. 2	Love Lifted Me
261	O For a Closer Walk with God
336	Stand Up and Bless the Lord
345	Take My Life and Let It Be

DEUTERONOMY 10:14–15

2	A Child of the King
283	O Worship the King
371	The Spacious Firmament
396	We Are God's People

DEUTERONOMY 10:17–21

66	Come, Thou Almighty King
107	God the Almighty One
137	Holy, Holy, Holy
283	O Worship the King
328	Sing Praise to God Who Reigns

DEUTERONOMY 11:1

245	My Jesus, I Love Thee
345	Take My Life and Let It Be
418	When We Walk with the Lord

DEUTERONOMY 11:11–31

| 286 | On Jordan's Stormy Banks I Stand |

DEUTERONOMY 11:13

222	Living for Jesus
313–St. 1	Rise Up, O Men of God
328–St. 4	Sing Praise to God Who Reigns
336–St. 1	Stand Up and Bless the Lord
345	Take My Life and Let It Be
421–St. 4	Wherever He Leads, I'll Go

DEUTERONOMY 11:16

| 67–St. 3 | Come, Thou Fount |
| 261 | O For a Closer Walk with God |

DEUTERONOMY 11:18

| 133 | Holy Bible, Book Divine |

DEUTERONOMY 11:23

| 418 | When We Walk with the Lord |

DEUTERONOMY 11:26–28

| 261 | O For a Closer Walk with God |

DEUTERONOMY 12:6

| 18 | All Things Are Thine |
| 398 | We Give Thee but Thine Own |

DEUTERONOMY 13:1–5

| 288 | Once to Every Man and Nation |

Before DEUTERONOMY 10:14–15, the right column begins with:

| 418 | When We Walk with the Lord |
| 421–St. 4 | Wherever He Leads, I'll Go |

DEUTERONOMY 13:3
245   My Jesus, I Love Thee

DEUTERONOMY 13:4
336   Stand Up and Bless the Lord

DEUTERONOMY 13:18
418   When We Walk with the Lord

DEUTERONOMY 14:2
396   We Are God's People

DEUTERONOMY 14:22–29
18   All Things Are Thine
398   We Give Thee but Thine Own

DEUTERONOMY 15:6
338   Standing on the Promises

DEUTERONOMY 16:15
329   Sing to the Lord of Harvest

DEUTERONOMY 16:17
398   We Give Thee but Thine Own

DEUTERONOMY 16:21–22
261   O For a Closer Walk with God

DEUTERONOMY 17:19
133   Holy Bible, Book Divine
430   Wonderful Words of Life

DEUTERONOMY 18:13
261   O For a Closer Walk with God

DEUTERONOMY 20:1
3   A Mighty Fortress Is Our God

DEUTERONOMY 20:8
86–St. 4   Fight the Good Fight

DEUTERONOMY 26:1–11
73   Come, Ye Thankful People, Come
329   Sing to the Lord of Harvest
400   We Plow the Fields

DEUTERONOMY 26:7
397   We Gather Together

DEUTERONOMY 26:10–15
398   We Give Thee but Thine Own

DEUTERONOMY 26:16
122   Have Thine Own Way, Lord

DEUTERONOMY 26:16–18
1   A Charge to Keep I Have
418   When We Walk with the Lord

DEUTERONOMY 26:18
396   We Are God's People

DEUTERONOMY 27:16
119   Happy the Home When God Is There

DEUTERONOMY 28:1
122   Have Thine Own Way, Lord
418   When We Walk with the Lord

DEUTERONOMY 28:2
67   Come, Thou Fount

DEUTERONOMY 28:6
74   Count Your Blessings
226   Lord, Dismiss Us

DEUTERONOMY 28:58
358   The God of Abraham Praise

DEUTERONOMY 28:65
230–St. 1   Love Divine, All Loves Excelling

DEUTERONOMY 29:10
101   God Himself Is with Us

DEUTERONOMY 29:29
103   God Moves in a Mysterious Way

DEUTERONOMY 30:2–6
79   Depth of Mercy! Can There Be?
261   O For a Closer Walk with God
262   O For a Heart to Praise My God
294   Out of My Bondage
345   Take My Life and Let It Be
419   Where Cross the Crowded Ways

DEUTERONOMY 30:10–14
418   When We Walk with the Lord

DEUTERONOMY 30:15–20
288   Once to Every Man and Nation
345   Take My Life and Let It Be

DEUTERONOMY 31:6–8

3	A Mighty Fortress Is Our God
17	All the Way My Savior Leads Me
104	God of Grace and God of Glory
109	God Will Take Care of You
114	Great Is Thy Faithfulness
115	Guide Me, O Thou Great Jehovah
125	He Leadeth Me
141	How Firm a Foundation
167	If Thou But Suffer God to Guide
173	In Heavenly Love Abiding
210	Lead, Kindly Light
238	Moment by Moment
268	O Jesus, I Have Promised
291–St. 1	Onward, Christian Soldiers
328–St. 3	Sing Praise to God Who Reigns
375–St. 1	There Is a Balm in Gilead
397	We Gather Together

DEUTERONOMY 31:10–12

53	Children of the Heavenly Father

DEUTERONOMY 31:16

67–St. 3	Come, Thou Fount

DEUTERONOMY 31:17–18

261	O For a Closer Walk with God

DEUTERONOMY 32:2

241	Morning Has Broken

DEUTERONOMY 32:3

142	How Great Thou Art
300	Praise the Lord Who Reigns Above
328	Sing Praise to God Who Reigns
358	The God of Abraham Praise
432	Ye Servants of God

DEUTERONOMY 32:3–4

137	Holy, Holy, Holy

DEUTERONOMY 32:4

170	Immortal, Invisible
314	Rock of Ages

DEUTERONOMY 32:6

114	Great Is Thy Faithfulness

DEUTERONOMY 32:10

156	I Love Thy Kingdom, Lord

DEUTERONOMY 32:10–12

17	All the Way My Savior Leads Me
109	God Will Take Care of You
115	Guide Me, O Thou Great Jehovah
124–St. 3	He Keeps Me Singing
125	He Leadeth Me
167	If Thou But Suffer God to Guide
341	Surely Goodness and Mercy
358	The God of Abraham Praise

DEUTERONOMY 32:15

67–St. 3	Come, Thou Fount
314	Rock of Ages

DEUTERONOMY 32:16–21

261	O For a Closer Walk with God

DEUTERONOMY 32:37

261	O For a Closer Walk with God

DEUTERONOMY 33:13

206–St. 2	Joyful, Joyful, We Adore Thee

DEUTERONOMY 33:13–16

89	For the Beauty of the Earth
160	I Sing the Almighty Power of God
400	We Plow the Fields

DEUTERONOMY 33:27

3	A Mighty Fortress Is Our God
100	God Be with You

DEUTERONOMY 33:27–29

53	Children of the Heavenly Father
109	God Will Take Care of You
213	Leaning on the Everlasting Arms
265	O God, Our Help in Ages Past
393	Under His Wings
397	We Gather Together

DEUTERONOMY 34:1

343–St. 3	Sweet Hour of Prayer

JOSHUA 1:5

76	Day by Day
114	Great Is Thy Faithfulness
141	How Firm a Foundation
167	If Thou But Suffer God to Guide

JOSHUA 1:8

122	Have Thine Own Way, Lord
418	When We Walk with the Lord

JOSHUA 1:9

| 109 | God Will Take Care of You |
| 375–St. 1 | There Is a Balm in Gilead |

JOSHUA 2:11

283	O Worship the King
304	Praise to the Lord, the Almighty
328	Sing Praise to God Who Reigns

JOSHUA 3:1–17

| 115–St. 3 | Guide Me, O Thou Great Jehovah |

JOSHUA 4:24

| 107 | God the Almighty One |
| 113 | Great God, We Sing Thy Mighty |

JOSHUA 7:6

| 70–St. 1 | Come, Ye Disconsolate |

JOSHUA 8:1

| 109 | God Will Take Care of You |

JOSHUA 21:44

| 105 | God of Our Fathers |

JOSHUA 21:45

| 114 | Great Is Thy Faithfulness |
| 338 | Standing on the Promises |

JOSHUA 22:5

1	A Charge to Keep I Have
122	Have Thine Own Way, Lord
222	Living for Jesus
245	My Jesus, I Love Thee
345	Take My Life and Let It Be

JOSHUA 22:29

| 67–St. 3 | Come, Thou Fount |

JOSHUA 23:5

| 286 | On Jordan's Stormy Banks I Stand |

JOSHUA 23:6

| 128 | He Who Would Valiant Be |
| 430 | Wonderful Words of Life |

JOSHUA 23:14

| 114 | Great Is Thy Faithfulness |

JOSHUA 23:15

| 338 | Standing on the Promises |

JOSHUA 24:14–24

1	A Charge to Keep I Have
261	O For a Closer Walk with God
288	Once to Every Man and Nation
345	Take My Life and Let It Be
426	Who Is on the Lord's Side?

JOSHUA 24:15

| 119 | Happy the Home When God Is There |
| 148 | I Have Decided to Follow Jesus |

JOSHUA 24:17

| 53 | Children of the Heavenly Father |

JOSHUA 24:24

| 426 | Who Is on the Lord's Side? |

JUDGES 2:1

| 338 | Standing on the Promises |
| 369–St. 3 | The Solid Rock |

JUDGES 2:10–19

| 261 | O For a Closer Walk with God |

JUDGES 5:2

| 345 | Take My Life and Let It Be |

JUDGES 5:3

300–St. 2	Praise the Lord Who Reigns Above
328	Sing Praise to God Who Reigns
401	We Praise Thee, O God
414	When in Our Music

JUDGES 6:23–24

| 429 | Wonderful Peace |

JUDGES 8:28

| 264 | O God of Love, O King of Peace |

JUDGES 10:10

| 261 | O For a Closer Walk with God |

JUDGES 20:26

| 248 | Nearer, My God, to Thee |

RUTH 1:6

| 53–St. 2 | Children of the Heavenly Father |

RUTH 1:16

| 358 | The God of Abraham Praise |

RUTH 2:12

10–St. 4	All for Jesus
100–St. 2	God Be with You
393	Under His Wings

1 SAMUEL 1:19

| 415 | When Morning Gilds the Skies |

1 SAMUEL 1:27

| 305 | Prayer Is the Soul's Sincere |

1 SAMUEL 2:1

| 309 | Rejoice, Ye Pure in Heart |

1 SAMUEL 2:2

4	A Shelter in the Time of Storm
134	Holy God, We Praise Thy Name
137	Holy, Holy, Holy

1 SAMUEL 2:8

| 383 | This Is My Father's World |

1 SAMUEL 2:30

| 418 | When We Walk with the Lord |

1 SAMUEL 3:9–10

168	I'll Go Where You Want Me To Go
229	Lord, Speak to Me
292	Open My Eyes

1 SAMUEL 6:20

| 134 | Holy God, We Praise Thy Name |
| 137 | Holy, Holy, Holy |

1 SAMUEL 7:3

| 261 | O For a Closer Walk with God |
| 262 | O For a Heart to Praise My God |

1 SAMUEL 7:12

67–St. 2	Come, Thou Fount
109	God Will Take Care of You
265	O God, Our Help in Ages Past

1 SAMUEL 10:6–10

| 63 | Come, Holy Ghost |

1 SAMUEL 12:10

| 261 | O For a Closer Walk with God |

1 SAMUEL 12:14

| 418 | When We Walk with the Lord |

1 SAMUEL 12:18

| 107–St. 1 | God the Almighty One |

1 SAMUEL 12:20

| 67–St. 3 | Come, Thou Fount |

1 SAMUEL 12:24

14	All People That On Earth
283	O Worship the King
336	Stand Up and Bless the Lord

1 SAMUEL 15:22

122	Have Thine Own Way, Lord
229	Lord, Speak to Me
418	When We Walk with the Lord
424–St. 2	Whiter Than Snow

1 SAMUEL 16:7

103	God Moves in a Mysterious Way
222–Refrain	Living for Jesus
231–St. 2	Love Lifted Me
262	O For a Heart to Praise My God
321–St. 3	Savior, Thy Dying Love

1 SAMUEL 16:13

| 335 | Spirit of the Living God |

1 SAMUEL 17:11

| 109 | God Will Take Care of You |

2 SAMUEL 5:24

| 397–St. 3 | We Gather Together |

2 SAMUEL 6:5

| 300–St. 2 | Praise the Lord Who Reigns Above |
| 414–St. 5 | When in Our Music |

2 SAMUEL 7:14

| 397–St. 1 | We Gather Together |

2 SAMUEL 7:18

| 253 | Now Thank We All Our God |

2 SAMUEL 7:18–29

| 74 | Count Your Blessings |

2 SAMUEL 7:22

142	How Great Thou Art
253–St. 3	Now Thank We All Our God
283	O Worship the King
300	Praise the Lord Who Reigns Above
432	Ye Servants of God

2 SAMUEL 7:28–29

338	Standing on the Promises

2 SAMUEL 7:29

123–St. 3	He Hideth My Soul

2 SAMUEL 22:1–51

3	A Mighty Fortress Is Our God
84	Faith Is the Victory
102	God Is My Strong Salvation
283	O Worship the King
397	We Gather Together

2 SAMUEL 22:2–4

3	A Mighty Fortress Is Our God
4	A Shelter in the Time of Storm
53	Children of the Heavenly Father
102	God Is My Strong Salvation
115–St. 2	Guide Me, O Thou Great Jehovah
167	If Thou But Suffer God to Guide
393	Under His Wings

2 SAMUEL 22:7

44–St. 3	Blessed Jesus, at Thy Word
56–St. 2	Christ Is Made the Sure
158	I Must Tell Jesus

2 SAMUEL 22:7–20

103	God Moves in a Mysterious Way

2 SAMUEL 22:7–47

107–St. 1	God the Almighty One

2 SAMUEL 22:17

141–St. 3	How Firm a Foundation

2 SAMUEL 22:29

44–St. 3	Blessed Jesus, at Thy Word
206–St. 1	Joyful, Joyful, We Adore Thee
210	Lead, Kindly Light
272–St. 2	O Love, That Will Not Let Me Go
278	O Splendor of God's Glory
387	Thou Whose Almighty Word

2 SAMUEL 22:29–33

102	God Is My Strong Salvation

2 SAMUEL 22:30–31

115–St. 2	Guide Me, O Thou Great Jehovah

2 SAMUEL 22:31

133	Holy Bible, Book Divine

137–St. 3	Holy, Holy, Holy

2 SAMUEL 22:31–33

3	A Mighty Fortress Is Our God
38	Be Thou My Vision
141	How Firm a Foundation
167	If Thou But Suffer God to Guide
393	Under His Wings

2 SAMUEL 22:47

107–Last st.	God the Almighty One

2 SAMUEL 22:50

299–St. 3	Praise, My Soul, the King
304	Praise to the Lord, the Almighty
328	Sing Praise to God Who Reigns
414	When in Our Music

2 SAMUEL 23:4

241	Morning Has Broken

2 SAMUEL 23:5

114	Great Is Thy Faithfulness

1 KINGS 2:3

1	A Charge to Keep I Have
418	When We Walk with the Lord

1 KINGS 3:8–9

105	God of Our Fathers

1 KINGS 3:9–12

104	God of Grace and God of Glory

1 KINGS 8:20–25

338	Standing on the Promises

1 KINGS 8:23

114	Great Is Thy Faithfulness
261	O For a Closer Walk with God
412	When All Thy Mercies, O My God
432	Ye Servants of God

1 KINGS 8:50–52

79	Depth of Mercy! Can There Be?
227	Lord, I'm Coming Home
261	O For a Closer Walk with God

1 KINGS 8:56

53	Children of the Heavenly Father
107–St. 3	God the Almighty One
114	Great Is Thy Faithfulness

299	Praise, My Soul, the King
338	Standing on the Promises

1 KINGS 8:57

85	Faith of Our Fathers
105	God of Our Fathers

1 KINGS 8:58

122	Have Thine Own Way, Lord
418	When We Walk with the Lord

1 KINGS 8:61

262	O For a Heart to Praise My God

1 KINGS 11:4–6

67–St. 3	Come, Thou Fount

1 KINGS 18:21

212	Lead On, O King Eternal
266	O Happy Day that Fixed My Choice
268	O Jesus, I Have Promised
288	Once to Every Man and Nation
345	Take My Life and Let It Be
426	Who Is on the Lord's Side?

1 KINGS 18:39

358	The God of Abraham Praise

1 KINGS 19:5

15	All Praise to Thee, My God

1 KINGS 19:9–13

78–St. 5	Dear Lord and Father of Mankind

1 KINGS 19:12

168	I'll Go Where You Want Me To Go
292–St. 2	Open My Eyes

2 KINGS 2:2

248–St. 4	Nearer, My God, to Thee

2 KINGS 5:17

358	The God of Abraham Praise

2 KINGS 6:16

96	Give to the Winds
104–St. 2	God of Grace and God of Glory

2 KINGS 8:19

338	Standing on the Promises

2 KINGS 13:23

114	Great Is Thy Faithfulness
299	Praise, My Soul, the King
381	There's a Wideness

2 KINGS 17:7–15

67–St. 3	Come, Thou Fount
261	O For a Closer Walk with God

2 KINGS 17:34–41

67–St. 3	Come, Thou Fount
261	O For a Closer Walk with God

2 KINGS 18:5–7

345	Take My Life and Let It Be
418	When We Walk with the Lord

2 KINGS 18:12

292–St. 2	Open My Eyes

2 KINGS 19:15

107	God the Almighty One
142	How Great Thou Art
160	I Sing the Almighty Power of God
283	O Worship the King
304	Praise to the Lord, the Almighty
328	Sing Praise to God Who Reigns
383	This Is My Father's World

2 KINGS 20:3

261	O For a Closer Walk with God

2 KINGS 23:3

261	O For a Closer Walk with God
345	Take My Life and Let It Be

2 KINGS 23:24

261	O For a Closer Walk with God

2 KINGS 23:25

345	Take My Life and Let It Be
418	When We Walk with the Lord

1 CHRONICLES 13:8

300–St. 2	Praise the Lord Who Reigns Above

1 CHRONICLES 15:16

62	Come, Christians, Join to Sing
300–St. 2	Praise the Lord Who Reigns Above

1 CHRONICLES 16:8–36

40	Begin, My Tongue, Some Heavenly

300	Praise the Lord Who Reigns Above
301	Praise the Lord! Ye Heavens
328	Sing Praise to God Who Reigns

1 CHRONICLES 16:9

62	Come, Christians, Join to Sing
67	Come, Thou Fount
414	When in Our Music

1 CHRONICLES 16:9–10

| 215 | Let All the World |
| 390 | To God Be the Glory |

1 CHRONICLES 16:23

| 414 | When in Our Music |

1 CHRONICLES 16:23–24

55	Christ for the World We Sing
399	We Have Heard the Joyful Sound
404	We've a Story to Tell

1 CHRONICLES 16:23–31

| 432 | Ye Servants of God |

1 CHRONICLES 16:23–33

9	All Creatures of Our God
206	Joyful, Joyful, We Adore Thee
215	Let All the World

1 CHRONICLES 16:23–36

14	All People That On Earth
299	Praise, My Soul, the King
301	Praise the Lord! Ye Heavens
304	Praise to the Lord, the Almighty
328	Sing Praise to God Who Reigns
336–St. 5	Stand Up and Bless the Lord
401	We Praise Thee, O God

1 CHRONICLES 16:24–25

| 390 | To God Be the Glory |

1 CHRONICLES 16:26

| 261 | O For a Closer Walk with God |

1 CHRONICLES 16:29–30

44	Blessed Jesus, at Thy Word
50	Brethren, We Have Met to Worship
101	God Himself Is with Us

1 CHRONICLES 16:30–33

| 383 | This Is My Father's World |

1 CHRONICLES 16:34

21	Amazing Grace
79	Depth of Mercy! Can There Be?
114	Great Is Thy Faithfulness
218	Let Us with a Gladsome Mind
303	Praise to God, Immortal Praise
412	When All Thy Mercies, O My God

1 CHRONICLES 16:34–35

| 381 | There's a Wideness |

1 CHRONICLES 16:34–36

| 253 | Now Thank We All Our God |

1 CHRONICLES 17:16–20

253	Now Thank We All Our God
261	O For a Closer Walk with God
432	Ye Servants of God

1 CHRONICLES 17:26

| 338 | Standing on the Promises |

1 CHRONICLES 19:13

| 128 | He Who Would Valiant Be |

1 CHRONICLES 21:13

| 381 | There's a Wideness |

1 CHRONICLES 22:13

| 109 | God Will Take Care of You |
| 128 | He Who Would Valiant Be |

1 CHRONICLES 23:30

77	Day Is Dying in the West
241	Morning Has Broken
253	Now Thank We All Our God
336	Stand Up and Bless the Lord
415	When Morning Gilds the Skies

1 CHRONICLES 25:6

| 300–St. 2 | Praise the Lord Who Reigns Above |

1 CHRONICLES 25:6–7

| 62 | Come, Christians, Join to Sing |

1 CHRONICLES 28:8–10

| 1 | A Charge to Keep I Have |

1 CHRONICLES 28:9

90	Forth in Thy Name, O Lord
122	Have Thine Own Way, Lord
222	Living for Jesus

229	Lord, Speak to Me
345	Take My Life and Let It Be
424–St. 4	Whiter Than Snow

1 CHRONICLES 28:20

3	A Mighty Fortress Is Our God
76	Day by Day
102	God Is My Strong Salvation
104	God of Grace and God of Glory
109	God Will Take Care of You
141	How Firm a Foundation
167	If Thou But Suffer God to Guide
265	O God, Our Help in Ages Past

1 CHRONICLES 29:5

122	Have Thine Own Way, Lord
345	Take My Life and Let It Be
426	Who Is on the Lord's Side?

1 CHRONICLES 29:10–13

1	A Charge to Keep I Have
66–St. 1	Come, Thou Almighty King
142	How Great Thou Art
160	I Sing the Almighty Power of God
170	Immortal, Invisible
212	Lead On, O King Eternal
283–St. 1	O Worship the King
299	Praise, My Soul, the King
300	Praise the Lord Who Reigns Above
304	Praise to the Lord, the Almighty
336	Stand Up and Bless the Lord

1 CHRONICLES 29:12

102	God Is My Strong Salvation
122–St. 3	Have Thine Own Way, Lord
167	If Thou But Suffer God to Guide
207	Just a Closer Walk with Thee
310–St. 4	Rescue the Perishing

1 CHRONICLES 29:13

73	Come, Ye Thankful People, Come
134	Holy God, We Praise Thy Name
253	Now Thank We All Our God
265	O God, Our Help in Ages Past

1 CHRONICLES 29:14

| 18 | All Things Are Thine |
| 398 | We Give Thee but Thine Own |

1 CHRONICLES 29:20

| 134 | Holy God, We Praise Thy Name |

2 CHRONICLES 1:10–11

| 104 | God of Grace and God of Glory |

2 CHRONICLES 2:4

| 18 | All Things Are Thine |

2 CHRONICLES 2:6

| 52 | Built on the Rock |

2 CHRONICLES 5:13–14

62	Come, Christians, Join to Sing
218	Let Us with a Gladsome Mind
300–St. 3	Praise the Lord Who Reigns Above
414	When in Our Music

2 CHRONICLES 6:14–16

| 338 | Standing on the Promises |

2 CHRONICLES 6:26–39

| 319–St. 3 | Savior, Like a Shepherd Lead Us |

2 CHRONICLES 7:3

| 218 | Let Us with a Gladsome Mind |
| 381 | There's a Wideness |

2 CHRONICLES 7:14–15

22	America the Beautiful
305	Prayer Is the Soul's Sincere
319–St. 3	Savior, Like a Shepherd Lead Us
343	Sweet Hour of Prayer
407	What a Friend We Have in Jesus

2 CHRONICLES 13:11

| 1 | A Charge to Keep I Have |

2 CHRONICLES 14:11

3	A Mighty Fortress Is Our God
76	Day by Day
84	Faith Is the Victory

2 CHRONICLES 15:2–8

| 261 | O For a Closer Walk with God |

2 CHRONICLES 15:15

| 266 | O Happy Day that Fixed My Choice |

2 CHRONICLES 16:7

| 102–St. 2 | God Is My Strong Salvation |

2 CHRONICLES 16:9

| 3 | A Mighty Fortress Is Our God |
| 319 | Savior, Like a Shepherd Lead Us |

2 CHRONICLES 19:3

262	O For a Heart to Praise My God

2 CHRONICLES 20:6

107	God the Almighty One
283	O Worship the King
304	Praise to the Lord, the Almighty
328	Sing Praise to God Who Reigns

2 CHRONICLES 20:6–7

358	The God of Abraham Praise

2 CHRONICLES 20:15–17

84	Faith Is the Victory
109	God Will Take Care of You
212	Lead On, O King Eternal
268	O Jesus, I Have Promised
291	Onward, Christian Soldiers
332	Soldiers of Christ, Arise
337–St. 3	Stand Up, Stand Up for Jesus
426	Who Is on the Lord's Side?

2 CHRONICLES 20:18

101	God Himself Is with Us

2 CHRONICLES 20:21

62	Come, Christians, Join to Sing
92	From All That Dwell Below
218	Let Us with a Gladsome Mind
283	O Worship the King
304	Praise to the Lord, the Almighty

2 CHRONICLES 21:7

338	Standing on the Promises

2 CHRONICLES 29:25–30

62	Come, Christians, Join to Sing
300	Praise the Lord Who Reigns Above
414	When in Our Music

2 CHRONICLES 30:8–9

79	Depth of Mercy! Can There Be?
163	I Surrender All
227	Lord, I'm Coming Home
261	O For a Closer Walk with God
331	Softly and Tenderly
412	When All Thy Mercies, O My God
418	When We Walk with the Lord

2 CHRONICLES 30:21

414	When in Our Music

2 CHRONICLES 31:4–11

18	All Things Are Thine
398	We Give Thee but Thine Own

2 CHRONICLES 32:7–8

3	A Mighty Fortress Is Our God
84	Faith Is the Victory
102	God Is My Strong Salvation
109	God Will Take Care of You
397–St. 3	We Gather Together

2 CHRONICLES 33:12–13

261	O For a Closer Walk with God

2 CHRONICLES 33:16

73	Come, Ye Thankful People, Come
253	Now Thank We All Our God

EZRA 3:10–11

300–St. 2	Praise the Lord Who Reigns Above
414	When in Our Music

EZRA 5:11

432	Ye Servants of God

EZRA 7:10

133	Holy Bible, Book Divine
430	Wonderful Words of Life

EZRA 7:27

105	God of Our Fathers

EZRA 8:22–23

141	How Firm a Foundation
305	Prayer Is the Soul's Sincere
393	Under His Wings

EZRA 9:6

227	Lord, I'm Coming Home
249	Nearer, Still Nearer
262	O For a Heart to Praise My God
311	Revive Us Again

EZRA 9:13

79	Depth of Mercy! Can There Be?
107	God the Almighty One
381	There's a Wideness
412	When All Thy Mercies, O My God

EZRA 9:15

107–St. 3	God the Almighty One
227	Lord, I'm Coming Home

261	O For a Closer Walk with God
262	O For a Heart to Praise My God
296	Pass Me Not, O Gentle Savior

NEHEMIAH 1:5

| 369 | The Solid Rock |

NEHEMIAH 1:5–7

79	Depth of Mercy! Can There Be?
227	Lord, I'm Coming Home
261	O For a Closer Walk with God

NEHEMIAH 1:10

| 396 | We Are God's People |
| 401 | We Praise Thee, O God |

NEHEMIAH 4:14

| 86 | Fight the Good Fight |

NEHEMIAH 8:1–6

133	Holy Bible, Book Divine
282	O Word of God Incarnate
430	Wonderful Words of Life

NEHEMIAH 8:6

| 101 | God Himself Is with Us |
| 401 | We Praise Thee, O God |

NEHEMIAH 8:10–11

206	Joyful, Joyful, We Adore Thee
238	Moment by Moment
272–St. 3	O Love, That Will Not Let Me Go
328–St. 4	Sing Praise to God Who Reigns

NEHEMIAH 9:5

| 265 | O God, Our Help in Ages Past |
| 336 | Stand Up and Bless the Lord |

NEHEMIAH 9:5–6

9	All Creatures of Our God
12	All Hail the Power of Jesus' Name
33	At the Name of Jesus
134	Holy God, We Praise Thy Name
137	Holy, Holy, Holy
142	How Great Thou Art
283	O Worship the King
299	Praise, My Soul, the King
304	Praise to the Lord, the Almighty
401	We Praise Thee, O God

NEHEMIAH 9:6

| 19 | All Things Bright and Beautiful |

| 160 | I Sing the Almighty Power of God |
| 301 | Praise the Lord! Ye Heavens |

NEHEMIAH 9:7–8

| 358 | The God of Abraham Praise |

NEHEMIAH 9:12

| 115–St. 2 | Guide Me, O Thou Great Jehovah |

NEHEMIAH 9:15

| 115–St. 1 | Guide Me, O Thou Great Jehovah |
| 316 | Satisfied |

NEHEMIAH 9:17

21	Amazing Grace
78–St. 1	Dear Lord and Father of Mankind
79	Depth of Mercy! Can There Be?
107–St. 2	God the Almighty One
206–St. 3	Joyful, Joyful, We Adore Thee
216	Let Jesus Come Into Your Heart
218	Let Us with a Gladsome Mind
244	My Faith Looks Up to Thee
359–St. 2	The Great Physician
381	There's a Wideness
412	When All Thy Mercies, O My God

NEHEMIAH 9:19–20

| 115–St. 2 | Guide Me, O Thou Great Jehovah |
| 125 | He Leadeth Me |

NEHEMIAH 9:20

| 316 | Satisfied |
| 334 | Spirit of God, Descend |

NEHEMIAH 9:21

| 53–St. 2 | Children of the Heavenly Father |
| 109 | God Will Take Care of You |

NEHEMIAH 9:27

21	Amazing Grace
305	Prayer Is the Soul's Sincere
407	What a Friend We Have in Jesus
412	When All Thy Mercies, O My God

NEHEMIAH 9:30

| 79 | Depth of Mercy! Can There Be? |

NEHEMIAH 9:31

21	Amazing Grace
381	There's a Wideness
412	When All Thy Mercies, O My God

NEHEMIAH 10:37–39

18	All Things Are Thine
398	We Give Thee but Thine Own

NEHEMIAH 12:27

300–St. 2	Praise the Lord Who Reigns Above
414	When in Our Music

NEHEMIAH 13:12

18	All Things Are Thine
79	Depth of Mercy! Can There Be?
398	We Give Thee but Thine Own

ESTHER 4:14

104	God of Grace and God of Glory

JOB 1:21

43	Blessed Be the Name
53–St. 4	Children of the Heavenly Father

JOB 3:17

199	Jesus, Still Lead On

JOB 4:3–6

53	Children of the Heavenly Father
103	God Moves in a Mysterious Way
109	God Will Take Care of You
115–St. 1	Guide Me, O Thou Great Jehovah
173	In Heavenly Love Abiding
177	In the Hour of Trial
393	Under His Wings

JOB 5:9

103	God Moves in a Mysterious Way

JOB 5:10

400	We Plow the Fields

JOB 5:11

70	Come, Ye Disconsolate
393	Under His Wings

JOB 5:17

397–St. 1	We Gather Together

JOB 7:4

208–St. 3	Just As I Am, Without One Plea

JOB 8:14–16

79	Depth of Mercy! Can There Be?

JOB 9:11

170	Immortal, Invisible

JOB 10:1

28	Are You (Art Thou) Weary?
122–St. 3	Have Thine Own Way, Lord

JOB 10:12

53	Children of the Heavenly Father
109	God Will Take Care of You
173	In Heavenly Love Abiding
319	Savior, Like a Shepherd Lead Us
393	Under His Wings

JOB 11:7

103	God Moves in a Mysterious Way

JOB 11:13–17

102	God Is My Strong Salvation
216	Let Jesus Come Into Your Heart
227	Lord, I'm Coming Home
294	Out of My Bondage
424	Whiter Than Snow

JOB 11:16

177–St. 3	In the Hour of Trial

JOB 11:17

129	Heaven Came Down

JOB 11:18

393	Under His Wings

JOB 12:7–10

114–St. 2	Great Is Thy Faithfulness
142	How Great Thou Art

JOB 12:13

103	God Moves in a Mysterious Way
170	Immortal, Invisible

JOB 12:22

129	Heaven Came Down
341–St. 3	Surely Goodness and Mercy

JOB 14:1

5	Abide with Me
177–St. 3	In the Hour of Trial

JOB 15:11

70	Come, Ye Disconsolate

JOB 19:25–27

39	Because He Lives
126	He Lives
152	I Know That My Redeemer Lives
153	I Know That My Redeemer Liveth
164	I Will Sing of My Redeemer

JOB 21:14

67–St. 3	Come, Thou Fount
177	In the Hour of Trial

JOB 22:23

67	Come, Thou Fount
227	Lord, I'm Coming Home
261	O For a Closer Walk with God
288	Once to Every Man and Nation
331	Softly and Tenderly

JOB 22:26

304	Praise to the Lord, the Almighty

JOB 23:3

70–St. 1	Come, Ye Disconsolate
93	From Every Stormy Wind
171–St. 2	Immortal Love, Forever Full

JOB 23:10

141–St. 4	How Firm a Foundation
319	Savior, Like a Shepherd Lead Us

JOB 23:12

48	Break Thou the Bread
133	Holy Bible, Book Divine
347–St. 1	Take Time to Be Holy
361	The Heavens Declare Thy Glory
430	Wonderful Words of Life

JOB 23:15

101	God Himself Is with Us

JOB 26:7–14

160	I Sing the Almighty Power of God
371	The Spacious Firmament

JOB 26:14

107–St. 1	God the Almighty One
283–St. 2	O Worship the King

JOB 28:28

104	God of Grace and God of Glory
288	Once to Every Man and Nation

JOB 32:8

49	Breathe on Me, Breath of God
104	God of Grace and God of Glory
334	Spirit of God, Descend

JOB 33:4

49	Breathe on Me, Breath of God
170–St. 3	Immortal, Invisible
334	Spirit of God, Descend

JOB 34:12

137	Holy, Holy, Holy
170	Immortal, Invisible

JOB 34:28

319	Savior, Like a Shepherd Lead Us

JOB 34:29

78	Dear Lord and Father of Mankind
103	God Moves in a Mysterious Way

JOB 35:10

15	All Praise to Thee, My God
106	God, That Madest Earth
339	Sun of My Soul, Thou Savior Dear

JOB 36:5

170	Immortal, Invisible

JOB 36:26

103	God Moves in a Mysterious Way
265	O God, Our Help in Ages Past

JOB 37:2–5

107–St. 1	God the Almighty One

JOB 37:9–13

283–St. 3	O Worship the King

JOB 37:14

74	Count Your Blessings
253	Now Thank We All Our God

JOB 37:14–16

103	God Moves in a Mysterious Way

JOB 37:21–24

170	Immortal, Invisible

JOB 38:1

78–St. 5	Dear Lord and Father of Mankind

JOB 38:4–13

371	The Spacious Firmament

JOB 38:4–41

19	All Things Bright and Beautiful
160	I Sing the Almighty Power of God
383	This Is My Father's World

JOB 38:7

206–St. 4	Joyful, Joyful, We Adore Thee

JOB 38:8

81–St. 1	Eternal Father, Strong to Save

JOB 38:12

34	Awake, My Soul, and with the Sun

JOB 38:35

107–St. 1	God the Almighty One

JOB 39:1–30

19	All Things Bright and Beautiful
160	I Sing the Almighty Power of God
383	This Is My Father's World

JOB 40:9

107–St. 1	God the Almighty One

PSALM 1:2

133	Holy Bible, Book Divine
361	The Heavens Declare Thy Glory

PSALM 2:6–7

69	Come, We That Love the Lord
75	Crown Him with Many Crowns
97	Glorious Things of Thee

PSALM 2:11

14	All People That On Earth
336–St. 2	Stand Up and Bless the Lord

PSALM 3:1–8

3	A Mighty Fortress Is Our God
53	Children of the Heavenly Father
397	We Gather Together

PSALM 3:5

15	All Praise to Thee, My God
106	God, That Madest Earth
254	Now the Day Is Over
318–St. 3	Savior, Again to Thy Dear Name

PSALM 3:8

74	Count Your Blessings
102	God Is My Strong Salvation
123–St. 3	He Hideth My Soul

PSALM 4:1–3

319–St. 2	Savior, Like a Shepherd Lead Us

PSALM 4:1–8

37	Be Still, My Soul
78	Dear Lord and Father of Mankind
339	Sun of My Soul, Thou Savior Dear
393	Under His Wings
429	Wonderful Peace

PSALM 4:5

86–St. 3	Fight the Good Fight
167	If Thou But Suffer God to Guide
290	Only Trust Him
418	When We Walk with the Lord

PSALM 4:8

5	Abide with Me
15	All Praise to Thee, My God
77	Day Is Dying in the West
106	God, That Madest Earth
254	Now the Day Is Over
318–St. 3	Savior, Again to Thy Dear Name
356	The Day Thou Gavest

PSALM 5:1–3

305	Prayer Is the Soul's Sincere
343	Sweet Hour of Prayer

PSALM 5:3

34	Awake, My Soul, and with the Sun
241	Morning Has Broken
415	When Morning Gilds the Skies

PSALM 5:7

101	God Himself Is with Us
336	Stand Up and Bless the Lord

PSALM 5:8

115	Guide Me, O Thou Great Jehovah
125	He Leadeth Me
397	We Gather Together

PSALM 5:11–12

43	Blessed Be the Name
123	He Hideth My Soul
188	Jesus Is All the World to Me

206	Joyful, Joyful, We Adore Thee		253	Now Thank We All Our God
309	Rejoice, Ye Pure in Heart		401	We Praise Thee, O God
393	Under His Wings			
397	We Gather Together			

PSALM 9:7–8

PSALM 5:12

			170–St. 2	Immortal, Invisible
283–St. 1	O Worship the King		299	Praise, My Soul, the King
			358	The God of Abraham Praise

PSALM 6:1–3

PSALM 9:9–10

79	Depth of Mercy! Can There Be?		76	Day by Day
107–St. 2	God the Almighty One		393	Under His Wings
115–St. 1	Guide Me, O Thou Great Jehovah		397	We Gather Together

PSALM 6:9

PSALM 9:9–11

305	Prayer Is the Soul's Sincere Desire		3	A Mighty Fortress Is Our God
343	Sweet Hour of Prayer		265	O God, Our Help in Ages Past
407	What a Friend We Have in Jesus			

PSALM 9:10

PSALM 7:1

			53–St. 4	Children of the Heavenly Father
102	God Is My Strong Salvation		114	Great Is Thy Faithfulness
299–St. 3	Praise, My Soul, the King		141–St. 5	How Firm a Foundation
			167	If Thou But Suffer God to Guide
			401	We Praise Thee, O God

PSALM 7:17

43	Blessed Be the Name			
215	Let All the World		**PSALM 9:11**	
263	O For a Thousand Tongues to Sing		69	Come, We That Love the Lord
298	Praise Him! Praise Him!		97	Glorious Things of Thee
304	Praise to the Lord, the Almighty		293	Open Now Thy Gates of Beauty
328	Sing Praise to God Who Reigns		328	Sing Praise to God Who Reigns
414	When in Our Music			
432	Ye Servants of God		**PSALM 9:13**	
			381	There's a Wideness

PSALM 8:1–9

9	All Creatures of Our God		**PSALM 10:1**	
77	Day Is Dying in the West		103	God Moves in a Mysterious Way
142–St. 1, 2	How Great Thou Art		137–St. 3	Holy, Holy, Holy
160	I Sing the Almighty Power of God			
304	Praise to the Lord, the Almighty		**PSALM 10:1–18**	
371	The Spacious Firmament		107	God the Almighty One
383	This Is My Father's World		259	O Day of God, Draw Nigh

PSALM 8:4

			PSALM 10:16	
23	And Can It Be That I Should Gain?		66–St. 1	Come, Thou Almighty King
208	Just As I Am, Without One Plea		283	O Worship the King
			299	Praise, My Soul, the King

PSALM 9:1–2

			PSALM 10:17	
390	To God Be the Glory		262	O For a Heart to Praise My God
414	When in Our Music			

PSALM 9:1–11

PSALM 11:1

40	Begin, My Tongue, Some Heavenly		53	Children of the Heavenly Father
206	Joyful, Joyful, We Adore Thee		283–St. 4	O Worship the King

393	Under His Wings

PSALM 11:1–7

107	God the Almighty One

PSALM 11:4

432–St. 3	Ye Servants of God

PSALM 12:6

338	Standing on the Promises

PSALM 13:1

103	God Moves in a Mysterious Way
137–St. 3	Holy, Holy, Holy

PSALM 13:5–6

23	And Can It Be That I Should Gain?
42	Blessed Assurance
43	Blessed Be the Name
124	He Keeps Me Singing
180	It Is Well with My Soul
263	O For a Thousand Tongues to Sing
283–St. 4	O Worship the King
290	Only Trust Him
298	Praise Him! Praise Him!
303	Praise to God, Immortal Praise
391	Trusting Jesus
401	We Praise Thee, O God
412	When All Thy Mercies, O My God
414	When in Our Music

PSALM 15:2

292	Open My Eyes

PSALM 16:1–2

3	A Mighty Fortress Is Our God
37	Be Still, My Soul
180	It Is Well with My Soul
290	Only Trust Him

PSALM 16:5–6

362	The King of Love My Shepherd Is
366	The Lord's My Shepherd

PSALM 16:8

76	Day by Day
145	I Am Thine, O Lord
247	Near to the Heart of God
248	Nearer, My God, to Thee
249	Nearer, Still Nearer
401–St. 2	We Praise Thee, O God

PSALM 16:8–9

273–St. 4	O Master, Let Me Walk with Thee
369	The Solid Rock

PSALM 16:8–11

61	Close to Thee
115	Guide Me, O Thou Great Jehovah
141	How Firm a Foundation
145	I Am Thine, O Lord
159	I Need Thee Every Hour
265	O God, Our Help in Ages Past
306	Precious Lord, Take My Hand
341	Surely Goodness and Mercy

PSALM 16:10–11

82	Face to Face
279	O That Will Be Glory For Me

PSALM 16:11

86–St. 2	Fight the Good Fight
125	He Leadeth Me
167	If Thou But Suffer God to Guide
206	Joyful, Joyful, We Adore Thee
213	Leaning on the Everlasting Arms
226	Lord, Dismiss Us
272–St. 3	O Love, That Will Not Let Me Go
340	Sunshine in My Soul
362	The King of Love My Shepherd Is
366	The Lord's My Shepherd

PSALM 17:1

336–St. 3	Stand Up and Bless the Lord

PSALM 17:3

122–St. 2	Have Thine Own Way, Lord
254	Now the Day Is Over

PSALM 17:5

124–St. 4	He Keeps Me Singing

PSALM 17:8

100–St. 2	God Be with You
109	God Will Take Care of You
123	He Hideth My Soul
124–St. 3	He Keeps Me Singing
304–St. 2	Praise to the Lord, the Almighty
393	Under His Wings

PSALM 17:8–9

3	A Mighty Fortress Is Our God
53	Children of the Heavenly Father
102	God Is My Strong Salvation

265–St. 2   O God, Our Help in Ages Past

PSALM 18:1

245   My Jesus, I Love Thee

PSALM 18:1–3

3   A Mighty Fortress Is Our God
115–St. 2   Guide Me, O Thou Great Jehovah
283   O Worship the King
304   Praise to the Lord, the Almighty
397   We Gather Together

PSALM 18:2

4   A Shelter in the Time of Storm
180   It Is Well with My Soul
290   Only Trust Him

PSALM 18:6

56–St. 2   Christ Is Made the Sure
141–St. 3   How Firm a Foundation
319–St. 2   Savior, Like a Shepherd Lead Us

PSALM 18:13–14

107–St. 1   God the Almighty One

PSALM 18:16–19

102   God Is My Strong Salvation

PSALM 18:28

44–St. 3   Blessed Jesus, at Thy Word
60   Christ Whose Glory Fills
102   God Is My Strong Salvation
165–St. 4   I Will Sing the Wondrous Story
201–St. 5   Jesus, Thou Joy of Loving Hearts
244–St. 3   My Faith Looks Up to Thee
267–St. 3   O, How I Love Jesus
339   Sun of My Soul, Thou Savior Dear

PSALM 18:28–50

3   A Mighty Fortress Is Our God

PSALM 18:31–32

4   A Shelter in the Time of Storm
100   God Be with You
283   O Worship the King
314   Rock of Ages
397–St. 3   We Gather Together

PSALM 18:46

42   Blessed Assurance

PSALM 18:46–49

102   God Is My Strong Salvation
283   O Worship the King
304   Praise to the Lord, the Almighty

PSALM 19:1

105   God of Our Fathers

PSALM 19:1–6

19   All Things Bright and Beautiful
77   Day Is Dying in the West
89   For the Beauty of the Earth
114–St. 2   Great Is Thy Faithfulness
137–St. 4   Holy, Holy, Holy
142–St. 1, 2   How Great Thou Art
160   I Sing the Almighty Power of God
206–St. 2   Joyful, Joyful, We Adore Thee
304   Praise to the Lord, the Almighty
371   The Spacious Firmament
383   This Is My Father's World

PSALM 19:1–14

361   The Heavens Declare Thy Glory

PSALM 19:7–11

133   Holy Bible, Book Divine
430   Wonderful Words of Life

PSALM 19:9

107–St. 3   God the Almighty One

PSALM 19:12–13

27   Are You Washed in the Blood?
58   Christ Receiveth Sinful Men
155–St. 1   I Lay My Sins on Jesus
208   Just As I Am, Without One Plea
249   Nearer, Still Nearer
319–St. 3   Savior, Like a Shepherd Lead Us
424   Whiter Than Snow

PSALM 19:14

229   Lord, Speak to Me

PSALM 20:1–9

3   A Mighty Fortress Is Our God

PSALM 20:4–5

309   Rejoice, Ye Pure in Heart

PSALM 20:5

291–St. 1   Onward, Christian Soldiers
308   Rejoice, the Lord Is King

337	Stand Up, Stand Up for Jesus

PSALM 20:7

84	Faith Is the Victory
369	The Solid Rock
391	Trusting Jesus

PSALM 21:4

102–St. 2	God Is My Strong Salvation

PSALM 21:13

283–St. 2	O Worship the King
300	Praise the Lord Who Reigns Above
301	Praise the Lord! Ye Heavens
328	Sing Praise to God Who Reigns
358	The God of Abraham Praise

PSALM 22:3

137	Holy, Holy, Holy
358	The God of Abraham Praise

PSALM 22:3–5

85	Faith of Our Fathers
88	For All the Saints
105	God of Our Fathers
265	O God, Our Help in Ages Past

PSALM 22:22–31

14	All People That On Earth
55	Christ for the World We Sing
66	Come, Thou Almighty King
283	O Worship the King
301	Praise the Lord! Ye Heavens
336	Stand Up and Bless the Lord

PSALM 22:23

358	The God of Abraham Praise

PSALM 23:1–6

17	All the Way My Savior Leads Me
61	Close to Thee
76	Day by Day
109	God Will Take Care of You
115	Guide Me, O Thou Great Jehovah
125	He Leadeth Me
159	I Need Thee Every Hour
167	If Thou But Suffer God to Guide
173	In Heavenly Love Abiding
319	Savior, Like a Shepherd Lead Us
324–St. 4	Shepherd of Tender Youth
341	Surely Goodness and Mercy
362	The King of Love My Shepherd Is

366	The Lord's My Shepherd

PSALM 23:4

5	Abide with Me
96	Give to the Winds
199	Jesus, Still Lead On
327–St. 3	Since Jesus Came Into My Heart

PSALM 23:6

14–St. 4	All People That On Earth
114	Great Is Thy Faithfulness
183	Jerusalem, My Happy Home
184	Jerusalem, the Golden
304–St. 3	Praise to the Lord, the Almighty
308–St. 4	Rejoice, the Lord Is King
342	Sweet By and By
417	When We All Get to Heaven

PSALM 24:1–2

89	For the Beauty of the Earth
160	I Sing the Almighty Power of God
371	The Spacious Firmament
383	This Is My Father's World

PSALM 24:1–5

108	God Who Touchest Earth

PSALM 24:1–10

9	All Creatures of Our God
66	Come, Thou Almighty King
283	O Worship the King
304	Praise to the Lord, the Almighty
309	Rejoice, Ye Pure in Heart

PSALM 24:7–10

116	Hail the Day That Sees Him Rise
220	Lift Up Your Heads
293	Open Now Thy Gates of Beauty

PSALM 25:1–2

159	I Need Thee Every Hour
180	It Is Well with My Soul
336	Stand Up and Bless the Lord
391	Trusting Jesus

PSALM 25:4

86–St. 2	Fight the Good Fight
90	Forth in Thy Name, O Lord

PSALM 25:4–10

125	He Leadeth Me
146	I Am Trusting Thee, Lord Jesus

167	If Thou But Suffer God to Guide
207	Just a Closer Walk with Thee
229	Lord, Speak to Me
261	O For a Closer Walk with God
268	O Jesus, I Have Promised
349	Teach Me Thy Way, O Lord
418	When We Walk with the Lord

PSALM 25:6

17	All the Way My Savior Leads Me
218	Let Us with a Gladsome Mind
412	When All Thy Mercies, O My God

PSALM 25:7

| 228 | Lord Jesus, Think on Me |

PSALM 25:8–10

341	Surely Goodness and Mercy
362	The King of Love My Shepherd Is
366	The Lord's My Shepherd

PSALM 25:9

| 166 | I Would Be True |
| 349 | Teach Me Thy Way, O Lord |

PSALM 25:11

78–St. 1	Dear Lord and Father of Mankind
192–St. 4	Jesus, Lover of My Soul
216	Let Jesus Come Into Your Heart
244	My Faith Looks Up to Thee
267	O, How I Love Jesus
294	Out of My Bondage
359–St. 2	The Great Physician
424	Whiter Than Snow

PSALM 25:12

| 418 | When We Walk with the Lord |

PSALM 25:14

| 103 | God Moves in a Mysterious Way |

PSALM 25:15–18

76	Day by Day
102	God Is My Strong Salvation
167	If Thou But Suffer God to Guide
207	Just a Closer Walk with Thee
306	Precious Lord, Take My Hand

PSALM 26:1

| 391 | Trusting Jesus |

PSALM 26:2

| 122–St. 2 | Have Thine Own Way, Lord |

PSALM 26:3

| 61 | Close to Thee |

PSALM 26:7

40	Begin, My Tongue, Some Heavenly
142	How Great Thou Art
300	Praise the Lord Who Reigns Above
303	Praise to God, Immortal Praise

PSALM 26:8

156	I Love Thy Kingdom, Lord
341–Refrain	Surely Goodness and Mercy
362–St. 6	The King of Love My Shepherd Is

PSALM 27:1

76	Day by Day
188	Jesus Is All the World to Me
213	Leaning on the Everlasting Arms
336–St. 4	Stand Up and Bless the Lord

PSALM 27:1–3

| 102 | God Is My Strong Salvation |
| 332 | Soldiers of Christ, Arise |

PSALM 27:1–4

| 341 | Surely Goodness and Mercy |

PSALM 27:1–14

3	A Mighty Fortress Is Our God
37	Be Still, My Soul
96	Give to the Winds
180	It Is Well with My Soul

PSALM 27:3

| 124–St. 1 | He Keeps Me Singing |

PSALM 27:3–4

| 93 | From Every Stormy Wind |

PSALM 27:4

293	Open Now Thy Gates of Beauty
341–Refrain	Surely Goodness and Mercy
362–St. 6	The King of Love My Shepherd Is

PSALM 27:4–6

| 115–St. 3 | Guide Me, O Thou Great Jehovah |

PSALM 27:5

| 53 | Children of the Heavenly Father |

123	He Hideth My Soul
249	Nearer, Still Nearer
393	Under His Wings

PSALM 27:5–9

| 4 | A Shelter in the Time of Storm |
| 265 | O God, Our Help in Ages Past |

PSALM 27:7

| 79 | Depth of Mercy! Can There Be? |

PSALM 27:9

| 137–St. 3 | Holy, Holy, Holy |

PSALM 27:11

17	All the Way My Savior Leads Me
125	He Leadeth Me
167	If Thou But Suffer God to Guide
239	More About Jesus
341	Surely Goodness and Mercy
349	Teach Me Thy Way, O Lord
362	The King of Love My Shepherd Is
366	The Lord's My Shepherd
397	We Gather Together

PSALM 27:13

| 86–St. 4 | Fight the Good Fight |

PSALM 28:1

| 314 | Rock of Ages |

PSALM 28:6–9

| 3 | A Mighty Fortress Is Our God |
| 141 | How Firm a Foundation |

PSALM 28:7–8

102	God Is My Strong Salvation
115	Guide Me, O Thou Great Jehovah
167	If Thou But Suffer God to Guide
180	It Is Well with My Soul
195–St. 1	Jesus Paid it All
206	Joyful, Joyful, We Adore Thee
207	Just a Closer Walk with Thee
328	Sing Praise to God Who Reigns
391	Trusting Jesus

PSALM 28:9

319	Savior, Like a Shepherd Lead Us
362	The King of Love My Shepherd Is
366	The Lord's My Shepherd

PSALM 29:1–2

1	A Charge to Keep I Have
50	Brethren, We Have Met to Worship
66	Come, Thou Almighty King
101	God Himself Is with Us
246	My Tribute
390	To God Be the Glory
432	Ye Servants of God

PSALM 29:1–11

170	Immortal, Invisible
206	Joyful, Joyful, We Adore Thee
304	Praise to the Lord, the Almighty

PSALM 29:4

| 292–St. 2 | Open My Eyes |

PSALM 29:10

| 253–St. 3 | Now Thank We All Our God |

PSALM 29:10–11

| 107 | God the Almighty One |
| 265 | O God, Our Help in Ages Past |

PSALM 29:11

75–St. 4	Crown Him with Many Crowns
102	God Is My Strong Salvation
105	God of Our Fathers
159	I Need Thee Every Hour
221	Like a River Glorious
264	O God of Love, O King of Peace
297	Peace, Perfect Peace
318	Savior, Again to Thy Dear Name
429	Wonderful Peace

PSALM 30:1–3

| 231 | Love Lifted Me |

PSALM 30:1–5

| 174 | In Loving Kindness Jesus Came |

PSALM 30:4

62	Come, Christians, Join to Sing
134	Holy God, We Praise Thy Name
137	Holy, Holy, Holy
215	Let All the World
358	The God of Abraham Praise
414	When in Our Music
432	Ye Servants of God

PSALM 30:4–5

| 15 | All Praise to Thee, My God |

415	When Morning Gilds the Skies

PSALM 30:5

5	Abide with Me
34	Awake, My Soul, and with the Sun
60	Christ Whose Glory Fills
70	Come, Ye Disconsolate
106	God, That Madest Earth
241	Morning Has Broken
395	Watchman, Tell Us of the Night

PSALM 30:8

305	Prayer Is the Soul's Sincere
343	Sweet Hour of Prayer
407	What a Friend We Have in Jesus

PSALM 30:8–10

79	Depth of Mercy! Can There Be?
381	There's a Wideness

PSALM 30:11–12

206	Joyful, Joyful, We Adore Thee
253	Now Thank We All Our God
258	O Could I Speak the Matchless
340	Sunshine in My Soul
414	When in Our Music

PSALM 31:1–5

283–St. 4	O Worship the King
290	Only Trust Him
314	Rock of Ages

PSALM 31:1–24

3	A Mighty Fortress Is Our God

PSALM 31:3

167	If Thou But Suffer God to Guide
173	In Heavenly Love Abiding
229	Lord, Speak to Me
362	The King of Love My Shepherd Is
366	The Lord's My Shepherd

PSALM 31:5

113	Great God, We Sing Thy Mighty
154	I Know Whom I Have Believed
163	I Surrender All

PSALM 31:6

261	O For a Closer Walk with God

PSALM 31:7–9

23	And Can It Be That I Should Gain?

381	There's a Wideness
412	When All Thy Mercies, O My God

PSALM 31:9

141–St. 3	How Firm a Foundation
294	Out of My Bondage

PSALM 31:14

146	I Am Trusting Thee, Lord Jesus
167	If Thou But Suffer God to Guide
180	It Is Well with My Soul
188	Jesus Is All the World to Me
391	Trusting Jesus

PSALM 31:19

67	Come, Thou Fount
412	When All Thy Mercies, O My God

PSALM 31:20–24

53	Children of the Heavenly Father
123	He Hideth My Soul
265	O God, Our Help in Ages Past
393	Under His Wings

PSALM 32:1–5

129	Heaven Came Down
155–St. 1	I Lay My Sins on Jesus
180	It Is Well with My Soul
208	Just As I Am, Without One Plea
244	My Faith Looks Up to Thee
294	Out of My Bondage
424	Whiter Than Snow

PSALM 32:7

3	A Mighty Fortress Is Our God
53	Children of the Heavenly Father
123	He Hideth My Soul
143	How Sweet the Name
192	Jesus, Lover of My Soul
265	O God, Our Help in Ages Past
307–St. 3	Redeemed, How I Love to Proclaim
326	Since I Have Been Redeemed
393	Under His Wings

PSALM 32:8

17	All the Way My Savior Leads Me
115	Guide Me, O Thou Great Jehovah
125	He Leadeth Me
167	If Thou But Suffer God to Guide
210	Lead, Kindly Light
349	Teach Me Thy Way, O Lord
397	We Gather Together

PSALM 32:10

23	And Can It Be That I Should Gain?

PSALM 32:11

206	Joyful, Joyful, We Adore Thee
266	O Happy Day that Fixed My Choice
309	Rejoice, Ye Pure in Heart
340	Sunshine in My Soul
414	When in Our Music

PSALM 33:1–3

62	Come, Christians, Join to Sing
69	Come, We That Love the Lord
134	Holy God, We Praise Thy Name
206	Joyful, Joyful, We Adore Thee
215	Let All the World
300–St. 2	Praise the Lord Who Reigns Above
309	Rejoice, Ye Pure in Heart
414	When in Our Music
415	When Morning Gilds the Skies

PSALM 33:1–5

299	Praise, My Soul, the King

PSALM 33:4

361	The Heavens Declare Thy Glory

PSALM 33:4–5

40	Begin, My Tongue, Some Heavenly
107	God the Almighty One
218	Let Us with a Gladsome Mind
381	There's a Wideness

PSALM 33:6–9

9	All Creatures of Our God
160	I Sing the Almighty Power of God
371	The Spacious Firmament

PSALM 33:8

101	God Himself Is with Us

PSALM 33:11

37	Be Still, My Soul
114	Great Is Thy Faithfulness
299	Praise, My Soul, the King

PSALM 33:12

22	America the Beautiful

PSALM 33:13–15

383	This Is My Father's World

PSALM 33:18–22

3	A Mighty Fortress Is Our God
42	Blessed Assurance
53	Children of the Heavenly Father
265	O God, Our Help in Ages Past
283–St. 4	O Worship the King
319	Savior, Like a Shepherd Lead Us
337–St. 3	Stand Up, Stand Up for Jesus
369	The Solid Rock
418	When We Walk with the Lord

PSALM 34:1–3

134	Holy God, We Praise Thy Name
263	O For a Thousand Tongues to Sing
299	Praise, My Soul, the King
336	Stand Up and Bless the Lord
415	When Morning Gilds the Skies

PSALM 34:1–22

3	A Mighty Fortress Is Our God
14	All People That On Earth

PSALM 34:4

3–St. 3	A Mighty Fortress Is Our God
102	God Is My Strong Salvation
104–St. 2	God of Grace and God of Glory
161	I Sought the Lord
326–St. 3	Since I Have Been Redeemed

PSALM 34:4–7

96	Give to the Winds

PSALM 34:6

141	How Firm a Foundation
174	In Loving Kindness Jesus Came
294	Out of My Bondage
310	Rescue the Perishing
407	What a Friend We Have in Jesus

PSALM 34:7

319	Savior, Like a Shepherd Lead Us

PSALM 34:8

53	Children of the Heavenly Father
192	Jesus, Lover of My Soul
213	Leaning on the Everlasting Arms
341	Surely Goodness and Mercy

PSALM 34:10

424–St. 4	Whiter Than Snow

PSALM 34:14

| 288 | Once to Every Man and Nation |

PSALM 34:15

| 44–St. 3 | Blessed Jesus, at Thy Word |

PSALM 34:17–19

28	Are You (Art Thou) Weary?
70	Come, Ye Disconsolate
145	I Am Thine, O Lord
158	I Must Tell Jesus
159	I Need Thee Every Hour
177–St. 3	In the Hour of Trial
200–St. 3	Jesus, the Very Thought of Thee
207	Just a Closer Walk with Thee
208	Just As I Am, Without One Plea
227	Lord, I'm Coming Home
247	Near to the Heart of God
248	Nearer, My God, to Thee
249–St. 2	Nearer, Still Nearer
261	O For a Closer Walk with God
262	O For a Heart to Praise My God
296	Pass Me Not, O Gentle Savior
305	Prayer Is the Soul's Sincere
310–St. 2	Rescue the Perishing
319	Savior, Like a Shepherd Lead Us
394–St. 2	Victory in Jesus

PSALM 34:22

| 167 | If Thou But Suffer God to Guide |
| 326 | Since I Have Been Redeemed |

PSALM 35:1–28

| 3 | A Mighty Fortress Is Our God |

PSALM 35:9

102	God Is My Strong Salvation
328–St. 4	Sing Praise to God Who Reigns
336	Stand Up and Bless the Lord

PSALM 35:18

253	Now Thank We All Our God
303	Praise to God, Immortal Praise
328	Sing Praise to God Who Reigns

PSALM 35:27–28

| 336 | Stand Up and Bless the Lord |

PSALM 35:28

40	Begin, My Tongue, Some Heavenly
263	O For a Thousand Tongues to Sing
328–St. 4	Sing Praise to God Who Reigns

| 401 | We Praise Thee, O God |

PSALM 36:1–4

| 288 | Once to Every Man and Nation |

PSALM 36:5

21	Amazing Grace
79	Depth of Mercy! Can There Be?
93	From Every Stormy Wind
381	There's a Wideness
412	When All Thy Mercies, O My God

PSALM 36:5–6

| 107 | God the Almighty One |

PSALM 36:5–7

| 114 | Great Is Thy Faithfulness |

PSALM 36:6

| 170–St. 2 | Immortal, Invisible |

PSALM 36:7

3	A Mighty Fortress Is Our God
100–St. 2	God Be with You
109	God Will Take Care of You
265	O God, Our Help in Ages Past
304–St. 2	Praise to the Lord, the Almighty
393	Under His Wings

PSALM 36:9

27–St. 4	Are You Washed in the Blood?
44–St. 3	Blessed Jesus, at Thy Word
80	Down at the Cross
115–St. 2	Guide Me, O Thou Great Jehovah
170–St. 3	Immortal, Invisible
278	O Splendor of God's Glory
340	Sunshine in My Soul
376	There Is a Fountain
387	Thou Whose Almighty Word

PSALM 36:9–10

| 272–St. 2 | O Love, That Will Not Let Me Go |
| 364 | The Light of the World Is Jesus |

PSALM 37:1–40

| 288 | Once to Every Man and Nation |

PSALM 37:3–6

76	Day by Day
96	Give to the Winds
103	God Moves in a Mysterious Way
146	I Am Trusting Thee, Lord Jesus

167	If Thou But Suffer God to Guide
244	My Faith Looks Up to Thee
283–St. 3, 4	O Worship the King
304–St. 2	Praise to the Lord, the Almighty
389	'Tis So Sweet To Trust in Jesus
391	Trusting Jesus
418	When We Walk with the Lord

PSALM 37:3–7

37	Be Still, My Soul
290	Only Trust Him

PSALM 37:7

28	Are You (Art Thou) Weary?
247	Near to the Heart of God
383–St. 3	This Is My Father's World

PSALM 37:17

109	God Will Take Care of You

PSALM 37:19

192	Jesus, Lover of My Soul

PSALM 37:23–24

17	All the Way My Savior Leads Me
115	Guide Me, O Thou Great Jehovah
125	He Leadeth Me
128	He Who Would Valiant Be
167	If Thou But Suffer God to Guide
341	Surely Goodness and Mercy
349	Teach Me Thy Way, O Lord

PSALM 37:24

113	Great God, We Sing Thy Mighty
123–Refrain	He Hideth My Soul
141–St. 2	How Firm a Foundation
221–St. 2	Like a River Glorious

PSALM 37:28

53–St. 4	Children of the Heavenly Father
88	For All the Saints
107	God the Almighty One
393	Under His Wings

PSALM 37:29

286	On Jordan's Stormy Banks I Stand
342	Sweet By and By

PSALM 37:39–40

3	A Mighty Fortress Is Our God
53	Children of the Heavenly Father
102	God Is My Strong Salvation

192	Jesus, Lover of My Soul
304	Praise to the Lord, the Almighty

PSALM 38:4

155	I Lay My Sins on Jesus
158	I Must Tell Jesus
209	Just When I Need Him

PSALM 38:15

132	Higher Ground
265	O God, Our Help in Ages Past
369	The Solid Rock

PSALM 38:17–18

70	Come, Ye Disconsolate

PSALM 39:7

138	Hope of the World
244	My Faith Looks Up to Thee
265	O God, Our Help in Ages Past
273–St. 4	O Master, Let Me Walk with Thee
369	The Solid Rock

PSALM 39:7–12

70	Come, Ye Disconsolate

PSALM 39:8

228	Lord Jesus, Think on Me
296	Pass Me Not, O Gentle Savior
424	Whiter Than Snow

PSALM 39:12

128	He Who Would Valiant Be
305	Prayer Is the Soul's Sincere

PSALM 40:1

347	Take Time to Be Holy

PSALM 40:1–5

67–St. 2	Come, Thou Fount
252	Now I Belong to Jesus
283–St. 4	O Worship the King
401	We Praise Thee, O God

PSALM 40:1–17

206	Joyful, Joyful, We Adore Thee

PSALM 40:2

174	In Loving Kindness Jesus Came

PSALM 40:2–3

310–St. 3	Rescue the Perishing

PSALM 40:2–4

369	The Solid Rock

PSALM 40:3

42	Blessed Assurance
55	Christ for the World We Sing
263	O For a Thousand Tongues to Sing
298	Praise Him! Praise Him!
336	Stand Up and Bless the Lord
432	Ye Servants of God

PSALM 40:3–4

290	Only Trust Him
418	When We Walk with the Lord

PSALM 40:5

74	Count Your Blessings
142	How Great Thou Art
253	Now Thank We All Our God
303	Praise to God, Immortal Praise

PSALM 40:6–8

122	Have Thine Own Way, Lord
145–St. 2	I Am Thine, O Lord
222	Living for Jesus
229	Lord, Speak to Me
239	More About Jesus
319–St. 4	Savior, Like a Shepherd Lead Us
345	Take My Life and Let It Be

PSALM 40:9–10

40	Begin, My Tongue, Some Heavenly
157	I Love to Tell the Story
292–St. 3	Open My Eyes

PSALM 40:10

114	Great Is Thy Faithfulness
326	Since I Have Been Redeemed
399	We Have Heard the Joyful Sound

PSALM 40:12–13

296	Pass Me Not, O Gentle Savior

PSALM 40:16

142	How Great Thou Art
246	My Tribute
390	To God Be the Glory

PSALM 40:17

102	God Is My Strong Salvation
109	God Will Take Care of You
158	I Must Tell Jesus

159	I Need Thee Every Hour
207	Just a Closer Walk with Thee
209	Just When I Need Him
228	Lord Jesus, Think on Me
238	Moment by Moment
283–St. 4	O Worship the King
306	Precious Lord, Take My Hand
317–St. 3	Saved! Saved! Saved!

PSALM 41:2

3	A Mighty Fortress Is Our God

PSALM 41:4

200–St. 3	Jesus, the Very Thought of Thee
249	Nearer, Still Nearer

PSALM 41:13

92	From All That Dwell Below
299	Praise, My Soul, the King
336	Stand Up and Bless the Lord
358	The God of Abraham Praise

PSALM 42:1–2

72–St. 2	Come, Ye Sinners, Poor and Needy
132	Higher Ground
159	I Need Thee Every Hour
239	More About Jesus
316	Satisfied

PSALM 42:1–11

3	A Mighty Fortress Is Our God

PSALM 42:5

37	Be Still, My Soul
70	Come, Ye Disconsolate
74–St. 1	Count Your Blessings
328–St. 3	Sing Praise to God Who Reigns
375	There Is a Balm in Gilead

PSALM 42:7–11

167	If Thou But Suffer God to Guide
177	In the Hour of Trial

PSALM 42:8

15	All Praise to Thee, My God
34	Awake, My Soul, and with the Sun
77	Day Is Dying in the West
106	God, That Madest Earth
254	Now the Day Is Over
339	Sun of My Soul, Thou Savior Dear
356	The Day Thou Gavest

PSALM 42:11

37	Be Still, My Soul
70	Come, Ye Disconsolate
74–St. 1	Count Your Blessings
328–St. 3	Sing Praise to God Who Reigns
375	There Is a Balm in Gilead

PSALM 43:1–5

| 3 | A Mighty Fortress Is Our God |

PSALM 43:3

130	Heavenly Sunlight
210	Lead, Kindly Light
292–St. 1	Open My Eyes
322	Send the Light

PSALM 43:4

| 300–St. 2 | Praise the Lord Who Reigns Above |
| 414 | When in Our Music |

PSALM 43:5

37	Be Still, My Soul
70	Come, Ye Disconsolate
74–St. 1	Count Your Blessings
328–St. 3	Sing Praise to God Who Reigns
375	There Is a Balm in Gilead

PSALM 44:1–3

| 105 | God of Our Fathers |

PSALM 44:4–7

66–St. 1	Come, Thou Almighty King
283	O Worship the King
304	Praise to the Lord, the Almighty

PSALM 44:5

| 84 | Faith Is the Victory |

PSALM 44:20–21

| 261 | O For a Closer Walk with God |

PSALM 44:21

| 122–St. 2 | Have Thine Own Way, Lord |

PSALM 44:26

23	And Can It Be That I Should Gain?
174	In Loving Kindness Jesus Came
307	Redeemed, How I Love to Proclaim

PSALM 45:6

| 299 | Praise, My Soul, the King |
| 358 | The God of Abraham Praise |

| 432–St. 3 | Ye Servants of God |

PSALM 45:6–7

| 107 | God the Almighty One |

PSALM 45:17

92	From All That Dwell Below
336	Stand Up and Bless the Lord
415–St. 3, 4	When Morning Gilds the Skies
432	Ye Servants of God

PSALM 46:1

76	Day by Day
159	I Need Thee Every Hour
207	Just a Closer Walk with Thee
209	Just When I Need Him

PSALM 46:1–11

3	A Mighty Fortress Is Our God
93	From Every Stormy Wind
96	Give to the Winds
102	God Is My Strong Salvation
124–St. 1	He Keeps Me Singing
141	How Firm a Foundation
158	I Must Tell Jesus
265	O God, Our Help in Ages Past
283	O Worship the King

PSALM 46:4–5

| 97 | Glorious Things of Thee |

PSALM 46:7

105	God of Our Fathers
265	O God, Our Help in Ages Past
401–St. 2	We Praise Thee, O God

PSALM 46:9

| 107 | God the Almighty One |
| 212 | Lead On, O King Eternal |

PSALM 46:9–11

| 264 | O God of Love, O King of Peace |

PSALM 46:10

37	Be Still, My Soul
78	Dear Lord and Father of Mankind
167	If Thou But Suffer God to Guide

PSALM 46:11

53	Children of the Heavenly Father
265	O God, Our Help in Ages Past
401–St. 2	We Praise Thee, O God

PSALM 47:1–9

66	Come, Thou Almighty King
134	Holy God, We Praise Thy Name
137	Holy, Holy, Holy
215	Let All the World
283	O Worship the King
304	Praise to the Lord, the Almighty
328	Sing Praise to God Who Reigns
358	The God of Abraham Praise

PSALM 47:6–7

66	Come, Thou Almighty King
299	Praise, My Soul, the King
401	We Praise Thee, O God
414	When in Our Music

PSALM 47:6–9

206	Joyful, Joyful, We Adore Thee

PSALM 47:7–8

300	Praise the Lord Who Reigns Above

PSALM 48:1–2

14	All People That On Earth
137	Holy, Holy, Holy
142	How Great Thou Art
300	Praise the Lord Who Reigns Above
304	Praise to the Lord, the Almighty

PSALM 48:1–14

69	Come, We That Love the Lord
97	Glorious Things of Thee
183	Jerusalem, My Happy Home
184	Jerusalem, the Golden
293	Open Now Thy Gates of Beauty

PSALM 48:9

171	Immortal Love, Forever Full
230	Love Divine, All Loves Excelling

PSALM 48:10

107–St. 3	God the Almighty One
134	Holy God, We Praise Thy Name
401	We Praise Thee, O God

PSALM 48:14

5	Abide with Me
17	All the Way My Savior Leads Me
115	Guide Me, O Thou Great Jehovah
125	He Leadeth Me
167	If Thou But Suffer God to Guide
173	In Heavenly Love Abiding

253	Now Thank We All Our God
265	O God, Our Help in Ages Past
268	O Jesus, I Have Promised
306	Precious Lord, Take My Hand
341	Surely Goodness and Mercy
347–St. 3	Take Time to Be Holy
358	The God of Abraham Praise
397–St. 2	We Gather Together

PSALM 49:3

292–St. 3	Open My Eyes

PSALM 49:15

5	Abide with Me
31	At Calvary
59–St. 2	Christ the Lord Is Risen Today
123	He Hideth My Soul
174	In Loving Kindness Jesus Came
279	O That Will Be Glory For Me
294–St. 4	Out of My Bondage
307	Redeemed, How I Love to Proclaim
326	Since I Have Been Redeemed
352	Ten Thousand Times Ten Thousand
417	When We All Get to Heaven

PSALM 50:2

69	Come, We That Love the Lord
97	Glorious Things of Thee
293	Open Now Thy Gates of Beauty

PSALM 50:10–12

19	All Things Bright and Beautiful
383	This Is My Father's World

PSALM 50:14

253	Now Thank We All Our God

PSALM 50:15

3	A Mighty Fortress Is Our God
70	Come, Ye Disconsolate
73	Come, Ye Thankful People, Come
102	God Is My Strong Salvation
177	In the Hour of Trial

PSALM 51:1–7

27	Are You Washed in the Blood?
58–St. 3	Christ Receiveth Sinful Men
79	Depth of Mercy! Can There Be?
80	Down at the Cross
112	Grace Greater Than Our Sin
192–St. 4	Jesus, Lover of My Soul
195	Jesus Paid it All

208	Just As I Am, Without One Plea
251	Nothing But the Blood
263–St. 3	O For a Thousand Tongues to Sing
376	There Is a Fountain
378	There Is Power in the Blood
424	Whiter Than Snow

PSALM 51:1–9

149	I Hear Thy Welcome Voice
155–St. 1	I Lay My Sins on Jesus
202	Jesus, Thy Blood and Righteousness
389–St. 2	'Tis So Sweet To Trust in Jesus
408	What a Wonderful Savior

PSALM 51:5

2–St. 3	A Child of the King
31	At Calvary

PSALM 51:7

112	Grace Greater Than Our Sin
122–St. 2	Have Thine Own Way, Lord
290–St. 2	Only Trust Him
424	Whiter Than Snow

PSALM 51:10

216	Let Jesus Come Into Your Heart
262	O For a Heart to Praise My God
424–St. 4	Whiter Than Snow

PSALM 51:10–12

255	O Breath of Life
311	Revive Us Again
334	Spirit of God, Descend

PSALM 51:10–17

261	O For a Closer Walk with God

PSALM 51:11

49	Breathe on Me, Breath of God
65	Come, Holy Spirit
135	Holy Spirit, Light Divine
335	Spirit of the Living God

PSALM 51:12

67	Come, Thou Fount
201	Jesus, Thou Joy of Loving Hearts
341–St. 2	Surely Goodness and Mercy
375–St. 1	There Is a Balm in Gilead
379	There Shall Be Showers

PSALM 51:14–15

43–St. 3	Blessed Be the Name

66	Come, Thou Almighty King
246	My Tribute
263	O For a Thousand Tongues to Sing
267	O, How I Love Jesus
326	Since I Have Been Redeemed
336	Stand Up and Bless the Lord
390	To God Be the Glory
401	We Praise Thee, O God

PSALM 51:15

292	Open My Eyes

PSALM 51:17

200–St. 3	Jesus, the Very Thought of Thee
249–St. 2	Nearer, Still Nearer
296–St. 3	Pass Me Not, O Gentle Savior
310–St. 2	Rescue the Perishing
394–St. 2	Victory in Jesus

PSALM 52:7

3–St. 2	A Mighty Fortress Is Our God

PSALM 52:8

146	I Am Trusting Thee, Lord Jesus
167	If Thou But Suffer God to Guide
180	It Is Well with My Soul

PSALM 52:8–9

114	Great Is Thy Faithfulness
283–St. 4	O Worship the King

PSALM 52:9

12	All Hail the Power of Jesus' Name
134	Holy God, We Praise Thy Name
246	My Tribute

PSALM 54:1–2

208	Just As I Am, Without One Plea
296	Pass Me Not, O Gentle Savior
424	Whiter Than Snow

PSALM 54:1–7

3	A Mighty Fortress Is Our God

PSALM 54:4

158	I Must Tell Jesus

PSALM 54:6

76	Day by Day
93	From Every Stormy Wind
109	God Will Take Care of You
265	O God, Our Help in Ages Past

PSALM 57:9

432	Ye Servants of God

PSALM 57:10

114	Great Is Thy Faithfulness
299–St. 2	Praise, My Soul, the King

PSALM 57:10–11

107	God the Almighty One

PSALM 57:11

160	I Sing the Almighty Power of God

PSALM 58:1–11

107	God the Almighty One

PSALM 59:9

3	A Mighty Fortress Is Our God
53	Children of the Heavenly Father
192	Jesus, Lover of My Soul
283	O Worship the King

PSALM 59:16–17

3	A Mighty Fortress Is Our God
53	Children of the Heavenly Father
160	I Sing the Almighty Power of God
192	Jesus, Lover of My Soul
283	O Worship the King
328	Sing Praise to God Who Reigns
414	When in Our Music
415	When Morning Gilds the Skies

PSALM 60:4

100–St. 4	God Be with You
291–St. 1	Onward, Christian Soldiers
309	Rejoice, Ye Pure in Heart
337–St. 1	Stand Up, Stand Up for Jesus

PSALM 60:5

67–St. 2	Come, Thou Fount
113	Great God, We Sing Thy Mighty
115	Guide Me, O Thou Great Jehovah
125	He Leadeth Me
141	How Firm a Foundation

PSALM 60:12

3	A Mighty Fortress Is Our God
128	He Who Would Valiant Be
426	Who Is on the Lord's Side?

PSALM 61:1–2

305	Prayer Is the Soul's Sincere

314	Rock of Ages
407	What a Friend We Have in Jesus

PSALM 61:1–4

3	A Mighty Fortress Is Our God
4	A Shelter in the Time of Storm
53	Children of the Heavenly Father
102	God Is My Strong Salvation
249	Nearer, Still Nearer
304–St. 2	Praise to the Lord, the Almighty
393	Under His Wings

PSALM 61:5

85	Faith of Our Fathers
105	God of Our Fathers

PSALM 61:8

34	Awake, My Soul, and with the Sun
62	Come, Christians, Join to Sing
134	Holy God, We Praise Thy Name
137	Holy, Holy, Holy
215	Let All the World
298	Praise Him! Praise Him!
304	Praise to the Lord, the Almighty
336	Stand Up and Bless the Lord
401	We Praise Thee, O God
414	When in Our Music
415	When Morning Gilds the Skies

PSALM 62:1–2

3	A Mighty Fortress Is Our God
221	Like a River Glorious
314	Rock of Ages
369	The Solid Rock

PSALM 62:5–8

3	A Mighty Fortress Is Our God
4	A Shelter in the Time of Storm
221	Like a River Glorious
314	Rock of Ages
369	The Solid Rock

PSALM 62:8

86–St. 3	Fight the Good Fight
146	I Am Trusting Thee, Lord Jesus
158	I Must Tell Jesus
163	I Surrender All
347	Take Time to Be Holy

PSALM 62:9–10

3–St. 2	A Mighty Fortress Is Our God

PSALM 62:11–12

107–St. 1	God the Almighty One
137	Holy, Holy, Holy
160	I Sing the Almighty Power of God

PSALM 63:1

41	Beneath the Cross of Jesus
123–St. 1	He Hideth My Soul
316	Satisfied

PSALM 63:2

104	God of Grace and God of Glory
304	Praise to the Lord, the Almighty
328	Sing Praise to God Who Reigns

PSALM 63:3–5

62	Come, Christians, Join to Sing
67	Come, Thou Fount
206	Joyful, Joyful, We Adore Thee
218	Let Us with a Gladsome Mind
253	Now Thank We All Our God
299	Praise, My Soul, the King
300	Praise the Lord Who Reigns Above
336	Stand Up and Bless the Lord
390	To God Be the Glory
412	When All Thy Mercies, O My God
432	Ye Servants of God

PSALM 63:4

| 92 | From All That Dwell Below |
| 415–St. 4 | When Morning Gilds the Skies |

PSALM 63:6

15	All Praise to Thee, My God
77	Day Is Dying in the West
106	God, That Madest Earth
339	Sun of My Soul, Thou Savior Dear
356	The Day Thou Gavest

PSALM 63:6–8

| 254 | Now the Day Is Over |
| 318–St. 3 | Savior, Again to Thy Dear Name |

PSALM 63:7

10–St. 4	All for Jesus
100–St. 2	God Be with You
109	God Will Take Care of You
123	He Hideth My Soul
124–St. 3	He Keeps Me Singing
304–St. 2	Praise to the Lord, the Almighty
393	Under His Wings

PSALM 63:8

67–St. 2	Come, Thou Fount
100–St. 3	God Be with You
115	Guide Me, O Thou Great Jehovah
132	Higher Ground
141–St. 2	How Firm a Foundation
249	Nearer, Still Nearer
268	O Jesus, I Have Promised

PSALM 64:1–10

| 3 | A Mighty Fortress Is Our God |
| 393 | Under His Wings |

PSALM 64:2

53	Children of the Heavenly Father
123	He Hideth My Soul
265	O God, Our Help in Ages Past

PSALM 64:10

42	Blessed Assurance
309	Rejoice, Ye Pure in Heart
328	Sing Praise to God Who Reigns

PSALM 65:1

| 97 | Glorious Things of Thee |

PSALM 65:1–13

14	All People That On Earth
73	Come, Ye Thankful People, Come
74	Count Your Blessings
89	For the Beauty of the Earth
303	Praise to God, Immortal Praise
329	Sing to the Lord of Harvest
400	We Plow the Fields

PSALM 65:2

305	Prayer Is the Soul's Sincere
343	Sweet Hour of Prayer
407	What a Friend We Have in Jesus

PSALM 65:3

27	Are You Washed in the Blood?
58	Christ Receiveth Sinful Men
112	Grace Greater Than Our Sin
155–St. 1	I Lay My Sins on Jesus
208	Just As I Am, Without One Plea
216	Let Jesus Come Into Your Heart
251	Nothing But the Blood
290	Only Trust Him
319–St. 3	Savior, Like a Shepherd Lead Us
424	Whiter Than Snow

PSALM 65:4

12–St. 2	All Hail the Power of Jesus' Name
53–St. 2	Children of the Heavenly Father
341	Surely Goodness and Mercy
362–St. 6	The King of Love My Shepherd Is
366	The Lord's My Shepherd

PSALM 65:5

| 81 | Eternal Father, Strong to Save |

PSALM 65:6–8

| 142 | How Great Thou Art |
| 160 | I Sing the Almighty Power of God |

PSALM 65:7

| 37–St. 2 | Be Still, My Soul |
| 197 | Jesus Savior, Pilot Me |

PSALM 65:11

| 113 | Great God, We Sing That Mighty Hand |

PSALM 66:1–4

12	All Hail the Power of Jesus' Name
43	Blessed Be the Name
62	Come, Christians, Join to Sing
67	Come, Thou Fount
215	Let All the World
263	O For a Thousand Tongues to Sing
298	Praise Him! Praise Him!

PSALM 66:1–9

14	All People That On Earth
134	Holy God, We Praise Thy Name
142	How Great Thou Art
283	O Worship the King
299	Praise, My Soul, the King
304	Praise to the Lord, the Almighty
328	Sing Praise to God Who Reigns

PSALM 66:2

200–St. 2	Jesus, the Very Thought of Thee
267	O, How I Love Jesus
414	When in Our Music

PSALM 66:12

| 124–St. 4 | He Keeps Me Singing |
| 141–St. 3, 4 | How Firm a Foundation |

PSALM 66:16–20

157	I Love to Tell the Story
174	In Loving Kindness Jesus Came
244	My Faith Looks Up to Thee

| 307 | Redeemed, How I Love to Proclaim |
| 317 | Saved! Saved! Saved! |

PSALM 67:1

21	Amazing Grace
79	Depth of Mercy! Can There Be?
100	God Be with You
226	Lord, Dismiss Us
236	May the Grace of Christ
397–St. 1	We Gather Together

PSALM 67:1–2

| 104 | God of Grace and God of Glory |

PSALM 67:1–7

14	All People That On Earth
55	Christ for the World We Sing
62	Come, Christians, Join to Sing
92	From All That Dwell Below
134	Holy God, We Praise Thy Name
215	Let All the World
283	O Worship the King
284	O Zion, Haste
303	Praise to God, Immortal Praise
328	Sing Praise to God Who Reigns
399	We Have Heard the Joyful Sound
401	We Praise Thee, O God

PSALM 67:2

| 404 | We've a Story to Tell |

PSALM 67:6–7

73	Come, Ye Thankful People, Come
329	Sing to the Lord of Harvest
400	We Plow the Fields

PSALM 68:3–4

215	Let All the World
328	Sing Praise to God Who Reigns
365	The Lily of the Valley
414	When in Our Music

PSALM 68:19–20

67	Come, Thou Fount
73	Come, Ye Thankful People, Come
74	Count Your Blessings
89	For the Beauty of the Earth
102	God Is My Strong Salvation
123–St. 3	He Hideth My Soul
253	Now Thank We All Our God
401	We Praise Thee, O God
432	Ye Servants of God

PSALM 68:26

358	The God of Abraham Praise

PSALM 68:32–35

160	I Sing the Almighty Power of God
206	Joyful, Joyful, We Adore Thee
215	Let All the World
283	O Worship the King
299	Praise, My Soul, the King
432	Ye Servants of God

PSALM 69:13–18

70	Come, Ye Disconsolate
102	God Is My Strong Salvation
174	In Loving Kindness Jesus Came
177	In the Hour of Trial

PSALM 69:16

107–St. 2	God the Almighty One

PSALM 69:30

73	Come, Ye Thankful People, Come
253	Now Thank We All Our God
414	When in Our Music

PSALM 69:33

209	Just When I Need Him
343	Sweet Hour of Prayer

PSALM 69:34

77	Day Is Dying in the West
215	Let All the World
301	Praise the Lord! Ye Heavens
383	This Is My Father's World
415	When Morning Gilds the Skies

PSALM 70:1–5

3	A Mighty Fortress Is Our God

PSALM 70:4

142	How Great Thou Art
246	My Tribute
340	Sunshine in My Soul

PSALM 70:5

207	Just a Closer Walk with Thee

PSALM 71:1–14

3	A Mighty Fortress Is Our God
53	Children of the Heavenly Father
102	God Is My Strong Salvation

PSALM 71:1–16

180	It Is Well with My Soul
265	O God, Our Help in Ages Past
290	Only Trust Him
314	Rock of Ages
418	When We Walk with the Lord

PSALM 71:5

138	Hope of the World
159	I Need Thee Every Hour
369	The Solid Rock

PSALM 71:5–8

76	Day by Day
283	O Worship the King
309	Rejoice, Ye Pure in Heart
401	We Praise Thee, O God

PSALM 71:5–9

109	God Will Take Care of You
167–St. 3	If Thou But Suffer God to Guide

PSALM 71:14

62	Come, Christians, Join to Sing
369	The Solid Rock

PSALM 71:14–24

265	O God, Our Help in Ages Past

PSALM 71:15–16

157	I Love to Tell the Story
399	We Have Heard the Joyful Sound

PSALM 71:16

90	Forth in Thy Name, O Lord

PSALM 71:22–24

43	Blessed Be the Name
263	O For a Thousand Tongues to Sing
298	Praise Him! Praise Him!
299	Praise, My Soul, the King
300–St. 2	Praise the Lord Who Reigns Above
401	We Praise Thee, O God
414	When in Our Music

PSALM 72:1–19

118	Hail to the Lord's Anointed
198	Jesus Shall Reign

PSALM 72:18–19

33	At the Name of Jesus
43	Blessed Be the Name

134	Holy God, We Praise Thy Name
170–St. 4	Immortal, Invisible
206	Joyful, Joyful, We Adore Thee
246	My Tribute
300	Praise the Lord Who Reigns Above
328	Sing Praise to God Who Reigns
336	Stand Up and Bless the Lord
358	The God of Abraham Praise
390	To God Be the Glory

PSALM 73:1

309	Rejoice, Ye Pure in Heart

PSALM 73:23–26

100	God Be with You
115	Guide Me, O Thou Great Jehovah
125	He Leadeth Me

PSALM 73:23–28

5	Abide with Me
61	Close to Thee
74–St. 4	Count Your Blessings
76	Day by Day
145	I Am Thine, O Lord
199	Jesus, Still Lead On
247	Near to the Heart of God
249	Nearer, Still Nearer
279	O That Will Be Glory For Me
418	When We Walk with the Lord

PSALM 73:24–28

244–St. 3	My Faith Looks Up to Thee

PSALM 73:25

132	Higher Ground

PSALM 73:26

3	A Mighty Fortress Is Our God
102	God Is My Strong Salvation
141	How Firm a Foundation
167	If Thou But Suffer God to Guide
195–St. 1	Jesus Paid it All
207	Just a Closer Walk with Thee
222	Living for Jesus
231–St. 2	Love Lifted Me
262	O For a Heart to Praise My God

PSALM 73:28

159	I Need Thee Every Hour
180	It Is Well with My Soul
182	I've Found a Friend
347	Take Time to Be Holy

PSALM 74:12

283	O Worship the King

PSALM 74:12–17

160	I Sing the Almighty Power of God
304	Praise to the Lord, the Almighty
328	Sing Praise to God Who Reigns

PSALM 74:16–17

9	All Creatures of Our God
34	Awake, My Soul, and with the Sun
206	Joyful, Joyful, We Adore Thee
339	Sun of My Soul, Thou Savior Dear
356	The Day Thou Gavest
383	This Is My Father's World

PSALM 75:1

73	Come, Ye Thankful People, Come
142	How Great Thou Art
246	My Tribute
253	Now Thank We All Our God
300	Praise the Lord Who Reigns Above

PSALM 75:9

358	The God of Abraham Praise

PSALM 76:11–12

237	Mine Eyes Have Seen the Glory

PSALM 77:11–14

74	Count Your Blessings
142	How Great Thou Art
253	Now Thank We All Our God

PSALM 77:13

101	God Himself Is with Us
137	Holy, Holy, Holy

PSALM 77:15

213	Leaning on the Everlasting Arms

PSALM 77:18

107–St. 1	God the Almighty One

PSALM 77:19

103	God Moves in a Mysterious Way
124–St. 4	He Keeps Me Singing

PSALM 77:20

17	All the Way My Savior Leads Me
115	Guide Me, O Thou Great Jehovah
125	He Leadeth Me

319	Savior, Like a Shepherd Lead Us
341	Surely Goodness and Mercy
362	The King of Love My Shepherd Is
366	The Lord's My Shepherd

PSALM 78:1–7

85	Faith of Our Fathers
105	God of Our Fathers
107	God the Almighty One
265	O God, Our Help in Ages Past

PSALM 78:7

1	A Charge to Keep I Have
369	The Solid Rock

PSALM 78:15–20

115–St. 2	Guide Me, O Thou Great Jehovah

PSALM 78:19–20

53–St. 2	Children of the Heavenly Father
109–St. 3	God Will Take Care of You

PSALM 78:23–29

109–St. 3	God Will Take Care of You
115–St. 2	Guide Me, O Thou Great Jehovah

PSALM 78:24

50	Brethren, We Have Met to Worship

PSALM 78:35

4	A Shelter in the Time of Storm
283	O Worship the King
314	Rock of Ages
369	The Solid Rock
401	We Praise Thee, O God

PSALM 78:38

58	Christ Receiveth Sinful Men
359–St. 2	The Great Physician

PSALM 78:38–40

79	Depth of Mercy! Can There Be?

PSALM 78:52

17	All the Way My Savior Leads Me
115–St. 1	Guide Me, O Thou Great Jehovah
125	He Leadeth Me
362	The King of Love My Shepherd Is
366	The Lord's My Shepherd

PSALM 78:53

213	Leaning on the Everlasting Arms

PSALM 79:8–9

58	Christ Receiveth Sinful Men
80	Down at the Cross
192–St. 4	Jesus, Lover of My Soul
216	Let Jesus Come Into Your Heart
244	My Faith Looks Up to Thee
319	Savior, Like a Shepherd Lead Us
359–St. 2	The Great Physician

PSALM 79:13

73	Come, Ye Thankful People, Come
253	Now Thank We All Our God
319	Savior, Like a Shepherd Lead Us
328	Sing Praise to God Who Reigns
362–St. 6	The King of Love My Shepherd Is
366	The Lord's My Shepherd

PSALM 80:1

115	Guide Me, O Thou Great Jehovah
125	He Leadeth Me
319	Savior, Like a Shepherd Lead Us
324	Shepherd of Tender Youth

PSALM 81:1

42	Blessed Assurance
62	Come, Christians, Join to Sing
67	Come, Thou Fount
206	Joyful, Joyful, We Adore Thee
215	Let All the World
304	Praise to the Lord, the Almighty
358	The God of Abraham Praise

PSALM 81:1–2

300–St. 2	Praise the Lord Who Reigns Above
414	When in Our Music

PSALM 81:9

261	O For a Closer Walk with God

PSALM 82:8

383	This Is My Father's World

PSALM 83:18

14	All People That On Earth
66–St. 1	Come, Thou Almighty King
160	I Sing the Almighty Power of God
283	O Worship the King

PSALM 84:1–4

67–St. 3	Come, Thou Fount
101	God Himself Is with Us
132	Higher Ground

262	O For a Heart to Praise My God
341	Surely Goodness and Mercy
362–St. 6	The King of Love My Shepherd Is

PSALM 84:1–12

53	Children of the Heavenly Father
69	Come, We That Love the Lord
97	Glorious Things of Thee
283	O Worship the King
293	Open Now Thy Gates of Beauty
304	Praise to the Lord, the Almighty

PSALM 84:10–12

104	God of Grace and God of Glory
288	Once to Every Man and Nation
341	Surely Goodness and Mercy

PSALM 84:11

21	Amazing Grace
115–St. 2	Guide Me, O Thou Great Jehovah
130	Heavenly Sunlight
267–St. 3	O, How I Love Jesus
272	O Love, That Will Not Let Me Go
278	O Splendor of God's Glory
283	O Worship the King
339	Sun of My Soul, Thou Savior Dear

PSALM 85:1–7

67	Come, Thou Fount
79	Depth of Mercy! Can There Be?
105	God of Our Fathers

PSALM 85:1–13

| 107 | God the Almighty One |

PSALM 85:2

112	Grace Greater Than Our Sin
155	I Lay My Sins on Jesus
206–St. 3	Joyful, Joyful, We Adore Thee
244	My Faith Looks Up to Thee
359–St. 2	The Great Physician

PSALM 85:6

151–St. 2	I Heard the Voice of Jesus Say
255	O Breath of Life
311	Revive Us Again
379	There Shall Be Showers

PSALM 85:8

292	Open My Eyes
297	Peace, Perfect Peace
318	Savior, Again to Thy Dear Name

PSALM 85:9

| 237 | Mine Eyes Have Seen the Glory |

PSALM 85:10

180	It Is Well with My Soul
221	Like a River Glorious
429	Wonderful Peace

PSALM 85:12

| 329 | Sing to the Lord of Harvest |

PSALM 86:1–7

23	And Can It Be That I Should Gain?
78–St. 1	Dear Lord and Father of Mankind
159	I Need Thee Every Hour
216	Let Jesus Come Into Your Heart
244	My Faith Looks Up to Thee
290	Only Trust Him
294	Out of My Bondage
359–St. 2	The Great Physician
381	There's a Wideness

PSALM 86:5

40	Begin, My Tongue, Some Heavenly
79	Depth of Mercy! Can There Be?
107–St. 2	God the Almighty One
206–St. 3	Joyful, Joyful, We Adore Thee
412	When All Thy Mercies, O My God

PSALM 86:8–10

40	Begin, My Tongue, Some Heavenly
137	Holy, Holy, Holy
142	How Great Thou Art
206	Joyful, Joyful, We Adore Thee
299	Praise, My Soul, the King
301	Praise the Lord! Ye Heavens
328	Sing Praise to God Who Reigns

PSALM 86:9

| 55 | Christ for the World We Sing |

PSALM 86:11

261	O For a Closer Walk with God
273	O Master, Let Me Walk with Thee
349	Teach Me Thy Way, O Lord

PSALM 86:12–13

23	And Can It Be That I Should Gain?
67	Come, Thou Fount
246	My Tribute
390	To God Be the Glory

PSALM 86:15

40	Begin, My Tongue, Some Heavenly
107–St. 2	God the Almighty One
230–St. 1	Love Divine, All Loves Excelling
381	There's a Wideness
412	When All Thy Mercies, O My God
419	Where Cross the Crowded Ways

PSALM 87:1–7

69	Come, We That Love the Lord
97	Glorious Things of Thee
293	Open Now Thy Gates of Beauty

PSALM 87:3

97	Glorious Things of Thee

PSALM 88:1–18

70	Come, Ye Disconsolate
305	Prayer Is the Soul's Sincere

PSALM 88:13

241	Morning Has Broken

PSALM 89:1–2

40	Begin, My Tongue, Some Heavenly
157	I Love to Tell the Story
164	I Will Sing of My Redeemer
165	I Will Sing the Wondrous Story
218	Let Us with a Gladsome Mind
292–St. 3	Open My Eyes
381	There's a Wideness
412	When All Thy Mercies, O My God

PSALM 89:1–18

114	Great Is Thy Faithfulness
283	O Worship the King

PSALM 89:1–52

105	God of Our Fathers
107	God the Almighty One

PSALM 89:5–18

160	I Sing the Almighty Power of God
215	Let All the World
301	Praise the Lord! Ye Heavens
371	The Spacious Firmament
432	Ye Servants of God

PSALM 89:7

101	God Himself Is with Us

PSALM 89:8

114	Great Is Thy Faithfulness

PSALM 89:9

37–St. 2	Be Still, My Soul
81–St. 1	Eternal Father, Strong to Save
93	From Every Stormy Wind
196–St. 3	Jesus, Priceless Treasure
197	Jesus Savior, Pilot Me

PSALM 89:13

113	Great God, We Sing That Mighty Hand
115–St. 1	Guide Me, O Thou Great Jehovah
123–Refrain	He Hideth My Soul
141–St. 2	How Firm a Foundation

PSALM 89:14–15

170	Immortal, Invisible

PSALM 89:21

3	A Mighty Fortress Is Our God
141–St. 2	How Firm a Foundation
207	Just a Closer Walk with Thee

PSALM 89:26

3	A Mighty Fortress Is Our God
4	A Shelter in the Time of Storm
314	Rock of Ages
369	The Solid Rock

PSALM 89:34

114	Great Is Thy Faithfulness

PSALM 90:1–6

105	God of Our Fathers
265	O God, Our Help in Ages Past
299	Praise, My Soul, the King

PSALM 90:1–17

107	God the Almighty One
265	O God, Our Help in Ages Past

PSALM 90:5–6

34	Awake, My Soul, and with the Sun

PSALM 90:10

222–St. 4	Living for Jesus

PSALM 90:12

104	God of Grace and God of Glory

PSALM 90:14

34	Awake, My Soul, and with the Sun
241	Morning Has Broken
319–St. 3	Savior, Like a Shepherd Lead Us
415	When Morning Gilds the Skies

PSALM 90:17

1	A Charge to Keep I Have
273	O Master, Let Me Walk with Thee
345	Take My Life and Let It Be

PSALM 91:1–4

4	A Shelter in the Time of Storm
100	God Be with You
109	God Will Take Care of You
192	Jesus, Lover of My Soul
393	Under His Wings

PSALM 91:1–16

3	A Mighty Fortress Is Our God
67–St. 2	Come, Thou Fount
81	Eternal Father, Strong to Save
102	God Is My Strong Salvation
123	He Hideth My Soul
265	O God, Our Help in Ages Past
304	Praise to the Lord, the Almighty

PSALM 91:5

| 254 | Now the Day Is Over |

PSALM 91:11

96	Give to the Winds
106	God, That Madest Earth
109	God Will Take Care of You

PSALM 91:15

| 407 | What a Friend We Have in Jesus |

PSALM 92:1–2

15	All Praise to Thee, My God
34	Awake, My Soul, and with the Sun
356	The Day Thou Gavest

PSALM 92:1–4

14	All People That On Earth
62	Come, Christians, Join to Sing
73	Come, Ye Thankful People, Come
253	Now Thank We All Our God
414	When in Our Music

PSALM 92:1–8

| 206–St. 2 | Joyful, Joyful, We Adore Thee |

299	Praise, My Soul, the King
300	Praise the Lord Who Reigns Above
328	Sing Praise to God Who Reigns

PSALM 92:2

5	Abide with Me
77	Day Is Dying in the West
106	God, That Madest Earth
114	Great Is Thy Faithfulness
254	Now the Day Is Over
339	Sun of My Soul, Thou Savior Dear

PSALM 92:13

| 156 | I Love Thy Kingdom, Lord |

PSALM 92:15

4	A Shelter in the Time of Storm
107–St. 3	God the Almighty One
167–St. 1	If Thou But Suffer God to Guide
369	The Solid Rock

PSALM 93:1–5

66	Come, Thou Almighty King
107	God the Almighty One
134	Holy God, We Praise Thy Name
137	Holy, Holy, Holy
160	I Sing the Almighty Power of God
283	O Worship the Lord
299	Praise, My Soul, the King
304	Praise to the Lord, the Almighty
358	The God of Abraham Praise

PSALM 94:1–23

| 107 | God the Almighty One |

PSALM 94:12

| 397–St. 1 | We Gather Together |

PSALM 94:14

| 141 | How Firm a Foundation |
| 401 | We Praise Thee, O God |

PSALM 94:17–19

53–St. 3	Children of the Heavenly Father
96	Give to the Winds
159	I Need Thee Every Hour
365	The Lily of the Valley

PSALM 94:22

3	A Mighty Fortress Is Our God
4	A Shelter in the Time of Storm
141	How Firm a Foundation

314	Rock of Ages
369	The Solid Rock

PSALM 95:1–2

42	Blessed Assurance
62	Come, Christians, Join to Sing
67–St. 1	Come, Thou Fount
215	Let All the World
253	Now Thank We All Our God
414	When in Our Music

PSALM 95:1–7

9	All Creatures of Our God
89	For the Beauty of the Earth
134	Holy God, We Praise Thy Name
300	Praise the Lord Who Reigns Above
304	Praise to the Lord, the Almighty
336	Stand Up and Bless the Lord
358	The God of Abraham Praise
401	We Praise Thee, O God

PSALM 95:3

142	How Great Thou Art
283	O Worship the King

PSALM 95:3–6

66	Come, Thou Almighty King
81	Eternal Father, Strong to Save
160	I Sing the Almighty Power of God
383	This Is My Father's World

PSALM 95:6

101	God Himself Is with Us

PSALM 95:6–7

44	Blessed Jesus, at Thy Word
50	Brethren, We Have Met to Worship

PSALM 95:7

100–St. 1	God Be with You
173	In Heavenly Love Abiding
319	Savior, Like a Shepherd Lead Us
362	The King of Love My Shepherd Is
366	The Lord's My Shepherd

PSALM 96:1–2

401	We Praise Thee, O God
414	When in Our Music

PSALM 96:1–4

263	O For a Thousand Tongues to Sing

PSALM 96:1–10

432	Ye Servants of God

PSALM 96:1–13

9	All Creatures of Our God
14	All People That On Earth
206	Joyful, Joyful, We Adore Thee
215	Let All the World
299	Praise, My Soul, the King
301	Praise the Lord! Ye Heavens
304	Praise to the Lord, the Almighty
328	Sing Praise to God Who Reigns
336	Stand Up and Bless the Lord
399	We Have Heard the Joyful Sound

PSALM 96:2–3

55	Christ for the World We Sing
404	We've a Story to Tell

PSALM 96:3–4

390	To God Be the Glory

PSALM 96:5

261	O For a Closer Walk with God

PSALM 96:8–9

1–St. 1	A Charge to Keep I Have
44	Blessed Jesus, at Thy Word
50	Brethren, We Have Met to Worship
101	God Himself Is with Us

PSALM 96:10

310	Rescue the Perishing
404	We've a Story to Tell

PSALM 96:10–13

383	This Is My Father's World

PSALM 97:1–12

9	All Creatures of Our God
14	All People That On Earth
66	Come, Thou Almighty King
107	God the Almighty One
134	Holy God, We Praise Thy Name
142	How Great Thou Art
170	Immortal, Invisible
283	O Worship the King
301	Praise the Lord! Ye Heavens
304	Praise to the Lord, the Almighty
328	Sing Praise to God Who Reigns
383	This Is My Father's World
432	Ye Servants of God

PSALM 97:2

137–St. 3	Holy, Holy, Holy

PSALM 97:10

53	Children of the Heavenly Father
104–St. 2	God of Grace and God of Glory
288	Once to Every Man and Nation

PSALM 97:11

60	Christ Whose Glory Fills
130	Heavenly Sunlight
340	Sunshine in My Soul

PSALM 98:1–6

14	All People That On Earth
283	O Worship the King
300–St. 2	Praise the Lord Who Reigns Above
390	To God Be the Glory
394	Victory in Jesus
414	When in Our Music

PSALM 98:1–9

9	All Creatures of Our God
205	Joy to the World
206	Joyful, Joyful, We Adore Thee
301	Praise the Lord! Ye Heavens

PSALM 98:9

107–St. 3	God the Almighty One
381	There's a Wideness

PSALM 99:1–5

43	Blessed Be the Name
66	Come, Thou Almighty King
206	Joyful, Joyful, We Adore Thee
299	Praise, My Soul, the King
358	The God of Abraham Praise

PSALM 99:1–9

304	Praise to the Lord, the Almighty

PSALM 99:2

97	Glorious Things of Thee

PSALM 99:5

101	God Himself Is with Us

PSALM 99:7

115	Guide Me, O Thou Great Jehovah

PSALM 99:9

77–Refrain	Day Is Dying in the West

134	Holy God, We Praise Thy Name
137	Holy, Holy, Holy

PSALM 100:1–2

62	Come, Christians, Join to Sing
309	Rejoice, Ye Pure in Heart

PSALM 100:1–5

9	All Creatures of Our God
14	All People That On Earth
67	Come, Thou Fount
206	Joyful, Joyful, We Adore Thee
215	Let All the World
253	Now Thank We All Our God
299	Praise, My Soul, the King
300	Praise the Lord Who Reigns Above
304	Praise to the Lord, the Almighty
319	Savior, Like a Shepherd Lead Us

PSALM 100:3

319	Savior, Like a Shepherd Lead Us
396	We Are God's People

PSALM 100:5

114	Great Is Thy Faithfulness
201–St. 2	Jesus, Thou Joy of Loving Hearts
218	Let Us with a Gladsome Mind

PSALM 101:1

414	When in Our Music

PSALM 102:11–12

114	Great Is Thy Faithfulness
299	Praise, My Soul, the King

PSALM 102:18

282	O Word of God Incarnate
361	The Heavens Declare Thy Glory

PSALM 102:21–22

69	Come, We That Love the Lord
97	Glorious Things of Thee

PSALM 102:24–27

9	All Creatures of Our God
75–St. 5	Crown Him with Many Crowns
113	Great God, We Sing That Mighty Hand
114–St. 2	Great Is Thy Faithfulness
142	How Great Thou Art
160	I Sing the Almighty Power of God
299	Praise, My Soul, the King
371	The Spacious Firmament

PSALM 103:1

134	Holy God, We Praise Thy Name
137	Holy, Holy, Holy

PSALM 103:1–5

14	All People That On Earth
43	Blessed Be the Name
74	Count Your Blessings
79	Depth of Mercy! Can There Be?
180	It Is Well with My Soul
206	Joyful, Joyful, We Adore Thee
218	Let Us with a Gladsome Mind
253	Now Thank We All Our God
263	O For a Thousand Tongues to Sing
299	Praise, My Soul, the King
304	Praise to the Lord, the Almighty
336	Stand Up and Bless the Lord
381	There's a Wideness
401	We Praise Thee, O God
412	When All Thy Mercies, O My God

PSALM 103:2

67	Come, Thou Fount
89	For the Beauty of the Earth
123–St. 3	He Hideth My Soul

PSALM 103:3

192	Jesus, Lover of My Soul
250–St. 1	No, Not One
359	The Great Physician

PSALM 103:6–18

79	Depth of Mercy! Can There Be?
107–St. 1	God the Almighty One
319–St. 3	Savior, Like a Shepherd Lead Us
359–St. 2	The Great Physician
412	When All Thy Mercies, O My God

PSALM 103:17

53	Children of the Heavenly Father
114	Great Is Thy Faithfulness
218	Let Us with a Gladsome Mind
341	Surely Goodness and Mercy

PSALM 103:18

166	I Would Be True

PSALM 103:19

66	Come, Thou Almighty King
184	Jerusalem, the Golden
283	O Worship the King

PSALM 103:19–22

14	All People That On Earth
134	Holy God, We Praise Thy Name
299	Praise, My Soul, the King
301	Praise the Lord! Ye Heavens
432	Ye Servants of God

PSALM 103:20

12	All Hail the Power of Jesus' Name

PSALM 104:1

283–St. 1, 2	O Worship the King
336	Stand Up and Bless the Lord

PSALM 104:1–5

170	Immortal, Invisible
206	Joyful, Joyful, We Adore Thee

PSALM 104:1–35

9	All Creatures of Our God
19	All Things Bright and Beautiful
89	For the Beauty of the Earth
92	From All That Dwell Below
114–St. 2	Great Is Thy Faithfulness
142	How Great Thou Art
160	I Sing the Almighty Power of God
304	Praise to the Lord, the Almighty
328	Sing Praise to God Who Reigns
371	The Spacious Firmament
383	This Is My Father's World
400	We Plow the Fields

PSALM 104:23

5	Abide with Me
15	All Praise to Thee, My God
106	God, That Madest Earth

PSALM 104:23–24

77	Day Is Dying in the West

PSALM 104:24

142	How Great Thou Art
160	I Sing the Almighty Power of God
383	This Is My Father's World

PSALM 104:33

62	Come, Christians, Join to Sing
414	When in Our Music

PSALM 104:33–35

336	Stand Up and Bless the Lord

PSALM 105:1–3

62	Come, Christians, Join to Sing
73	Come, Ye Thankful People, Come
215	Let All the World
253	Now Thank We All Our God
300	Praise the Lord Who Reigns Above
304	Praise to the Lord, the Almighty
414	When in Our Music

PSALM 105:1–5

105	God of Our Fathers
142	How Great Thou Art
265	O God, Our Help in Ages Past
283	O Worship the King
358	The God of Abraham Praise

PSALM 105:7

| 259 | O Day of God, Draw Nigh |

PSALM 105:39

| 115–St. 2 | Guide Me, O Thou Great Jehovah |

PSALM 105:42

| 338 | Standing on the Promises |

PSALM 105:43

| 336 | Stand Up and Bless the Lord |

PSALM 106:1–5

40	Begin, My Tongue, Some Heavenly
105	God of Our Fathers
114	Great Is Thy Faithfulness
206	Joyful, Joyful, We Adore Thee
218	Let Us with a Gladsome Mind
283	O Worship the King
301	Praise the Lord! Ye Heavens
304–St. 3	Praise to the Lord, the Almighty
341	Surely Goodness and Mercy

PSALM 106:4–5

79	Depth of Mercy! Can There Be?
228	Lord Jesus, Think on Me
230–St. 1	Love Divine, All Loves Excelling
319	Savior, Like a Shepherd Lead Us

PSALM 106:25

| 292–St. 2 | Open My Eyes |

PSALM 106:47–48

92	From All That Dwell Below
253	Now Thank We All Our God
299	Praise, My Soul, the King

304–St. 4	Praise to the Lord, the Almighty
336	Stand Up and Bless the Lord
358	The God of Abraham Praise
432	Ye Servants of God

PSALM 107:1

| 253 | Now Thank We All Our God |

PSALM 107:1–2

| 303 | Praise to God, Immortal Praise |

PSALM 107:1–9

| 316 | Satisfied |

PSALM 107:1–43

14	All People That On Earth
67	Come, Thou Fount
109	God Will Take Care of You
114	Great Is Thy Faithfulness
201	Jesus, Thou Joy of Loving Hearts
381	There's a Wideness

PSALM 107:2

42	Blessed Assurance
174	In Loving Kindness Jesus Came
252	Now I Belong to Jesus
307	Redeemed, How I Love to Proclaim
317	Saved! Saved! Saved!
326	Since I Have Been Redeemed

PSALM 107:7

115	Guide Me, O Thou Great Jehovah
125	He Leadeth Me
341	Surely Goodness and Mercy

PSALM 107:8

| 67 | Come, Thou Fount |
| 89 | For the Beauty of the Earth |

PSALM 107:8–9

| 218 | Let Us with a Gladsome Mind |

PSALM 107:15

89	For the Beauty of the Earth
218	Let Us with a Gladsome Mind
253	Now Thank We All Our God

PSALM 107:21–22

89	For the Beauty of the Earth
218	Let Us with a Gladsome Mind
253	Now Thank We All Our God

PSALM 107:22

73	Come, Ye Thankful People, Come
309	Rejoice, Ye Pure in Heart

PSALM 107:23–32

81–St. 1, 4	Eternal Father, Strong to Save

PSALM 107:28–30

37	Be Still, My Soul
93	From Every Stormy Wind
197	Jesus Savior, Pilot Me
204–St. 4	Jesus, What a Friend for Sinners

PSALM 107:31–32

218	Let Us with a Gladsome Mind
253	Now Thank We All Our God

PSALM 107:32

156	I Love Thy Kingdom, Lord
336	Stand Up and Bless the Lord

PSALM 108:1

414	When in Our Music

PSALM 108:1–5

62	Come, Christians, Join to Sing
107	God the Almighty One
134	Holy God, We Praise Thy Name
206	Joyful, Joyful, We Adore Thee
300	Praise the Lord Who Reigns Above
336	Stand Up and Bless the Lord
390	To God Be the Glory
415	When Morning Gilds the Skies

PSALM 108:2–3

34	Awake, My Soul, and with the Sun

PSALM 108:4

79	Depth of Mercy! Can There Be?
114	Great Is Thy Faithfulness

PSALM 108:12–13

3	A Mighty Fortress Is Our God
128	He Who Would Valiant Be

PSALM 109:21

230	Love Divine, All Loves Excelling

PSALM 109:21–31

3	A Mighty Fortress Is Our God

PSALM 109:22

55–St. 1	Christ for the World We Sing
72	Come, Ye Sinners, Poor and Needy
122–St. 3	Have Thine Own Way, Lord
238–St. 3	Moment by Moment
294	Out of My Bondage

PSALM 111:1–10

114	Great Is Thy Faithfulness
142	How Great Thou Art
253	Now Thank We All Our God
299	Praise, My Soul, the King
301	Praise the Lord! Ye Heavens
304	Praise to the Lord, the Almighty
336	Stand Up and Bless the Lord
401	We Praise Thee, O God

PSALM 111:3

107–St. 3	God the Almighty One

PSALM 111:5

109	God Will Take Care of You
338	Standing on the Promises

PSALM 111:9

137	Holy, Holy, Holy

PSALM 111:9–10

134	Holy God, We Praise Thy Name

PSALM 111:10

104	God of Grace and God of Glory

PSALM 112:1–10

107	God the Almighty One
419	Where Cross the Crowded Ways

PSALM 112:4

201–St. 5	Jesus, Thou Joy of Loving Hearts
267–St. 3	O, How I Love Jesus
364	The Light of the World Is Jesus

PSALM 112:7

3	A Mighty Fortress Is Our God
76	Day by Day
86–St. 3	Fight the Good Fight
96	Give to the Winds
104–St. 2	God of Grace and God of Glory
290	Only Trust Him
418–St. 4	When We Walk with the Lord

PSALM 113:1–5

300	Praise the Lord Who Reigns Above
328	Sing Praise to God Who Reigns
358	The God of Abraham Praise

PSALM 113:1–9

283	O Worship the King
299	Praise, My Soul, the King
304	Praise to the Lord, the Almighty
336	Stand Up and Bless the Lord

PSALM 113:2–3

356	The Day Thou Gavest

PSALM 113:3

33	At the Name of Jesus
134	Holy God, We Praise Thy Name
137	Holy, Holy, Holy

PSALM 115:1

336	Stand Up and Bless the Lord
432	Ye Servants of God

PSALM 115:1–18

304	Praise to the Lord, the Almighty

PSALM 115:9–13

3	A Mighty Fortress Is Our God
109	God Will Take Care of You
115–St. 2	Guide Me, O Thou Great Jehovah
167	If Thou But Suffer God to Guide
265	O God, Our Help in Ages Past
283	O Worship the King

PSALM 115:15–16

89	For the Beauty of the Earth

PSALM 115:18

415–St. 4	When Morning Gilds the Skies

PSALM 116:1–19

67	Come, Thou Fount
238	Moment by Moment
362–St. 4	The King of Love My Shepherd Is
381	There's a Wideness

PSALM 116:6

53	Children of the Heavenly Father
115–St. 1	Guide Me, O Thou Great Jehovah
207	Just a Closer Walk with Thee
306	Precious Lord, Take My Hand
391	Trusting Jesus

PSALM 116:7

221	Like a River Glorious
247	Near to the Heart of God
249	Nearer, Still Nearer

PSALM 116:12

74	Count Your Blessings

PSALM 116:16

294	Out of My Bondage
310–St. 3	Rescue the Perishing

PSALM 116:17

73	Come, Ye Thankful People, Come
253	Now Thank We All Our God

PSALM 117:1–2

9	All Creatures of Our God
14	All People That On Earth
66	Come, Thou Almighty King
67	Come, Thou Fount
92	From All That Dwell Below
114	Great Is Thy Faithfulness
134	Holy God, We Praise Thy Name
218	Let Us with a Gladsome Mind
246	My Tribute
304	Praise to the Lord, the Almighty
328	Sing Praise to God Who Reigns

PSALM 118:1–4

92–St. 2	From All That Dwell Below
171	Immortal Love, Forever Full
203	Jesus, Thy Boundless Love to Me
218	Let Us with a Gladsome Mind
253	Now Thank We All Our God
381	There's a Wideness

PSALM 118:1–29

283	O Worship the King
304	Praise to the Lord, the Almighty
328	Sing Praise to God Who Reigns

PSALM 118:5

294	Out of My Bondage

PSALM 118:6–9

3	A Mighty Fortress Is Our God
37	Be Still, My Soul
76	Day by Day
102	God Is My Strong Salvation
182	I've Found a Friend
188	Jesus Is All the World to Me

244	My Faith Looks Up to Thee
268	O Jesus, I Have Promised
290	Only Trust Him
347	Take Time to Be Holy
389	'Tis So Sweet To Trust in Jesus
391	Trusting Jesus
418	When We Walk with the Lord

PSALM 118:14

102	God Is My Strong Salvation
213	Leaning on the Everlasting Arms
340	Sunshine in My Soul

PSALM 118:15

123	He Hideth My Soul
141–St. 2	How Firm a Foundation

PSALM 118:18

397–St. 1	We Gather Together

PSALM 118:19–21

293	Open Now Thy Gates of Beauty

PSALM 118:22

52	Built on the Rock
56	Christ Is Made the Sure
141	How Firm a Foundation
314	Rock of Ages
353	The Church's One Foundation
396–St. 1	We Are God's People

PSALM 118:24

241	Morning Has Broken
384	This Is the Day

PSALM 118:28–29

171	Immortal Love, Forever Full
203	Jesus, Thy Boundless Love to Me
218	Let Us with a Gladsome Mind
253	Now Thank We All Our God
358	The God of Abraham Praise
381	There's a Wideness

PSALM 119:1–8

115	Guide Me, O Thou Great Jehovah
122	Have Thine Own Way, Lord
167–St. 3	If Thou But Suffer God to Guide
418	When We Walk with the Lord

PSALM 119:1–176

48	Break Thou the Bread
133	Holy Bible, Book Divine

282	O Word of God Incarnate
361	The Heavens Declare Thy Glory
430	Wonderful Words of Life

PSALM 119:12–13

229	Lord, Speak to Me

PSALM 119:18

292–St. 1	Open My Eyes

PSALM 119:30

288	Once to Every Man and Nation

PSALM 119:33–34

48–St. 3	Break Thou the Bread
122	Have Thine Own Way, Lord
345	Take My Life and Let It Be

PSALM 119:41

141	How Firm a Foundation
338	Standing on the Promises

PSALM 119:49–50

40–St. 3	Begin, My Tongue, Some Heavenly
141	How Firm a Foundation
154	I Know Whom I Have Believed
338	Standing on the Promises

PSALM 119:64

381	There's a Wideness

PSALM 119:68

362	The King of Love My Shepherd Is
366	The Lord's My Shepherd

PSALM 119:81

154–St. 2	I Know Whom I Have Believed

PSALM 119:89

153–St. 2	I Know That My Redeemer Liveth
361	The Heavens Declare Thy Glory

PSALM 119:90–91

114	Great Is Thy Faithfulness

PSALM 119:103–105

48	Break Thou the Bread
133	Holy Bible, Book Divine
141–St. 1	How Firm a Foundation
282	O Word of God Incarnate
361	The Heavens Declare Thy Glory

PSALM 119:114–116

3	A Mighty Fortress Is Our God
123	He Hideth My Soul
265	O God, Our Help in Ages Past
369	The Solid Rock

PSALM 119:134

397–St. 1	We Gather Together

PSALM 119:137–142

107–St. 3	God the Almighty One

PSALM 119:143

177–St. 3	In the Hour of Trial

PSALM 119:151

159	I Need Thee Every Hour
247	Near to the Heart of God

PSALM 119:160

282	O Word of God Incarnate

PSALM 119:165

297	Peace, Perfect Peace
429	Wonderful Peace

PSALM 119:172

430	Wonderful Words of Life

PSALM 119:176

67–St. 3	Come, Thou Fount
165–St. 2	I Will Sing the Wondrous Story
227	Lord, I'm Coming Home
341	Surely Goodness and Mercy
362–St. 3	The King of Love My Shepherd Is

PSALM 121:1–8

3	A Mighty Fortress Is Our God
53	Children of the Heavenly Father
76	Day by Day
96	Give to the Winds
109	God Will Take Care of You
114	Great Is Thy Faithfulness
115	Guide Me, O Thou Great Jehovah
173	In Heavenly Love Abiding
283	O Worship the King

PSALM 121:4

328–St. 2	Sing Praise to God Who Reigns

PSALM 122:1

50	Brethren, We Have Met to Worship

PSALM 122:1–9

293	Open Now Thy Gates of Beauty

PSALM 122:6–8

107	God the Almighty One
264	O God of Love, O King of Peace

PSALM 123:1–4

79	Depth of Mercy! Can There Be?
381	There's a Wideness
412	When All Thy Mercies, O My God

PSALM 124:1–8

3	A Mighty Fortress Is Our God
283	O Worship the King

PSALM 124:8

76	Day by Day
265	O God, Our Help in Ages Past

PSALM 125:1

97	Glorious Things of Thee
146	I Am Trusting Thee, Lord Jesus
369	The Solid Rock
389	'Tis So Sweet To Trust in Jesus

PSALM 125:1–5

3	A Mighty Fortress Is Our God
283–St. 4	O Worship the King

PSALM 125:2

5	Abide with Me
173	In Heavenly Love Abiding

PSALM 125:5

264	O God of Love, O King of Peace

PSALM 126:1–6

105	God of Our Fathers

PSALM 126:2–3

246	My Tribute
253	Now Thank We All Our God
390	To God Be the Glory

PSALM 127:1–2

395	Watchman, Tell Us of the Night
15	All Praise to Thee, My God
254	Now the Day Is Over

PSALM 127:1–3

119	Happy the Home When God Is There

PSALM 128:1

1	A Charge to Keep I Have
61	Close to Thee

PSALM 128:5

97	Glorious Things of Thee

PSALM 129:5

69	Come, We That Love the Lord

PSALM 130:1–2

81	Eternal Father, Strong to Save
305	Prayer Is the Soul's Sincere
343	Sweet Hour of Prayer
407	What a Friend We Have in Jesus

PSALM 130:3–4

78	Dear Lord and Father of Mankind
244	My Faith Looks Up to Thee

PSALM 130:5

347	Take Time to Be Holy

PSALM 130:6

34	Awake, My Soul, and with the Sun
254	Now the Day Is Over
395	Watchman, Tell Us of the Night

PSALM 130:7–8

23	And Can It Be That I Should Gain?
31	At Calvary
67	Come, Thou Fount
200–St. 3	Jesus, the Very Thought of Thee
298–St. 2	Praise Him! Praise Him!
319–St. 3	Savior, Like a Shepherd Lead Us
326	Since I Have Been Redeemed
369	The Solid Rock
412	When All Thy Mercies, O My God

PSALM 131:1–3

78	Dear Lord and Father of Mankind
283–St. 4	O Worship the King

PSALM 132:13

69	Come, We That Love the Lord
97	Glorious Things of Thee

PSALM 133:1

46	Blest Be the Tie
172	In Christ There Is No East
206–St. 3	Joyful, Joyful, We Adore Thee
344	Sweet, Sweet Spirit

PSALM 134:1–3

336	Stand Up and Bless the Lord

PSALM 135:1–21

134	Holy God, We Praise Thy Name
142	How Great Thou Art
160	I Sing the Almighty Power of God
206	Joyful, Joyful, We Adore Thee
299	Praise, My Soul, the King
304	Praise to the Lord, the Almighty
336	Stand Up and Bless the Lord
358	The God of Abraham Praise

PSALM 135:3

43	Blessed Be the Name
300	Praise the Lord Who Reigns Above
414	When in Our Music

PSALM 135:13

85	Faith of Our Fathers
105	God of Our Fathers
265	O God, Our Help in Ages Past

PSALM 136:1–9

9	All Creatures of Our God
19	All Things Bright and Beautiful

PSALM 136:1–26

40	Begin, My Tongue, Some Heavenly
92–St. 2	From All That Dwell Below
107	God the Almighty One
114	Great Is Thy Faithfulness
171	Immortal Love, Forever Full
218	Let Us with a Gladsome Mind
230	Love Divine, All Loves Excelling
381	There's a Wideness

PSALM 136:25

400	We Plow the Fields

PSALM 137:3

69	Come, We That Love the Lord

PSALM 137:5–6

156	I Love Thy Kingdom, Lord

PSALM 138:1–2

230–St. 3	Love Divine, All Loves Excelling
262	O For a Heart to Praise My God
283	O Worship the King
303	Praise to God, Immortal Praise
309	Rejoice, Ye Pure in Heart

| 336 | Stand Up and Bless the Lord |

PSALM 138:3

76	Day by Day
141–St. 2	How Firm a Foundation
167	If Thou But Suffer God to Guide

PSALM 138:5

328	Sing Praise to God Who Reigns
390	To God Be the Glory
414	When in Our Music

PSALM 138:7

177	In the Hour of Trial
221	Like a River Glorious
238	Moment by Moment

PSALM 138:8

21	Amazing Grace
79	Depth of Mercy! Can There Be?
218	Let Us with a Gladsome Mind
381	There's a Wideness
412	When All Thy Mercies, O My God

PSALM 139:1–12

5	Abide with Me
17	All the Way My Savior Leads Me
101	God Himself Is with Us
102	God Is My Strong Salvation
115–St. 1	Guide Me, O Thou Great Jehovah
125	He Leadeth Me
167	If Thou But Suffer God to Guide
171	Immortal Love, Forever Full
247	Near to the Heart of God
319	Savior, Like a Shepherd Lead Us
328–St. 3	Sing Praise to God Who Reigns
341	Surely Goodness and Mercy
362	The King of Love My Shepherd Is
366	The Lord's My Shepherd

PSALM 139:1–24

| 37 | Be Still, My Soul |
| 141–St. 2 | How Firm a Foundation |

PSALM 139:11–12

15	All Praise to Thee, My God
77	Day Is Dying in the West
130	Heavenly Sunlight
201–St. 5	Jesus, Thou Joy of Loving Hearts
206–St. 1	Joyful, Joyful, We Adore Thee
244–St. 3	My Faith Looks Up to Thee
254	Now the Day Is Over

267–St. 3	O, How I Love Jesus
339	Sun of My Soul, Thou Savior Dear
415	When Morning Gilds the Skies

PSALM 139:14

| 142 | How Great Thou Art |
| 206 | Joyful, Joyful, We Adore Thee |

PSALM 139:17–18

74	Count Your Blessings
106	God, That Madest Earth
228	Lord Jesus, Think on Me
412	When All Thy Mercies, O My God

PSALM 139:23

| 122–St. 2 | Have Thine Own Way, Lord |

PSALM 139:24

17	All the Way My Savior Leads Me
115	Guide Me, O Thou Great Jehovah
167	If Thou But Suffer God to Guide
306	Precious Lord, Take My Hand
341	Surely Goodness and Mercy
385	Thou Art the Way: to Thee Alone

PSALM 140:1–13

| 3 | A Mighty Fortress Is Our God |
| 230–St. 3 | Love Divine, All Loves Excelling |

PSALM 140:7

| 268 | O Jesus, I Have Promised |
| 337 | Stand Up, Stand Up for Jesus |

PSALM 140:13

5	Abide with Me
101	God Himself Is with Us
253	Now Thank We All Our God
293	Open Now Thy Gates of Beauty

PSALM 141:1–2

| 305 | Prayer Is the Soul's Sincere |
| 343 | Sweet Hour of Prayer |

PSALM 141:8

3	A Mighty Fortress Is Our God
53	Children of the Heavenly Father
290	Only Trust Him

PSALM 142:1–7

3	A Mighty Fortress Is Our God
53	Children of the Heavenly Father
158	I Must Tell Jesus

381	There's a Wideness

PSALM 143:1

229	Lord, Speak to Me
305	Prayer Is the Soul's Sincere
343	Sweet Hour of Prayer

PSALM 143:4

70	Come, Ye Disconsolate

PSALM 143:5

105	God of Our Fathers

PSALM 143:6

316	Satisfied

PSALM 143:8–10

3	A Mighty Fortress Is Our God
49	Breathe on Me, Breath of God
53	Children of the Heavenly Father
115	Guide Me, O Thou Great Jehovah
122	Have Thine Own Way, Lord
123	He Hideth My Soul
125	He Leadeth Me
145–St. 2	I Am Thine, O Lord
239	More About Jesus
319–St. 4	Savior, Like a Shepherd Lead Us
347–St. 4	Take Time to Be Holy
349	Teach Me Thy Way, O Lord
391	Trusting Jesus
418	When We Walk with the Lord

PSALM 144:1–2

3	A Mighty Fortress Is Our God

PSALM 144:9

67	Come, Thou Fount
164	I Will Sing of My Redeemer
263	O For a Thousand Tongues to Sing
300–St. 2	Praise the Lord Who Reigns Above
309	Rejoice, Ye Pure in Heart
326	Since I Have Been Redeemed
414	When in Our Music

PSALM 144:15

42	Blessed Assurance
124	He Keeps Me Singing
144	I Am His and He Is Mine
266	O Happy Day that Fixed My Choice
340	Sunshine in My Soul

PSALM 145:1–3

21–Last st.	Amazing Grace
62	Come, Christians, Join to Sing
92	From All That Dwell Below
134	Holy God, We Praise Thy Name
160	I Sing the Almighty Power of God
230–St. 3	Love Divine, All Loves Excelling
300	Praise the Lord Who Reigns Above
308	Rejoice, the Lord Is King
336	Stand Up and Bless the Lord
401	We Praise Thee, O God
415–St. 4	When Morning Gilds the Skies
432	Ye Servants of God

PSALM 145:1–21

40	Begin, My Tongue, Some Heavenly
137	Holy, Holy, Holy
142	How Great Thou Art
206	Joyful, Joyful, We Adore Thee
283	O Worship the King
304	Praise to the Lord, the Almighty
328	Sing Praise to God Who Reigns

PSALM 145:4

85	Faith of Our Fathers
105	God of Our Fathers
134–St. 3	Holy God, We Praise Thy Name

PSALM 145:7–9

74	Count Your Blessings
218	Let Us with a Gladsome Mind
341	Surely Goodness and Mercy
362	The King of Love My Shepherd Is
366	The Lord's My Shepherd
381	There's a Wideness
412	When All Thy Mercies, O My God

PSALM 145:10–13

9	All Creatures of Our God
160	I Sing the Almighty Power of God
206–St. 2	Joyful, Joyful, We Adore Thee
253	Now Thank We All Our God
298	Praise Him! Praise Him!
301	Praise the Lord! Ye Heavens
383	This Is My Father's World

PSALM 145:13

114	Great Is Thy Faithfulness
198	Jesus Shall Reign
299	Praise, My Soul, the King
308	Rejoice, the Lord Is King

356–Last st.   The Day Thou Gavest
358   The God of Abraham Praise
397–St. 2   We Gather Together

PSALM 145:16

206–St. 3   Joyful, Joyful, We Adore Thee
400   We Plow the Fields

PSALM 145:18–20

28   Are You (Art Thou) Weary?
103   God Moves in a Mysterious Way
145   I Am Thine, O Lord
159   I Need Thee Every Hour
244   My Faith Looks Up to Thee
247   Near to the Heart of God
248   Nearer, My God, to Thee
249   Nearer, Still Nearer
328–St. 3   Sing Praise to God Who Reigns
331   Softly and Tenderly
381   There's a Wideness

PSALM 145:21

12   All Hail the Power of Jesus' Name
43   Blessed Be the Name
92   From All That Dwell Below
134   Holy God, We Praise Thy Name
215   Let All the World
301   Praise the Lord! Ye Heavens
336   Stand Up and Bless the Lord
432   Ye Servants of God

PSALM 146:1–2

230–St. 3   Love Divine, All Loves Excelling
336   Stand Up and Bless the Lord
414   When in Our Music

PSALM 146:1–10

283   O Worship the King
299   Praise, My Soul, the King
328   Sing Praise to God Who Reigns

PSALM 146:5

76   Day by Day
138   Hope of the World
265   O God, Our Help in Ages Past
369   The Solid Rock

PSALM 146:8

208–St. 4   Just As I Am, Without One Plea
263–St. 4   O For a Thousand Tongues to Sing

PSALM 146:10

265   O God, Our Help in Ages Past
300   Praise the Lord Who Reigns Above
358   The God of Abraham Praise

PSALM 147:1

62   Come, Christians, Join to Sing
215   Let All the World
300   Praise the Lord Who Reigns Above
301   Praise the Lord! Ye Heavens
309   Rejoice, Ye Pure in Heart
336   Stand Up and Bless the Lord
414   When in Our Music
415   When Morning Gilds the Skies

PSALM 147:1–20

9   All Creatures of Our God
328   Sing Praise to God Who Reigns

PSALM 147:3

122–St. 3   Have Thine Own Way, Lord
165–St. 3   I Will Sing the Wondrous Story
192–St. 3   Jesus, Lover of My Soul

PSALM 147:5

103   God Moves in a Mysterious Way
170   Immortal, Invisible

PSALM 147:7

73   Come, Ye Thankful People, Come
253   Now Thank We All Our God
300–St. 2   Praise the Lord Who Reigns Above
309   Rejoice, Ye Pure in Heart
414   When in Our Music

PSALM 147:12

69   Come, We That Love the Lord
336   Stand Up and Bless the Lord

PSALM 147:14

264   O God of Love, O King of Peace

PSALM 148:1–2

299–St. 4   Praise, My Soul, the King

PSALM 148:1–6

371   The Spacious Firmament

PSALM 148:1–14

9   All Creatures of Our God
92   From All That Dwell Below
134   Holy God, We Praise Thy Name

137–St. 4   Holy, Holy, Holy
206   Joyful, Joyful, We Adore Thee
301   Praise the Lord! Ye Heavens
304   Praise to the Lord, the Almighty
328   Sing Praise to God Who Reigns
415   When Morning Gilds the Skies

PSALM 148:2

12   All Hail the Power of Jesus' Name
298   Praise Him! Praise Him!

PSALM 148:12–13

309   Rejoice, Ye Pure in Heart

PSALM 148:13–14

77–Refrain   Day Is Dying in the West
137   Holy, Holy, Holy
300   Praise the Lord Who Reigns Above
358   The God of Abraham Praise

PSALM 149:1–3

62   Come, Christians, Join to Sing
69   Come, We That Love the Lord
206   Joyful, Joyful, We Adore Thee
246   My Tribute
300–St. 2   Praise the Lord Who Reigns Above
304   Praise to the Lord, the Almighty
328   Sing Praise to God Who Reigns
390   To God Be the Glory
414   When in Our Music

PSALM 150:1–6

134   Holy God, We Praise Thy Name
137   Holy, Holy, Holy
206   Joyful, Joyful, We Adore Thee
298   Praise Him! Praise Him!
300   Praise the Lord Who Reigns Above
301   Praise the Lord! Ye Heavens
304   Praise to the Lord, the Almighty
328   Sing Praise to God Who Reigns
414   When in Our Music
415   When Morning Gilds the Skies

PSALM 150:2

40   Begin, My Tongue, Some Heavenly
142   How Great Thou Art
160   I Sing the Almighty Power of God

PSALM 150:6

9   All Creatures of Our God
14   All People That On Earth
62   Come, Christians, Join to Sing

92   From All That Dwell Below
215   Let All the World

PROVERBS 1:2–7

104   God of Grace and God of Glory

PROVERBS 1:8–9

119   Happy the Home When God Is There

PROVERBS 1:33

37   Be Still, My Soul
78   Dear Lord and Father of Mankind
102   God Is My Strong Salvation
104–St. 2   God of Grace and God of Glory

PROVERBS 2:3–5

239   More About Jesus

PROVERBS 2:6–9

341   Surely Goodness and Mercy

PROVERBS 2:8

53–St. 4   Children of the Heavenly Father
109   God Will Take Care of You
362–St. 2   The King of Love My Shepherd Is

PROVERBS 3:5–7

17   All the Way My Savior Leads Me
76   Day by Day
86–St. 3   Fight the Good Fight
103   God Moves in a Mysterious Way
115   Guide Me, O Thou Great Jehovah
125   He Leadeth Me
146   I Am Trusting Thee, Lord Jesus
163   I Surrender All
167   If Thou But Suffer God to Guide
173–St. 2   In Heavenly Love Abiding
231–St. 2   Love Lifted Me
268   O Jesus, I Have Promised
321–St. 3   Savior, Thy Dying Love
347–St. 3   Take Time to Be Holy
349   Teach Me Thy Way, O Lord
389   'Tis So Sweet To Trust in Jesus
391   Trusting Jesus

PROVERBS 3:9–10

73   Come, Ye Thankful People, Come
398   We Give Thee but Thine Own

PROVERBS 3:11–12

397–St. 1   We Gather Together

PROVERBS 3:13–18

104	God of Grace and God of Glory

PROVERBS 3:19–20

371	The Spacious Firmament
383	This Is My Father's World

PROVERBS 3:24

15	All Praise to Thee, My God
106	God, That Madest Earth
254	Now the Day Is Over

PROVERBS 3:26

76	Day by Day
96	Give to the Winds
102	God Is My Strong Salvation
159	I Need Thee Every Hour
167	If Thou But Suffer God to Guide
265	O God, Our Help in Ages Past

PROVERBS 3:32

103	God Moves in a Mysterious Way

PROVERBS 3:34

378–St. 2	There Is Power in the Blood

PROVERBS 4:1

119	Happy the Home When God Is There

PROVERBS 4:5

239	More About Jesus

PROVERBS 4:5–10

104	God of Grace and God of Glory

PROVERBS 4:10

113	Great God, We Sing That Mighty Hand

PROVERBS 4:11–12

86–St. 2	Fight the Good Fight
349	Teach Me That Way, O Lord
362	The King of Love My Shepherd Is
366	The Lord's My Shepherd

PROVERBS 4:14–15

288	Once to Every Man and Nation

PROVERBS 4:18

60	Christ Whose Glory Fills
86–St. 2	Fight the Good Fight
130	Heavenly Sunlight
239	More About Jesus

261	O For a Closer Walk with God
268	O Jesus, I Have Promised
341	Surely Goodness and Mercy

PROVERBS 4:19

248–St. 2	Nearer, My God, to Thee

PROVERBS 4:20

292	Open My Eyes

PROVERBS 4:23

262	O For a Heart to Praise My God
321–St. 3	Savior, Thy Dying Love

PROVERBS 4:27

288	Once to Every Man and Nation

PROVERBS 9:10

104	God of Grace and God of Glory
239	More About Jesus

PROVERBS 10:7

85	Faith of Our Fathers

PROVERBS 10:22

74	Count Your Blessings
123–St. 3	He Hideth My Soul

PROVERBS 10:27

102–St. 2	God Is My Strong Salvation

PROVERBS 10:28

369	The Solid Rock

PROVERBS 10:31

292–St. 3	Open My Eyes

PROVERBS 13:10

57–St. 3	Christ Is the World's
378–St. 2	There Is Power in the Blood

PROVERBS 14:26

3	A Mighty Fortress Is Our God
53	Children of the Heavenly Father
78	Dear Lord and Father of Mankind
265	O God, Our Help in Ages Past
393	Under His Wings

PROVERBS 14:34

22	America the Beautiful

PROVERBS 15:1–33
288   Once to Every Man and Nation

PROVERBS 15:8
305   Prayer Is the Soul's Sincere
343   Sweet Hour of Prayer
407   What a Friend We Have in Jesus

PROVERBS 15:14
239   More About Jesus

PROVERBS 15:29
319–St. 2   Savior, Like a Shepherd Lead Us

PROVERBS 16:2
122–St. 2   Have Thine Own Way, Lord

PROVERBS 16:5
57–St. 3   Christ Is the World's
378–St. 2   There Is Power in the Blood

PROVERBS 16:6
78   Dear Lord and Father of Mankind
107   God the Almighty One
244   My Faith Looks Up to Thee

PROVERBS 16:7
102   God Is My Strong Salvation

PROVERBS 16:8
288   Once to Every Man and Nation

PROVERBS 16:9
37   Be Still, My Soul
115   Guide Me, O Thou Great Jehovah
125   He Leadeth Me

PROVERBS 16:16
239   More About Jesus

PROVERBS 16:18
57–St. 3   Christ Is the World's
378–St. 2   There Is Power in the Blood

PROVERBS 16:19
262   O For a Heart to Praise My God

PROVERBS 16:20
167   If Thou But Suffer God to Guide
290   Only Trust Him
389   'Tis So Sweet To Trust in Jesus
391   Trusting Jesus

418   When We Walk with the Lord

PROVERBS 17:3
262   O For a Heart to Praise My God

PROVERBS 17:17
182   I've Found a Friend

PROVERBS 18:10
3   A Mighty Fortress Is Our God
43   Blessed Be the Name
143   How Sweet the Name
265   O God, Our Help in Ages Past
346   Take the Name of Jesus with You

PROVERBS 18:22
274   O Perfect Love

PROVERBS 18:24
182   I've Found a Friend
188   Jesus Is All the World to Me
204   Jesus, What a Friend for Sinners
250   No, Not One
407   What a Friend We Have in Jesus

PROVERBS 19:17
398   We Give Thee but Thine Own

PROVERBS 20:12
292   Open My Eyes

PROVERBS 20:24
103   God Moves in a Mysterious Way
229   Lord, Speak to Me
319   Savior, Like a Shepherd Lead Us
349   Teach Me Thy Way, O Lord
362   The King of Love My Shepherd Is
366   The Lord's My Shepherd

PROVERBS 21:4
57–St. 3   Christ Is the World's
378–St. 2   There Is Power in the Blood

PROVERBS 21:10
230–St. 2   Love Divine, All Loves Excelling

PROVERBS 21:17
177–St. 2   In the Hour of Trial

PROVERBS 21:24
57–St. 3   Christ Is the World's

378–St. 2   There Is Power in the Blood

PROVERBS 21:30

103   God Moves in a Mysterious Way

PROVERBS 22:2

74–St. 3   Count Your Blessings

PROVERBS 22:4

166   I Would Be True
262   O For a Heart to Praise My God
281   O to Be Like Thee!

PROVERBS 22:6

119   Happy the Home When God Is There
324–St. 1   Shepherd of Tender Youth

PROVERBS 22:9

419   Where Cross the Crowded Ways

PROVERBS 24:3–5

104   God of Grace and God of Glory

PROVERBS 25:2

103   God Moves in a Mysterious Way

PROVERBS 27:1

34   Awake, My Soul, and With the Sun
76   Day by Day
113   Great God, We Sing That Mighty Hand

PROVERBS 27:8

67–St. 3   Come, Thou Fount
248–St. 2   Nearer, My God, to Thee
331   Softly and Tenderly
362–St. 3   The King of Love My Shepherd Is

PROVERBS 28:14

261   O For a Closer Walk with God

PROVERBS 28:27

419   Where Cross the Crowded Ways

PROVERBS 29:7

55–St. 1   Christ for the World We Sing
87–St. 3   Footsteps of Jesus

PROVERBS 29:18

38   Be Thou My Vision
133   Holy Bible, Book Divine

PROVERBS 29:25

221   Like a River Glorious
389   'Tis So Sweet To Trust in Jesus

PROVERBS 30:5

76   Day by Day
123   He Hideth My Soul
133   Holy Bible, Book Divine
192   Jesus, Lover of My Soul
265   O God, Our Help in Ages Past
282   O Word of God Incarnate
361   The Heavens Declare Thy Glory

PROVERBS 31:10–31

119   Happy the Home When God Is There

ECCLESIASTES 1:4

85   Faith of Our Fathers
105   God of Our Fathers

ECCLESIASTES 2:23

177   In the Hour of Trial

ECCLESIASTES 3:2

400   We Plow the Fields

ECCLESIASTES 3:8

107   God the Almighty One
264   O God of Love, O King of Peace

ECCLESIASTES 3:11

19   All Things Bright and Beautiful
89   For the Beauty of the Earth
103   God Moves in a Mysterious Way
108   God Who Touchest Earth
206–St. 2   Joyful, Joyful, We Adore Thee
383   This Is My Father's World

ECCLESIASTES 3:14

114   Great Is Thy Faithfulness
137–St. 3   Holy, Holy, Holy
253–St. 3   Now Thank We All Our God

ECCLESIASTES 5:10

74–St. 3   Count Your Blessings
316   Satisfied

ECCLESIASTES 11:5

103   God Moves in a Mysterious Way

ECCLESIASTES 12:13

1   A Charge to Keep I Have

ISAIAH 6:6

336–St. 3	Stand Up and Bless the Lord

ISAIAH 6:7

27	Are You Washed in the Blood?
58–St. 3	Christ Receiveth Sinful Men
112	Grace Greater Than Our Sin
155–St. 1	I Lay My Sins on Jesus
202	Jesus, Thy Blood and Righteousness
216	Let Jesus Come Into Your Heart
251	Nothing But the Blood
378	There Is Power in the Blood
389–St. 2	'Tis So Sweet To Trust in Jesus
424	Whiter Than Snow

ISAIAH 6:8

1	A Charge to Keep I Have
55	Christ for the World We Sing
121	Hark, the Voice of Jesus Calling
157	I Love to Tell the Story
168	I'll Go Where You Want Me To Go
229	Lord, Speak to Me
233	Make Me a Blessing
268	O Jesus, I Have Promised
284	O Zion, Haste
295	Pass It On
310	Rescue the Perishing
330	So Send I You
345	Take My Life and Let It Be
373	The Vision of a Dying World
399	We Have Heard the Joyful Sound
404	We've a Story to Tell
426	Who Is on the Lord's Side?

ISAIAH 7:4

118	Hail to the Lord's Anointed

ISAIAH 7:14

24	Angels from the Realms of Glory
68	Come, Thou Long-Expected Jesus
95	Gentle Mary Laid Her Child
120	Hark! The Herald Angels Sing
143	How Sweet the Name
257	O Come, O Come, Emmanuel
270–St. 4	O Little Town of Bethlehem
289–St. 1	One Day
325	Silent Night! Holy Night

ISAIAH 8:11

292–St. 2	Open My Eyes

ISAIAH 8:13

134	Holy God, We Praise Thy Name
137	Holy, Holy, Holy
336–St. 2	Stand Up and Bless the Lord

ISAIAH 9:2

60	Christ, Whose Glory Fills
118	Hail to the Lord's Anointed
129–St. 1	Heaven Came Down
151–St. 3	I Heard the Voice of Jesus Say
170	Immortal, Invisible
206–St. 1	Joyful, Joyful, We Adore Thee
244–St. 3	My Faith Looks Up to Thee
272–St. 2	O Love, That Will Not Let Me Go
311–St. 2	Revive Us Again
322	Send the Light
340	Sunshine in My Soul
364	The Light of the World Is Jesus
387	Thou Whose Almighty Word
392	Turn Your Eyes Upon Jesus

ISAIAH 9:3

129	Heaven Came Down
390	To God Be the Glory

ISAIAH 9:6

12	All Hail the Power of Jesus' Name
43–St. 4	Blessed Be the Name
120	Hark! The Herald Angels Sing
143	How Sweet the Name
224	Lo, How a Rose E'er Blooming
232	Majestic Sweetness
289	One Day

ISAIAH 9:6–7

68	Come, Thou Long–Expected Jesus
75–St. 4	Crown Him with Many Crowns
118	Hail to the Lord's Anointed
198	Jesus Shall Reign

ISAIAH 10:22

202–St. 4	Jesus, Thy Blood and Righteousness

ISAIAH 11:1–2

224	Lo, How a Rose E'er Blooming
257–St. 2	O Come, O Come, Emmanuel

ISAIAH 11:5

114	Great Is Thy Faithfulness

ISAIAH 12:1–6

40	Begin, My Tongue, Some Heavenly

42	Blessed Assurance
102	God Is My Strong Salvation
401	We Praise Thee, O God
432	Ye Servants of God

ISAIAH 12:2

3	A Mighty Fortress Is Our God
96	Give to the Winds
336–St. 4	Stand Up and Bless the Lord
391	Trusting Jesus

ISAIAH 12:2–3

146	I Am Trusting Thee, Lord Jesus
266	O Happy Day that Fixed My Choice
294	Out of My Bondage
307	Redeemed, How I Love to Proclaim
316	Satisfied
326	Since I Have Been Redeemed
376	There Is a Fountain

ISAIAH 12:4–6

43	Blessed Be the Name
134	Holy God, We Praise Thy Name
142	How Great Thou Art
253	Now Thank We All Our God
263	O For a Thousand Tongues to Sing
414	When in Our Music

ISAIAH 13:2–4

291–St. 1	Onward, Christian Soldiers

ISAIAH 13:11

378–St. 2	There Is Power in the Blood
383–St. 3	This Is My Father's World

ISAIAH 14:3

28	Are You (Art Thou) Weary?
70	Come, Ye Disconsolate
96	Give to the Winds
151–St. 1	I Heard the Voice of Jesus Say
247	Near to the Heart of God

ISAIAH 18:4

78	Dear Lord and Father of Mankind

ISAIAH 21:11–12

34	Awake, My Soul, and With the Sun
395	Watchman, Tell Us of the Night

ISAIAH 24:14–16

14	All People That On Earth
92	From All That Dwell Below

358	The God of Abraham Praise

ISAIAH 24:23

223	Lo, He Comes with Clouds

ISAIAH 25:1

92	From All That Dwell Below
105	God of Our Fathers
142	How Great Thou Art
300	Praise the Lord Who Reigns Above
328	Sing Praise to God Who Reigns
358	The God of Abraham Praise

ISAIAH 25:1–4

3	A Mighty Fortress Is Our God
40	Begin, My Tongue, Some Heavenly
114	Great Is Thy Faithfulness
206	Joyful, Joyful, We Adore Thee
304	Praise to the Lord, the Almighty

ISAIAH 25:4

4	A Shelter in the Time of Storm
53	Children of the Heavenly Father
74	Count Your Blessings
93	From Every Stormy Wind
109	God Will Take Care of You
123	He Hideth My Soul
158	I Must Tell Jesus
173	In Heavenly Love Abiding
192	Jesus, Lover of My Soul
265	O God, Our Help in Ages Past
294	Out of My Bondage
393	Under His Wings

ISAIAH 25:7–9

42	Blessed Assurance
59	Christ the Lord Is Risen Today
75–St. 6	Crown Him with Many Crowns
82	Face to Face
102	God Is My Strong Salvation
138–Last st.	Hope of the World
238	Moment by Moment
244	My Faith Looks Up to Thee
277	O Sons and Daughters
286	On Jordan's Stormy Banks I Stand
297	Peace, Perfect Peace
317	Saved! Saved! Saved!
352	Ten Thousand Times Ten Thousand
372	The Strife Is O'er
405	Welcome, Happy Morning
410	What If It Were Today?

ISAIAH 26:2

22	America the Beautiful
288	Once to Every Man and Nation

ISAIAH 26:3

75–St. 4	Crown Him with Many Crowns
221	Like a River Glorious
297	Peace, Perfect Peace
429	Wonderful Peace

ISAIAH 26:3–4

3	A Mighty Fortress Is Our God
76	Day by Day
78	Dear Lord and Father of Mankind
102	God Is My Strong Salvation
146	I Am Trusting Thee, Lord Jesus
159	I Need Thee Every Hour
167	If Thou But Suffer God to Guide
188	Jesus Is All the World to Me
192	Jesus, Lover of My Soul
265	O God, Our Help in Ages Past
283–St. 4	O Worship the King
290	Only Trust Him
314	Rock of Ages
318	Savior, Again to Thy Dear Name
389	'Tis So Sweet To Trust in Jesus
391	Trusting Jesus

ISAIAH 26:7

362	The King of Love My Shepherd Is
366	The Lord's My Shepherd

ISAIAH 26:9

356	The Day Thou Gavest

ISAIAH 26:12–13

264	O God of Love, O King of Peace
318	Savior, Again to Thy Dear Name
429	Wonderful Peace

ISAIAH 28:5

75	Crown Him with Many Crowns

ISAIAH 28:12

28	Are You (Art Thou) Weary?
151–St. 1	I Heard the Voice of Jesus Say

ISAIAH 28:16

52	Built on the Rock
56	Christ Is Made the Sure
141	How Firm a Foundation
248–St. 2	Nearer, My God, to Thee

298–St. 2	Praise Him! Praise Him!
314	Rock of Ages
353	The Church's One Foundation

ISAIAH 29:6

78–St. 5	Dear Lord and Father of Mankind

ISAIAH 29:16

122–St. 1	Have Thine Own Way, Lord

ISAIAH 29:18

208	Just As I Am, Without One Plea
292	Open My Eyes

ISAIAH 30:15

28	Are You (Art Thou) Weary?
37	Be Still, My Soul
78	Dear Lord and Father of Mankind
151–St. 1	I Heard the Voice of Jesus Say
167–St. 2	If Thou But Suffer God to Guide
247	Near to the Heart of God
249	Nearer, Still Nearer

ISAIAH 30:18

79	Depth of Mercy! Can There Be?
259	O Day of God, Draw Nigh
319–St. 3	Savior, Like a Shepherd Lead Us
347	Take Time to Be Holy
381	There's a Wideness

ISAIAH 30:20

177	In the Hour of Trial

ISAIAH 30:21

397–St. 2	We Gather Together

ISAIAH 31:5

3	A Mighty Fortress Is Our God
53	Children of the Heavenly Father
123	He Hideth My Soul
393	Under His Wings
397–St. 3	We Gather Together

ISAIAH 32:17–18

37	Be Still, My Soul
78	Dear Lord and Father of Mankind
107	God the Almighty One
247	Near to the Heart of God
264	O God of Love, O King of Peace
265	O God, Our Help in Ages Past
273	O Master, Let Me Walk with Thee
297	Peace, Perfect Peace

429	Wonderful Peace

ISAIAH 33:2

3	A Mighty Fortress Is Our God
76	Day by Day
96	Give to the Winds
265	O God, Our Help in Ages Past
306	Precious Lord, Take My Hand

ISAIAH 33:5

259	O Day of God, Draw Nigh
383	This Is My Father's World

ISAIAH 33:6

104	God of Grace and God of Glory

ISAIAH 33:17

286	On Jordan's Stormy Banks I Stand

ISAIAH 33:20–21

97	Glorious Things of Thee

ISAIAH 33:22

66	Come, Thou Almighty King
170	Immortal, Invisible
283	O Worship the King

ISAIAH 34:4

180–St. 4	It Is Well with My Soul

ISAIAH 35:1–2

224	Lo, How a Rose E'er Blooming

ISAIAH 35:4

3–St. 3	A Mighty Fortress Is Our God
53	Children of the Heavenly Father
81	Eternal Father, Strong to Save
96	Give to the Winds

ISAIAH 35:5–6

263–St. 4	O For a Thousand Tongues to Sing

ISAIAH 35:8

347	Take Time to Be Holy

ISAIAH 35:10

16–St. 5	All That Thrills My Soul
17–St. 3	All the Way My Savior Leads Me
42	Blessed Assurance
55–St. 4	Christ for the World We Sing
62–St. 3	Come, Christians, Join to Sing
69	Come, We That Love the Lord

82	Face to Face
97	Glorious Things of Thee
162–St. 5	I Stand Amazed in the Presence
164	I Will Sing of My Redeemer
165	I Will Sing the Wondrous Story
181–St. 4	It May Be at Morn
184	Jerusalem, the Golden
206	Joyful, Joyful, We Adore Thee
235–St. 5	"Man of Sorrows," What a Name
244–St. 4	My Faith Looks Up to Thee
263	O For a Thousand Tongues to Sing
266	O Happy Day that Fixed My Choice
279	O That Will Be Glory For Me
286	On Jordan's Stormy Banks I Stand
307	Redeemed, How I Love to Proclaim
326	Since I Have Been Redeemed
340	Sunshine in My Soul
352	Ten Thousand Times Ten Thousand
417	When We All Get to Heaven

ISAIAH 37:16

107	God the Almighty One
137	Holy, Holy, Holy
170	Immortal, Invisible
304	Praise to the Lord, the Almighty

ISAIAH 37:35

3	A Mighty Fortress Is Our God
397–St. 3	We Gather Together

ISAIAH 38:19

119	Happy the Home When God Is There

ISAIAH 38:20

62	Come, Christians, Join to Sing
300–St. 2	Praise the Lord Who Reigns Above
340	Sunshine in My Soul
414	When in Our Music

ISAIAH 40:3–5

68	Come, Thou Long–Expected Jesus
82–St. 3	Face to Face
205	Joy to the World

ISAIAH 40:8

133	Holy Bible, Book Divine
282	O Word of God Incarnate
430	Wonderful Words of Life

ISAIAH 40:9–10

97	Glorious Things of Thee
141–St. 2	How Firm a Foundation

284	O Zion, Haste

ISAIAH 40:11

100–St. 1	God Be with You
141	How Firm a Foundation
173	In Heavenly Love Abiding
298–St. 1	Praise Him! Praise Him!
319	Savior, Like a Shepherd Lead Us
324	Shepherd of Tender Youth
341	Surely Goodness and Mercy
362	The King of Love My Shepherd Is
366	The Lord's My Shepherd

ISAIAH 40:21–31

3	A Mighty Fortress Is Our God
160	I Sing the Almighty Power of God
371	The Spacious Firmament
383	This Is My Father's World

ISAIAH 40:26–31

328	Sing Praise to God Who Reigns

ISAIAH 40:28

103	God Moves in a Mysterious Way
114	Great Is Thy Faithfulness

ISAIAH 40:29–31

76	Day by Day
86–St. 4	Fight the Good Fight
102	God Is My Strong Salvation
167–St. 1	If Thou But Suffer God to Guide
188–St. 1	Jesus Is All the World to Me
244–St. 2	My Faith Looks Up to Thee
310–St. 4	Rescue the Perishing

ISAIAH 40:30–31

306	Precious Lord, Take My Hand

ISAIAH 40:31

35	Awake, My Soul, Stretch
81–St. 3	Eternal Father, Strong to Save
86–St. 2	Fight the Good Fight
108	God Who Touchest Earth
207	Just a Closer Walk with Thee
341–St. 2	Surely Goodness and Mercy

ISAIAH 41:8–10

12–St. 2	All Hail the Power of Jesus' Name
358	The God of Abraham Praise

ISAIAH 41:10–14

3	A Mighty Fortress Is Our God
74–St. 4	Count Your Blessings
76	Day by Day
93–Last St.	From Every Stormy Wind
96	Give to the Winds
103	God Moves in a Mysterious Way
104	God of Grace and God of Glory
109	God Will Take Care of You
124	He Keeps Me Singing
125	He Leadeth Me
141–St. 2	How Firm a Foundation
158	I Must Tell Jesus
173	In Heavenly Love Abiding
177	In the Hour of Trial
188	Jesus Is All the World to Me
192	Jesus, Lover of My Soul
207	Just a Closer Walk with Thee
306	Precious Lord, Take My Hand

ISAIAH 41:17

316–St. 1	Satisfied
407	What a Friend We Have in Jesus

ISAIAH 42:10–12

9	All Creatures of Our God
215	Let All the World

ISAIAH 42:10–13

237	Mine Eyes Have Seen the Glory

ISAIAH 42:12

55	Christ for the World We Sing
62	Come, Christians, Join to Sing
92	From All That Dwell Below
399	We Have Heard the Joyful Sound

ISAIAH 42:16

17	All the Way My Savior Leads Me
82–St. 3	Face to Face
115	Guide Me, O Thou Great Jehovah
125	He Leadeth Me
167	If Thou But Suffer God to Guide
210	Lead, Kindly Light
341	Surely Goodness and Mercy
397–St. 2	We Gather Together

ISAIAH 42:18

292	Open My Eyes

ISAIAH 43:1–3

67	Come, Thou Fount
93	From Every Stormy Wind
96	Give to the Winds
124–St. 1	He Keeps Me Singing
141–St. 3, 4	How Firm a Foundation
177–St. 3	In the Hour of Trial
197	Jesus Savior, Pilot Me
326	Since I Have Been Redeemed

ISAIAH 43:3

| 134 | Holy God, We Praise Thy Name |
| 137 | Holy, Holy, Holy |

ISAIAH 43:10–11

102	God Is My Strong Salvation
157	I Love to Tell the Story
233	Make Me a Blessing
284	O Zion, Haste
326–St. 3	Since I Have Been Redeemed
336	Stand Up and Bless the Lord
404	We've a Story to Tell
432–St. 1	Ye Servants of God

ISAIAH 43:15

9	All Creatures of Our God
299	Praise, My Soul, the King
304	Praise to the Lord, the Almighty
328	Sing Praise to God Who Reigns

ISAIAH 43:21

55	Christ for the World We Sing
62	Come, Christians, Join to Sing
112	Grace Greater Than Our Sin
155	I Lay My Sins on Jesus
215	Let All the World
244	My Faith Looks Up to Thee
300	Praise the Lord Who Reigns Above

ISAIAH 43:25

| 331–St. 4 | Softly and Tenderly |

ISAIAH 44:6

| 253–St. 3 | Now Thank We All Our God |
| 283 | O Worship the King |

ISAIAH 44:21–24

| 142 | How Great Thou Art |
| 301 | Praise the Lord! Ye Heavens |

ISAIAH 44:22

21	Amazing Grace
79	Depth of Mercy! Can There Be?
112	Grace Greater Than Our Sin
155–St. 1	I Lay My Sins on Jesus
192	Jesus, Lover of My Soul
244	My Faith Looks Up to Thee
290	Only Trust Him
331–St. 4	Softly and Tenderly
359–St. 2	The Great Physician
381	There's a Wideness
408	What a Wonderful Savior

ISAIAH 44:22–23

129	Heaven Came Down
164	I Will Sing of My Redeemer
206	Joyful, Joyful, We Adore Thee
298	Praise Him! Praise Him!

ISAIAH 45:5–6

17	All the Way My Savior Leads Me
76	Day by Day
102	God Is My Strong Salvation
122–St. 1	Have Thine Own Way, Lord
167–St. 1	If Thou But Suffer God to Guide

ISAIAH 45:7

304	Praise to the Lord, the Almighty
371	The Spacious Firmament
383	This Is My Father's World

ISAIAH 45:11–19

| 103 | God Moves in a Mysterious Way |

ISAIAH 45:12

142	How Great Thou Art
160	I Sing the Almighty Power of God
328	Sing Praise to God Who Reigns

ISAIAH 45:15

| 137–St. 3 | Holy, Holy, Holy |
| 170 | Immortal, Invisible |

ISAIAH 45:18

19	All Things Bright and Beautiful
160	I Sing the Almighty Power of God
328	Sing Praise to God Who Reigns
383	This Is My Father's World

ISAIAH 45:22

14	All People That On Earth
55	Christ for the World We Sing
58	Christ Receiveth Sinful Men
138	Hope of the World

149	I Hear Thy Welcome Voice
315	Room at the Cross for You
368	The Savior Is Waiting
392	Turn Your Eyes Upon Jesus

ISAIAH 45:24

102	God Is My Strong Salvation

ISAIAH 47:4

43	Blessed Be the Name
137	Holy, Holy, Holy
401–St. 1	We Praise Thee, O God

ISAIAH 47:10

3–St. 2	A Mighty Fortress Is Our God

ISAIAH 48:13

142	How Great Thou Art
160	I Sing the Almighty Power of God
371	The Spacious Firmament
383	This Is My Father's World

ISAIAH 48:17

17	All the Way My Savior Leads Me
115	Guide Me, O Thou Great Jehovah
125	He Leadeth Me
167	If Thou But Suffer God to Guide
173	In Heavenly Love Abiding
212	Lead On, O King Eternal
349	Teach Me Thy Way, O Lord
397–St. 2	We Gather Together

ISAIAH 48:18

197	Jesus Savior, Pilot Me
221	Like a River Glorious

ISAIAH 48:21

123	He Hideth My Soul
316–St. 1	Satisfied

ISAIAH 49:4

375–St. 1	There Is a Balm in Gilead

ISAIAH 49:6

322	Send the Light

ISAIAH 49:8–10

17	All the Way My Savior Leads Me
56	Christ Is Made the Sure
115–St. 2	Guide Me, O Thou Great Jehovah
125	He Leadeth Me
167	If Thou But Suffer God to Guide

173	In Heavenly Love Abiding
316	Satisfied
341–St. 2	Surely Goodness and Mercy
362–St. 2	The King of Love My Shepherd Is
366	The Lord's My Shepherd

ISAIAH 49:13

9	All Creatures of Our God
301	Praise the Lord! Ye Heavens

ISAIAH 49:16

156–St. 2	I Love Thy Kingdom, Lord

ISAIAH 50:4

34	Awake, My Soul, and With the Sun
40	Begin, My Tongue, Some Heavenly

ISAIAH 50:5

292–St. 2	Open My Eyes

ISAIAH 50:7

154	I Know Whom I Have Believed

ISAIAH 50:8

247	Near to the Heart of God

ISAIAH 50:10

3	A Mighty Fortress Is Our God
261	O For a Closer Walk with God
346	Take the Name of Jesus with You
347–St. 3	Take Time to Be Holy

ISAIAH 51:3

42	Blessed Assurance
69	Come, We That Love the Lord
124	He Keeps Me Singing

ISAIAH 51:4–5

259	O Day of God, Draw Nigh

ISAIAH 51:6–8

85	Faith of Our Fathers
105	God of Our Fathers
114	Great Is Thy Faithfulness

ISAIAH 51:11

16–St. 5	All That Thrills My Soul
17–St. 3	All the Way My Savior Leads Me
31	At Calvary
42	Blessed Assurance
55–St. 4	Christ for the World We Sing
62–St. 3	Come, Christians, Join to Sing

69	Come, We That Love the Lord
82	Face to Face
97	Glorious Things of Thee
162–St. 5	I Stand Amazed in the Presence
164	I Will Sing of My Redeemer
165	I Will Sing the Wondrous Story
181–St. 4	It May Be at Morn
184	Jerusalem, the Golden
206	Joyful, Joyful, We Adore Thee
235–St. 5	"Man of Sorrows," What a Name
244–St. 4	My Faith Looks Up to Thee
263	O For a Thousand Tongues to Sing
266	O Happy Day that Fixed My Choice
279	O That Will Be Glory For Me
286	On Jordan's Stormy Banks I Stand
307	Redeemed, How I Love to Proclaim
326	Since I Have Been Redeemed
340	Sunshine in My Soul
352	Ten Thousand Times Ten Thousand
417	When We All Get to Heaven

ISAIAH 51:12

70	Come, Ye Disconsolate
96	Give to the Winds

ISAIAH 51:16

109	God Will Take Care of You
115–St. 1	Guide Me, O Thou Great Jehovah
123	He Hideth My Soul
125	He Leadeth Me
141	How Firm a Foundation

ISAIAH 52:7–10

75–St. 4	Crown Him with Many Crowns
284	O Zion, Haste
399	We Have Heard the Joyful Sound
404	We've a Story to Tell

ISAIAH 53:1–12

7	Ah, Holy Jesus
8	Alas! And Did My Savior Bleed?
32	At the Cross
45	Blessed Redeemer
99	Go to Dark Gethsemane
117	Hail, Thou Once Despised Jesus
162	I Stand Amazed in the Presence
164	I Will Sing of My Redeemer
235	"Man of Sorrows," What a Name
275	O Sacred Head, Now Wounded
298–St. 2	Praise Him! Praise Him!
406	Were You There?

ISAIAH 53:2–6

33–St. 3	At the Name of Jesus

ISAIAH 53:3

289–St. 2	One Day
351–St. 2	Tell Me the Story of Jesus

ISAIAH 53:4–6

31	At Calvary
75–St. 2	Crown Him with Many Crowns
147	I Gave My Life for Thee
174–St. 3	In Loving Kindness Jesus Came
195	Jesus Paid it All
202	Jesus, Thy Blood and Righteousness
211	Lead Me to Calvary
222	Living for Jesus
275	O Sacred Head, Now Wounded

ISAIAH 53:6

67–St. 3	Come, Thou Fount
155	I Lay My Sins on Jesus
165–St. 2	I Will Sing the Wondrous Story
362–St. 3	The King of Love My Shepherd Is

ISAIAH 53:12

195	Jesus Paid it All
202	Jesus, Thy Blood and Righteousness

ISAIAH 54:7–8

79	Depth of Mercy! Can There Be?
412	When All Thy Mercies, O My God

ISAIAH 54:7–10

381	There's a Wideness

ISAIAH 54:8

107–St. 2	God the Almighty One

ISAIAH 54:10

218	Let Us with a Gladsome Mind

ISAIAH 54:14

102	God Is My Strong Salvation

ISAIAH 55:1–2

72–St. 2	Come, Ye Sinners, Poor and Needy
362–St. 2	The King of Love My Shepherd Is
427	Whosoever Will

ISAIAH 55:3

72	Come, Ye Sinners, Poor and Needy
149	I Hear Thy Welcome Voice

| 190 | Jesus Is Tenderly Calling |
| 331 | Softly and Tenderly |

ISAIAH 55:6

61	Close to Thee
159	I Need Thee Every Hour
247	Near to the Heart of God
248	Nearer, My God, to Thee

ISAIAH 55:7

58	Christ Receiveth Sinful Men
78–St. 1	Dear Lord and Father of Mankind
79	Depth of Mercy! Can There Be?
107	God the Almighty One
129	Heaven Came Down
155–St. 1	I Lay My Sins on Jesus
208	Just As I Am, Without One Plea
216	Let Jesus Come Into Your Heart
227	Lord, I'm Coming Home
244	My Faith Looks Up to Thee
261	O For a Closer Walk with God
315	Room at the Cross for You
319–St. 3	Savior, Like a Shepherd Lead Us
331	Softly and Tenderly
389–St. 3	'Tis So Sweet To Trust in Jesus

ISAIAH 55:8–9

| 103 | God Moves in a Mysterious Way |

ISAIAH 55:10

| 400 | We Plow the Fields |

ISAIAH 56:2

| 260 | O Day of Rest and Gladness |

ISAIAH 56:7

| 101 | God Himself Is with Us |
| 343 | Sweet Hour of Prayer |

ISAIAH 57:2

5	Abide with Me
145–St. 4	I Am Thine, O Lord
199	Jesus, Still Lead On
318	Savior, Again to Thy Dear Name
429	Wonderful Peace

ISAIAH 57:15

134	Holy God, We Praise Thy Name
137	Holy, Holy, Holy
170	Immortal, Invisible
200–St. 3	Jesus, the Very Thought of Thee
249–St. 2	Nearer, Still Nearer

261	O For a Closer Walk with God
296	Pass Me Not, O Gentle Savior
310	Rescue the Perishing
311	Revive Us Again

ISAIAH 57:18

| 125 | He Leadeth Me |
| 341–St. 2 | Surely Goodness and Mercy |

ISAIAH 57:19

| 297 | Peace, Perfect Peace |
| 429 | Wonderful Peace |

ISAIAH 58:6–8

| 166 | I Would Be True |

ISAIAH 58:9

| 343 | Sweet Hour of Prayer |
| 407 | What a Friend We Have in Jesus |

ISAIAH 58:11

17	All the Way My Savior Leads Me
109	God Will Take Care of You
115	Guide Me, O Thou Great Jehovah
125	He Leadeth Me
167	If Thou But Suffer God to Guide
173	In Heavenly Love Abiding
210	Lead, Kindly Light
265	O God, Our Help in Ages Past
316	Satisfied
328–St. 3	Sing Praise to God Who Reigns
341	Surely Goodness and Mercy

ISAIAH 58:13

| 260 | O Day of Rest and Gladness |

ISAIAH 59:1

| 44–St. 3 | Blessed Jesus, at Thy Word |
| 141–St. 2 | How Firm a Foundation |

ISAIAH 59:7

| 230–St. 2 | Love Divine, All Loves Excelling |

ISAIAH 59:21

| 85 | Faith of Our Fathers |

ISAIAH 60:1–3

44–St. 3	Blessed Jesus, at Thy Word
57	Christ Is the World's
83–St. 3	Fairest Lord Jesus
129	Heaven Came Down
272–St. 2	O Love, That Will Not Let Me Go

184	Jerusalem, the Golden
383–St. 3	This Is My Father's World

ISAIAH 65:24

44–St. 3	Blessed Jesus, at Thy Word
305	Prayer Is the Soul's Sincere
391	Trusting Jesus

ISAIAH 66:2

261	O For a Closer Walk with God

ISAIAH 66:13–14

70	Come, Ye Disconsolate
74–St. 4	Count Your Blessings
96	Give to the Winds
109	God Will Take Care of You

ISAIAH 66:18

105	God of Our Fathers
237	Mine Eyes Have Seen the Glory

ISAIAH 66:22

383–St. 3	This Is My Father's World

ISAIAH 66:23

260	O Day of Rest and Gladness

JEREMIAH 1:7–8

1	A Charge to Keep I Have
168	I'll Go Where You Want Me To Go

JEREMIAH 1:8

3	A Mighty Fortress Is Our God

JEREMIAH 2:19

67–St. 3	Come, Thou Fount

JEREMIAH 3:4

17	All the Way My Savior Leads Me
115	Guide Me, O Thou Great Jehovah
125	He Leadeth Me
265	O God, Our Help in Ages Past
324	Shepherd of Tender Youth

JEREMIAH 3:12

79	Depth of Mercy! Can There Be?
319–St. 3	Savior, Like a Shepherd Lead Us

JEREMIAH 3:14

67–St. 3	Come, Thou Fount
362–St. 3	The King of Love My Shepherd Is

JEREMIAH 3:17

183	Jerusalem, My Happy Home
184	Jerusalem, the Golden

JEREMIAH 3:22

67–St. 3	Come, Thou Fount
102	God Is My Strong Salvation
341–St. 2	Surely Goodness and Mercy

JEREMIAH 4:1–2

261–St. 3	O For a Closer Walk with God

JEREMIAH 4:4

107	God the Almighty One

JEREMIAH 4:14

58	Christ Receiveth Sinful Men
216	Let Jesus Come Into Your Heart
424	Whiter Than Snow

JEREMIAH 7:13

185	Jesus Calls Us

JEREMIAH 7:23

122	Have Thine Own Way, Lord
418	When We Walk with the Lord

JEREMIAH 8:22

375	There Is a Balm in Gilead

JEREMIAH 9:7

283	O Worship the King

JEREMIAH 10:6–7

66	Come, Thou Almighty King
170	Immortal, Invisible
283	O Worship the King
299	Praise, My Soul, the King
301	Praise the Lord! Ye Heavens

JEREMIAH 10:10

66	Come, Thou Almighty King
253–St. 3	Now Thank We All Our God
283	O Worship the King

JEREMIAH 10:12–13

160	I Sing the Almighty Power of God
328	Sing Praise to God Who Reigns
371	The Spacious Firmament
383	This Is My Father's World

JEREMIAH 10:23

17	All the Way My Savior Leads Me
115	Guide Me, O Thou Great Jehovah
122	Have Thine Own Way, Lord
125	He Leadeth Me
167	If Thou But Suffer God to Guide
173	In Heavenly Love Abiding
397–St. 2	We Gather Together

JEREMIAH 10:24

| 107 | God the Almighty One |

JEREMIAH 12:1

| 107 | God the Almighty One |

JEREMIAH 14:19

| 264 | O God of Love, O King of Peace |

JEREMIAH 14:20

| 228 | Lord Jesus, Think on Me |
| 261 | O For a Closer Walk with God |

JEREMIAH 15:16

48	Break Thou the Bread
133	Holy Bible, Book Divine
282	O Word of God Incarnate
347–St. 1	Take Time to Be Holy
361	The Heavens Declare Thy Glory
430	Wonderful Words of Life

JEREMIAH 16:19

3	A Mighty Fortress Is Our God
53	Children of the Heavenly Father
81	Eternal Father, Strong to Save
102	God Is My Strong Salvation
393	Under His Wings

JEREMIAH 16:20

| 261 | O For a Closer Walk with God |

JEREMIAH 16:21

283	O Worship the King
299	Praise, My Soul, the King
328	Sing Praise to God Who Reigns

JEREMIAH 17:5

| 3–St. 2 | A Mighty Fortress Is Our God |
| 67–St. 3 | Come, Thou Fount |

JEREMIAH 17:7

| 30 | Ask Ye What Great Things I Know |
| 103 | God Moves in a Mysterious Way |

138	Hope of the World
146	I Am Trusting Thee, Lord Jesus
167	If Thou But Suffer God to Guide
200–St. 3	Jesus, the Very Thought of Thee
265	O God, Our Help in Ages Past
283–St. 4	O Worship the King
290	Only Trust Him
369	The Solid Rock
389	'Tis So Sweet To Trust in Jesus
418	When We Walk with the Lord

JEREMIAH 17:10

| 122–St. 2 | Have Thine Own Way, Lord |

JEREMIAH 17:14

| 102 | God Is My Strong Salvation |
| 432 | Ye Servants of God |

JEREMIAH 18:3–6

| 122–St. 1 | Have Thine Own Way, Lord |

JEREMIAH 20:11–13

3	A Mighty Fortress Is Our God
76	Day by Day
102	God Is My Strong Salvation

JEREMIAH 20:13

| 263 | O For a Thousand Tongues to Sing |

JEREMIAH 21:8

86–St. 2	Fight the Good Fight
261	O For a Closer Walk with God
262	O For a Heart to Praise My God
268	O Jesus, I Have Promised

JEREMIAH 22:29

| 292–St. 2 | Open My Eyes |

JEREMIAH 23:3–4

| 109 | God Will Take Care of You |
| 319 | Savior, Like a Shepherd Lead Us |

JEREMIAH 23:5–6

107–St. 3	God the Almighty One
118	Hail to the Lord's Anointed
257	O Come, O Come, Emmanuel

JEREMIAH 23:12

| 248–St. 2 | Nearer, My God, to Thee |

JEREMIAH 24:7

| 216 | Let Jesus Come Into Your Heart |

227	Lord, I'm Coming Home
262	O For a Heart to Praise My God
396	We Are God's People

JEREMIAH 26:4

| 418 | When We Walk with the Lord |

JEREMIAH 27:5

160	I Sing the Almighty Power of God
328	Sing Praise to God Who Reigns
371	The Spacious Firmament
383	This Is My Father's World

JEREMIAH 29:11

| 103 | God Moves in a Mysterious Way |
| 228 | Lord Jesus, Think on Me |

JEREMIAH 29:13

161	I Sought the Lord
171–St. 2	Immortal Love, Forever Full
201	Jesus, Thou Joy of Loving Hearts
305	Prayer Is the Soul's Sincere
319–St. 4	Savior, Like a Shepherd Lead Us
424–St. 4	Whiter Than Snow

JEREMIAH 30:8–9

| 118 | Hail to the Lord's Anointed |
| 384–St. 3 | This Is the Day |

JEREMIAH 30:10

| 109 | God Will Take Care of You |
| 264 | O God of Love, O King of Peace |

JEREMIAH 30:17

| 122–St. 3 | Have Thine Own Way, Lord |
| 341–St. 2 | Surely Goodness and Mercy |

JEREMIAH 31:1

| 396 | We Are God's People |

JEREMIAH 31:2

| 15 | All Praise to Thee, My God |

JEREMIAH 31:3

144	I Am His and He Is Mine
145	I Am Thine, O Lord
161	I Sought the Lord
171	Immortal Love, Forever Full
173	In Heavenly Love Abiding
182	I've Found a Friend
203	Jesus, Thy Boundless Love to Me
230	Love Divine, All Loves Excelling

231	Love Lifted Me
272–St. 1	O Love, That Will Not Let Me Go
319–St. 4	Savior, Like a Shepherd Lead Us
320	Savior, Teach Me Day by Day
411	What Wondrous Love Is This?

JEREMIAH 31:9–12

53	Children of the Heavenly Father
319	Savior, Like a Shepherd Lead Us
362	The King of Love My Shepherd Is

JEREMIAH 31:12

70	Come, Ye Disconsolate
141–St. 3	How Firm a Foundation
286	On Jordan's Stormy Banks I Stand

JEREMIAH 31:13

| 244–St. 3 | My Faith Looks Up to Thee |

JEREMIAH 31:19

| 227 | Lord, I'm Coming Home |
| 261 | O For a Closer Walk with God |

JEREMIAH 31:25

| 207 | Just a Closer Walk with Thee |
| 306 | Precious Lord, Take My Hand |

JEREMIAH 31:33–34

78–St. 1	Dear Lord and Father of Mankind
192–St. 4	Jesus, Lover of My Soul
216	Let Jesus Come Into Your Heart
359–St. 2	The Great Physician
369–St. 3	The Solid Rock
396	We Are God's People

JEREMIAH 31:35

| 9 | All Creatures of Our God |
| 301 | Praise the Lord! Ye Heavens |

JEREMIAH 32:17–20

9	All Creatures of Our God
40	Begin, My Tongue, Some Heavenly
105	God of Our Fathers
142	How Great Thou Art
160	I Sing the Almighty Power of God
206	Joyful, Joyful, We Adore Thee
304	Praise to the Lord, the Almighty
328	Sing Praise to God Who Reigns
371	The Spacious Firmament

JEREMIAH 32:40

| 114 | Great Is Thy Faithfulness |

299   Praise, My Soul, the King

JEREMIAH 32:42

338   Standing on the Promises

JEREMIAH 33:6

102–St. 2   God Is My Strong Salvation
264   O God of Love, O King of Peace
429   Wonderful Peace

JEREMIAH 33:8

78–St. 1   Dear Lord and Father of Mankind
112   Grace Greater Than Our Sin
129   Heaven Came Down
155–St. 1   I Lay My Sins on Jesus
235   "Man of Sorrows," What a Name
244   My Faith Looks Up to Thee
331–St. 4   Softly and Tenderly
408   What a Wonderful Savior

JEREMIAH 33:11

14   All People That On Earth
206   Joyful, Joyful, We Adore Thee
283   O Worship the King
299   Praise, My Soul, the King
328   Sing Praise to God Who Reigns
341   Surely Goodness and Mercy
362   The King of Love My Shepherd Is
366   The Lord's My Shepherd
381   There's a Wideness

JEREMIAH 33:14

338   Standing on the Promises

JEREMIAH 33:15–17

118   Hail to the Lord's Anointed
257   O Come, O Come, Emmanuel

JEREMIAH 35:15

216   Let Jesus Come Into Your Heart
331   Softly and Tenderly

JEREMIAH 36:2

133   Holy Bible, Book Divine
282   O Word of God Incarnate

JEREMIAH 42:6

168   I'll Go Where You Want Me To Go
292–St. 2   Open My Eyes
418   When We Walk with the Lord

JEREMIAH 46:11

375   There Is a Balm in Gilead

JEREMIAH 46:27

109   God Will Take Care of You
264   O God of Love, O King of Peace

JEREMIAH 49:4

3–St. 2   A Mighty Fortress Is Our God

JEREMIAH 50:5

69   Come, We That Love the Lord
268   O Jesus, I Have Promised
369–St. 3   The Solid Rock

JEREMIAH 50:6

14–St. 2   All People That On Earth
67–St. 3   Come, Thou Fount
248–St. 2   Nearer, My God, to Thee
319   Savior, Like a Shepherd Lead Us
362–St. 3   The King of Love My Shepherd Is

JEREMIAH 50:34

43   Blessed Be the Name
102   God Is My Strong Salvation
107   God the Almighty One
283   O Worship the King
304   Praise to the Lord, the Almighty

JEREMIAH 51:5

107–St. 2   God the Almighty One
299   Praise, My Soul, The King

JEREMIAH 51:8

375   There Is a Balm in Gilead

JEREMIAH 51:15–19

9   All Creatures of Our God
160   I Sing the Almighty Power of God
383   This Is My Father's World

JEREMIAH 51:17

261   O For a Closer Walk with God

LAMENTATIONS 3:21–26

37   Be Still, My Soul
107   God the Almighty One
114   Great Is Thy Faithfulness
218   Let Us with a Gladsome Mind
265   O God, Our Help in Ages Past
299   Praise, My Soul, the King
369   The Solid Rock

381	There's a Wideness

LAMENTATIONS 3:22

23	And Can It Be That I Should Gain?
319–St. 3	Savior, Like a Shepherd Lead Us

LAMENTATIONS 3:22–23

79	Depth of Mercy! Can There Be?
93	From Every Stormy Wind
412	When All Thy Mercies, O My God

LAMENTATIONS 3:23

34	Awake, My Soul, and With the Sun
241	Morning Has Broken

LAMENTATIONS 3:26

37	Be Still, My Soul
102	God Is My Strong Salvation
132	Higher Ground
138	Hope of the World

LAMENTATIONS 3:31–32

107	God the Almighty One
171	Immortal Love, Forever Full
272	O Love, That Will Not Let Me Go
381	There's a Wideness

LAMENTATIONS 3:40

79	Depth of Mercy! Can There Be
261	O For a Closer Walk with God
262	O For a Heart to Praise My God
296	Pass Me Not, O Gentle Savior

LAMENTATIONS 3:55–58

3–St. 3	A Mighty Fortress Is Our God
96	Give to the Winds
102	God Is My Strong Salvation

LAMENTATIONS 4:2

122–St. 1	Have Thine Own Way, Lord

LAMENTATIONS 4:14

248–St. 2	Nearer, My God, to Thee
341–St. 1	Surely Goodness and Mercy

LAMENTATIONS 5:19

66	Come, Thou Almighty King
114	Great Is Thy Faithfulness
265	O God, Our Help in Ages Past
283	O Worship the King
299	Praise, My Soul, the King
356–Last st.	The Day Thou Gavest

358	The God of Abraham Praise

LAMENTATIONS 5:21

311	Revive Us Again
375–St. 1	There Is a Balm in Gilead

EZEKIEL 2:3

399	We Have Heard the Joyful Sound

EZEKIEL 3:12

137	Holy, Holy, Holy
300	Praise the Lord Who Reigns Above

EZEKIEL 3:19

284	O Zion, Haste

EZEKIEL 10:5

134–St. 2	Holy God, We Praise Thy Name
137–St. 2	Holy, Holy, Holy

EZEKIEL 10:20

134–St. 2	Holy God, We Praise Thy Name
137–St. 2	Holy, Holy, Holy

EZEKIEL 11:15–17

286	On Jordan's Stormy Banks I Stand

EZEKIEL 11:19

195–St. 2	Jesus Paid it All
216	Let Jesus Come Into Your Heart
262	O For a Heart to Praise My God
311	Revive Us Again
424	Whiter Than Snow

EZEKIEL 11:20

396	We Are God's People

EZEKIEL 11:22

134–St. 2	Holy God, We Praise Thy Name
137–St. 2	Holy, Holy, Holy

EZEKIEL 12:2

292	Open My Eyes

EZEKIEL 12:8

241	Morning Has Broken

EZEKIEL 14:5–6

67–St. 3	Come, Thou Fount
261	O For a Closer Walk with God

EZEKIEL 16:60–62

114	Great Is Thy Faithfulness

EZEKIEL 17:23

53–St. 1	Children of the Heavenly Father

EZEKIEL 18:5–9

262	O For a Heart to Praise My God
418	When We Walk with the Lord

EZEKIEL 18:21–23

79	Depth of Mercy! Can There Be?
261	O For a Closer Walk with God
262	O For a Heart to Praise My God
284	O Zion, Haste
331	Softly and Tenderly
389–St. 3	'Tis So Sweet To Trust in Jesus

EZEKIEL 18:31–32

216	Let Jesus Come Into Your Heart
227	Lord, I'm Coming Home
261	O For a Closer Walk with God
262	O For a Heart to Praise My God
284	O Zion, Haste
331	Softly and Tenderly

EZEKIEL 20:11

418	When We Walk with the Lord

EZEKIEL 20:12

260	O Day of Rest and Gladness

EZEKIEL 28:26

3	A Mighty Fortress Is Our God

EZEKIEL 29:16

3–St. 2	A Mighty Fortress Is Our God

EZEKIEL 33:11

79	Depth of Mercy! Can There Be?
149	I Hear Thy Welcome Voice
261	O For a Closer Walk with God
315	Room at the Cross for You
331	Softly and Tenderly
389–St. 3	'Tis So Sweet To Trust in Jesus
392	Turn Your Eyes Upon Jesus

EZEKIEL 34:1–31

125	He Leadeth Me
319	Savior, Like a Shepherd Lead Us
324	Shepherd of Tender Youth
362	The King of Love My Shepherd Is

366	The Lord's My Shepherd

EZEKIEL 34:6

248–St. 2	Nearer, My God, to Thee
341	Surely Goodness and Mercy

EZEKIEL 34:12–16

298–St. 1	Praise Him! Praise Him!

EZEKIEL 34:14

100–St. 1	God Be with You

EZEKIEL 34:25

297	Peace, Perfect Peace

EZEKIEL 34:26

379	There Shall Be Showers

EZEKIEL 34:31

362	The King of Love My Shepherd Is
366	The Lord's My Shepherd

EZEKIEL 36:23

33	At the Name of Jesus

EZEKIEL 36:25–26

27	Are You Washed in the Blood?
58	Christ Receiveth Sinful Men
80	Down at the Cross
112	Grace Greater Than Our Sin
129	Heaven Came Down
155–St. 1	I Lay My Sins on Jesus
195	Jesus Paid it All
208	Just As I Am, Without One Plea
216	Let Jesus Come Into Your Heart
251	Nothing But the Blood
262	O For a Heart to Praise My God
311	Revive Us Again
378	There Is Power in the Blood
424	Whiter Than Snow
431	Ye Must Be Born Again

EZEKIEL 36:25–27

108	God Who Touchest Earth

EZEKIEL 36:26–27

44–St. 2	Blessed Jesus, at Thy Word
49	Breathe on Me, Breath of God
63	Come, Holy Ghost
122–St. 4	Have Thine Own Way, Lord
135	Holy Spirit, Light Divine
136	Holy Spirit, Truth Divine

140	Hover O'er Me, Holy Spirit
292	Open My Eyes
333	Spirit Divine, Attend Our Prayer
334	Spirit of God, Descend
335	Spirit of the Living God
344	Sweet, Sweet Spirit

EZEKIEL 36:28

396	We Are God's People

EZEKIEL 37:9–10

49	Breathe on Me, Breath of God

EZEKIEL 37:10

291	Onward, Christian Soldiers

EZEKIEL 37:14

49	Breathe on Me, Breath of God
333	Spirit Divine, Attend Our Prayer

EZEKIEL 37:23

27	Are You Washed in the Blood?
112	Grace Greater Than Our Sin

EZEKIEL 38:23

77–Refrain	Day Is Dying in the West
134	Holy God, We Praise Thy Name
137	Holy, Holy, Holy
142	How Great Thou Art

EZEKIEL 39:7

77–Refrain	Day Is Dying in the West
134	Holy God, We Praise Thy Name
137	Holy, Holy, Holy
142	How Great Thou Art

EZEKIEL 39:29

63	Come, Holy Ghost
137–St. 3	Holy, Holy, Holy
333	Spirit Divine, Attend Our Prayer

EZEKIEL 43:1–5

293	Open Now Thy Gates of Beauty

EZEKIEL 44:4

293	Open Now Thy Gates of Beauty

EZEKIEL 46:1

293	Open Now Thy Gates of Beauty

DANIEL 2:20

33	At the Name of Jesus

328	Sing Praise to God Who Reigns
358	The God of Abraham Praise

DANIEL 2:20–23

38	Be Thou My Vision
103	God Moves in a Mysterious Way
104	God of Grace and God of Glory
170	Immortal, Invisible
253	Now Thank We All Our God

DANIEL 3:17

67–St. 2	Come, Thou Fount

DANIEL 4:3

3–St. 4	A Mighty Fortress Is Our God
66	Come, Thou Almighty King
85	Faith of Our Fathers
105	God of Our Fathers
283	O Worship the King
299	Praise, My Soul, the King

DANIEL 4:27

389–St. 3	'Tis So Sweet To Trust in Jesus

DANIEL 4:34–37

3	A Mighty Fortress Is Our God
103	God Moves in a Mysterious Way
283	O Worship the King
299	Praise, My Soul, the King
304	Praise to the Lord, the Almighty
358	The God of Abraham Praise

DANIEL 6:10

33	At the Name of Jesus
253	Now Thank We All Our God
305	Prayer Is the Soul's Sincere
343	Sweet Hour of Prayer
407	What a Friend We Have in Jesus

DANIEL 6:26–27

3	A Mighty Fortress Is Our God
114	Great Is Thy Faithfulness
253–St. 3	Now Thank We All Our God
283	O Worship the King
358	The God of Abraham Praise

DANIEL 7:3–4

262–St. 2	O For a Heart to Praise My God
305	Prayer Is the Soul's Sincere

DANIEL 7:9

66–St. 1	Come, Thou Almighty King

170–St. 1   Immortal, Invisible
283–St. 1   O Worship the King
358   The God of Abraham Praise

DANIEL 7:10
352   Ten Thousand Times Ten Thousand

DANIEL 7:13
66–St. 1   Come, Thou Almighty King
170–St. 1   Immortal, Invisible
283–St. 1   O Worship the King

DANIEL 7:13–14
223   Lo, He Comes with Clouds

DANIEL 7:18
352   Ten Thousand Times Ten Thousand

DANIEL 7:22
66–St. 1   Come, Thou Almighty King
170–St. 1   Immortal, Invisible
283–St. 1   O Worship the King

DANIEL 9:4
114   Great Is Thy Faithfulness

DANIEL 9:9
78–St. 1   Dear Lord and Father of Mankind
107   God the Almighty One
192   Jesus, Lover of My Soul
206–St. 3   Joyful, Joyful, We Adore Thee
216   Let Jesus Come Into Your Heart
359–St. 2   The Great Physician

DANIEL 9:18
79   Depth of Mercy! Can There Be?
381   There's a Wideness

DANIEL 9:24
118   Hail to the Lord's Anointed

DANIEL 10:18–19
3–St. 3   A Mighty Fortress Is Our God
195–St. 1   Jesus Paid it All

DANIEL 11:35
141–St. 4   How Firm a Foundation

DANIEL 12:3
284   O Zion, Haste
310   Rescue the Perishing
404   We've a Story to Tell

DANIEL 12:10
27   Are You Washed in the Blood?
58–St. 3   Christ Receiveth Sinful Men
202   Jesus, Thy Blood and Righteousness
378   There Is Power in the Blood
424   Whiter Than Snow

HOSEA 1:10
202–St. 4   Jesus, Thy Blood and Righteousness

HOSEA 2:15
309   Rejoice, Ye Pure in Heart

HOSEA 2:18
264   O God of Love, O King of Peace

HOSEA 2:19
412   When All Thy Mercies, O My God

HOSEA 2:23
40–St. 4   Begin, My Tongue, Some Heavenly
79   Depth of Mercy! Can There Be?
396   We Are God's People

HOSEA 6:1
72   Come, Ye Sinners, Poor and Needy
149   I Hear Thy Welcome Voice
208   Just As I Am, Without One Plea
216   Let Jesus Come Into Your Heart
290   Only Trust Him
331   Softly and Tenderly

HOSEA 6:3
379   There Shall Be Showers

HOSEA 6:4
350–St. 2   Tell Me the Old, Old Story

HOSEA 10:12
73   Come, Ye Thankful People, Come
379   There Shall Be Showers
424–St. 4   Whiter Than Snow

HOSEA 11:1–8
272   O Love, That Will Not Let Me Go

HOSEA 13:4
261   O For a Closer Walk with God
350–St. 2   Tell Me the Old, Old Story

HOSEA 13:9
265   O God, Our Help in Ages Past

HOSEA 13:14

59–St. 2	Christ the Lord Is Risen Today
75–St. 6	Crown Him with Many Crowns
202	Jesus, Thy Blood and Righteousness
232	Majestic Sweetness
351–St. 3	Tell Me the Story of Jesus

HOSEA 14:1

67–St. 3	Come, Thou Fount
227	Lord, I'm Coming Home

HOSEA 14:2

79	Depth of Mercy! Can There Be?
208	Just As I Am, Without One Plea
261	O For a Closer Walk with God

HOSEA 14:4

67–St. 3	Come, Thou Fount
216	Let Jesus Come Into Your Heart
341–St. 2	Surely Goodness and Mercy

HOSEA 14:9

86–St. 2	Fight the Good Fight
90	Forth in Thy Name, O Lord
128	He Who Would Valiant Be
167	If Thou But Suffer God to Guide
268	O Jesus, I Have Promised
349	Teach Me Thy Way, O Lord

JOEL 2:12–13

79	Depth of Mercy! Can There Be?
107	God the Almighty One
122	Have Thine Own Way, Lord
227	Lord, I'm Coming Home
261	O For a Closer Walk with God
381	There's a Wideness

JOEL 2:23

379	There Shall Be Showers

JOEL 2:28–29

38	Be Thou My Vision
63	Come, Holy Ghost
333	Spirit Divine, Attend Our Prayer

JOEL 3:10

57–St. 2	Christ Is the World's
207	Just a Closer Walk with Thee

JOEL 3:13

121	Hark, the Voice of Jesus Calling

JOEL 3:16

265	O God, Our Help in Ages Past
369	The Solid Rock

AMOS 2:11

284–St. 4	O Zion, Haste

AMOS 4:13

107	God the Almighty One
160	I Sing the Almighty Power of God
301	Praise the Lord! Ye Heavens
328	Sing Praise to God Who Reigns
383	This Is My Father's World

AMOS 5:4

58	Christ Receiveth Sinful Men
161	I Sought the Lord
331	Softly and Tenderly
424–St. 4	Whiter Than Snow

AMOS 5:8

371	The Spacious Firmament

AMOS 5:23

65–St. 2	Come, Holy Spirit
414	When in Our Music

AMOS 8:11

292–St. 2	Open My Eyes

OBADIAH 1:17

2	A Child of the King

JONAH 1:9

142	How Great Thou Art
304	Praise to the Lord, the Almighty
383	This Is My Father's World

JONAH 2:5–6

177–St. 3	In the Hour of Trial

JONAH 2:7

70	Come, Ye Disconsolate

JONAH 2:9

62	Come, Christians, Join to Sing
67	Come, Thou Fount
73	Come, Ye Thankful People, Come
246	My Tribute
253	Now Thank We All Our God

JONAH 4:2

21	Amazing Grace
112	Grace Greater Than Our Sin
381	There's a Wideness
412	When All Thy Mercies, O My God

MICAH 2:12–13

17	All the Way My Savior Leads Me
319	Savior, Like a Shepherd Leads Us
341	Surely Goodness and Mercy

MICAH 3:8

284	O Zion, Haste
404	We've a Story to Tell

MICAH 4:3

107	God the Almighty One
404	We've a Story to Tell

MICAH 4:5

50	Brethren, We Have Met to Worship
207	Just a Closer Walk with Thee
261	O For a Closer Walk with God
283	O Worship the King

MICAH 4:7

328	Sing Praise to God Who Reigns
432–St. 2	Ye Servants of God

MICAH 5:2

270	O Little Town of Bethlehem
276	O Sing a Song of Bethlehem
422–St. 2	While By the Sheep

MICAH 5:4

206	Joyful, Joyful, We Adore Thee
265	O God, Our Help in Ages Past
298–St. 1	Praise Him! Praise Him!
299	Praise, My Soul, the King

MICAH 5:5

150	I Heard the Bells on Christmas

MICAH 6:6–8

1	A Charge to Keep I Have
222	Living for Jesus
261	O For a Closer Walk with God
321	Savior, Thy Dying Love
334	Spirit of God, Descend

MICAH 7:7–8

102	God Is My Strong Salvation

130	Heavenly Sunlight
173–St. 3	In Heavenly Love Abiding
206–St. 1	Joyful, Joyful, We Adore Thee
244	My Faith Looks Up to Thee
319–St. 2	Savior, Like a Shepherd Lead Us
340	Sunshine in My Soul
364	The Light of the World Is Jesus
387	Thou Whose Almighty Word

MICAH 7:18–20

21	Amazing Grace
58	Christ Receiveth Sinful Men
67	Come, Thou Fount
79	Depth of Mercy! Can There Be?
107	God the Almighty One
114	Great Is Thy Faithfulness
129	Heaven Came Down
192–St. 4	Jesus, Lover of My Soul
216	Let Jesus Come Into Your Heart
244	My Faith Looks Up to Thee
267	O, How I Love Jesus
331	Softly and Tenderly
359–St. 2	The Great Physician
381	There's a Wideness
412	When All Thy Mercies, O My God

MICAH 7:19

341	Surely Goodness and Mercy

MICAH 7:20

358–St. 2	The God of Abraham Praise

NAHUM 1:2–7

103	God Moves in a Mysterious Way

NAHUM 1:3

93	From Every Stormy Wind
107	God the Almighty One

NAHUM 1:7

53	Children of the Heavenly Father
74	Count Your Blessings
100	God Be with You
109	God Will Take Care of You
114	Great Is Thy Faithfulness
124–St. 4	He Keeps Me Singing
141	How Firm a Foundation
146	I Am Trusting Thee, Lord Jesus
158	I Must Tell Jesus
173	In Heavenly Love Abiding
188	Jesus Is All the World to Me
192	Jesus, Lover of My Soul

221	Like a River Glorious
238	Moment by Moment
265	O God, Our Help in Ages Past
294	Out of My Bondage
341	Surely Goodness and Mercy
362	The King of Love My Shepherd Is
366	The Lord's My Shepherd
389	'Tis So Sweet To Trust in Jesus

NAHUM 1:13

104–St. 2	God of Grace and God of Glory

HABAKKUK 1:2–5

3	A Mighty Fortress Is Our God
167	If Thou But Suffer God to Guide
383–St. 3	This Is My Father's World

HABAKKUK 1:12

137	Holy, Holy, Holy
170	Immortal, Invisible
283	O Worship the King

HABAKKUK 2:1

395	Watchman, Tell Us of the Night

HABAKKUK 2:14

104	God of Grace and God of Glory
137	Holy, Holy, Holy

HABAKKUK 2:18

261	O For a Closer Walk with God

HABAKKUK 2:20

78	Dear Lord and Father of Mankind
101	God Himself Is with Us
214	Let All Mortal Flesh

HABAKKUK 3:2

40	Begin, My Tongue, Some Heavenly
103	God Moves in a Mysterious Way
113	Great God, We Sing That Mighty Hand
255	O Breath of Life
311	Revive Us Again
373	The Vision of a Dying World
375–St. 1	There Is a Balm in Gilead

HABAKKUK 3:3

206–St. 2	Joyful, Joyful, We Adore Thee

HABAKKUK 3:4

283–St. 2	O Worship the King

HABAKKUK 3:18–19

3	A Mighty Fortress Is Our God
67	Come, Thou Fount
76	Day by Day
102	God Is My Strong Salvation
167–St. 1	If Thou But Suffer God to Guide
206	Joyful, Joyful, We Adore Thee
298–St. 2	Praise Him! Praise Him!
304	Praise to the Lord, the Almighty
310–St. 4	Rescue the Perishing

ZEPHANIAH 1:7

293	Open Now Thy Gates of Beauty

ZEPHANIAH 2:3

79	Depth of Mercy! Can There Be?
227	Lord, I'm Coming Home
261	O For a Closer Walk with God
262	O For a Heart to Praise My God
288	Once to Every Man and Nation
331	Softly and Tenderly

ZEPHANIAH 2:11

288	Once to Every Man and Nation
404	We've a Story to Tell

ZEPHANIAH 3:5

114	Great Is Thy Faithfulness
170–St. 2	Immortal, Invisible
259	O Day of God, Draw Nigh

ZEPHANIAH 3:9

288	Once to Every Man and Nation

ZEPHANIAH 3:12

166–St. 2	I Would Be True

ZEPHANIAH 3:12–17

67	Come, Thou Fount
265	O God, Our Help in Ages Past

ZEPHANIAH 3:14–17

206	Joyful, Joyful, We Adore Thee
309	Rejoice, Ye Pure in Heart

ZEPHANIAH 3:17

31	At Calvary
42	Blessed Assurance
102	God Is My Strong Salvation
204	Jesus, What a Friend for Sinners
319–St. 4	Savior, Like a Shepherd Lead Us
390	To God Be the Glory

HAGGAI 1:13

5	Abide with Me
114	Great Is Thy Faithfulness

HAGGAI 2:4–5

5	Abide with Me
114	Great Is Thy Faithfulness
310–St. 4	Rescue the Perishing
334	Spirit of God, Descend

HAGGAI 2:7

24–St. 3	Angels from the Realms of Glory
68	Come, Thou Long–Expected Jesus
257–St. 5	O Come, O Come, Emmanuel

HAGGAI 2:8

18	All Things Are Thine
345	Take My Life and Let It Be
398	We Give Thee but Thine Own

ZECHARIAH 1:3

79	Depth of Mercy! Can There Be?
261	O For a Closer Walk with God
331	Softly and Tenderly

ZECHARIAH 1:11

264	O God of Love, O King of Peace

ZECHARIAH 1:17

97	Glorious Things of Thee

ZECHARIAH 2:5

3	A Mighty Fortress Is Our God

ZECHARIAH 2:10

238	Moment by Moment
309	Rejoice, Ye Pure in Heart

ZECHARIAH 2:11

57	Christ Is the World's
288	Once to Every Man and Nation

ZECHARIAH 2:13

101	God Himself Is with Us
214	Let All Mortal Flesh

ZECHARIAH 3:4

78–St. 1	Dear Lord and Father of Mankind

ZECHARIAH 4:6

135	Holy Spirit, Light Divine
136–St. 3	Holy Spirit, Truth Divine

334	Spirit of God, Descend
335	Spirit of the Living God

ZECHARIAH 6:15

292–St. 2	Open My Eyes

ZECHARIAH 7:9–10

46	Blest Be the Tie
206–St. 3	Joyful, Joyful, We Adore Thee
273	O Master, Let Me Walk with Thee
419	Where Cross the Crowded Ways

ZECHARIAH 8:2–8

97	Glorious Things of Thee
183	Jerusalem, My Happy Home
184	Jerusalem, the Golden

ZECHARIAH 8:13

233	Make Me a Blessing

ZECHARIAH 8:16

292	Open My Eyes

ZECHARIAH 9:9

11	All Glory, Laud and Honor
66	Come, Thou Almighty King
312	Ride On, Ride On in Majesty!

ZECHARIAH 9:11

8	Alas! And Did My Savior Bleed?
251	Nothing But the Blood
369	The Solid Rock

ZECHARIAH 9:14

237	Mine Eyes Have Seen the Glory

ZECHARIAH 9:15–16

3	A Mighty Fortress Is Our God
265	O God, Our Help in Ages Past
319	Savior, Like a Shepherd Lead Us
362	The King of Love My Shepherd Is
366	The Lord's My Shepherd

ZECHARIAH 10:1

400	We Plow the Fields

ZECHARIAH 10:2–6

67–St. 3	Come, Thou Fount
165–St. 2	I Will Sing the Wondrous Story
319	Savior, Like a Shepherd Lead Us

ZECHARIAH 10:5

3	A Mighty Fortress Is Our God
84	Faith Is the Victory
212	Lead On, O King Eternal
291	Onward, Christian Soldiers
337	Stand Up, Stand Up for Jesus
397–St. 3	We Gather Together
401–St. 2	We Praise Thee, O God

ZECHARIAH 10:11

197	Jesus Savior, Pilot Me

ZECHARIAH 10:12

3	A Mighty Fortress Is Our God
265	O God, Our Help in Ages Past
418	When We Walk with the Lord

ZECHARIAH 12:1

142	How Great Thou Art
160	I Sing the Almighty Power of God
304	Praise to the Lord, the Almighty
383	This Is My Father's World

ZECHARIAH 12:8

3	A Mighty Fortress Is Our God
265	O God, Our Help in Ages Past
397	We Gather Together

ZECHARIAH 13:1

27–St. 4	Are You Washed in the Blood?
43–St. 3	Blessed Be the Name
58	Christ Receiveth Sinful Men
80	Down at the Cross
112	Grace Greater Than Our Sin
115–St. 2	Guide Me, O Thou Great Jehovah
191	Jesus, Keep Me Near the Cross
192–St. 4	Jesus, Lover of My Soul
251	Nothing But the Blood
257	O Come, O Come, Emmanuel
263–St. 3	O For a Thousand Tongues to Sing
267–St. 2	O, How I Love Jesus
319–St. 3	Savior, Like a Shepherd Lead Us
376	There Is a Fountain
378	There Is Power in the Blood
424	Whiter Than Snow

ZECHARIAH 13:9

40–St. 4	Begin, My Tongue, Some Heavenly
141–St. 4	How Firm a Foundation

ZECHARIAH 14:3

397–St. 3	We Gather Together

ZECHARIAH 14:9

12	All Hail the Power of Jesus' Name
66	Come, Thou Almighty King
170	Immortal, Invisible
223–Last st.	Lo, He Comes with Clouds
283	O Worship the King
299	Praise, My Soul, the King
304	Praise to the Lord, the Almighty
308	Rejoice, the Lord Is King

MALACHI 1:2

114	Great Is Thy Faithfulness
230	Love Divine, All Loves Excelling
381	There's a Wideness

MALACHI 1:6

432	Ye Servants of God

MALACHI 1:11

33	At the Name of Jesus
34	Awake, My Soul, and With the Sun
43	Blessed Be the Name
142	How Great Thou Art
346	Take the Name of Jesus with You
399	We Have Heard the Joyful Sound

MALACHI 1:14

66	Come, Thou Almighty King
212	Lead On, O King Eternal
283	O Worship the King
299	Praise, My Soul, the King

MALACHI 2:1–7

1	A Charge to Keep I Have
288	Once to Every Man and Nation
292	Open My Eyes

MALACHI 2:10

85	Faith of Our Fathers
105	God of Our Fathers
206–St. 3	Joyful, Joyful, We Adore Thee

MALACHI 3:1

24–St. 4	Angels from the Realms of Glory
68	Come, Thou Long–Expected Jesus
230–St. 3	Love Divine, All Loves Excelling
257	O Come, O Come, Emmanuel

MALACHI 3:2–3

27	Are You Washed in the Blood?
58	Christ Receiveth Sinful Men
112	Grace Greater Than Our Sin
141–St. 4	How Firm a Foundation
251	Nothing But the Blood

MALACHI 3:6

5	Abide with Me
37	Be Still, My Soul
114	Great Is Thy Faithfulness
170–St. 3	Immortal, Invisible
173	In Heavenly Love Abiding
253–St. 3	Now Thank We All Our God
265	O God, Our Help in Ages Past
280	O the Deep, Deep Love of Jesus
358	The God of Abraham Praise

MALACHI 3:7

67–St. 3	Come, Thou Fount
79	Depth of Mercy! Can There Be?
261	O For a Closer Walk with God

MALACHI 3:8–10

18	All Things Are Thine
345	Take My Life and Let It Be
398	We Give Thee but Thine Own

MALACHI 3:10

| 74 | Count Your Blessings |

MALACHI 3:14–18

1	A Charge to Keep I Have
273	O Master, Let Me Walk with Thee
288	Once to Every Man and Nation
383–St. 3	This Is My Father's World

MALACHI 4:2

60	Christ Whose Glory Fills
83–St. 3	Fairest Lord Jesus
120–St. 3	Hark! The Herald Angels Sing
124–St. 3	He Keeps Me Singing
130	Heavenly Sunlight
257	O Come, O Come, Emmanuel
387–St. 2	Thou Whose Almighty Word

MALACHI 4:3

| 84 | Faith Is the Victory |
| 383 | This Is My Father's World |

MALACHI 4:6

85	Faith of Our Fathers
105	God of Our Fathers
119	Happy the Home When God Is There

New Testament

MATTHEW 1:18–25

68	Come, Thou Long-Expected Jesus
120	Hark! The Herald Angels Sing
257	O Come, O Come, Emmanuel
270	O Little Town of Bethlehem
285	Of the Father's Love Begotten
289–St. 1	One Day

MATTHEW 1:21

43	Blessed Be the Name
200–St. 2	Jesus, the Very Thought of Thee
235	"Man of Sorrows," What a Name
263–St. 2	O For a Thousand Tongues to Sing
267	O, How I Love Jesus
346	Take the Name of Jesus with You

MATTHEW 2:1–11

13	All My Heart This Night
24–St. 3	Angels from the Realms of Glory
29	As With Gladness Men of Old
51	Brightest and Best
95–St. 2	Gentle Mary Laid Her Child
110	Good Christian Men, Rejoice
256	O Come, All Ye Faithful
270	O Little Town of Bethlehem
276	O Sing a Song of Bethlehem
357	The First Noel
380	There's a Song in the Air
402	We Three Kings
403–St. 1	We Would See Jesus; Lo! His Star
409	What Child Is This?

MATTHEW 2:23

162–St. 1	I Stand Amazed in the Presence
276–St. 2	O Sing a Song of Bethlehem

MATTHEW 3:3

205	Joy to the World

MATTHEW 3:11

49	Breathe on Me, Breath of God
63	Come, Holy Ghost
66–St. 3	Come, Thou Almighty King
140	Hover O'er Me, Holy Spirit
311	Revive Us Again
333	Spirit Divine, Attend Our Prayer
335	Spirit of the Living God
354	The Comforter Has Come

MATTHEW 3:13–17

64	Come, Holy Spirit, Dove Divine
65	Come, Holy Spirit
271–St. 2	O Love How Deep, How Broad

MATTHEW 4:1–11

159–St. 2	I Need Thee Every Hour
271–St. 2	O Love How Deep, How Broad
351–St. 2	Tell Me the Story of Jesus
425–St. 1	Who Is He in Yonder Stall?

MATTHEW 4:4

17–St. 2	All the Way My Savior Leads Me
20–St. 4	Am I a Soldier of the Cross?
48	Break Thou the Bread
115–St. 1	Guide Me, O Thou Great Jehovah
133	Holy Bible, Book Divine
347–St. 1	Take Time to Be Holy
430	Wonderful Words of Life

MATTHEW 4:16

5	Abide with Me
129–St. 1	Heaven Came Down
130	Heavenly Sunlight
151–St. 3	I Heard the Voice of Jesus Say
170	Immortal, Invisible
206–St. 1	Joyful, Joyful, We Adore Thee
278	O Splendor of God's Glory
322	Send the Light!

327–St. 1	Since Jesus Came Into My Heart
340	Sunshine in My Soul
364	The Light of the World Is Jesus
387	Thou Whose Almighty Word
395	Watchman, Tell Us of the Night

MATTHEW 4:17

185	Jesus Calls Us
368	The Savior Is Waiting
424	Whiter Than Snow

MATTHEW 4:18–22

78–St. 2	Dear Lord and Father of Mankind
121	Hark, the Voice of Jesus Calling
148	I Have Decided to Follow Jesus
185	Jesus Calls Us
273	O Master, Let Me Walk with Thee
403–St. 4	We Would See Jesus; Lo! His Star
420	Where He Leads Me
421	Wherever He Leads, I'll Go

MATTHEW 4:19

222–St. 2	Living for Jesus
233	Make Me a Blessing
284	O Zion, Haste
310	Rescue the Perishing

MATTHEW 4:23–24

55	Christ for the World We Sing
238	Moment by Moment
243–St. 4	My Faith Has Found
250	No, Not One
351	Tell Me the Story of Jesus
359	The Great Physician
394–St. 2	Victory in Jesus
425–St. 2	Who Is He in Yonder Stall?

MATTHEW 5:1

| 419–St. 4 | Where Cross the Crowded Ways |

MATTHEW 5:1–12

| 403–St. 3 | We Would See Jesus; Lo! His Star |

MATTHEW 5:2

| 425–St. 2 | Who Is He in Yonder Stall? |

MATTHEW 5:4

96	Give to the Winds
238	Moment by Moment
393–St. 2	Under His Wings

MATTHEW 5:5

| 200–St. 3 | Jesus, the Very Thought of Thee |

MATTHEW 5:6

72	Come, Ye Sinners, Poor and Needy
151–St. 2	I Heard the Voice of Jesus Say
201	Jesus, Thou Joy of Loving Hearts
239	More About Jesus
316	Satisfied

MATTHEW 5:8

108	God Who Touchest Earth
262	O For a Heart to Praise My God
309	Rejoice, Ye Pure in Heart

MATTHEW 5:14–16

1	A Charge to Keep I Have
35–St. 2	Awake, My Soul, Stretch
233	Make Me a Blessing

MATTHEW 5:18

| 167 | If Thou But Suffer God to Guide |
| 259–Last St. | O Day of God, Draw Nigh |

MATTHEW 5:29

| 177–St. 2 | In the Hour of Trial |

MATTHEW 5:30

| 345 | Take My Life and Let It Be |

MATTHEW 5:43–48

65	Come, Holy Spirit
295	Pass It On
320	Savior, Teach Me Day by Day

MATTHEW 5:48

| 38 | Be Thou My Vision |
| 137–St. 3 | Holy, Holy, Holy |

MATTHEW 6:5–13

305	Prayer Is the Soul's Sincere
343	Sweet Hour of Prayer
407	What a Friend We Have in Jesus

MATTHEW 6:6

| 347–St. 2 | Take Time to Be Holy |

MATTHEW 6:8

| 53 | Children of the Heavenly Father |
| 109 | God Will Take Care of You |

MATTHEW 6:9–10

33–St. 1	At the Name of Jesus
66–St. 1	Come, Thou Almighty King
134	Holy God, We Praise Thy Name
300–St. 3	Praise the Lord Who Reigns Above

MATTHEW 6:10

49	Breathe on Me, Breath of God
122	Have Thine Own Way, Lord
145–St. 2	I Am Thine, O Lord
404	We've a Story to Tell

MATTHEW 6:11

400–St. 2	We Plow the Fields

MATTHEW 6:13

3	A Mighty Fortress Is Our God
159–St. 2	I Need Thee Every Hour
177	In the Hour of Trial
382	Thine Is the Glory

MATTHEW 6:19–21

38–St. 3	Be Thou My Vision
74–St. 3	Count Your Blessings
173–St. 3	In Heavenly Love Abiding

MATTHEW 6:21

163	I Surrender All
262	O For a Heart to Praise My God

MATTHEW 6:23

129–St. 1	Heaven Came Down
165–St. 4	I Will Sing the Wondrous Story
364	The Light of the World Is Jesus

MATTHEW 6:24

145–St. 2	I Am Thine, O Lord
147	I Gave My Life for Thee
148	I Have Decided to Follow Jesus
222	Living for Jesus
268	O Jesus, I Have Promised
288	Once to Every Man and Nation
345	Take My Life and Let It Be

MATTHEW 6:26–34

17	All the Way My Savior Leads Me
53	Children of the Heavenly Father
86–St. 3	Fight the Good Fight
109	God Will Take Care of You
167	If Thou But Suffer God to Guide
206–St. 2	Joyful, Joyful, We Adore Thee
283–St. 3	O Worship the King

347	Take Time to Be Holy
391	Trusting Jesus

MATTHEW 7:7–8

201–St. 2	Jesus, Thou Joy of Loving Hearts

MATTHEW 7:11

74	Count Your Blessings
383	This Is My Father's World

MATTHEW 7:13–14

86–St. 2	Fight the Good Fight
213–St. 2	Leaning on the Everlasting Arms
268	O Jesus, I Have Promised
310–St. 4	Rescue the Perishing

MATTHEW 7:20

233	Make Me a Blessing

MATTHEW 7:21

1	A Charge to Keep I Have
49	Breathe on Me, Breath of God
122	Have Thine Own Way, Lord
171–Last St.	Immortal Love, Forever Full
418	When We Walk with the Lord

MATTHEW 7:24–25

97–St. 1	Glorious Things of Thee
141	How Firm a Foundation
167	If Thou But Suffer God to Guide
369	The Solid Rock

MATTHEW 7:28

154	I Know Whom I Have Believed

MATTHEW 8:2–3

27	Are You Washed in the Blood?
192–St. 3	Jesus, Lover of My Soul
195–St. 2	Jesus Paid it All
208	Just As I Am, Without One Plea
243–St. 4	My Faith Has Found
394–St. 2	Victory in Jesus

MATTHEW 8:3

80	Down at the Cross
122–St. 2	Have Thine Own Way, Lord
155	I Lay My Sins on Jesus
228	Lord Jesus, Think on Me
290	Only Trust Him
389–St. 2	'Tis So Sweet To Trust in Jesus
424	Whiter Than Snow

MATTHEW 8:16–17

122–St. 2	Have Thine Own Way, Lord
162–St. 4	I Stand Amazed in the Presence
243–St. 4	My Faith Has Found
267–St. 4	O, How I Love Jesus
359	The Great Physician
394–St. 2	Victory in Jesus

MATTHEW 8:19–22

87	Footsteps of Jesus
90	Forth in Thy Name, O Lord
121	Hark, the Voice of Jesus Calling
148	I Have Decided to Follow Jesus
185	Jesus Calls Us
188–St. 3	Jesus Is All the World to Me
222–St. 2	Living for Jesus
268	O Jesus, I Have Promised
273	O Master, Let Me Walk with Thee
321	Savior, Thy Dying Love
348	"Take Up Thy Cross"
403–St. 4	We Would See Jesus; Lo! His Star
420	Where He Leads Me
421	Wherever He Leads, I'll Go

MATTHEW 8:20

351–St. 2	Tell Me the Story of Jesus
386	Thou Didst Leave Thy Throne

MATTHEW 8:23–27

37–St. 2	Be Still, My Soul
81–St. 2	Eternal Father, Strong to Save
93	From Every Stormy Wind
196–St. 3	Jesus, Priceless Treasure
197	Jesus Savior, Pilot Me
204–St. 4	Jesus, What a Friend for Sinners
231	Love Lifted Me
310	Rescue the Perishing

MATTHEW 9:1–8

155–St. 2	I Lay My Sins on Jesus
165–St. 3	I Will Sing the Wondrous Story
192–St. 3	Jesus, Lover of My Soul
243–St. 4	My Faith Has Found
263	O For a Thousand Tongues to Sing
359	The Great Physician
394–St. 2	Victory in Jesus

MATTHEW 9:9

148	I Have Decided to Follow Jesus
185	Jesus Calls Us
222–St. 2	Living for Jesus

348	"Take Up Thy Cross"
403–St. 4	We Would See Jesus; Lo! His Star
420	Where He Leads Me
421	Wherever He Leads, I'll Go

MATTHEW 9:10–13

204	Jesus, What a Friend for Sinners

MATTHEW 9:12

359	The Great Physician

MATTHEW 9:13

190	Jesus Is Tenderly Calling
222–St. 2	Living for Jesus

MATTHEW 9:20–22

171	Immortal Love, Forever Full

MATTHEW 9:22

243–St. 4	My Faith Has Found
359–St. 1	The Great Physician
394–St. 2	Victory in Jesus
424	Whiter Than Snow

MATTHEW 9:27–35

192–St. 3	Jesus, Lover of My Soul
243–St. 4	My Faith Has Found
394–St. 2	Victory in Jesus

MATTHEW 9:28–29

146	I Am Trusting Thee, Lord Jesus
244	My Faith Looks Up to Thee
389	'Tis So Sweet To Trust in Jesus
391	Trusting Jesus

MATTHEW 9:36

138–St. 1	Hope of the World

MATTHEW 9:37–38

73	Come, Ye Thankful People, Come
121	Hark, the Voice of Jesus Calling
125	He Leadeth Me
165–St. 2	I Will Sing the Wondrous Story
168	I'll Go Where You Want Me To Go
230	Love Divine, All Loves Excelling
284	O Zion, Haste
298–St. 1	Praise Him! Praise Him!
310	Rescue the Perishing
329	Sing to the Lord of Harvest
330	So Send I You
373	The Vision of a Dying World
399	We Have Heard the Joyful Sound

| 404 | We've a Story to Tell |
| 419 | Where Cross the Crowded Ways |

MATTHEW 10:8

| 233 | Make Me a Blessing |
| 295 | Pass It On |

MATTHEW 10:16

| 288 | Once to Every Man and Nation |
| 319 | Savior, Like a Shepherd Lead Us |

MATTHEW 10:20

| 292–St. 3 | Open My Eyes |
| 321–St. 2 | Savior, Thy Dying Love |

MATTHEW 10:22

| 20 | Am I a Soldier of the Cross? |

MATTHEW 10:29–31

| 53 | Children of the Heavenly Father |
| 109 | God Will Take Care of You |

MATTHEW 10:32

| 88–St. 1 | For All the Saints |
| 427 | Whosoever Will |

MATTHEW 10:33

| 177–St. 1 | In the Hour of Trial |
| 188–St. 3 | Jesus Is All the World to Me |

MATTHEW 10:34

| 212 | Lead On, O King Eternal |

MATTHEW 10:37–39

185	Jesus Calls Us
240	More Love to Thee, O Christ
245	My Jesus, I Love Thee

MATTHEW 10:38

148	I Have Decided to Follow Jesus
187	Jesus, I My Cross Have Taken
188	Jesus Is All the World to Me
211–St. 4	Lead Me to Calvary
242	Must Jesus Bear the Cross Alone?
321–St. 2	Savior, Thy Dying Love
374	The Way of the Cross Leads Home
403–St. 4	We Would See Jesus; Lo! His Star
420	Where He Leads Me

MATTHEW 10:38–39

| 1 | A Charge to Keep I Have |
| 26 | "Are Ye Able," Said the Master |

41	Beneath the Cross of Jesus
90	Forth in Thy Name, O Lord
121	Hark, the Voice of Jesus Calling
222	Living for Jesus
268	O Jesus, I Have Promised
273	O Master, Let Me Walk with Thee
348	"Take Up Thy Cross"
421	Wherever He Leads, I'll Go

MATTHEW 10:39

| 234 | Make Me a Captive, Lord |

MATTHEW 10:42

1	A Charge to Keep I Have
90	Forth in Thy Name, O Lord
121	Hark, the Voice of Jesus Calling
268	O Jesus, I Have Promised
419	Where Cross the Crowded Ways

MATTHEW 11:3

| 68 | Come, Thou Long-Expected Jesus |
| 118 | Hail to the Lord's Anointed |

MATTHEW 11:5

165–St. 3	I Will Sing the Wondrous Story
208	Just As I Am, Without One Plea
263–St. 4	O For a Thousand Tongues to Sing
394–St. 2	Victory in Jesus

MATTHEW 11:15

| 190 | Jesus Is Tenderly Calling |
| 292–St. 2 | Open My Eyes |

MATTHEW 11:18–30

| 76 | Day by Day |

MATTHEW 11:19

182	I've Found a Friend
188	Jesus Is All the World to Me
204	Jesus, What a Friend for Sinners
250	No, Not One
407	What a Friend We Have in Jesus

MATTHEW 11:25–26

| 103 | God Moves in a Mysterious Way |

MATTHEW 11:28

72	Come, Ye Sinners, Poor and Needy
91–St. 2	Free From the Law
149–St. 1	I Hear Thy Welcome Voice
159	I Need Thee Every Hour
216	Let Jesus Come Into Your Heart

137–St. 2	Holy, Holy, Holy
190	Jesus Is Tenderly Calling
235–St. 5	"Man of Sorrows," What a Name
292–St. 2	Open My Eyes
299–St. 4	Praise, My Soul, the King
352	Ten Thousand Times Ten Thousand
404	We've a Story to Tell
417	When We All Get to Heaven

MATTHEW 13:44

196	Jesus, Priceless Treasure

MATTHEW 14:14

138–St. 1	Hope of the World
155–St. 2	I Lay My Sins on Jesus
230–St. 1	Love Divine, All Loves Excelling
243–St. 4	My Faith Has Found
359–St. 1	The Great Physician
394–St. 2	Victory in Jesus
419	Where Cross the Crowded Ways

MATTHEW 14:15–21

48	Break Thou the Bread

MATTHEW 14:22–32

197	Jesus Savior, Pilot Me

MATTHEW 14:24–32

276–St. 3	O Sing a Song of Bethlehem

MATTHEW 14:27

188	Jesus Is All the World to Me
192	Jesus, Lover of My Soul

MATTHEW 14:28–33

161–St. 2	I Sought the Lord

MATTHEW 14:30–32

17	All the Way My Savior Leads Me
37–St. 2	Be Still, My Soul

MATTHEW 14:33

235	"Man of Sorrows," What a Name

MATTHEW 14:35–36

243–St. 4	My Faith Has Found
359–St. 1	The Great Physician
365–St. 1	The Lily of the Valley
424	Whiter Than Snow

MATTHEW 15:8

67–St. 3	Come, Thou Fount

262	O For a Heart to Praise My God

MATTHEW 15:18

262	O For a Heart to Praise My God

MATTHEW 15:24

165–St. 2	I Will Sing the Wondrous Story
319	Savior, Like a Shepherd Lead Us

MATTHEW 15:28

424	Whiter Than Snow

MATTHEW 15:29–38

48	Break Thou the Bread

MATTHEW 15:30–31

243–St. 4	My Faith Has Found
394–St. 2	Victory in Jesus

MATTHEW 15:32

138–St. 1	Hope of the World
230–St. 1	Love Divine, All Loves Excelling
419	Where Cross the Crowded Ways

MATTHEW 16:13

75–St. 6	Crown Him with Many Crowns

MATTHEW 16:15–18

52	Built on the Rock
56	Christ Is Made the Sure
156	I Love Thy Kingdom, Lord
235	"Man of Sorrows," What a Name
353	The Church's One Foundation

MATTHEW 16:18

97–St. 1	Glorious Things of Thee
291	Onward, Christian Soldiers

MATTHEW 16:19

308–St. 3	Rejoice, the Lord Is King

MATTHEW 16:21

117	Hail, Thou Once Despised Jesus

MATTHEW 16:24

26	"Are Ye Able," Said the Master
41	Beneath the Cross of Jesus
148	I Have Decided to Follow Jesus
171–Last st.	Immortal Love, Forever Full
185	Jesus Calls Us
188–St. 3	Jesus Is All the World to Me
211–St. 4	Lead Me to Calvary

321–St. 2	Savior, Thy Dying Love
370	The Son of God Goes Forth to War
374	The Way of the Cross Leads Home
421	Wherever He Leads, I'll Go

MATTHEW 16:24–25

121	Hark, the Voice of Jesus Calling
187	Jesus, I My Cross Have Taken
222	Living for Jesus
234	Make Me a Captive, Lord
268	O Jesus, I Have Promised
273	O Master, Let Me Walk with Thee
420	Where He Leads Me

MATTHEW 16:24–27

177–St. 2	In the Hour of Trial
242	Must Jesus Bear the Cross Alone?
348	"Take Up Thy Cross"
403–St. 4	We Would See Jesus; Lo! His Star

MATTHEW 16:27–28

33	At the Name of Jesus
82–St. 2	Face to Face
124–St. 5	He Keeps Me Singing
181	It May Be at Morn
189	Jesus Is Coming Again
223	Lo, He Comes with Clouds
289–St. 5	One Day
410	What If It Were Today?

MATTHEW 17:2

60	Christ, Whose Glory Fills
124–St. 3	He Keeps Me Singing
130	Heavenly Sunlight
151–St. 3	I Heard the Voice of Jesus Say
340	Sunshine in My Soul
364	The Light of the World Is Jesus

MATTHEW 17:12

| 211 | Lead Me to Calvary |
| 275 | O Sacred Head, Now Wounded |

MATTHEW 17:18

| 394–St. 2 | Victory in Jesus |

MATTHEW 17:20

| 84 | Faith Is the Victory |
| 391 | Trusting Jesus |

MATTHEW 18:3

| 36 | Away in a Manger |
| 53 | Children of the Heavenly Father |

| 320–St. 2 | Savior, Teach Me Day by Day |

MATTHEW 18:8

| 177–St. 2 | In the Hour of Trial |

MATTHEW 18:11–14

53	Children of the Heavenly Father
165–St. 2	I Will Sing the Wondrous Story
193	Jesus Loves Even Me
194	Jesus Loves Me
222–St. 4	Living for Jesus
243–St. 4	My Faith Has Found
284–St. 1	O Zion, Haste
298–St. 2	Praise Him! Praise Him!
319–St. 2	Savior, Like a Shepherd Lead Us
362–St. 3	The King of Love My Shepherd Is

MATTHEW 18:20

33	At the Name of Jesus
46	Blest Be the Tie
52	Built on the Rock
143	How Sweet the Name
156	I Love Thy Kingdom, Lord
344	Sweet, Sweet Spirit
346	Take the Name of Jesus with You

MATTHEW 19:2

155–St. 2	I Lay My Sins on Jesus
243–St. 4	My Faith Has Found
394–St. 2	Victory in Jesus

MATTHEW 19:4–6

| 119 | Happy the Home When God Is There |
| 274 | O Perfect Love |

MATTHEW 19:13–14

36	Away in a Manger
53	Children of the Heavenly Father
194	Jesus Loves Me

MATTHEW 19:21

38–St. 3	Be Thou My Vision
87	Footsteps of Jesus
148	I Have Decided to Follow Jesus
185	Jesus Calls Us
188–St. 3	Jesus Is All the World to Me
222–St. 2	Living for Jesus
419	Where Cross the Crowded Ways

MATTHEW 19:26

| 207 | Just a Closer Walk with Thee |

MATTHEW 19:26–28

| 90 | Forth in Thy Name, O Lord |
| 229 | Lord, Speak to Me |

MATTHEW 19:28

198	Jesus Shall Reign
232	Majestic Sweetness
308	Rejoice, the Lord Is King

MATTHEW 19:29

| 230 | Love Divine, All Loves Excelling |

MATTHEW 20:17–19

| 289–St. 2 | One Day |

MATTHEW 20:19

| 225–St. 3 | Look, Ye Saints! |
| 372–St. 3 | The Strife Is O'er |

MATTHEW 20:22

26	"Are Ye Able," Said the Master
211–St. 4	Lead Me to Calvary
242	Must Jesus Bear the Cross Alone?
420	Where He Leads Me

MATTHEW 20:22–23

| 370 | The Son of God Goes Forth to War |

MATTHEW 20:26–28

1	A Charge to Keep I Have
147	I Gave My Life for Thee
252	Now I Belong to Jesus
273	O Master, Let Me Walk with Thee
348	"Take Up Thy Cross"

MATTHEW 20:28

31	At Calvary
164–St. 2	I Will Sing of My Redeemer
174	In Loving Kindness Jesus Came
202	Jesus, Thy Blood and Righteousness
235	"Man of Sorrows," What a Name
289	One Day
390	To God Be the Glory
394–St. 1	Victory in Jesus
408	What a Wonderful Savior

MATTHEW 20:30–34

| 394–St. 2 | Victory in Jesus |

MATTHEW 20:33

| 292–St. 1 | Open My Eyes |

MATTHEW 20:34

| 138–St. 1 | Hope of the World |
| 230–St. 1 | Love Divine, All Loves Excelling |

MATTHEW 21:1–11

11	All Glory, Laud and Honor
139	Hosanna, Loud Hosanna
312	Ride On, Ride On in Majesty!

MATTHEW 21:5

| 155–St. 3 | I Lay My Sins on Jesus |

MATTHEW 21:9

| 118 | Hail to the Lord's Anointed |

MATTHEW 21:11

| 276–St. 2, 3 | O Sing a Song of Bethlehem |

MATTHEW 21:14

155–St. 2	I Lay My Sins on Jesus
165–St. 3	I Will Sing the Wondrous Story
243–St. 4	My Faith Has Found
263	O For a Thousand Tongues to Sing
394–St. 2	Victory in Jesus

MATTHEW 21:15–16

11	All Glory, Laud and Honor
139	Hosanna, Loud Hosanna
198	Jesus Shall Reign
324–St. 1	Shepherd of Tender Youth

MATTHEW 21:21–22

37	Be Still, My Soul
84	Faith Is the Victory
391	Trusting Jesus

MATTHEW 21:22

| 407 | What a Friend We Have in Jesus |

MATTHEW 21:31–32

| 290 | Only Trust Him |
| 389 | 'Tis So Sweet To Trust in Jesus |

MATTHEW 21:42

52	Built on the Rock
56	Christ Is Made the Sure
396–St. 1	We Are God's People

MATTHEW 22:1–4

58	Christ Receiveth Sinful Men
72	Come, Ye Sinners, Poor and Needy
315	Room at the Cross for You

368	The Savior Is Waiting
427	Whosoever Will

MATTHEW 22:1–14

208	Just As I Am, Without One Plea
331	Softly and Tenderly

MATTHEW 22:9

284	O Zion, Haste
310	Rescue the Perishing
399	We Have Heard the Joyful Sound
404	We've a Story to Tell

MATTHEW 22:16

320	Savior, Teach Me Day by Day
385–St. 2	Thou Art the Way: to Thee Alone

MATTHEW 22:18

159–St. 2	I Need Thee Every Hour

MATTHEW 22:29

48	Break Thou the Bread
103	God Moves in a Mysterious Way
282	O Word of God Incarnate

MATTHEW 22:37–39

10	All for Jesus
65	Come, Holy Spirit
163	I Surrender All
169	I'll Live for Him
240	More Love to Thee, O Christ
245	My Jesus, I Love Thee
262	O For a Heart to Praise My God
313–St. 1	Rise Up, O Men of God
320	Savior, Teach Me Day by Day
334	Spirit of God, Descend
345	Take My Life and Let It Be
421–St. 4	Wherever He Leads, I'll Go

MATTHEW 22:42

75–St. 2	Crown Him with Many Crowns
142–St. 2	How Great Thou Art
384–St. 3	This Is the Day

MATTHEW 23:8–12

46	Blest Be the Tie
166	I Would Be True
171–Last St.	Immortal Love, Forever Full
172	In Christ There Is No East
206–St. 3	Joyful, Joyful, We Adore Thee
222	Living for Jesus
268	O Jesus, I Have Promised

273	O Master, Let Me Walk with Thee
291–St. 1	Onward, Christian Soldiers
421–St. 4	Wherever He Leads, I'll Go
432	Ye Servants of God

MATTHEW 23:23

321	Savior, Thy Dying Love
345	Take My Life and Let It Be
398	We Give Thee but Thine Own

MATTHEW 23:34

370	The Son of God Goes Forth to War

MATTHEW 23:37

10–St. 4	All for Jesus
53	Children of the Heavenly Father
109	God Will Take Care of You
393	Under His Wings
419	Where Cross the Crowded Ways

MATTHEW 23:39

33	At the Name of Jesus
43	Blessed Be the Name

MATTHEW 24:13

20	Am I a Soldier of the Cross?
35	Awake, My Soul, Stretch
212	Lead On, O King Eternal
242	Must Jesus Bear the Cross Alone
337	Stand Up, Stand Up for Jesus

MATTHEW 24:14

55	Christ for the World We Sing
138	Hope of the World
284	O Zion, Haste
322	Send the Light
399	We Have Heard the Joyful Sound
404	We've a Story to Tell

MATTHEW 24:27–44

33–St. 5	At the Name of Jesus
107–St. 1	God the Almighty One
124–St. 5	He Keeps Me Singing
154–St. 4	I Know Whom I Have Believed
180–St. 4	It Is Well with My Soul
181–St. 2	It May Be at Morn
189	Jesus Is Coming Again
223	Lo, He Comes with Clouds
289–St. 5	One Day
298–St. 3	Praise Him! Praise Him!
363	The King Shall Come When Morning
410	What If It Were Today?

416	When the Roll Is Called

MATTHEW 24:35

66–St. 2	Come, Thou Almighty King
133	Holy Bible, Book Divine
141–St. 1	How Firm a Foundation
153–St. 2	I Know That My Redeemer Liveth
282	O Word of God Incarnate
389–St. 1	'Tis So Sweet To Trust in Jesus
430	Wonderful Words of Life

MATTHEW 24:50

154–St. 4	I Know Whom I Have Believed
410	What If It Were Today?

MATTHEW 25:1–13

27–St. 3	Are You Washed in the Blood
154–St. 4	I Know Whom I Have Believed
181	It May Be at Morn
189	Jesus Is Coming Again
410	What If It Were Today?

MATTHEW 25:21

40–St. 4	Begin, My Tongue, Some Heavenly
42	Blessed Assurance
321–St. 4	Savior, Thy Dying Love

MATTHEW 25:24–30

419	Where Cross the Crowded Ways

MATTHEW 25:31

75	Crown Him with Many Crowns
181	It May Be at Morn
225	Look, Ye Saints!
232	Majestic Sweetness
298–St. 3	Praise Him! Praise Him!
363	The King Shall Come When Morning
432–St. 3	Ye Servants of God

MATTHEW 25:31–34

235–St. 5	"Man of Sorrows," What a Name
410	What If It Were Today?

MATTHEW 25:31–46

223	Lo, He Comes with Clouds

MATTHEW 25:34

190	Jesus Is Tenderly Calling
279	O That Will Be Glory For Me
294–St. 4	Out of My Bondage

MATTHEW 25:34–46

121	Hark, the Voice of Jesus Calling
206–St. 3	Joyful, Joyful, We Adore Thee
233	Make Me a Blessing
313	Rise Up, O Men of God
330	So Send I You
419	Where Cross the Crowded Ways

MATTHEW 25:46

286	On Jordan's Stormy Banks I Stand
417	When We All Get to Heaven

MATTHEW 26:26

48	Break Thou the Bread

MATTHEW 26:26–29

6	According to Thy Gracious Word
47	Bread of the World
131	Here, O My Lord, I See Thee
217	Let Us Break Bread Together

MATTHEW 26:28

27	Are You Washed in the Blood
80	Down at the Cross
91–St. 1	Free From the Law
117–St. 2	Hail, Thou Once Despised Jesus
202	Jesus, Thy Blood and Righteousness
235–St. 2	"Man of Sorrows," What a Name
251	Nothing But the Blood
267–St. 2	O, How I Love Jesus
376	There Is a Fountain
378	There Is Power in the Blood

MATTHEW 26:30

414	When in Our Music

MATTHEW 26:31–32

319	Savior, Like a Shepherd Lead Us
362–St. 3	The King of Love My Shepherd Is

MATTHEW 26:32

126	He Lives

MATTHEW 26:34

177–St. 1	In the Hour of Trial
188–St. 3	Jesus Is All the World to Me

MATTHEW 26:36

177–St. 2	In the Hour of Trial

MATTHEW 26:36–45

99–St. 1	Go to Dark Gethsemane

162–St. 2   I Stand Amazed in the Presence
388   'Tis Midnight and on Olive's Brow
425–St. 4   Who Is He in Yonder Stall?

MATTHEW 26:36–68

211   Lead Me to Calvary
275   O Sacred Head, Now Wounded
420–St. 2   Where He Leads Me

MATTHEW 26:39

26   "Are Ye Able," Said the Master
122   Have Thine Own Way, Lord
211–St. 4   Lead Me to Calvary

MATTHEW 26:39–41

177   In the Hour of Trial
305   Prayer Is the Soul's Sincere
343   Sweet Hour of Prayer
407   What a Friend We Have in Jesus

MATTHEW 26:42

211–St. 4   Lead Me to Calvary

MATTHEW 26:47–75

99–St. 2   Go to Dark Gethsemane

MATTHEW 26:57–68

420–St. 3   Where He Leads Me

MATTHEW 26:63–64

308   Rejoice, the Lord Is King

MATTHEW 26:64

181   It May Be at Morn
189   Jesus Is Coming Again
363   The King Shall Come When Morning
410   What If It Were Today?

MATTHEW 26:69–75

177–St. 1   In the Hour of Trial

MATTHEW 27:1–31

99–St. 2   Go to Dark Gethsemane

MATTHEW 27:1–66

211   Lead Me to Calvary
351–St. 3   Tell Me the Story of Jesus

MATTHEW 27:11–26

420–St. 3   Where He Leads Me

MATTHEW 27:24–54

7   Ah, Holy Jesus
8   Alas! And Did My Savior Bleed?
32   At the Cross
117   Hail, Thou Once Despised Jesus
275   O Sacred Head, Now Wounded
289–St. 2   One Day
298–St. 2   Praise Him! Praise Him!
360   The Head That Once Was Crowned
406   Were You There?

MATTHEW 27:29–31

28–St. 3   Are You (Art Thou) Weary
225–St. 3   Look, Ye Saints!
275–St. 1   O Sacred Head, Now Wounded
413–St. 3   When I Survey the Wondrous Cross

MATTHEW 27:31–50

99–St. 3   Go to Dark Gethsemane

MATTHEW 27:32–33

41   Beneath the Cross of Jesus
367   The Old Rugged Cross

MATTHEW 27:54

75–St. 2   Crown Him with Many Crowns
235   "Man of Sorrows," What a Name

MATTHEW 27:57–66

54   Christ Arose
99–St. 4   Go to Dark Gethsemane
211–St. 2   Lead Me to Calvary
289–St. 3   One Day
406   Were You There?

MATTHEW 28:1–10

39   Because He Lives
43   Blessed Be the Name
54   Christ Arose
59   Christ the Lord Is Risen Today
62   Come, Christians, Join to Sing
71   Come, Ye Faithful, Raise
99–St. 4   Go to Dark Gethsemane
111   Good Christian Men, Rejoice and Sing
126   He Lives
152   I Know That My Redeemer Lives
153   I Know That My Redeemer Liveth
186   Jesus Christ Is Risen Today
211–St. 3   Lead Me to Calvary
277   O Sons and Daughters
289–St. 4   One Day

351–St. 3	Tell Me the Story of Jesus
355	The Day of Resurrection
382	Thine Is the Glory
384	This Is the Day
399	We Have Heard the Joyful Sound
405	Welcome, Happy Morning
415	When Morning Gilds the Skies

MATTHEW 28:18

12	All Hail the Power of Jesus' Name
43	Blessed Be the Name
75	Crown Him with Many Crowns
198	Jesus Shall Reign
232	Majestic Sweetness
298–St. 3	Praise Him! Praise Him!
308	Rejoice, the Lord Is King
425–St. 5	Who Is He in Yonder Stall?

MATTHEW 28:19

66	Come, Thou Almighty King
284	O Zion, Haste
322	Send the Light
373	The Vision of a Dying World

MATTHEW 28:19–20

55	Christ for the World We Sing
168	I'll Go Where You Want Me To Go
229	Lord, Speak to Me
310	Rescue the Perishing
404	We've a Story to Tell

MATTHEW 28:20

126	He Lives
201–St. 4	Jesus, Thou Joy of Loving Hearts
250	No, Not One
365–St. 3	The Lily of the Valley
389–St. 4	'Tis So Sweet To Trust in Jesus

MARK 1:1–3

68	Come, Thou Long-Expected Jesus
118	Hail to the Lord's Anointed
220	Lift Up Your Heads

MARK 1:1–12

171	Immortal Love, Forever Full
394	Victory in Jesus

MARK 1:8

135	Holy Spirit, Light Divine
335	Spirit of the Living God
354	The Comforter Has Come

MARK 1:8–10

49	Breathe on Me, Breath of God

MARK 1:8–13

271–St. 2	O Love How Deep, How Broad
351–St. 2	Tell Me the Story of Jesus

MARK 1:10

65	Come, Holy Spirit
333	Spirit Divine, Attend Our Prayer

MARK 1:11

83	Fairest Lord Jesus

MARK 1:15–20

78	Dear Lord and Father of Mankind
121	Hark, the Voice of Jesus Calling
185	Jesus Calls Us
268	O Jesus, I Have Promised
290	Only Trust Him
403–St. 4	We Would See Jesus; Lo! His Star

MARK 1:32–42

155–St. 2	I Lay My Sins on Jesus
171	Immortal Love, Forever Full
238	Moment by Moment
243–St. 4	My Faith Has Found
263	O For a Thousand Tongues to Sing
359–St. 1	The Great Physician
394–St. 2	Victory in Jesus

MARK 1:35

305	Prayer Is the Soul's Sincere
343	Sweet Hour of Prayer

MARK 1:39–42

55–St. 1	Christ for the World We Sing
138–St. 1	Hope of the World
192–St. 3	Jesus, Lover of My Soul
195–St. 2	Jesus Paid it All
230–St. 1	Love Divine, All Loves Excelling
250–St. 1	No, Not One
359–St. 1	The Great Physician

MARK 2:1–12

155	I Lay My Sins on Jesus
162–St. 1	I Stand Amazed in the Presence
165–St. 3	I Will Sing the Wondrous Story
192	Jesus, Lover of My Soul
263	O For a Thousand Tongues to Sing
359–St. 2	The Great Physician

MARK 2:14

78–St. 2	Dear Lord and Father of Mankind
148	I Have Decided to Follow Jesus
222–St. 2	Living for Jesus
403–St. 4	We Would See Jesus; Lo! His Star
420	Where He Leads Me
421	Wherever He Leads, I'll Go

MARK 2:16

204	Jesus, What a Friend for Sinners

MARK 2:17

58	Christ Receiveth Sinful Men
72	Come, Ye Sinners, Poor and Needy
190	Jesus Is Tenderly Calling
200–St. 3	Jesus, the Very Thought of Thee
208	Just As I Am, Without One Plea
222–St. 2	Living for Jesus
331	Softly and Tenderly
368	The Savior Is Waiting

MARK 2:27–28

260	O Day of Rest and Gladness
384	This Is the Day

MARK 3:1–10

192–St. 3	Jesus, Lover of My Soul
394–St. 2	Victory in Jesus

MARK 3:11

83	Fairest Lord Jesus
235	"Man of Sorrows," What a Name

MARK 3:35

145–St. 2	I Am Thine, O Lord
313–St. 4	Rise Up, O Men of God

MARK 4:2

320	Savior, Teach Me Day by Day

MARK 4:9

190	Jesus Is Tenderly Calling
292	Open My Eyes

MARK 4:11

103	God Moves in a Mysterious Way
137–St. 3	Holy, Holy, Holy

MARK 4:23

190	Jesus Is Tenderly Calling
292	Open My Eyes

MARK 4:26–29

73	Come, Ye Thankful People, Come

MARK 4:35–41

37–St. 2	Be Still, My Soul
81	Eternal Father, Strong to Save
197	Jesus Savior, Pilot Me
204–St. 4	Jesus, What a Friend for Sinners
231	Love Lifted Me

MARK 4:38–41

17	All the Way My Savior Leads Me
96	Give to the Winds
104–St. 2	God of Grace and God of Glory
109	God Will Take Care of You
158	I Must Tell Jesus
159–St. 2	I Need Thee Every Hour
297	Peace, Perfect Peace
391	Trusting Jesus

MARK 5:15

78–St. 1	Dear Lord and Father of Mankind

MARK 5:19–20

16	All That Thrills My Soul
157	I Love to Tell the Story
230–St. 1	Love Divine, All Loves Excelling
246	My Tribute
350	Tell Me the Old, Old Story
390	To God Be the Glory

MARK 5:21–43

155–St. 2	I Lay My Sins on Jesus
171	Immortal Love, Forever Full
238	Moment by Moment
394–St. 2	Victory in Jesus

MARK 5:34

243–St. 4	My Faith Has Found
424	Whiter Than Snow

MARK 5:36

86–St. 4	Fight the Good Fight
310–St. 2	Rescue the Perishing
359–St. 3	The Great Physician

MARK 6:12–13

72	Come, Ye Sinners, Poor and Needy
394	Victory in Jesus

MARK 6:34

230–St. 1	Love Divine, All Loves Excelling

319	Savior, Like a Shepherd Lead Us
324	Shepherd of Tender Youth
341	Surely Goodness and Mercy
362	The King of Love My Shepherd Is
366	The Lord's My Shepherd

MARK 6:35–44

| 48 | Break Thou the Bread |

MARK 6:45–51

| 197 | Jesus Savior, Pilot Me |

MARK 6:51

| 162–St. 1 | I Stand Amazed in the Presence |

MARK 6:55–57

171	Immortal Love, Forever Full
238	Moment by Moment
243–St. 4	My Faith Has Found
263	O For a Thousand Tongues to Sing
394–St. 2	Victory in Jesus

MARK 7:6

| 262 | O For a Heart to Praise My God |
| 424 | Whiter Than Snow |

MARK 7:16

| 190 | Jesus Is Tenderly Calling |
| 238 | Moment by Moment |

MARK 7:20–21

| 262 | O For a Heart to Praise My God |
| 424 | Whiter Than Snow |

MARK 7:31–37

238	Moment by Moment
243–St. 4	My Faith Has Found
263–St. 4	O For a Thousand Tongues to Sing
394–St. 2	Victory in Jesus

MARK 8:2

| 230–St. 1 | Love Divine, All Loves Excelling |

MARK 8:18

| 292 | Open My Eyes |

MARK 8:22–25

243–St. 4	My Faith Has Found
263	O For a Thousand Tongues to Sing
394–St. 2	Victory in Jesus

MARK 8:29

| 75 | Crown Him with Many Crowns |
| 83 | Fairest Lord Jesus |

MARK 8:31

7	Ah, Holy Jesus
8	Alas! And Did My Savior Bleed?
235	"Man of Sorrows," What a Name
275	O Sacred Head, Now Wounded
289–St. 2	One Day
351–St. 2	Tell Me the Story of Jesus

MARK 8:34–38

26	"Are Ye Able," Said the Master
121	Hark, the Voice of Jesus Calling
148	I Have Decided to Follow Jesus
185	Jesus Calls Us
187	Jesus, I My Cross Have Taken
188–St. 3	Jesus Is All the World to Me
211–St. 4	Lead Me to Calvary
222	Living for Jesus
242	Must Jesus Bear the Cross Alone
268	O Jesus; I Have Promised
348	"Take Up Thy Cross"
370	The Son of God Goes Forth to War
374	The Way of the Cross Leads Home
403–St. 4	We Would See Jesus, Lo! His Star
420	Where He Leads Me
421	Wherever He Leads, I'll Go

MARK 9:22

| 228 | Lord Jesus, Think on Me |

MARK 9:23

| 389 | 'Tis So Sweet To Trust in Jesus |

MARK 9:23–24

60–St. 3	Christ Whose Glory Fills
84	Faith Is the Victory
359–St. 3	The Great Physician

MARK 9:24

290	Only Trust Him
296–St. 2	Pass Me Not, O Gentle Savior
310–St. 2	Rescue the Perishing

MARK 9:29

| 407 | What a Friend We Have in Jesus |

MARK 9:35

| 273 | O Master, Let Me Walk with Thee |
| 313 | Rise Up, O Men of God |

348	"Take Up Thy Cross"	286	On Jordan's Stormy Banks I Stand

MARK 9:37

204–St. 5   Jesus, What a Friend for Sinners

MARK 9:41

268   O Jesus, I Have Promised
419   Where Cross the Crowded Ways

MARK 10:7–9

119   Happy the Home When God Is There
274   O Perfect Love

MARK 10:13–16

36   Away in a Manger

MARK 10:14

194   Jesus Loves Me
320–St. 2   Savior, Teach Me Day by Day
324–St. 1   Shepherd of Tender Youth

MARK 10:16

72   Come, Ye Sinners, Poor and Needy
165–St. 2   I Will Sing the Wondrous Story

MARK 10:21

26   "Are Ye Able," Said the Master
41   Beneath the Cross of Jesus
90   Forth in Thy Name, O Lord
148   I Have Decided to Follow Jesus
185   Jesus Calls Us
187   Jesus, I My Cross Have Taken
211–St. 4   Lead Me to Calvary
222   Living for Jesus
268   O Jesus, I Have Promised
320   Savior, Teach Me Day by Day
403–St. 4   We Would See Jesus; Lo! His Star
419   Where Cross the Crowded Ways
420   Where He Leads Me
421   Wherever He Leads, I'll Go

MARK 10:24–25

74–St. 3   Count Your Blessings

MARK 10:28–30

10   All for Jesus
26   "Are Ye Able," Said the Master
148   I Have Decided to Follow Jesus
163   I Surrender All
182   I've Found a Friend
187   Jesus, I My Cross Have Taken
222   Living for Jesus

286	On Jordan's Stormy Banks I Stand
345	Take My Life and Let It Be
418	When We Walk with the Lord

MARK 10:32

17   All the Way My Savior Leads Me
162–St. 1   I Stand Amazed in the Presence

MARK 10:33–34

225–St. 3   Look, Ye Saints!

MARK 10:38–39

26   "Are Ye Able," Said the Master
211–St. 4   Lead Me to Calvary
370   The Son of God Goes Forth to War

MARK 10:43–45

1   A Charge to Keep I Have
233   Make Me a Blessing
273   O Master, Let Me Walk with Thee

MARK 10:45

147   I Gave My Life for Thee
164–St. 2   I Will Sing of My Redeemer
202   Jesus, Thy Blood and Righteousness
235   "Man of Sorrows," What a Name
252   Now I Belong to Jesus
351   Tell Me the Story of Jesus
408   What a Wonderful Savior

MARK 10:46–52

192–St. 3   Jesus, Lover of My Soul
208   Just As I Am, Without One Plea
238   Moment by Moment
243–St. 4   My Faith Has Found
263   O For a Thousand Tongues to Sing
359–St. 1   The Great Physician
394–St. 2   Victory in Jesus

MARK 10:49

185   Jesus Calls Us
190   Jesus Is Tenderly Calling

MARK 10:52

148   I Have Decided to Follow Jesus

MARK 11:1–10

11   All Glory, Laud and Honor
139   Hosanna, Loud Hosanna
312   Ride On, Ride On in Majesty!

MARK 11:22

| 17 | All the Way My Savior Leads Me |
| 244 | My Faith Looks Up to Thee |

MARK 11:24

305	Prayer Is the Soul's Sincere
343	Sweet Hour of Prayer
407	What a Friend We Have in Jesus

MARK 12:10–11

52	Built on the Rock
56	Christ Is Made the Sure
353	The Church's One Foundation

MARK 12:24

| 48 | Break Thou the Bread |

MARK 12:29

| 57–St. 3 | Christ Is the World's |
| 253–St. 3 | Now Thank We All Our God |

MARK 12:30–34

10	All for Jesus
57–St. 3	Christ Is the World's
65	Come, Holy Spirit
163	I Surrender All
169	I'll Live for Him
185	Jesus Calls Us
222	Living for Jesus
240	More Love to Thee, O Christ
245	My Jesus, I Love Thee
262	O For a Heart to Praise My God
320	Savior, Teach Me Day by Day
321	Savior, Thy Dying Love
334	Spirit of God, Descend
432	Ye Servants of God

MARK 12:42–44

18	All Things Are Thine
147	I Gave My Life for Thee
321	Savior, Thy Dying Love
345	Take My Life and Let It Be
398	We Give Thee but Thine Own

MARK 13:8

| 141–St. 3 | How Firm a Foundation |

MARK 13:10

55	Christ for the World We Sing
284	O Zion, Haste
310	Rescue the Perishing
373	The Vision of a Dying World

| 399 | We Have Heard the Joyful Sound |
| 404 | We've a Story to Tell |

MARK 13:11

| 63 | Come, Holy Ghost |
| 292–St. 3 | Open My Eyes |

MARK 13:26–37

154–St. 4	I Know Whom I Have Believed
181	It May Be at Morn
189	Jesus Is Coming Again
223	Lo, He Comes with Clouds
289–St. 4	One Day
363	The King Shall Come When Morning
410	What If It Were Today?

MARK 13:31

66	Come, Thou Almighty King
141	How Firm a Foundation
153–St. 2	I Know That My Redeemer Liveth
282	O Word of God Incarnate
290	Only Trust Him
430	Wonderful Words of Life

MARK 14:22

| 48 | Break Thou the Bread |

MARK 14:22–25

6	According to Thy Gracious Word
47	Bread of the World
131	Here, O My Lord, I See Thee
217	Let Us Break Bread Together

MARK 14:24

27	Are You Washed in the Blood
202	Jesus, Thy Blood and Righteousness
235–St. 2	"Man of Sorrows," What a Name
251	Nothing But the Blood
267–St. 2	O, How I Love Jesus
290–St. 2	Only Trust Him
378	There Is Power in the Blood

MARK 14:26

| 414 | When in Our Music |

MARK 14:30–31

| 177–St. 1 | In the Hour of Trial |

MARK 14:32

| 177–St. 2 | In the Hour of Trial |

MARK 14:32–34

425–St. 4	Who Is He in Yonder Stall?

MARK 14:32–36

162	I Stand Amazed in the Presence

MARK 14:32–41

99–St. 1	Go to Dark Gethsemane
388	'Tis Midnight and on Olive's Brow

MARK 14:32–50

420–St. 2	Where He Leads Me

MARK 14:38

177	In the Hour of Trial

MARK 14:42–65

99–St. 2	Go to Dark Gethsemane

MARK 14:53–65

420–St. 3	Where He Leads Me

MARK 14:62

181	It May Be at Morn
189	Jesus Is Coming Again
223	Lo, He Comes with Clouds
225	Look, Ye Saints!
298–St. 3	Praise Him! Praise Him!
308	Rejoice, the Lord Is King
363	The King Shall Come When Morning
410	What If It Were Today?

MARK 14:66–72

177	In the Hour of Trial

MARK 15:1–15

99–St. 2	Go to Dark Gethsemane
420–St. 3	Where He Leads Me

MARK 15:1–39

7	Ah, Holy Jesus
32	At the Cross

MARK 15:1–47

211	Lead Me to Calvary
351–St. 3	Tell Me the Story of Jesus

MARK 15:15–37

275	O Sacred Head, Now Wounded
289–St. 2	One Day

MARK 15:15–47

406	Were You There?

MARK 15:16–19

225–St. 3	Look, Ye Saints!
360	The Head That Once Was Crowned

MARK 15:20–38

99–St. 3	Go to Dark Gethsemane

MARK 15:21–22

211	Lead Me to Calvary
367	The Old Rugged Cross

MARK 15:25

41	Beneath the Cross of Jesus

MARK 15:39

235	"Man of Sorrows," What a Name

MARK 15:40–47

99–St. 4	Go to Dark Gethsemane
211–St. 2	Lead Me to Calvary
289–St. 3	One Day

MARK 15:46–47

54	Christ Arose

MARK 16:1–6

39	Because He Lives
54	Christ Arose
59	Christ the Lord Is Risen Today
71	Come, Ye Faithful, Raise
99–St. 4	Go to Dark Gethsemane
126	He Lives
152	I Know That My Redeemer Lives
153	I Know That My Redeemer Liveth
186	Jesus Christ Is Risen Today
289–St. 4	One Day
351–St. 3	Tell Me the Story of Jesus
355	The Day of Resurrection
372	The Strife Is O'er
382	Thine Is the Glory

MARK 16:1–8

211–St. 3	Lead Me to Calvary
277	O Sons and Daughters
384	This Is the Day
405	Welcome, Happy Morning

MARK 16:2

260–St. 2	O Day of Rest and Gladness

MARK 16:15–16

21	Amazing Grace
55	Christ for the World We Sing
86–St. 4	Fight the Good Fight
154–St. 2	I Know Whom I Have Believed
168	I'll Go Where You Want Me To Go
284	O Zion, Haste
290	Only Trust Him
310	Rescue the Perishing
322	Send the Light
359–St. 3	The Great Physician
373	The Vision of a Dying World
399	We Have Heard the Joyful Sound
404	We've a Story to Tell

MARK 16:19

43–St. 2	Blessed Be the Name
116	Hail the Day That Sees Him Rise
225	Look, Ye Saints!
232	Majestic Sweetness
289–St. 4	One Day

LUKE 1:14

13	All My Heart This Night

LUKE 1:26–38

68	Come, Thou Long-Expected Jesus
95	Gentle Mary Laid Her Child
120	Hark! The Herald Angels Sing
270–St. 2	O Little Town of Bethlehem

LUKE 1:30–33

94	From Heaven Above to Earth
289–St. 1	One Day

LUKE 1:31–33

43	Blessed Be the Name
118	Hail to the Lord's Anointed
143	How Sweet the Name

LUKE 1:32–33

75	Crown Him with Many Crowns
83	Fairest Lord Jesus
184–St. 3	Jerusalem, the Golden
198	Jesus Shall Reign
235	"Man of Sorrows," What a Name
257	O Come, O Come, Emmanuel
258	O Could I Speak the Matchless
308	Rejoice, the Lord Is King
357–Refrain	The First Noel
432–St. 3	Ye Servants of God

LUKE 1:33–35

120–St. 2	Hark! The Herald Angels Sing

LUKE 1:35

83	Fairest Lord Jesus

LUKE 1:46–55

205	Joy to the World

LUKE 1:47

201	Jesus, Thou Joy of Loving Hearts
235	"Man of Sorrows," What a Name
308	Rejoice, the Lord Is King

LUKE 1:49–50

107	God the Almighty One

LUKE 1:50

79	Depth of Mercy! Can There Be
319–St. 3	Savior, Like a Shepherd Lead Us
381	There's a Wideness
412	When All Thy Mercies, O My God

LUKE 1:54–55

105	God of Our Fathers

LUKE 1:68–69

42	Blessed Assurance
164	I Will Sing of My Redeemer
205	Joy to the World
246	My Tribute
256	O Come, All Ye Faithful
380	There's a Song in the Air
390	To God Be the Glory
401	We Praise Thee, O God

LUKE 1:68–73

68	Come, Thou Long-Expected Jesus
114	Great Is Thy Faithfulness

LUKE 1:74–75

347	Take Time to Be Holy

LUKE 1:76–79

214	Let All Mortal Flesh

LUKE 1:77–79

60	Christ Whose Glory Fills
120–St. 3	Hark! The Herald Angels Sing
325	Silent Night! Holy Night
364	The Light of the World Is Jesus

LUKE 1:78–79

57	Christ Is the World's
125	He Leadeth Me
257–St. 3	O Come, O Come, Emmanuel
381	There's a Wideness
387	Thou Whose Almighty Word

LUKE 1:79

75–St. 4	Crown Him with Many Crowns
102	God Is My Strong Salvation
151–St. 3	I Heard the Voice of Jesus Say
165–St. 4	I Will Sing the Wondrous Story
201	Jesus, Thou Joy of Loving Hearts
297	Peace, Perfect Peace
318–St. 4	Savior, Again to Thy Dear Name
340	Sunshine in My Soul

LUKE 2:1–7

68	Come, Thou Long-Expected Jesus
270	O Little Town of Bethlehem
289–St. 1	One Day
386	Thou Didst Leave Thy Throne

LUKE 2:1–20

178	Infant Holy, Infant Lowly
256	O Come, All Ye Faithful
285	Of the Father's Love Begotten
422	While By the Sheep

LUKE 2:4–7

287	Once in Royal David's City

LUKE 2:4–20

276	O Sing a Song of Bethlehem

LUKE 2:6–20

409	What Child Is This?
425–St. 1	Who Is He in Yonder Stall?

LUKE 2:7

36	Away in a Manger
403–St. 1	We Would See Jesus; Lo! His Star

LUKE 2:7–14

94	From Heaven Above to Earth

LUKE 2:7–20

13	All My Heart This Night
24	Angels from the Realms of Glory
25	Angels We Have Heard on High
95	Gentle Mary Laid Her Child
179	It Came Upon a Midnight Clear

325	Silent Night! Holy Night
380	There's a Song in the Air

LUKE 2:8–14

179	It Came Upon a Midnight Clear
423	While Shepherds Watched

LUKE 2:8–20

98	Go, Tell It on the Mountain
357	The First Noel

LUKE 2:10–11

120	Hark! The Herald Angels Sing

LUKE 2:10–20

110	Good Christian Men, Rejoice

LUKE 2:11

13	All My Heart This Night
205	Joy to the World
270	O Little Town of Bethlehem

LUKE 2:11–12

287	Once in Royal David's City

LUKE 2:12

36	Away in a Manger

LUKE 2:13–14

120	Hark! The Herald Angels Sing
351	Tell Me the Story of Jesus
403–St. 1	We Would See Jesus; Lo! His Star

LUKE 2:14

25	Angels We Have Heard on High
150	I Heard the Bells on Christmas

LUKE 2:16

36	Away in a Manger

LUKE 2:21

43	Blessed Be the Name
143	How Sweet the Name

LUKE 2:29–32

364	The Light of the World Is Jesus
380	There's a Song in the Air

LUKE 2:32

60	Christ, Whose Glory Fills
151–St. 3	I Heard the Voice of Jesus Say
257–St. 3	O Come, O Come, Emmanuel

322	Send the Light!

LUKE 2:39

276–St. 2	O Sing a Song of Bethlehem

LUKE 2:40

287	Once in Royal David's City

LUKE 2:51

276–St. 2	O Sing a Song of Bethlehem

LUKE 2:52

287	Once in Royal David's City
403–St. 2	We Would See Jesus; Lo! His Star

LUKE 3:5

82–St. 3	Face to Face
124–St. 4	He Keeps Me Singing

LUKE 3:16

140	Hover O'er Me, Holy Spirit
333	Spirit Divine, Attend Our Prayer
354	The Comforter Has Come

LUKE 3:21–22

64	Come, Holy Spirit, Dove Divine
271–St. 2	O Love How Deep, How Broad

LUKE 3:22

63	Come, Holy Ghost
65	Come, Holy Spirit
333	Spirit Divine, Attend Our Prayer

LUKE 4:1–2

425–St. 1	Who Is He in Yonder Stall?

LUKE 4:1–14

271–St. 2	O Love How Deep, How Broad
351–St. 2	Tell Me the Story of Jesus

LUKE 4:4

48	Break Thou the Bread
133	Holy Bible, Book Divine
347–St. 1	Take Time to Be Holy
361	The Heavens Declare Thy Glory
430	Wonderful Words of Life

LUKE 4:8

358	The God of Abraham Praise

LUKE 4:12–13

159–St. 2	I Need Thee Every Hour

LUKE 4:16

260	O Day of Rest and Gladness
276–St. 2	O Sing a Song of Bethlehem

LUKE 4:18

165–St. 3	I Will Sing the Wondrous Story
238	Moment by Moment
243	My Faith Has Found
294	Out of My Bondage
310	Rescue the Perishing
330	So Send I You
375	There Is a Balm in Gilead
394–St. 2	Victory in Jesus

LUKE 4:22

425–St. 2	Who Is He in Yonder Stall?

LUKE 4:32

66–St. 2	Come, Thou Almighty King
389–St. 1	'Tis So Sweet To Trust in Jesus
430	Wonderful Words of Life

LUKE 4:33–41

155–St. 2	I Lay My Sins on Jesus
171	Immortal Love, Forever Full
243–St. 4	My Faith Has Found
394–St. 2	Victory in Jesus

LUKE 4:36

162–St. 1	I Stand Amazed in the Presence

LUKE 4:41

83	Fairest Lord Jesus
235	"Man of Sorrows," What a Name

LUKE 5:3

320	Savior, Teach Me Day by Day

LUKE 5:8

192–St. 3	Jesus, Lover of My Soul

LUKE 5:10–11

78–St. 2	Dear Lord and Father of Mankind

LUKE 5:11

10	All for Jesus
26	"Are Ye Able," Said the Master
87	Footsteps of Jesus
163	I Surrender All
187	Jesus, I My Cross Have Taken
222	Living for Jesus

LUKE 5:12–26

155–St. 2	I Lay My Sins on Jesus
243–St. 4	My Faith Has Found
359	The Great Physician
394–St. 2	Victory in Jesus

LUKE 5:17

165–St. 3	I Will Sing the Wondrous Story
192–St. 3	Jesus, Lover of My Soul

LUKE 5:20–24

165–St. 3	I Will Sing the Wondrous Story
192–St. 3	Jesus, Lover of My Soul
263	O For a Thousand Tongues to Sing

LUKE 5:26

162–St. 1	I Stand Amazed in the Presence

LUKE 5:27

222–St. 2	Living for Jesus
403–St. 4	We Would See Jesus; Lo! His Star

LUKE 5:27–28

87	Footsteps of Jesus
148	I Have Decided to Follow Jesus
163	I Surrender All
185	Jesus Calls Us
268	O Jesus, I Have Promised
420	Where He Leads Me
421	Wherever He Leads, I'll Go

LUKE 5:30–32

204	Jesus, What a Friend for Sinners

LUKE 5:32

58	Christ Receiveth Sinful Men
72	Come, Ye Sinners, Poor and Needy
151	I Heard the Voice of Jesus Say
185	Jesus Calls Us
190	Jesus Is Tenderly Calling
216	Let Jesus Come Into Your Heart
222–St. 2	Living for Jesus
331	Softly and Tenderly
368	The Savior Is Waiting

LUKE 6:1–9

260	O Day of Rest and Gladness

LUKE 6:12

78–St. 3	Dear Lord and Father of Mankind
305	Prayer Is the Soul's Sincere
343	Sweet Hour of Prayer

LUKE 6:17–19

155–St. 2	I Lay My Sins on Jesus
165–St. 3	I Will Sing the Wondrous Story
171	Immortal Love, Forever Full
192–St. 3	Jesus, Lover of My Soul
208–St. 4	Just As I Am, Without One Plea
238	Moment by Moment
243–St. 4	My Faith Has Found
250–St. 1	No, Not One
359–St. 1	The Great Physician
394–St. 2	Victory in Jesus

LUKE 6:21

238	Moment by Moment
316	Satisfied

LUKE 6:23

279	O That Will Be Glory For Me
286	On Jordan's Stormy Banks I Stand

LUKE 6:24

74–St. 3	Count Your Blessings

LUKE 6:36

218	Let Us with a Gladsome Mind
381	There's a Wideness
412	When All Thy Mercies, O My God

LUKE 6:38

398	We Give Thee but Thine Own

LUKE 6:40

273	O Master, Let Me Walk with Thee
349	Teach Me Thy Way, O Lord

LUKE 6:45

262	O For a Heart to Praise My God
334	Spirit of God, Descend
424	Whiter Than Snow

LUKE 6:46–49

141	How Firm a Foundation
167–St. 1	If Thou But Suffer God to Guide
171–Last St.	Immortal Love, Forever Full
185	Jesus Calls Us
292	Open My Eyes
321	Savior, Thy Dying Love
349	Teach Me Thy Way, O Lord
418	When We Walk with the Lord

LUKE 7:13

230–St. 1	Love Divine, All Loves Excelling

359–St. 1	The Great Physician
419	Where Cross the Crowded Ways

LUKE 7:16

162	I Stand Amazed in the Presence

LUKE 7:21–22

165–St. 3	I Will Sing the Wondrous Story
192–St. 3	Jesus, Lover of My Soul
208–St. 4	Just As I Am, Without One Plea
238	Moment by Moment
243–St. 4	My Faith Has Found
250–St. 1	No, Not One
263–St. 4	O For a Thousand Tongues to Sing
359–St. 1	The Great Physician
394–St. 2	Victory in Jesus

LUKE 7:34

182	I've Found a Friend
204	Jesus, What a Friend for Sinners
250	No, Not One
365–St. 1	The Lily of the Valley
407	What a Friend We Have in Jesus

LUKE 7:41–50

23	And Can It Be That I Should Gain
112	Grace Greater Than Our Sin
252	Now I Belong to Jesus
263–St. 3	O For a Thousand Tongues to Sing
267	O, How I Love Jesus
359–St. 2	The Great Physician
413–St. 4	When I Survey the Wondrous Cross

LUKE 8:8–10

190	Jesus Is Tenderly Calling
292	Open My Eyes

LUKE 8:11

48	Break Thou the Bread

LUKE 8:14

177	In the Hour of Trial

LUKE 8:15

273–St. 3	O Master, Let Me Walk with Thee
430	Wonderful Words of Life

LUKE 8:21

171–Last St.	Immortal Love, Forever Full
206–St. 3	Joyful, Joyful, We Adore Thee

LUKE 8:22–25

37–St. 2	Be Still, My Soul
204–St. 4	Jesus, What a Friend for Sinners
231	Love Lifted Me
244	My Faith Looks Up to Thee

LUKE 8:35

78–St. 1	Dear Lord and Father of Mankind

LUKE 8:36

155–St. 2	I Lay My Sins on Jesus

LUKE 8:39

16	All That Thrills My Soul
129	Heaven Came Down
157	I Love to Tell the Story
162	I Stand Amazed in the Presence
174	In Loving Kindness Jesus Came
238	Moment by Moment
284	O Zion, Haste
394	Victory in Jesus

LUKE 8:41–56

155–St. 2	I Lay My Sins on Jesus
208–St. 4	Just As I Am, Without One Plea
238	Moment by Moment
263	O For a Thousand Tongues to Sing
359	The Great Physician
394–St. 2	Victory in Jesus
424	Whiter Than Snow

LUKE 9:2–6

121	Hark, the Voice of Jesus Calling
284	O Zion, Haste

LUKE 9:11

155–St. 2	I Lay My Sins on Jesus
243–St. 4	My Faith Has Found
394–St. 2	Victory in Jesus

LUKE 9:12–17

48	Break Thou the Bread

LUKE 9:22–26

26	"Are Ye Able," Said the Master
41	Beneath the Cross of Jesus
78–St. 2	Dear Lord and Father of Mankind
90	Forth in Thy Name, O Lord
117	Hail, Thou Once Despised Jesus
148	I Have Decided to Follow Jesus
185	Jesus Calls Us
187	Jesus, I My Cross Have Taken

188–St. 3	Jesus Is All the World to Me
211–St. 4	Lead Me to Calvary
222	Living for Jesus
242	Must Jesus Bear the Cross Alone
268	O Jesus, I Have Promised
348	"Take Up Thy Cross"
370	The Son of God Goes Forth to War
374	The Way of the Cross Leads Home
403–St. 4	We Would See Jesus; Lo! His Star
420	Where He Leads Me
421	Wherever He Leads, I'll Go

LUKE 9:42

155–St. 2	I Lay My Sins on Jesus
243–St. 4	My Faith Has Found
394–St. 2	Victory in Jesus

LUKE 9:43

162–St. 1	I Stand Amazed in the Presence

LUKE 9:48

234	Make Me a Captive, Lord

LUKE 9:56

294	Out of My Bondage
310	Rescue the Perishing

LUKE 9:57–62

1	A Charge to Keep I Have
26	"Are Ye Able," Said the Master
87	Footsteps of Jesus
90	Forth in Thy Name, O Lord
148	I Have Decided to Follow Jesus
168	I'll Go Where You Want Me To Go
185	Jesus Calls Us
187	Jesus, I My Cross Have Taken
188–St. 3	Jesus Is All the World to Me
222–St. 2	Living for Jesus
268	O Jesus, I Have Promised
284	O Zion, Haste
310	Rescue the Perishing
348	"Take Up Thy Cross"
351–St. 2	Tell Me the Story of Jesus
404	We've a Story to Tell
420	Where He Leads Me
421	Wherever He Leads, I'll Go

LUKE 10:2

73	Come, Ye Thankful People, Come
121	Hark, the Voice of Jesus Calling
168	I'll Go Where You Want Me To Go
295	Pass It On

330	So Send I You
373	The Vision of a Dying World
404	We've a Story to Tell

LUKE 10:17

12	All Hail the Power of Jesus' Name
43	Blessed Be the Name
143	How Sweet the Name
263	O For a Thousand Tongues to Sing
267	O, How I Love Jesus
359	The Great Physician

LUKE 10:19

84	Faith Is the Victory
204	Jesus, What a Friend for Sinners

LUKE 10:20

129–St. 3	Heaven Came Down
266	O Happy Day that Fixed My Choice
309	Rejoice, Ye Pure in Heart

LUKE 10:21–24

103	God Moves in a Mysterious Way

LUKE 10:23

292–St. 1	Open My Eyes

LUKE 10:27

245	My Jesus, I Love Thee
262	O For a Heart to Praise My God
321	Savior, Thy Dying Love
334	Spirit of God, Descend

LUKE 11:1–4

305	Prayer Is the Soul's Sincere
343	Sweet Hour of Prayer
407	What a Friend We Have in Jesus

LUKE 11:2

145–St. 2	I Am Thine, O Lord
300–St. 3	Praise the Lord Who Reigns Above

LUKE 11:3

17–St. 2	All the Way My Savior Leads Me
400–St. 2	We Plow the Fields

LUKE 11:4

78–St. 1	Dear Lord and Father of Mankind

LUKE 11:10

427	Whosoever Will

LUKE 11:10–11

244	My Faith Looks Up to Thee

LUKE 11:13

49	Breathe on Me, Breath of God
63	Come, Holy Ghost
135	Holy Spirit, Light Divine
136	Holy Spirit, Truth Divine
140	Hover O'er Me, Holy Spirit
333	Spirit Divine, Attend Our Prayer
334	Spirit of God, Descend
335	Spirit of the Living God

LUKE 11:20

3–St. 3	A Mighty Fortress Is Our God

LUKE 11:28

239	More About Jesus
282	O Word of God Incarnate
430	Wonderful Words of Life

LUKE 11:34

292	Open My Eyes

LUKE 11:35

130	Heavenly Sunlight
165–St. 4	I Will Sing the Wondrous Story
322	Send the Light
364	The Light of the World Is Jesus

LUKE 11:42

321	Savior, Thy Dying Love
398	We Give Thee but Thine Own

LUKE 12:6–7

53	Children of the Heavenly Father
109	God Will Take Care of You
393	Under His Wings

LUKE 12:8

30	Ask Ye What Great Things I Know
40	Begin, My Tongue, Some Heavenly
157	I Love to Tell the Story
165	I Will Sing the Wondrous Story
307	Redeemed, How I Love to Proclaim
427	Whosoever Will

LUKE 12:9

177–St. 1	In the Hour of Trial

LUKE 12:12

63	Come, Holy Ghost

LUKE 12:19

292–St. 3	Open My Eyes
177–St. 2	In the Hour of Trial

LUKE 12:27

83–St. 2	Fairest Lord Jesus

LUKE 12:27–28

53	Children of the Heavenly Father
74	Count Your Blessings
109	God Will Take Care of You
391	Trusting Jesus
393	Under His Wings

LUKE 12:29–32

17	All the Way My Savior Leads Me

LUKE 12:32

141–St. 2	How Firm a Foundation

LUKE 12:33

398	We Give Thee but Thine Own

LUKE 12:33–34

38–St. 3	Be Thou My Vision

LUKE 12:34

173–St. 3	In Heavenly Love Abiding
196	Jesus, Priceless Treasure

LUKE 12:35–40

142–St. 4	How Great Thou Art
154–St. 4	I Know Whom I Have Believed
181	It May Be at Morn
189	Jesus Is Coming Again
223	Lo, He Comes with Clouds
289	One Day
363	The King Shall Come When Morning
395	Watchman, Tell Us of the Night
410	What If It Were Today?

LUKE 12:47–48

418	When We Walk with the Lord

LUKE 12:48

398	We Give Thee but Thine Own

LUKE 12:49

49	Breathe on Me, Breath of God

LUKE 13:3–5

72	Come, Ye Sinners, Poor and Needy
294	Out of My Bondage
296	Pass Me Not, O Gentle Savior
310	Rescue the Perishing
331	Softly and Tenderly
424	Whiter Than Snow
431	Ye Must Be Born Again

LUKE 13:10–13

208–St. 4	Just As I Am, Without One Plea
243–St. 4	My Faith Has Found
394–St. 2	Victory in Jesus

LUKE 13:10–17

260	O Day of Rest and Gladness

LUKE 13:34

53	Children of the Heavenly Father
109	God Will Take Care of You
123	He Hideth My Soul
362	The King of Love My Shepherd Is
393	Under His Wings

LUKE 14:1–6

260	O Day of Rest and Gladness

LUKE 14:4

243–St. 4	My Faith Has Found
394–St. 2	Victory in Jesus

LUKE 14:13–17

58	Christ Receiveth Sinful Men
72	Come, Ye Sinners, Poor and Needy
149	I Hear Thy Welcome Voice
151	I Heard the Voice of Jesus Say
208	Just As I Am, Without One Plea
341–Refrain	Surely Goodness and Mercy

LUKE 14:23

233	Make Me a Blessing
310	Rescue the Perishing
404	We've a Story to Tell

LUKE 14:27

26	"Are Ye Able," Said the Master
41	Beneath the Cross of Jesus
187	Jesus, I My Cross Have Taken
211–St. 4	Lead Me to Calvary
222–St. 3	Living for Jesus
242	Must Jesus Bear the Cross Alone
268	O Jesus, I Have Promised

297	Peace, Perfect Peace
348	"Take Up Thy Cross"
370	The Son of God Goes Forth to War
374	The Way of the Cross Leads Home
420	Where He Leads Me
421	Wherever He Leads, I'll Go

LUKE 14:35

292	Open My Eyes

LUKE 15:2

58	Christ Receiveth Sinful Men
250–St. 4	No, Not One

LUKE 15:4–7

165–St. 2	I Will Sing the Wondrous Story
200–St. 3	Jesus, the Very Thought of Thee
319	Savior, Like a Shepherd Lead Us
362	The King of Love My Shepherd Is
366	The Lord's My Shepherd

LUKE 15:11–24

190	Jesus Is Tenderly Calling
200–St. 3	Jesus, the Very Thought of Thee
208	Just As I Am, Without One Plea
227	Lord, I'm Coming Home

LUKE 16:10

18	All Things Are Thine
166	I Would Be True
398	We Give Thee but Thine Own

LUKE 16:13

145–St. 2	I Am Thine, O Lord
268	O Jesus, I Have Promised
288	Once to Every Man and Nation
421	Wherever He Leads, I'll Go

LUKE 16:17

282	O Word of God Incarnate

LUKE 17:5

244	My Faith Looks Up to Thee

LUKE 17:10

1	A Charge to Keep I Have
90	Forth in Thy Name, O Lord
121	Hark, the Voice of Jesus Calling
222–St. 3	Living for Jesus
268	O Jesus, I Have Promised
273	O Master, Let Me Walk with Thee
313	Rise Up, O Men of God

LUKE 17:11–15

243–St. 4	My Faith Has Found
394–St. 2	Victory in Jesus

LUKE 17:11–19

155–St. 2	I Lay My Sins on Jesus
294	Out of My Bondage
359–St. 1	The Great Physician

LUKE 17:24

142–St. 4	How Great Thou Art
181	It May Be at Morn
223	Lo, He Comes with Clouds
289–St. 5	One Day
363	The King Shall Come When Morning
410	What If It Were Today?

LUKE 17:25

7	Ah, Holy Jesus
235	"Man of Sorrows," What a Name
275	O Sacred Head, Now Wounded

LUKE 18:1

86–St. 4	Fight the Good Fight
305	Prayer Is the Soul's Sincere
343	Sweet Hour of Prayer
407	What a Friend We Have in Jesus

LUKE 18:8

84	Faith Is the Victory
180	It Is Well with My Soul
391	Trusting Jesus
410–St. 3	What If It Were Today?

LUKE 18:12

18	All Things Are Thine
398	We Give Thee but Thine Own

LUKE 18:13

78–St. 1	Dear Lord and Father of Mankind
79	Depth of Mercy! Can There Be
208	Just As I Am, Without One Plea
244	My Faith Looks Up to Thee
261	O For a Closer Walk with God
296	Pass Me Not, O Gentle Savior
359–St. 2	The Great Physician

LUKE 18:14

166	I Would Be True
262	O For a Heart to Praise My God

LUKE 18:22

26	"Are Ye Able," Said the Master
87	Footsteps of Jesus
128	He Who Would Valiant Be
148	I Have Decided to Follow Jesus
185	Jesus Calls Us
188–St. 3	Jesus Is All the World to Me
222–St. 2	Living for Jesus
268	O Jesus, I Have Promised
403–St. 4	We Would See Jesus; Lo! His Star
420	Where He Leads Me
421	Wherever He Leads, I'll Go

LUKE 18:27

103	God Moves in a Mysterious Way

LUKE 18:28

148	I Have Decided to Follow Jesus
187	Jesus, I My Cross Have Taken
188–St. 3	Jesus Is All the World to Me

LUKE 18:31–33

7	Ah, Holy Jesus
8	Alas! And Did My Savior Bleed?
45	Blessed Redeemer
117	Hail, Thou Once Despised Jesus
211	Lead Me to Calvary
225–St. 3	Look, Ye Saints!
235	"Man of Sorrows," What a Name
388	'Tis Midnight and on Olive's Brow

LUKE 18:35–43

208–St. 4	Just As I Am, Without One Plea
243–St. 4	My Faith Has Found
263	O For a Thousand Tongues to Sing
394–St. 2	Victory in Jesus

LUKE 19:9

119	Happy the Home When God Is There
266	O Happy Day that Fixed My Choice

LUKE 19:10

161	I Sought the Lord
165–St. 2	I Will Sing the Wondrous Story
174	In Loving Kindness Jesus Came
193	Jesus Loves Even Me
194	Jesus Loves Me
222–St. 4	Living for Jesus
235	"Man of Sorrows," What a Name
243–St. 4	My Faith Has Found
310	Rescue the Perishing

362–St. 3   The King of Love My Shepherd Is

LUKE 19:29–38
11	All Glory, Laud and Honor
139	Hosanna, Loud Hosanna
312	Ride On, Ride On in Majesty!

LUKE 19:37–38
40	Begin, My Tongue, Some Heavenly
298	Praise Him! Praise Him!
390	To God Be the Glory

LUKE 19:41
419	Where Cross the Crowded Ways

LUKE 20:17
52	Built on the Rock
56	Christ Is Made the Sure
353	The Church's One Foundation

LUKE 20:21
320	Savior, Teach Me Day by Day

LUKE 20:23
159–St. 2	I Need Thee Every Hour

LUKE 20:35–38
88	For All the Saints

LUKE 20:36
53	Children of the Heavenly Father
417	When We All Get to Heaven

LUKE 20:38
169	I'll Live for Him
170–St. 3	Immortal, Invisible
222	Living for Jesus
238	Moment by Moment

LUKE 21:1–4
18	All Things Are Thine
147	I Gave My Life for Thee
321	Savior, Thy Dying Love
398	We Give Thee but Thine Own

LUKE 21:4
345	Take My Life and Let It Be

LUKE 21:19
35	Awake, My Soul, Stretch
242	Must Jesus Bear the Cross Alone
273–St. 3	O Master, Let Me Walk with Thee

337   Stand Up, Stand Up for Jesus

LUKE 21:27–28
33–St. 5	At the Name of Jesus
124–St. 5	He Keeps Me Singing
181	It May Be at Morn
189	Jesus Is Coming Again
220	Lift Up Your Heads
223	Lo, He Comes with Clouds
289–St. 5	One Day
410	What If It Were Today?
416	When the Roll Is Called

LUKE 21:33
107–St. 3	God the Almighty One
141–St. 1	How Firm a Foundation
153–St. 2	I Know That My Redeemer Liveth
430	Wonderful Words of Life

LUKE 21:36
343	Sweet Hour of Prayer

LUKE 22:14–20
6	According to Thy Gracious Word
47	Bread of the World
131	Here, O My Lord, I See Thee
217	Let Us Break Bread Together

LUKE 22:19
48	Break Thou the Bread

LUKE 22:20
8	Alas! And Did My Savior Bleed?
27	Are You Washed in the Blood
202	Jesus, Thy Blood and Righteousness
251	Nothing But the Blood
267–St. 2	O, How I Love Jesus
307	Redeemed, How I Love to Proclaim

LUKE 22:27
242	Must Jesus Bear the Cross Alone
273	O Master, Let Me Walk with Thee

LUKE 22:30
50–Last St.	Brethren, We Have Met

LUKE 22:31–32
177–St. 1	In the Hour of Trial

LUKE 22:32
46	Blest Be the Tie

LUKE 22:37

7	Ah, Holy Jesus
8	Alas! And Did My Savior Bleed?
33–St. 3	At the Name of Jesus
117	Hail, Thou Once Despised Jesus
204	Jesus, What a Friend for Sinners

LUKE 22:39–46

99–St. 1	Go to Dark Gethsemane
388	'Tis Midnight and on Olive's Brow
420–St. 2	Where He Leads Me
425–St. 4	Who Is He in Yonder Stall?

LUKE 22:39–54

211	Lead Me to Calvary

LUKE 22:40

159–St. 2	I Need Thee Every Hour

LUKE 22:41

78–St. 2	Dear Lord and Father of Mankind

LUKE 22:41–44

162–St. 2	I Stand Amazed in the Presence

LUKE 22:42

122	Have Thine Own Way, Lord

LUKE 22:43

162–St. 3	I Stand Amazed in the Presence

LUKE 22:51

155–St. 2	I Lay My Sins on Jesus
359–St. 1	The Great Physician

LUKE 22:54–62

7	Ah, Holy Jesus
177–St. 1	In the Hour of Trial

LUKE 22:63–65

225–St. 3	Look, Ye Saints!

LUKE 22:66–71

420–St. 3	Where He Leads Me

LUKE 22:69–70

43–St. 2	Blessed Be the Name
83	Fairest Lord Jesus
198	Jesus Shall Reign
225	Look, Ye Saints!
232	Majestic Sweetness
235	"Man of Sorrows," What a Name

308	Rejoice, the Lord Is King

LUKE 23:1–25

99–St. 2	Go to Dark Gethsemane
420–St. 3	Where He Leads Me

LUKE 23:1–46

7	Ah, Holy Jesus
8	Alas! And Did My Savior Bleed?
32	At the Cross

LUKE 23:1–56

211	Lead Me to Calvary
351–St. 3	Tell Me the Story of Jesus

LUKE 23:26–49

99–St. 3	Go to Dark Gethsemane
289–St. 2	One Day

LUKE 23:33–46

31	At Calvary
45–St. 2	Blessed Redeemer
165–St. 1	I Will Sing the Wondrous Story
177–St. 2	In the Hour of Trial
211	Lead Me to Calvary
222–St. 2	Living for Jesus
367	The Old Rugged Cross
377	There Is a Green Hill Far Away
425–St. 4	Who Is He in Yonder Stall?

LUKE 23:33–53

406	Were You There?

LUKE 23:34

359–St. 2	The Great Physician

LUKE 23:38

43	Blessed Be the Name
198	Jesus Shall Reign
298	Praise Him! Praise Him!

LUKE 23:39–43

6–St. 5	According to Thy Gracious Word
26–St. 2	"Are Ye Able," Said the Master
58–St. 4	Christ Receiveth Sinful Men
59–St. 3	Christ the Lord Is Risen Today
82	Face to Face
279	O That Will Be Glory For Me
286	On Jordan's Stormy Banks I Stand
342	Sweet By and By
376–St. 2	There Is a Fountain
417	When We All Get to Heaven

LUKE 23:48–56

54	Christ Arose
289–St. 3	One Day
406	Were You There?

LUKE 24:1–8

39	Because He Lives
54	Christ Arose
59	Christ the Lord Is Risen Today
99–St. 4	Go to Dark Gethsemane
111	Good Christian Men, Rejoice and Sing
117–St. 1	Hail, Thou Once Despised Jesus
126	He Lives
152	I Know That My Redeemer Lives
186	Jesus Christ Is Risen Today
211	Lead Me to Calvary
277	O Sons and Daughters
289–St. 4	One Day
351–St. 3	Tell Me the Story of Jesus
372	The Strife Is O'er
382	Thine Is the Glory
384	This Is the Day

LUKE 24:8

389–St. 1	'Tis So Sweet To Trust in Jesus

LUKE 24:26

117	Hail, Thou Once Despised Jesus
211	Lead Me to Calvary
235	"Man of Sorrows," What a Name
275	O Sacred Head, Now Wounded
289	One Day

LUKE 24:27

282	O Word of God Incarnate

LUKE 24:29

5	Abide with Me
15	All Praise to Thee, My God
77	Day Is Dying in the West
106	God, That Madest Earth
254	Now the Day Is Over

LUKE 24:32

48	Break Thou the Bread
282	O Word of God Incarnate
361	The Heavens Declare Thy Glory
430	Wonderful Words of Life

LUKE 24:34

54	Christ Arose

59	Christ the Lord Is Risen Today
71	Come, Ye Faithful, Raise
126	He Lives
152	I Know That My Redeemer Lives
153–St. 3	I Know That My Redeemer Liveth
186	Jesus Christ Is Risen Today
355	The Day of Resurrection

LUKE 24:36

297	Peace, Perfect Peace
318	Savior, Again to Thy Dear Name

LUKE 24:45

48	Break Thou the Bread
282	O Word of God Incarnate

LUKE 24:46

186	Jesus Christ Is Risen Today
289	One Day
351–St. 3	Tell Me the Story of Jesus

LUKE 24:46–48

30	Ask Ye What Great Things I Know
31	At Calvary
55	Christ for the World We Sing
284	O Zion, Haste
310	Rescue the Perishing
322	Send the Light
346	Take the Name of Jesus with You
373	The Vision of a Dying World
399	We Have Heard the Joyful Sound
404	We've a Story to Tell

LUKE 24:49

135	Holy Spirit, Light Divine
136–St. 3	Holy Spirit, Truth Divine
333	Spirit Divine, Attend Our Prayer
335	Spirit of the Living God
339	Sun of My Soul, Thou Savior Dear

LUKE 24:50–53

43	Blessed Be the Name
59–St. 4	Christ the Lord Is Risen Today
116	Hail the Day That Sees Him Rise
215	Let All the World
289–St. 4	One Day
304	Praise to the Lord, the Almighty
308	Rejoice, the Lord Is King
360	The Head That Once Was Crowned

JOHN 1:1

66–St. 2	Come, Thou Almighty King

324–St. 2	Shepherd of Tender Youth

JOHN 1:1–5

33	At the Name of Jesus
170	Immortal, Invisible
282	O Word of God Incarnate

JOHN 1:1–14

60	Christ Whose Glory Fills
278	O Splendor of God's Glory

JOHN 1:3

19	All Things Bright and Beautiful
75–St. 5	Crown Him with Many Crowns
89	For the Beauty of the Earth
389–St. 3	'Tis So Sweet To Trust in Jesus

JOHN 1:4

30–St. 3	Ask Ye What Great Thing I Know
75–St. 6	Crown Him with Many Crowns
385–St. 3	Thou Art the Way: to Thee Alone

JOHN 1:4–5

129	Heaven Came Down
214	Let All Mortal Flesh
267–St. 3	O, How I Love Jesus
272–St. 2	O Love, That Will Not Let Me Go
311–St. 2	Revive Us Again
325	Silent Night! Holy Night
403–St. 2	We Would See Jesus; Lo! His Star

JOHN 1:4–9

24–St. 2	Angels from the Realms of Glory
57	Christ Is the World's
118	Hail to the Lord's Anointed
130	Heavenly Sunlight
151–St. 3	I Heard the Voice of Jesus Say
201	Jesus, Thou Joy of Loving Hearts
340	Sunshine in My Soul
364	The Light of the World Is Jesus
387	Thou Whose Almighty Word
392–St. 1	Turn Your Eyes Upon Jesus

JOHN 1:11

117	Hail, Thou Once Despised Jesus
147	I Gave My Life for Thee
386	Thou Didst Leave Thy Throne

JOHN 1:12–13

2	A Child of the King
38–St. 2	Be Thou My Vision
53	Children of the Heavenly Father

91–St. 3	Free From the Law
129	Heaven Came Down
143	How Sweet the Name
204	Jesus, What a Friend for Sinners
290	Only Trust Him
307	Redeemed, How I Love to Proclaim
346	Take the Name of Jesus with You
389	'Tis So Sweet To Trust in Jesus
431	Ye Must Be Born Again

JOHN 1:14

66–St. 2	Come, Thou Almighty King
75–St. 2	Crown Him with Many Crowns
94	From Heaven Above to Earth
120–St. 2	Hark! The Herald Angels Sing
214	Let All Mortal Flesh
224	Lo, How a Rose E'er Blooming
256	O Come, All Ye Faithful
258	O Could I Speak the Matchless
282	O Word of God Incarnate
285	Of the Father's Love Begotten
289–St. 1	One Day
385–St. 2	Thou Art the Way: to Thee Alone
390	To God Be the Glory

JOHN 1:16–17

16	All That Thrills My Soul
21	Amazing Grace
58	Christ Receiveth Sinful Men
91	Free From the Law
112	Grace Greater Than Our Sin
154–St. 1	I Know Whom I Have Believed
195	Jesus Paid it All
258	O Could I Speak the Matchless
289	One Day
385–St. 2	Thou Art the Way: to Thee Alone
420–St. 4	Where He Leads Me
428	Wonderful Grace of Jesus

JOHN 1:18

170	Immortal, Invisible

JOHN 1:23

68	Come, Thou Long-Expected Jesus

JOHN 1:29

75–St. 1	Crown Him with Many Crowns
117–St. 2	Hail, Thou Once Despised Jesus
118	Hail to the Lord's Anointed
155	I Lay My Sins on Jesus
162	I Stand Amazed in the Presence
169	I'll Live for Him

208	Just As I Am, Without One Plea
244	My Faith Looks Up to Thee
311–St. 2	Revive Us Again
359–St. 3	The Great Physician
376–St. 3	There Is a Fountain
411	What Wondrous Love Is This?

JOHN 1:32–33

63	Come, Holy Ghost
65	Come, Holy Spirit
333	Spirit Divine, Attend Our Prayer
387–St. 3	Thou Whose Almighty Word

JOHN 1:34

75–St. 2	Crown Him with Many Crowns
83	Fairest Lord Jesus
235	"Man of Sorrows," What a Name

JOHN 1:35–43

78–St. 2	Dear Lord and Father of Mankind

JOHN 1:36

155–St. 1	I Lay My Sins on Jesus
235–St. 3	"Man of Sorrows," What a Name
359–St. 3	The Great Physician
376–St. 3	There Is a Fountain

JOHN 1:37

17	All the Way My Savior Leads Me
87	Footsteps of Jesus
148	I Have Decided to Follow Jesus

JOHN 1:43

87	Footsteps of Jesus
148	I Have Decided to Follow Jesus
222–St. 2	Living for Jesus
403–St. 4	We Would See Jesus; Lo! His Star

JOHN 1:45–46

276–St. 2	O Sing a Song of Bethlehem

JOHN 2:22

153	I Know That My Redeemer Liveth

JOHN 2:23

143	How Sweet the Name
346	Take the Name of Jesus with You

JOHN 3:1–7

129–St. 2	Heaven Came Down
431	Ye Must Be Born Again

JOHN 3:3

230–St. 4	Love Divine, All Loves Excelling

JOHN 3:3–5

353–St. 2	The Church's One Foundation

JOHN 3:5–7

49	Breathe on Me, Breath of God
63	Come, Holy Ghost
108	God Who Touchest Earth

JOHN 3:11

157	I Love to Tell the Story
229	Lord, Speak to Me

JOHN 3:13–17

30	Ask Ye What Great Thing I Know
235–St. 4	"Man of Sorrows," What a Name
289	One Day
359–St. 2	The Great Physician
390	To God Be the Glory

JOHN 3:15–17

284	O Zion, Haste
310–St. 2	Rescue the Perishing
389	'Tis So Sweet To Trust in Jesus
427	Whosoever Will

JOHN 3:16–17

8	Alas! And Did My Savior Bleed?
211	Lead Me to Calvary
411	What Wondrous Love Is This?

JOHN 3:16–18

23	And Can It Be That I Should Gain
43–St. 3	Blessed Be the Name
67–St. 2	Come, Thou Fount
142–St. 3	How Great Thou Art
143	How Sweet the Name
154	I Know Whom I Have Believed
157	I Love to Tell the Story
162	I Stand Amazed in the Presence
164	I Will Sing of My Redeemer
174	In Loving Kindness Jesus Came
230	Love Divine, All Loves Excelling
231	Love Lifted Me
267	O, How I Love Jesus
271	O Love How Deep, How Broad
290	Only Trust Him
315	Room at the Cross for You
381	There's a Wideness

399	We Have Heard the Joyful Sound
404–St. 3	We've a Story to Tell
411	What Wondrous Love Is This?

JOHN 3:19–21

57	Christ Is the World's
129	Heaven Came Down
130	Heavenly Sunlight
278	O Splendor of God's Glory
340	Sunshine in My Soul
364	The Light of the World Is Jesus

JOHN 3:29

| 27–St. 3 | Are You Washed in the Blood |

JOHN 3:30–35

43	Blessed Be the Name
298–St. 3	Praise Him! Praise Him!
308	Rejoice, the Lord Is King

JOHN 3:36

86–St. 4	Fight the Good Fight
123	He Hideth My Soul
243	My Faith Has Found
290	Only Trust Him
310	Rescue the Perishing
359–St. 2	The Great Physician
389	'Tis So Sweet To Trust in Jesus

JOHN 4:10–14

17–St. 2	All the Way My Savior Leads Me
72–St. 2	Come, Ye Sinners, Poor and Needy
97–St. 2	Glorious Things of Thee
115–St. 2	Guide Me, O Thou Great Jehovah
151–St. 2	I Heard the Voice of Jesus Say
201	Jesus, Thou Joy of Loving Hearts
206–St. 3	Joyful, Joyful, We Adore Thee
250–St. 5	No, Not One
316	Satisfied
362–St. 2	The King of Love My Shepherd Is
427	Whosoever Will

JOHN 4:23–24

44	Blessed Jesus, at Thy Word
50	Brethren, We Have Met to Worship
66	Come, Thou Almighty King
101	God Himself Is with Us
283	O Worship the King

JOHN 4:34

| 90 | Forth in Thy Name, O Lord |
| 351 | Tell Me the Story of Jesus |

JOHN 4:35–38

73	Come, Ye Thankful People, Come
121	Hark, the Voice of Jesus Calling
373	The Vision of a Dying World

JOHN 4:42

| 408 | What a Wonderful Savior |

JOHN 4:46–53

243–St. 4	My Faith Has Found
359	The Great Physician
394–St. 2	Victory in Jesus

JOHN 5:1–9

243–St. 4	My Faith Has Found
359	The Great Physician
394–St. 2	Victory in Jesus
424	Whiter Than Snow

JOHN 5:5–9

| 192–St. 3 | Jesus, Lover of My Soul |

JOHN 5:17

| 351 | Tell Me the Story of Jesus |

JOHN 5:19–27

43	Blessed Be the Name
75–St. 6	Crown Him with Many Crowns
83	Fairest Lord Jesus
91	Free From the Law
154	I Know Whom I Have Believed
164–St. 4	I Will Sing of My Redeemer
263	O For a Thousand Tongues to Sing
290	Only Trust Him
298	Praise Him! Praise Him!
308–St. 4	Rejoice, the Lord Is King
385	Thou Art the Way: to Thee Alone
389	'Tis So Sweet To Trust in Jesus
415	When Morning Gilds the Skies
430	Wonderful Words of Life
431	Ye Must Be Born Again
432	Ye Servants of God

JOHN 5:32

| 258 | O Could I Speak the Matchless |

JOHN 5:37

| 170 | Immortal, Invisible |

JOHN 5:39

| 48 | Break Thou the Bread |
| 133 | Holy Bible, Book Divine |

193	Jesus Loves Even Me
194	Jesus Loves Me
239–St. 3	More About Jesus
282	O Word of God Incarnate
361	The Heavens Declare Thy Glory
430	Wonderful Words of Life

JOHN 6:2

243–St. 4	My Faith Has Found
250	No, Not One
359–St. 1	The Great Physician
394–St. 2	Victory in Jesus

JOHN 6:5–13

48	Break Thou the Bread

JOHN 6:15

78–St. 3	Dear Lord and Father of Mankind

JOHN 6:16–20

276–St. 3	O Sing a Song of Bethlehem

JOHN 6:28–29

86–St. 4	Fight the Good Fight
146	I Am Trusting Thee, Lord Jesus
154	I Know Whom I Have Believed
244	My Faith Looks Up to Thee
290	Only Trust Him
389	'Tis So Sweet To Trust in Jesus
391	Trusting Jesus
418	When We Walk with the Lord

JOHN 6:31

50	Brethren, We Have Met to Worship

JOHN 6:31–35

17–St. 2	All the Way My Savior Leads Me
48	Break Thou the Bread
70–St. 3	Come, Ye Disconsolate
100–St. 2	God Be with You

JOHN 6:35

138–St. 2	Hope of the World
151–St. 2	I Heard the Voice of Jesus Say
188	Jesus Is All the World to Me
201	Jesus, Thou Joy of Loving Hearts
316	Satisfied

JOHN 6:35–58

47	Bread of the World
48	Break Thou the Bread
131	Here, O My Lord, I See Thee

JOHN 6:37–40

58	Christ Receiveth Sinful Men
72	Come, Ye Sinners, Poor and Needy
147	I Gave My Life for Thee
208	Just As I Am, Without One Plea
250–St. 4	No, Not One
294	Out of My Bondage
296	Pass Me Not, O Gentle Savior
319–St. 3	Savior, Like a Shepherd Lead Us
365	The Lily of the Valley

JOHN 6:40

30–St. 3	Ask Ye What Great Thing I Know
279	O That Will Be Glory For Me
286	On Jordan's Stormy Banks I Stand
290	Only Trust Him
352	Ten Thousand Times Ten Thousand

JOHN 6:41

138–St. 2	Hope of the World

JOHN 6:45

320	Savior, Teach Me Day by Day

JOHN 6:46

137–St. 3	Holy, Holy, Holy
170	Immortal, Invisible

JOHN 6:47–58

70–St. 3	Come, Ye Disconsolate
100–St. 2	God Be with You
115–St. 1	Guide Me, O Thou Great Jehovah
138–St. 2	Hope of the World
290	Only Trust Him
316	Satisfied

JOHN 6:51

17–St. 2	All the Way My Savior Leads Me
48	Break Thou the Bread

JOHN 6:53–58

6	According to Thy Gracious Word
27	Are You Washed in the Blood
38	Be Thou My Vision
80	Down at the Cross
144	I Am His and He Is Mine
217	Let Us Break Bread Together
251	Nothing But the Blood
378	There Is Power in the Blood

JOHN 6:58

17–St. 2	All the Way My Savior Leads Me

48	Break Thou the Bread
50	Brethren, We Have Met to Worship
100–St. 2	God Be with You

JOHN 6:63

49	Breathe on Me, Breath of God
65	Come, Holy Spirit
129–St. 2	Heaven Came Down
335	Spirit of the Living God
430	Wonderful Words of Life

JOHN 6:66–67

67–St. 3	Come, Thou Fount

JOHN 6:68–69

86–St. 4	Fight the Good Fight
153	I Know That My Redeemer Liveth
235	"Man of Sorrows," What a Name
243–St. 3	My Faith Has Found
244	My Faith Looks Up to Thee
359–St. 3	The Great Physician
389	'Tis So Sweet To Trust in Jesus
430	Wonderful Words of Life

JOHN 7:17

122	Have Thine Own Way, Lord
239	More About Jesus
292	Open My Eyes

JOHN 7:37–38

58	Christ Receiveth Sinful Men
72–St. 2	Come, Ye Sinners, Poor and Needy
86–St. 4	Fight the Good Fight
149	I Hear Thy Welcome Voice
151–St. 2	I Heard the Voice of Jesus Say
190	Jesus Is Tenderly Calling
201	Jesus, Thou Joy of Loving Hearts
208	Just As I Am, Without One Plea
290	Only Trust Him
294	Out of My Bondage
427	Whosoever Will

JOHN 7:41–42

276	O Sing a Song of Bethlehem

JOHN 7:42

118	Hail to the Lord's Anointed

JOHN 7:46

258	O Could I Speak the Matchless
430	Wonderful Words of Life

JOHN 8:2

320	Savior, Teach Me Day by Day

JOHN 8:9

154–St. 3	I Know Whom I Have Believed

JOHN 8:11

58–St. 3	Christ Receiveth Sinful Men
79	Depth of Mercy! Can There Be
112	Grace Greater Than Our Sin
115	Guide Me, O Thou Great Jehovah
174	In Loving Kindness Jesus Came
359–St. 2	The Great Physician
424	Whiter Than Snow

JOHN 8:12

57	Christ Is the World's
60	Christ Whose Glory Fills
83–St. 3	Fairest Lord Jesus
129	Heaven Came Down
130	Heavenly Sunlight
151–St. 3	I Heard the Voice of Jesus Say
165–St. 4	I Will Sing the Wondrous Story
170	Immortal, Invisible
188	Jesus Is All the World to Me
201–St. 5	Jesus, Thou Joy of Loving Hearts
250–St. 3	No, Not One
267–St. 3	O, How I Love Jesus
272–St. 2	O Love, That Will Not Let Me Go
278	O Splendor of God's Glory
311–St. 2	Revive Us Again
327	Since Jesus Came Into My Heart
340	Sunshine in My Soul
364	The Light of the World Is Jesus
387	Thou Whose Almighty Word
392–St. 1	Turn Your Eyes Upon Jesus

JOHN 8:28

235–St. 4	"Man of Sorrows," What a Name

JOHN 8:29–30

229	Lord, Speak to Me

JOHN 8:30

389	'Tis So Sweet To Trust in Jesus

JOHN 8:31–32

20–St. 4	Am I a Soldier of the Cross?
128	He Who Would Valiant Be
145	I Am Thine, O Lord
222	Living for Jesus

268	O Jesus, I Have Promised
345	Take My Life and Let It Be
418	When We Walk with the Lord

JOHN 8:32

48–St. 2	Break Thou the Bread
282	O Word of God Incarnate
292	Open My Eyes
385–St. 2	Thou Art the Way: to Thee Alone

JOHN 8:34–36

23–St. 4	And Can It Be That I Should Gain
30	Ask Ye What Great Thing I Know
48–St. 2, 3	Break Thou the Bread
91	Free From the Law
164	I Will Sing of My Redeemer
202	Jesus, Thy Blood and Righteousness
263–St. 3	O For a Thousand Tongues to Sing
267–St. 2	O, How I Love Jesus
294	Out of My Bondage
319–St. 3	Savior, Like a Shepherd Lead Us
326	Since I Have Been Redeemed
428	Wonderful Grace of Jesus

JOHN 8:46

154–St. 3	I Know Whom I Have Believed

JOHN 8:51

141	How Firm a Foundation
290	Only Trust Him
389–St. 1	'Tis So Sweet To Trust in Jesus
430	Wonderful Words of Life

JOHN 8:54–56

232	Majestic Sweetness

JOHN 8:58

75–St. 2	Crown Him with Many Crowns
358	The God of Abraham Praise

JOHN 9:1–11

87–St. 2	Footsteps of Jesus

JOHN 9:4

15	All Praise to Thee, My God
28	Are You (Art Thou) Weary
34	Awake, My Soul, and With the Sun
168	I'll Go Where You Want Me To Go
279	O That Will Be Glory For Me

JOHN 9:5

60	Christ Whose Glory Fills

151–St. 3	I Heard the Voice of Jesus Say

JOHN 9:31

305	Prayer Is the Soul's Sincere

JOHN 9:35

154	I Know Whom I Have Believed
290	Only Trust Him

JOHN 9:38

359–St. 3	The Great Physician
415	When Morning Gilds the Skies

JOHN 9:39

394–St. 2	Victory in Jesus

JOHN 10:1–16

100–St. 1	God Be with You
192	Jesus, Lover of My Soul
269	O Jesus, Thou Art Standing
298–St. 1	Praise Him! Praise Him!
319	Savior, Like a Shepherd Lead Us
324	Shepherd of Tender Youth
362	The King of Love My Shepherd Is
366	The Lord's My Shepherd

JOHN 10:3–5

17	All the Way My Savior Leads Me
78–St. 2	Dear Lord and Father of Mankind
87	Footsteps of Jesus
115	Guide Me, O Thou Great Jehovah
125	He Leadeth Me
151	I Heard the Voice of Jesus Say
185	Jesus Calls Us
188–St. 3	Jesus Is All the World to Me
190	Jesus Is Tenderly Calling
222	Living for Jesus
331	Softly and Tenderly
359–St. 1	The Great Physician
391–St. 2	Trusting Jesus
403–St. 4	We Would See Jesus; Lo! His Star

JOHN 10:9–11

7	Ah, Holy Jesus
30–St. 3	Ask Ye What Great Thing I Know
58	Christ Receiveth Sinful Men
75–St. 6	Crown Him with Many Crowns
147	I Gave My Life for Thee
149	I Hear Thy Welcome Voice
169	I'll Live for Him
173–St. 3	In Heavenly Love Abiding
174	In Loving Kindness Jesus Came

184–St. 2	Jerusalem, the Golden
195	Jesus Paid it All
196	Jesus, Priceless Treasure
206	Joyful, Joyful, We Adore Thee
216	Let Jesus Come Into Your Heart
222	Living for Jesus
250	No, Not One
275	O Sacred Head, Now Wounded
362–St. 2	The King of Love My Shepherd Is
385	Thou Art the Way: to Thee Alone
392	Turn Your Eyes Upon Jesus

JOHN 10:16

57	Christ Is the World's
359–St. 1	The Great Physician

JOHN 10:17–18

7	Ah, Holy Jesus
30	Ask Ye What Great Thing I Know
195	Jesus Paid it All
235	"Man of Sorrows," What a Name
275	O Sacred Head, Now Wounded
289	One Day
394–St. 1	Victory in Jesus

JOHN 10:27–28

87	Footsteps of Jesus
100–St. 1	God Be with You
151	I Heard the Voice of Jesus Say
185	Jesus Calls Us
188	Jesus Is All the World to Me
222	Living for Jesus
319	Savior, Like a Shepherd Lead Us
324	Shepherd of Tender Youth
331	Softly and Tenderly
359–St. 1	The Great Physician
362	The King of Love My Shepherd Is
366	The Lord's My Shepherd
420	Where He Leads Me

JOHN 10:28–29

53–St. 3	Children of the Heavenly Father
75–St. 6	Crown Him with Many Crowns
141–St. 5	How Firm a Foundation
153–St. 1	I Know That My Redeemer Liveth
221–St. 2	Like a River Glorious
279	O That Will Be Glory For Me
286	On Jordan's Stormy Banks I Stand
352	Ten Thousand Times Ten Thousand
417	When We All Get to Heaven

JOHN 11:25–27

59–St. 4	Christ the Lord Is Risen Today
69	Come, We That Love the Lord
75–St. 6	Crown Him with Many Crowns
146	I Am Trusting Thee, Lord Jesus
152	I Know That My Redeemer Lives
153	I Know That My Redeemer Liveth
154	I Know Whom I Have Believed
279	O That Will Be Glory For Me
290	Only Trust Him
310–St. 2	Rescue the Perishing
342	Sweet By and By
359–St. 3	The Great Physician
385–St. 3	Thou Art the Way: to Thee Alone
390	To God Be the Glory
392	Turn Your Eyes Upon Jesus
417	When We All Get to Heaven

JOHN 11:27

235	"Man of Sorrows," What a Name

JOHN 11:28

83	Fairest Lord Jesus

JOHN 11:35–36

182	I've Found a Friend
359–St. 1	The Great Physician
419	Where Cross the Crowded Ways

JOHN 11:40

290	Only Trust Him
391	Trusting Jesus

JOHN 11:50–52

53	Children of the Heavenly Father
55	Christ for the World We Sing
57	Christ Is the World's
162	I Stand Amazed in the Presence
353–St. 2	The Church's One Foundation
408	What a Wonderful Savior

JOHN 12:9

425–St. 3	Who Is He in Yonder Stall?

JOHN 12:12–15

11	All Glory, Laud and Honor
139	Hosanna, Loud Hosanna
312	Ride On, Ride On in Majesty!

JOHN 12:13

43	Blessed Be the Name

JOHN 12:24–26

234	Make Me a Captive, Lord

JOHN 12:26

17	All the Way My Savior Leads Me
26	"Are Ye Able," Said the Master
87	Footsteps of Jesus
90	Forth in Thy Name, O Lord
121	Hark, the Voice of Jesus Calling
145–St. 2	I Am Thine, O Lord
148	I Have Decided to Follow Jesus
168	I'll Go Where You Want Me To Go
185	Jesus Calls Us
188–St. 3	Jesus Is All the World to Me
222	Living for Jesus
268	O Jesus, I Have Promised
273	O Master, Let Me Walk with Thee
313	Rise Up, O Men of God
348	"Take Up Thy Cross"
403–St. 5	We Would See Jesus; Lo! His Star
420	Where He Leads Me
421	Wherever He Leads, I'll Go

JOHN 12:27

275	O Sacred Head, Now Wounded

JOHN 12:28

43	Blessed Be the Name
134	Holy God, We Praise Thy Name
206	Joyful, Joyful, We Adore Thee
358	The God of Abraham Praise
390	To God Be the Glory

JOHN 12:29

107–St. 1	God the Almighty One

JOHN 12:32

201	Jesus, Thou Joy of Loving Hearts
219	Lift High the Cross
272	O Love, That Will Not Let Me Go
298	Praise Him! Praise Him!
360	The Head That Once Was Crowned

JOHN 12:32–34

235–St. 4	"Man of Sorrows," What a Name
289–St. 2	One Day

JOHN 12:35–36

130	Heavenly Sunlight
165–St. 4	I Will Sing the Wondrous Story
206–St. 1	Joyful, Joyful, We Adore Thee

364	The Light of the World Is Jesus
387	Thou Whose Almighty Word

JOHN 12:46–47

8	Alas! And Did My Savior Bleed?
57	Christ Is the World's
60	Christ Whose Glory Fills
118	Hail to the Lord's Anointed
129	Heaven Came Down
130	Heavenly Sunlight
151–St. 3	I Heard the Voice of Jesus Say
162	I Stand Amazed in the Presence
164	I Will Sing of My Redeemer
165–St. 4	I Will Sing the Wondrous Story
174	In Loving Kindness Jesus Came
201	Jesus, Thou Joy of Loving Hearts
235	"Man of Sorrows," What a Name
243	My Faith Has Found
244–St. 3	My Faith Looks Up to Thee
250–St. 3	No, Not One
272–St. 2	O Love, That Will Not Let Me Go
278	O Splendor of God's Glory
311–St. 2	Revive Us Again
322	Send the Light
327	Since Jesus Came Into My Heart
340	Sunshine in My Soul
364	The Light of the World Is Jesus
368–St. 2	The Savior Is Waiting
387	Thou Whose Almighty Word
392	Turn Your Eyes Upon Jesus
394	Victory in Jesus
404	We've a Story to Tell
408	What a Wonderful Savior

JOHN 12:48

216	Let Jesus Come Into Your Heart
430	Wonderful Words of Life

JOHN 13:1

45	Blessed Redeemer
144	I Am His and He Is Mine
162	I Stand Amazed in the Presence
171	Immortal Love, Forever Full
174	In Loving Kindness Jesus Came
182	I've Found a Friend
192	Jesus, Lover of My Soul
193	Jesus Loves Even Me
194	Jesus Loves Me
203	Jesus, Thy Boundless Love to Me
272	O Love, That Will Not Let Me Go
280	O the Deep, Deep Love of Jesus

320	Savior, Teach Me Day by Day
377	There Is a Green Hill Far Away
411	What Wondrous Love Is This?

JOHN 13:3–9

| 424 | Whiter Than Snow |

JOHN 13:3–17

| 348 | "Take Up Thy Cross" |

JOHN 13:7

| 103 | God Moves in a Mysterious Way |

JOHN 13:13

| 75 | Crown Him with Many Crowns |
| 421–St. 4 | Wherever He Leads, I'll Go |

JOHN 13:13–17

38	Be Thou My Vision
171–Last St.	Immortal Love, Forever Full
222	Living for Jesus
273	O Master, Let Me Walk with Thee
320	Savior, Teach Me Day by Day
349	Teach Me Thy Way, O Lord

JOHN 13:15

155–St. 3	I Lay My Sins on Jesus
229	Lord, Speak to Me
281	O to Be Like Thee!
289–St. 1	One Day
321–St. 3	Savior, Thy Dying Love
347–St. 2	Take Time to Be Holy

JOHN 13:16–17

20	Am I a Soldier of the Cross?
243	My Faith Has Found
273	O Master, Let Me Walk with Thee

JOHN 13:31–32

12	All Hail the Power of Jesus' Name
13	All My Heart This Night
258	O Could I Speak the Matchless

JOHN 13:34–35

46	Blest Be the Tie
50–Last St.	Brethren, We Have Met
65	Come, Holy Spirit
136–St. 2	Holy Spirit, Truth Divine
206–St. 3	Joyful, Joyful, We Adore Thee
233	Make Me a Blessing
273–St. 2	O Master, Let Me Walk with Thee
295	Pass It On

320	Savior, Teach Me Day by Day
334	Spirit of God, Descend
336–St. 4	Stand Up and Bless the Lord
419	Where Cross the Crowded Ways

JOHN 13:38

| 177–St. 1 | In the Hour of Trial |

JOHN 14:1

70	Come, Ye Disconsolate
86–St. 4	Fight the Good Fight
96	Give to the Winds
141–St. 3	How Firm a Foundation
146	I Am Trusting Thee, Lord Jesus
158	I Must Tell Jesus
188	Jesus Is All the World to Me
192	Jesus, Lover of My Soul
201	Jesus, Thou Joy of Loving Hearts
204	Jesus, What a Friend for Sinners
230–St. 2	Love Divine, All Loves Excelling
247	Near to the Heart of God
267–St. 4	O, How I Love Jesus
389	'Tis So Sweet To Trust in Jesus
391	Trusting Jesus

JOHN 14:1–4

17–St. 3	All the Way My Savior Leads Me
37–St. 3	Be Still, My Soul
286	On Jordan's Stormy Banks I Stand

JOHN 14:2–4

82	Face to Face
129–St. 3	Heaven Came Down
142–St. 4	How Great Thou Art
152	I Know That My Redeemer Lives
153–St. 3	I Know That My Redeemer Liveth
235–St. 5	"Man of Sorrows," What a Name
245–Last St.	My Jesus, I Love Thee
279	O That Will Be Glory For Me
326–St. 4	Since I Have Been Redeemed
341–St. 3	Surely Goodness and Mercy
394–St. 3	Victory in Jesus
410	What If It Were Today?
416	When the Roll Is Called
417	When We All Get to Heaven

JOHN 14:6

86–St. 2	Fight the Good Fight
143	How Sweet the Name
149	I Hear Thy Welcome Voice
269	O Jesus, Thou Art Standing
290	Only Trust Him

305–Last st.   Prayer Is the Soul's Sincere
314   Rock of Ages
369   The Solid Rock
385   Thou Art the Way: to Thee Alone
390   To God Be the Glory
392   Turn Your Eyes Upon Jesus
403–St. 2   We Would See Jesus; Lo! His Star

JOHN 14:12

86–St. 4   Fight the Good Fight
229   Lord, Speak to Me
418   When We Walk with the Lord

JOHN 14:13

33   At the Name of Jesus
124–Refrain   He Keeps Me Singing
267   O, How I Love Jesus

JOHN 14:13–14

143   How Sweet the Name
346   Take the Name of Jesus with You

JOHN 14:15

320   Savior, Teach Me Day by Day

JOHN 14:16

63   Come, Holy Ghost
96   Give to the Winds
122–St. 4   Have Thine Own Way, Lord

JOHN 14:16–17

49   Breathe on Me, Breath of God
135   Holy Spirit, Light Divine
136   Holy Spirit, Truth Divine
140   Hover O'er Me, Holy Spirit
334   Spirit of God, Descend
335   Spirit of the Living God
354   The Comforter Has Come

JOHN 14:16–18

66–St. 3   Come, Thou Almighty King
70–St. 2   Come, Ye Disconsolate
76   Day by Day

JOHN 14:17

44–St. 2   Blessed Jesus, at Thy Word
154–St. 3   I Know Whom I Have Believed

JOHN 14:18

17   All the Way My Savior Leads Me
165–St. 4   I Will Sing the Wondrous Story
192   Jesus, Lover of My Soul

201   Jesus, Thou Joy of Loving Hearts
204–St. 3   Jesus, What a Friend for Sinners
267–St. 4   O, How I Love Jesus
298–St. 3   Praise Him! Praise Him!
365   The Lily of the Valley

JOHN 14:18–19

188   Jesus Is All the World to Me
238   Moment by Moment

JOHN 14:19

30–St. 3   Ask Ye What Great Things I Know
39   Because He Lives
75–St. 6   Crown Him with Many Crowns
126   He Lives
144   I Am His and He Is Mine
147   I Gave My Life for Thee
152   I Know That My Redeemer Lives
279   O That Will Be Glory For Me
385–St. 3   Thou Art the Way: to Thee Alone

JOHN 14:19–21

38–St. 2   Be Thou My Vision
153   I Know That My Redeemer Liveth
169   I'll Live for Him
193   Jesus Loves Even Me
230   Love Divine, All Loves Excelling

JOHN 14:23–26

44   Blessed Jesus, at Thy Word
229   Lord, Speak to Me
245   My Jesus, I Love Thee
320   Savior, Teach Me Day by Day
396–St. 3   We Are God's People
430   Wonderful Words of Life

JOHN 14:26

49   Breathe on Me, Breath of God
63   Come, Holy Ghost
66–St. 3   Come, Thou Almighty King
140   Hover O'er Me, Holy Spirit
154–St. 3   I Know Whom I Have Believed
239   More About Jesus
335   Spirit of the Living God
354   The Comforter Has Come

JOHN 14:27

17   All the Way My Savior Leads Me
28   Are You (Art Thou) Weary
70–St. 2   Come, Ye Disconsolate
75–St. 4   Crown Him with Many Crowns
76   Day by Day

78	Dear Lord and Father of Mankind
96	Give to the Winds
107	God the Almighty One
124–St. 1	He Keeps Me Singing
159–St. 1	I Need Thee Every Hour
180	It Is Well with My Soul
221	Like a River Glorious
247	Near to the Heart of God
297	Peace, Perfect Peace
318	Savior, Again to Thy Dear Name
389–St. 3	'Tis So Sweet To Trust in Jesus
429	Wonderful Peace

JOHN 15:1–15

| 38 | Be Thou My Vision |

JOHN 15:4–8

1	A Charge to Keep I Have
80	Down at the Cross
144	I Am His and He Is Mine
163	I Surrender All
203	Jesus, Thy Boundless Love to Me
222	Living for Jesus
233	Make Me a Blessing
252	Now I Belong to Jesus
347–St. 2	Take Time to Be Holy
418	When We Walk with the Lord

JOHN 15:9–11

16	All That Thrills My Soul
127	He the Pearly Gates Will Open
171	Immortal Love, Forever Full
173	In Heavenly Love Abiding
182	I've Found a Friend
200–St. 4	Jesus, the Very Thought of Thee
201	Jesus, Thou Joy of Loving Hearts
203	Jesus, Thy Boundless Love to Me
231	Love Lifted Me
239	More About Jesus
267	O, How I Love Jesus
272	O Love, That Will Not Let Me Go
280	O the Deep, Deep Love of Jesus
320	Savior, Teach Me Day by Day
418	When We Walk with the Lord

JOHN 15:11

17–St. 2	All the Way My Savior Leads Me
124	He Keeps Me Singing
145–St. 4	I Am Thine, O Lord
188	Jesus Is All the World to Me
192	Jesus, Lover of My Soul

240–St. 2	More Love to Thee, O Christ
266	O Happy Day that Fixed My Choice
340	Sunshine in My Soul
349–St. 2	Teach Me Thy Way, O Lord

JOHN 15:13

23	And Can It Be That I Should Gain
62–St. 2	Come, Christians, Join to Sing
162	I Stand Amazed in the Presence
193	Jesus Loves Even Me
194	Jesus Loves Me
195	Jesus Paid it All
203	Jesus, Thy Boundless Love to Me
231	Love Lifted Me
267	O, How I Love Jesus
280	O the Deep, Deep Love of Jesus
411	What Wondrous Love Is This?
413–St. 4	When I Survey the Wondrous Cross

JOHN 15:13–17

37–St. 1	Be Still, My Soul
167–St. 2	If Thou But Suffer God to Guide
182	I've Found a Friend
188	Jesus Is All the World to Me
204	Jesus, What a Friend for Sinners
250	No, Not One
268	O Jesus, I Have Promised
317–St. 1	Saved! Saved! Saved!
346	Take the Name of Jesus with You
365	The Lily of the Valley
407	What a Friend We Have in Jesus

JOHN 15:17–19

| 273 | O Master, Let Me Walk with Thee |

JOHN 15:26

44–St. 2	Blessed Jesus, at Thy Word
66–St. 3	Come, Thou Almighty King
70–St. 2	Come, Ye Disconsolate
135	Holy Spirit, Light Divine
136–St. 1	Holy Spirit, Truth Divine
140	Hover O'er Me, Holy Spirit
154–St. 3	I Know Whom I Have Believed
334	Spirit of God, Descend
354	The Comforter Has Come

JOHN 16:7–8

63	Come, Holy Ghost
66–St. 3	Come, Thou Almighty King
70–St. 2	Come, Ye Disconsolate
76	Day by Day
140	Hover O'er Me, Holy Spirit

335	Spirit of the Living God		201	Jesus, Thou Joy of Loving Hearts
354	The Comforter Has Come		209	Just When I Need Him
			221	Like a River Glorious

JOHN 16:7–14

154–St. 3	I Know Whom I Have Believed		238	Moment by Moment
			247	Near to the Heart of God
			294	Out of My Bondage

JOHN 16:13–15

44–St. 2	Blessed Jesus, at Thy Word		297	Peace, Perfect Peace
49	Breathe on Me, Breath of God		308	Rejoice, the Lord Is King
63	Come, Holy Ghost		383–St. 3	This Is My Father's World
66–St. 3	Come, Thou Almighty King		390	To God Be the Glory
125	He Leadeth Me		397	We Gather Together
135	Holy Spirit, Light Divine		429	Wonderful Peace
136	Holy Spirit, Truth Divine			

JOHN 17:1–5

167	If Thou But Suffer God to Guide		12	All Hail the Power of Jesus' Name
239–St. 2	More About Jesus		17–St. 3	All the Way My Savior Leads Me
292	Open My Eyes		33	At the Name of Jesus
335	Spirit of the Living God		60	Christ Whose Glory Fills
347–St. 4	Take Time to Be Holy		75–St. 2	Crown Him with Many Crowns
385–St. 2	Thou Art the Way: to Thee Alone		153–St. 1	I Know That My Redeemer Liveth
			232	Majestic Sweetness

JOHN 16:19–22

70	Come, Ye Disconsolate		258	O Could I Speak the Matchless
96	Give to the Winds		298–St. 3	Praise Him! Praise Him!
126–St. 3	He Lives		390	To God Be the Glory
152	I Know That My Redeemer Lives			

JOHN 17:8

206–St. 1	Joyful, Joyful, We Adore Thee		142	How Great Thou Art
244–St. 3	My Faith Looks Up to Thee		390	To God Be the Glory
307–St. 2	Redeemed, How I Love to Proclaim			
308	Rejoice, the Lord Is King			

JOHN 17:10

340	Sunshine in My Soul		204–St. 5	Jesus, What a Friend for Sinners
360	The Head That Once Was Crowned			
410	What If It Were Today?			

JOHN 17:13

			188	Jesus Is All the World to Me
			200	Jesus, the Very Thought of Thee

JOHN 16:23–24

143	How Sweet the Name		201	Jesus, Thou Joy of Loving Hearts
305	Prayer Is the Soul's Sincere			

JOHN 17:15

407	What a Friend We Have in Jesus		21–St. 3	Amazing Grace
			268	O Jesus, I Have Promised

JOHN 16:33

			393	Under His Wings
17	All the Way My Savior Leads Me			
20	Am I a Soldier of the Cross?			

JOHN 17:17

75–St. 4	Crown Him with Many Crowns		48	Break Thou the Bread
78	Dear Lord and Father of Mankind		282	O Word of God Incarnate
84	Faith Is the Victory		292	Open My Eyes
124	He Keeps Me Singing		389–St. 1	'Tis So Sweet To Trust in Jesus
141	How Firm a Foundation		430	Wonderful Words of Life
158	I Must Tell Jesus			
159–St. 1	I Need Thee Every Hour			

JOHN 17:18

162–St. 4	I Stand Amazed in the Presence		55	Christ for the World We Sing
175	In the Cross of Christ I Glory		168	I'll Go Where You Want Me To Go
200	Jesus, the Very Thought of Thee			

284	O Zion, Haste
310	Rescue the Perishing
330	So Send I You
399	We Have Heard the Joyful Sound
404	We've a Story to Tell

JOHN 17:19

| 385–St. 2 | Thou Art the Way: to Thee Alone |

JOHN 17:21–23

38–St. 2	Be Thou My Vision
57	Christ Is the World's
122–St. 4	Have Thine Own Way, Lord
144	I Am His and He Is Mine
353–St. 2	The Church's One Foundation
420–St. 4	Where He Leads Me

JOHN 17:24

82	Face to Face
232	Majestic Sweetness
279	O That Will Be Glory For Me

JOHN 18:1

| 388 | 'Tis Midnight and on Olive's Brow |

JOHN 18:1–12

| 420–St. 2 | Where He Leads Me |

JOHN 18:1–40

| 211 | Lead Me to Calvary |

JOHN 18:11

| 211–St. 4 | Lead Me to Calvary |

JOHN 18:19–24

| 99–St. 2 | Go to Dark Gethsemane |

JOHN 18:25–27

| 177–St. 1 | In the Hour of Trial |

JOHN 18:28–40

| 99–St. 2 | Go to Dark Gethsemane |

JOHN 18:36

| 225 | Look, Ye Saints! |
| 308 | Rejoice, the Lord Is King |

JOHN 18:37

190	Jesus Is Tenderly Calling
292	Open My Eyes
385–St. 2	Thou Art the Way: to Thee Alone

JOHN 19:1–5

28–St. 3	Are You (Art Thou) Weary
211–St. 1	Lead Me to Calvary
235–St. 2	"Man of Sorrows," What a Name
275–St. 1	O Sacred Head, Now Wounded
360	The Head That Once Was Crowned

JOHN 19:1–16

| 99–St. 2 | Go to Dark Gethsemane |
| 420–St. 3 | Where He Leads Me |

JOHN 19:1–42

| 211 | Lead Me to Calvary |
| 351–St. 3 | Tell Me the Story of Jesus |

JOHN 19:16–30

7	Ah, Holy Jesus
8	Alas! And Did My Savior Bleed?
32	At the Cross
41	Beneath the Cross of Jesus
80	Down at the Cross
99–St. 3	Go to Dark Gethsemane
175	In the Cross of Christ I Glory
191	Jesus, Keep Me Near the Cross
211	Lead Me to Calvary
289–St. 2	One Day
367	The Old Rugged Cross
377	There Is a Green Hill Far Away
406	Were You There?
413	When I Survey the Wondrous Cross

JOHN 19:30

| 235–St. 4 | "Man of Sorrows," What a Name |

JOHN 19:31–42

211–St. 2	Lead Me to Calvary
289–St. 3	One Day
406	Were You There?

JOHN 19:34

27	Are You Washed in the Blood
28–St. 2	Are You (Art Thou) Weary
80	Down at the Cross
145–Refrain	I Am Thine, O Lord
174–St. 3	In Loving Kindness Jesus Came
251	Nothing But the Blood
314	Rock of Ages
376	There Is a Fountain
378	There Is Power in the Blood
413–St. 3	When I Survey the Wondrous Cross

JOHN 19:37

413   When I Survey the Wondrous Cross

JOHN 19:41–42

54   Christ Arose

JOHN 20:1

260–St. 2   O Day of Rest and Gladness

JOHN 20:1–18

54   Christ Arose
59   Christ the Lord Is Risen Today
71   Come, Ye Faithful, Raise
99–St. 4   Go to Dark Gethsemane
211–St. 3   Lead Me to Calvary
289–St. 4   One Day
355   The Day of Resurrection

JOHN 20:1–21

186   Jesus Christ Is Risen Today
384   This Is the Day

JOHN 20:1–29

277   O Sons and Daughters

JOHN 20:10–18

176   In the Garden

JOHN 20:19–22

260–St. 2   O Day of Rest and Gladness

JOHN 20:20

75–St. 3   Crown Him with Many Crowns

JOHN 20:21

55   Christ for the World We Sing
168   I'll Go Where You Want Me To Go
284   O Zion, Haste
295   Pass It On
310   Rescue the Perishing
322   Send the Light
330   So Send I You
399   We Have Heard the Joyful Sound
404   We've a Story to Tell

JOHN 20:22

49   Breathe on Me, Breath of God
66–St. 3   Come, Thou Almighty King
230–St. 2   Love Divine, All Loves Excelling
255   O Breath of Life
333   Spirit Divine, Attend Our Prayer
335   Spirit of the Living God

JOHN 20:25–28

28–St. 2   Are You (Art Thou) Weary
75–St. 3   Crown Him with Many Crowns

JOHN 20:29–31

33   At the Name of Jesus
43   Blessed Be the Name
80   Down at the Cross
86–St. 4   Fight the Good Fight
133   Holy Bible, Book Divine
143   How Sweet the Name
154–St. 2   I Know Whom I Have Believed
157–St. 1   I Love to Tell the Story
243–St. 3   My Faith Has Found
263   O For a Thousand Tongues to Sing
267   O, How I Love Jesus
290   Only Trust Him
346   Take the Name of Jesus with You
359–St. 3   The Great Physician
369   The Solid Rock
385–St. 3   Thou Art the Way: to Thee Alone
389   'Tis So Sweet To Trust in Jesus
391   Trusting Jesus
430   Wonderful Words of Life

JOHN 21:15–17

1   A Charge to Keep I Have
185   Jesus Calls Us
233   Make Me a Blessing
240   More Love to Thee, O Christ
245   My Jesus, I Love Thee
268   O Jesus, I Have Promised
313   Rise Up, O Men of God
320   Savior, Teach Me Day by Day

JOHN 21:15–19

26   "Are Ye Able," Said the Master
78–St. 2   Dear Lord and Father of Mankind
90   Forth in Thy Name, O Lord
148   I Have Decided to Follow Jesus
222–St. 2   Living for Jesus
420   Where He Leads Me
421   Wherever He Leads, I'll Go

ACTS 1:3

39   Because He Lives
126   He Lives
152   I Know That My Redeemer Lives

ACTS 1:4–5

49   Breathe on Me, Breath of God

63	Come, Holy Ghost
65	Come, Holy Spirit
66–St. 3	Come, Thou Almighty King
135	Holy Spirit, Light Divine
140	Hover O'er Me, Holy Spirit
230–St. 2	Love Divine, All Loves Excelling
354	The Comforter Has Come

ACTS 1:8

55	Christ for the World We Sing
63	Come, Holy Ghost
66–St. 3	Come, Thou Almighty King
135	Holy Spirit, Light Divine
136	Holy Spirit, Truth Divine
157	I Love to Tell the Story
229	Lord, Speak to Me
233	Make Me a Blessing
284	O Zion, Haste
310	Rescue the Perishing
326–St. 3	Since I Have Been Redeemed
333	Spirit Divine, Attend Our Prayer
399	We Have Heard the Joyful Sound
404	We've a Story to Tell

ACTS 1:9–11

33–St. 5	At the Name of Jesus
116	Hail the Day That Sees Him Rise
124–St. 5	He Keeps Me Singing
189	Jesus Is Coming Again
223	Lo, He Comes with Clouds
225	Look, Ye Saints!
289–St. 4, 5	One Day
308	Rejoice, the Lord Is King
360	The Head That Once Was Crowned
363	The King Shall Come When Morning
410	What If It Were Today?

ACTS 1:14

| 305 | Prayer Is the Soul's Sincere |
| 343 | Sweet Hour of Prayer |

ACTS 2:1–4

49	Breathe on Me, Breath of God
63	Come, Holy Ghost
65	Come, Holy Spirit
66–St. 3	Come, Thou Almighty King
122–St. 4	Have Thine Own Way, Lord
140	Hover O'er Me, Holy Spirit
255	O Breath of Life
333	Spirit Divine, Attend Our Prayer
336–St. 2	Stand Up and Bless the Lord

| 354 | The Comforter Has Come |

ACTS 2:17–18

49	Breathe on Me, Breath of God
63	Come, Holy Ghost
65	Come, Holy Spirit
140	Hover O'er Me, Holy Spirit
255	O Breath of Life
335	Spirit of the Living God
354	The Comforter Has Come

ACTS 2:21

30	Ask Ye What Great Things I Know
129	Heaven Came Down
143	How Sweet the Name
294	Out of My Bondage
307	Redeemed, How I Love to Proclaim
331	Softly and Tenderly
346	Take the Name of Jesus with You
368	The Savior Is Waiting
399	We Have Heard the Joyful Sound
427	Whosoever Will

ACTS 2:24–32

39	Because He Lives
54	Christ Arose
59	Christ the Lord Is Risen Today
71	Come, Ye Faithful, Raise
111	Good Christian Men, Rejoice and Sing
126	He Lives
152	I Know That My Redeemer Lives
232	Majestic Sweetness
289–St. 4	One Day
355	The Day of Resurrection
372	The Strife Is O'er
382	Thine Is the Glory

ACTS 2:25

53–St. 2	Children of the Heavenly Father
192	Jesus, Lover of My Soul
397	We Gather Together

ACTS 2:26–28

| 200 | Jesus, the Very Thought of Thee |
| 262 | O For a Heart to Praise My God |

ACTS 2:27

| 141–St. 5 | How Firm a Foundation |

ACTS 2:28–29

| 39 | Because He Lives |
| 72 | Come, Ye Sinners, Poor and Needy |

79	Depth of Mercy! Can There Be
153	I Know That My Redeemer Liveth
382	Thine Is the Glory
394	Victory in Jesus
424	Whiter Than Snow
431	Ye Must Be Born Again

ACTS 2:30–36

75	Crown Him with Many Crowns
152	I Know That My Redeemer Lives
153	I Know That My Redeemer Liveth

ACTS 2:32–34

432	Ye Servants of God

ACTS 2:32–36

30	Ask Ye What Great Things I Know
43	Blessed Be the Name
66–St. 3	Come, Thou Almighty King
126	He Lives
225	Look, Ye Saints!
230–St. 2	Love Divine, All Loves Excelling
235–St. 4	"Man of Sorrows," What a Name
258	O Could I Speak the Matchless
289–St. 4	One Day
298	Praise Him! Praise Him!
338	Standing on the Promises
360	The Head That Once Was Crowned

ACTS 2:37

154–St. 3	I Know Whom I Have Believed

ACTS 2:38–39

49	Breathe on Me, Breath of God
63	Come, Holy Ghost
135	Holy Spirit, Light Divine
136	Holy Spirit, Truth Divine
140	Hover O'er Me, Holy Spirit
216	Let Jesus Come Into Your Heart
230–St. 2	Love Divine, All Loves Excelling
338	Standing on the Promises
359–St. 2	The Great Physician
389–St. 3	'Tis So Sweet To Trust in Jesus

ACTS 2:46–47

156	I Love Thy Kingdom, Lord

ACTS 3:1

305	Prayer Is the Soul's Sincere
343	Sweet Hour of Prayer

ACTS 3:6

192–St. 3	Jesus, Lover of My Soul

ACTS 3:15

126	He Lives
152	I Know That My Redeemer Lives

ACTS 3:16

243	My Faith Has Found
346	Take the Name of Jesus with You

ACTS 3:18

7	Ah, Holy Jesus
8	Alas! And Did My Savior Bleed?
117	Hail, Thou Once Despised Jesus
235–St. 2	"Man of Sorrows," What a Name
275	O Sacred Head, Now Wounded

ACTS 3:19

162	I Stand Amazed in the Presence
208	Just As I Am, Without One Plea
227	Lord, I'm Coming Home
266	O Happy Day that Fixed My Choice
319–St. 3	Savior, Like a Shepherd Lead Us
331	Softly and Tenderly
379	There Shall Be Showers
394–St. 1	Victory in Jesus

ACTS 4:4–20

30	Ask Ye What Great Thing I Know
129	Heaven Came Down
307	Redeemed, How I Love to Proclaim
399	We Have Heard the Joyful Sound

ACTS 4:10–12

143	How Sweet the Name
359	The Great Physician
424	Whiter Than Snow

ACTS 4:11

52	Built on the Rock
56	Christ Is Made the Sure
141	How Firm a Foundation
396	We Are God's People

ACTS 4:12

33	At the Name of Jesus
43	Blessed Be the Name
80	Down at the Cross
124–Refrain	He Keeps Me Singing
129–St. 2	Heaven Came Down
190	Jesus Is Tenderly Calling

200–St. 2	Jesus, the Very Thought of Thee
243–St. 3	My Faith Has Found
263–St. 2	O For a Thousand Tongues to Sing
267	O, How I Love Jesus
290	Only Trust Him
296–St. 4	Pass Me Not, O Gentle Savior
302–St. 2	Praise the Savior, Ye Who Know
314	Rock of Ages
346	Take the Name of Jesus with You
369	The Solid Rock
394	Victory in Jesus
399	We Have Heard the Joyful Sound

ACTS 4:20

157	I Love to Tell the Story
295	Pass It On

ACTS 4:24

19	All Things Bright and Beautiful
142	How Great Thou Art
160	I Sing the Almighty Power of God
328	Sing Praise to God Who Reigns
383	This Is My Father's World

ACTS 4:29

229	Lord, Speak to Me

ACTS 4:30

346	Take the Name of Jesus with You

ACTS 4:31

135	Holy Spirit, Light Divine
136	Holy Spirit, Truth Divine
140	Hover O'er Me, Holy Spirit
305	Prayer Is the Soul's Sincere
333	Spirit Divine, Attend Our Prayer
335	Spirit of the Living God

ACTS 4:32

57	Christ Is the World's
172	In Christ There Is No East
344	Sweet, Sweet Spirit

ACTS 4:33

16	All That Thrills My Soul
21	Amazing Grace
31	At Calvary
91	Free From the Law
129	Heaven Came Down
152	I Know That My Redeemer Lives
154	I Know Whom I Have Believed
157	I Love to Tell the Story

317	Saved! Saved! Saved!
369	The Solid Rock

ACTS 5:21

34	Awake, My Soul, and With the Sun

ACTS 5:29

1	A Charge to Keep I Have
122	Have Thine Own Way, Lord
148	I Have Decided to Follow Jesus
169	I'll Live for Him
418	When We Walk with the Lord

ACTS 5:30–31

43	Blessed Be the Name
57–St. 3	Christ Is the World's
83	Fairest Lord Jesus
232	Majestic Sweetness
235–St. 4	"Man of Sorrows," What a Name
258	O Could I Speak the Matchless
298–St. 3	Praise Him! Praise Him!
324–St. 3	Shepherd of Tender Youth
360	The Head That Once Was Crowned
432	Ye Servants of God

ACTS 5:32

63	Come, Holy Ghost
135	Holy Spirit, Light Divine
136	Holy Spirit, Truth Divine
140	Hover O'er Me, Holy Spirit
354	The Comforter Has Come

ACTS 5:42

157	I Love to Tell the Story
233	Make Me a Blessing
295	Pass It On
399	We Have Heard the Joyful Sound
404	We've a Story to Tell

ACTS 6:8–15

370–St. 2	The Son of God Goes Forth to War

ACTS 7:5

338	Standing on the Promises

ACTS 7:32

358	The God of Abraham Praise

ACTS 7:48–50

52	Built on the Rock
66	Come, Thou Almighty King
160	I Sing the Almighty Power of God

ACTS 7:51

| 65 | Come, Holy Spirit |
| 334 | Spirit of God, Descend |

ACTS 7:54–60

| 370–St. 2 | The Son of God Goes Forth to War |

ACTS 7:55

| 104 | God of Grace and God of Glory |

ACTS 7:56

| 425–St. 5 | Who Is He in Yonder Stall? |

ACTS 8:1–3

| 85 | Faith of Our Fathers |

ACTS 8:15–17

49	Breathe on Me, Breath of God
63	Come, Holy Ghost
65	Come, Holy Spirit
135	Holy Spirit, Light Divine
136	Holy Spirit, Truth Divine
333	Spirit Divine, Attend Our Prayer
335	Spirit of the Living God

ACTS 8:20

164	I Will Sing of My Redeemer
310	Rescue the Perishing
404	We've a Story to Tell

ACTS 8:23

| 294 | Out of My Bondage |

ACTS 8:25

| 157 | I Love to Tell the Story |

ACTS 8:32–33

7	Ah, Holy Jesus
33–St. 3	At the Name of Jesus
117	Hail, Thou Once Despised Jesus
235–St. 2	"Man of Sorrows," What a Name
275	O Sacred Head, Now Wounded

ACTS 8:35

| 351 | Tell Me the Story of Jesus |

ACTS 8:37

83	Fairest Lord Jesus
86–St. 4	Fight the Good Fight
154	I Know Whom I Have Believed
389	'Tis So Sweet To Trust in Jesus

ACTS 9:16

| 222–St. 3 | Living for Jesus |

ACTS 9:20

83–St. 1	Fairest Lord Jesus
142	How Great Thou Art
390	To God Be the Glory

ACTS 9:31

| 333 | Spirit Divine, Attend Our Prayer |

ACTS 9:34

192–St. 3	Jesus, Lover of My Soul
250–St. 1	No, Not One
359–St. 1	The Great Physician

ACTS 10:9

| 305 | Prayer Is the Soul's Sincere |
| 343 | Sweet Hour of Prayer |

ACTS 10:34–35

| 427 | Whosoever Will |

ACTS 10:36

221	Like a River Glorious
297	Peace, Perfect Peace
429	Wonderful Peace

ACTS 10:38

118	Hail to the Lord's Anointed
238	Moment by Moment
243–St. 4	My Faith Has Found
263	O For a Thousand Tongues to Sing
359–St. 1	The Great Physician
394–St. 2	Victory in Jesus
425–St. 2	Who Is He in Yonder Stall?

ACTS 10:39–43

58	Christ Receiveth Sinful Men
126	He Lives
143	How Sweet the Name
152	I Know That My Redeemer Lives
154	I Know Whom I Have Believed
157	I Love to Tell the Story
192	Jesus, Lover of My Soul
202	Jesus, Thy Blood and Righteousness
208	Just As I Am, Without One Plea
244	My Faith Looks Up to Thee
263	O For a Thousand Tongues to Sing
267	O, How I Love Jesus
290	Only Trust Him
310	Rescue the Perishing

346	Take the Name of Jesus with You
351	Tell Me the Story of Jesus
359	The Great Physician
389	'Tis So Sweet To Trust in Jesus
427	Whosoever Will

ACTS 10:44–45

49	Breathe on Me, Breath of God
63	Come, Holy Ghost
65	Come, Holy Spirit
66–St. 3	Come, Thou Almighty King
135	Holy Spirit, Light Divine
136	Holy Spirit, Truth Divine
140	Hover O'er Me, Holy Spirit
334	Spirit of God, Descend
335	Spirit of the Living God
354	The Comforter Has Come

ACTS 11:15–17

49	Breathe on Me, Breath of God
63	Come, Holy Ghost
66–St. 3	Come, Thou Almighty King
135	Holy Spirit, Light Divine
333	Spirit Divine, Attend Our Prayer
335	Spirit of the Living God
354	The Comforter Has Come

ACTS 11:18

427	Whosoever Will

ACTS 11:19–21

370	The Son of God Goes Forth to War

ACTS 11:23

166	I Would Be True

ACTS 11:26

156	I Love Thy Kingdom, Lord

ACTS 12:1–3

85	Faith of Our Fathers
370	The Son of God Goes Forth to War

ACTS 12:13–23

68	Come, Thou Long-Expected Jesus

ACTS 13:23

43	Blessed Be the Name
338	Standing on the Promises

ACTS 13:29–38

39	Because He Lives

54	Christ Arose
83	Fairest Lord Jesus
126	He Lives
284	O Zion, Haste
308	Rejoice, the Lord Is King
382	Thine Is the Glory
394	Victory in Jesus

ACTS 13:39

27	Are You Washed in the Blood
72	Come, Ye Sinners, Poor and Needy
112	Grace Greater Than Our Sin
129–St. 2	Heaven Came Down
195	Jesus Paid it All
251	Nothing But the Blood
290	Only Trust Him
376	There Is a Fountain
389	'Tis So Sweet To Trust in Jesus
394	Victory in Jesus
408	What a Wonderful Savior

ACTS 13:47

60	Christ Whose Glory Fills
322	Send the Light
340	Sunshine in My Soul
364	The Light of the World Is Jesus

ACTS 13:49

284	O Zion, Haste
404	We've a Story to Tell

ACTS 13:52

135–St. 3	Holy Spirit, Light Divine
136–St. 6	Holy Spirit, Truth Divine
140	Hover O'er Me, Holy Spirit
335	Spirit of the Living God
344	Sweet, Sweet Spirit

ACTS 14:15

9	All Creatures of Our God
160	I Sing the Almighty Power of God
304	Praise to the Lord, the Almighty
371	The Spacious Firmament
383	This Is My Father's World

ACTS 14:17

329	Sing to the Lord of Harvest
400	We Plow the Fields

ACTS 14:22

157	I Love to Tell the Story
166	I Would Be True

177	In the Hour of Trial	368	The Savior Is Waiting
242	Must Jesus Bear the Cross Alone		
337	Stand Up, Stand Up for Jesus	**ACTS 16:25**	
397	We Gather Together	62	Come, Christians, Join to Sing
		69	Come, We That Love the Lord
ACTS 14:27		164	I Will Sing of My Redeemer
269	O Jesus, Thou Art Standing	414	When in Our Music

ACTS 15:7

229	Lord, Speak to Me	**ACTS 16:30–31**
233	Make Me a Blessing	

229	Lord, Speak to Me	86–St. 4	Fight the Good Fight
233	Make Me a Blessing	146	I Am Trusting Thee, Lord Jesus
284	O Zion, Haste	154	I Know Whom I Have Believed
295	Pass It On	216	Let Jesus Come Into Your Heart
310	Rescue the Perishing	244	My Faith Looks Up to Thee
404	We've a Story to Tell	252	Now I Belong to Jesus
		266	O Happy Day that Fixed My Choice
ACTS 15:8		290	Only Trust Him
49	Breathe on Me, Breath of God	294	Out of My Bondage
66–St. 3	Come, Thou Almighty King	310–St. 2	Rescue the Perishing
135	Holy Spirit, Light Divine	359–St. 3	The Great Physician
		368	The Savior Is Waiting
		389	'Tis So Sweet To Trust in Jesus
ACTS 15:11		431	Ye Must Be Born Again
21	Amazing Grace		
58	Christ Receiveth Sinful Men	**ACTS 17:3**	
91	Free From the Law	30	Ask Ye What Great Thing I Know
112	Grace Greater Than Our Sin	83	Fairest Lord Jesus
129	Heaven Came Down	162	I Stand Amazed in the Presence
192–St. 4	Jesus, Lover of My Soul	235	"Man of Sorrows," What a Name
195	Jesus Paid it All	289	One Day
244	My Faith Looks Up to Thee	351–St. 3	Tell Me the Story of Jesus
290	Only Trust Him		
381	There's a Wideness	**ACTS 17:11**	
428	Wonderful Grace of Jesus	48	Break Thou the Bread
		133	Holy Bible, Book Divine
ACTS 15:26		282	O Word of God Incarnate
370	The Son of God Goes Forth to War	430	Wonderful Words of Life

ACTS 16:5		**ACTS 17:24**	
156	I Love Thy Kingdom, Lord	9	All Creatures of Our God
		52	Built on the Rock
ACTS 16:9–10		160	I Sing the Almighty Power of God
55	Christ for the World We Sing	293	Open Now Thy Gates of Beauty
168	I'll Go Where You Want Me To Go	371	The Spacious Firmament
284	O Zion, Haste		
310	Rescue the Perishing	**ACTS 17:25**	
322–St. 2	Send the Light	170–St. 3	Immortal, Invisible
373	The Vision of a Dying World	321–St. 4	Savior, Thy Dying Love
399	We Have Heard the Joyful Sound	400	We Plow the Fields
404	We've a Story to Tell		
		ACTS 17:26	
ACTS 16:14		22	America the Beautiful
269	O Jesus, Thou Art Standing		

57	Christ Is the World's

ACTS 17:27–28

5	Abide with Me
61	Close to Thee
100	God Be with You
101	God Himself Is with Us
145	I Am Thine, O Lord
159	I Need Thee Every Hour
161	I Sought the Lord
169	I'll Live for Him
170–St. 3	Immortal, Invisible
171–St. 2	Immortal Love, Forever Full
222	Living for Jesus
247	Near to the Heart of God
248	Nearer, My God, to Thee
249	Nearer, Still Nearer
261	O For a Closer Walk with God
265	O God, Our Help in Ages Past
284–St. 3	O Zion, Haste
300–St. 3	Praise the Lord Who Reigns Above
328–St. 3	Sing Praise to God Who Reigns
424–St. 4	Whiter Than Snow

ACTS 17:30

72	Come, Ye Sinners, Poor and Needy
262	O For a Heart to Praise My God
294	Out of My Bondage
310–St. 2	Rescue the Perishing
424	Whiter Than Snow
431	Ye Must Be Born Again

ACTS 17:31

42	Blessed Assurance
202	Jesus, Thy Blood and Righteousness
369	The Solid Rock

ACTS 18:9

157	I Love to Tell the Story
229	Lord, Speak to Me
292	Open My Eyes

ACTS 18:10

102	God Is My Strong Salvation
123	He Hideth My Soul
393	Under His Wings

ACTS 18:28

133	Holy Bible, Book Divine
282	O Word of God Incarnate

ACTS 19:2–6

49	Breathe on Me, Breath of God
63	Come, Holy Ghost
135	Holy Spirit, Light Divine
136	Holy Spirit, Truth Divine
140	Hover O'er Me, Holy Spirit
335	Spirit of the Living God

ACTS 19:17

12	All Hail the Power of Jesus' Name
33	At the Name of Jesus
43	Blessed Be the Name
143	How Sweet the Name
200	Jesus, the Very Thought of Thee
258	O Could I Speak the Matchless
263	O For a Thousand Tongues to Sing
298	Praise Him! Praise Him!
302	Praise the Savior, Ye Who Know
336	Stand Up and Bless the Lord
346	Take the Name of Jesus with You

ACTS 19:20

66–St. 2	Come, Thou Almighty King
282	O Word of God Incarnate

ACTS 20:7

260	O Day of Rest and Gladness

ACTS 20:21

30	Ask Ye What Great Thing I Know
72	Come, Ye Sinners, Poor and Needy
208	Just As I Am, Without One Plea
369	The Solid Rock
427	Whosoever Will
431	Ye Must Be Born Again

ACTS 20:24

21	Amazing Grace
35	Awake, My Soul, Stretch
86	Fight the Good Fight
157	I Love to Tell the Story
233	Make Me a Blessing
307	Redeemed, How I Love to Proclaim
349–St. 4	Teach Me Thy Way, O Lord

ACTS 20:28–29

1	A Charge to Keep I Have
27	Are You Washed in the Blood
156	I Love Thy Kingdom, Lord
313–St. 3	Rise Up, O Men of God
319	Savior, Like a Shepherd Lead Us

| 353–St. 1 | The Church's One Foundation |
| 376–St. 3 | There Is a Fountain |

ACTS 20:32

21	Amazing Grace
58	Christ Receiveth Sinful Men
88	For All the Saints
100	God Be with You
133	Holy Bible, Book Divine
279	O That Will Be Glory For Me
417	When We All Get to Heaven
428	Wonderful Grace of Jesus
430	Wonderful Words of Life

ACTS 20:33

| 74–St. 3 | Count Your Blessings |

ACTS 20:35

| 347–St. 1 | Take Time to Be Holy |

ACTS 21:13

| 370 | The Son of God Goes Forth to War |

ACTS 21:14

122	Have Thine Own Way, Lord
163	I Surrender All
292	Open My Eyes
418	When We Walk with the Lord

ACTS 22:11

229	Lord, Speak to Me
284	O Zion, Haste
292	Open My Eyes
404	We've a Story to Tell

ACTS 22:14

| 358 | The God of Abraham Praise |

ACTS 22:15

157	I Love to Tell the Story
229	Lord, Speak to Me
233	Make Me a Blessing
284	O Zion, Haste
326–St. 3	Since I Have Been Redeemed
351	Tell Me the Story of Jesus

ACTS 22:16

27	Are You Washed in the Blood
58	Christ Receiveth Sinful Men
112	Grace Greater Than Our Sin
129	Heaven Came Down
143	How Sweet the Name

155–St. 1	I Lay My Sins on Jesus
195	Jesus Paid it All
251	Nothing But the Blood
376	There Is a Fountain
408	What a Wonderful Savior
424	Whiter Than Snow

ACTS 23:11

| 157 | I Love to Tell the Story |

ACTS 24:14

| 432 | Ye Servants of God |

ACTS 24:15

138	Hope of the World
265	O God, Our Help in Ages Past
369	The Solid Rock

ACTS 25:19

| 126 | He Lives |
| 152 | I Know That My Redeemer Lives |

ACTS 26:6

| 338 | Standing on the Promises |

ACTS 26:13–15

| 60 | Christ Whose Glory Fills |

ACTS 26:16–18

55	Christ for the World We Sing
57	Christ Is the World's
88	For All the Saints
157	I Love to Tell the Story
284	O Zion, Haste
310	Rescue the Perishing
322	Send the Light
330	So Send I You
373	The Vision of a Dying World
399	We Have Heard the Joyful Sound
404	We've a Story to Tell

ACTS 26:20

389	'Tis So Sweet To Trust in Jesus
418	When We Walk with the Lord
424	Whiter Than Snow
431	Ye Must Be Born Again

ACTS 26:22–23

57	Christ Is the World's
113	Great God, We Sing That Mighty Hand
130	Heavenly Sunlight
151	I Heard the Voice of Jesus Say

152	I Know That My Redeemer Lives
201	Jesus, Thou Joy of Loving Hearts
278	O Splendor of God's Glory
340	Sunshine in My Soul
351–St. 3	Tell Me the Story of Jesus
364	The Light of the World Is Jesus

ACTS 28:23

157	I Love to Tell the Story

ACTS 28:27

292	Open My Eyes

ROMANS 1:2–4

12	All Hail the Power of Jesus' Name
43	Blessed Be the Name
75	Crown Him with Many Crowns
83	Fairest Lord Jesus
118	Hail to the Lord's Anointed
142	How Great Thou Art
152	I Know That My Redeemer Lives
235	"Man of Sorrows," What a Name
289	One Day
338	Standing on the Promises
390	To God Be the Glory
425–St. 5	Who Is He in Yonder Stall?

ROMANS 1:5

90	Forth in Thy Name, O Lord

ROMANS 1:6

185	Jesus Calls Us
190	Jesus Is Tenderly Calling
252	Now I Belong to Jesus
269	O Jesus, Thou Art Standing
331	Softly and Tenderly
368	The Savior Is Waiting

ROMANS 1:12

46	Blest Be the Tie

ROMANS 1:16–17

57	Christ Is the World's
86–St. 4	Fight the Good Fight
141	How Firm a Foundation
154	I Know Whom I Have Believed
243	My Faith Has Found
244	My Faith Looks Up to Thee
290	Only Trust Him
326	Since I Have Been Redeemed
359–St. 3	The Great Physician
369	The Solid Rock

389	'Tis So Sweet To Trust in Jesus
394	Victory in Jesus
399	We Have Heard the Joyful Sound
404	We've a Story to Tell

ROMANS 1:17

84	Faith Is the Victory
391	Trusting Jesus

ROMANS 1:20

9	All Creatures of Our God
19	All Things Bright and Beautiful
142	How Great Thou Art
160	I Sing the Almighty Power of God
170	Immortal, Invisible
371	The Spacious Firmament

ROMANS 2:4–5

21	Amazing Grace
67	Come, Thou Fount
79	Depth of Mercy! Can There Be
310	Rescue the Perishing
341	Surely Goodness and Mercy
362–St. 3	The King of Love My Shepherd Is
368	The Savior Is Waiting
412	When All Thy Mercies, O My God

ROMANS 2:11

427	Whosoever Will

ROMANS 2:29

262	O For a Heart to Praise My God

ROMANS 3:3

154–St. 2	I Know Whom I Have Believed

ROMANS 3:20–26

91	Free From the Law

ROMANS 3:21–26

21	Amazing Grace
27	Are You Washed in the Blood
30	Ask Ye What Great Thing I Know
43–St. 3	Blessed Be the Name
58	Christ Receiveth Sinful Men
112	Grace Greater Than Our Sin
117	Hail, Thou Once Despised Jesus
164	I Will Sing of My Redeemer
192	Jesus, Lover of My Soul
195	Jesus Paid it All
202	Jesus, Thy Blood and Righteousness
208	Just As I Am, Without One Plea

251	Nothing But the Blood
263–St. 3	O For a Thousand Tongues to Sing
266	O Happy Day that Fixed My Choice
267–St. 2	O, How I Love Jesus
290	Only Trust Him
307	Redeemed, How I Love to Proclaim
326	Since I Have Been Redeemed
350	Tell Me the Old, Old Story
376	There Is a Fountain
378	There Is Power in the Blood
389	'Tis So Sweet To Trust in Jesus
390	To God Be the Glory
408	What a Wonderful Savior
424	Whiter Than Snow
428	Wonderful Grace of Jesus

ROMANS 3:27–28

91	Free From the Law
129–St. 2	Heaven Came Down
154–St. 2	I Know Whom I Have Believed
243	My Faith Has Found
244	My Faith Looks Up to Thee
290	Only Trust Him
314	Rock of Ages
389	'Tis So Sweet To Trust in Jesus

ROMANS 4:4–5

21	Amazing Grace
154–St. 2	I Know Whom I Have Believed
243	My Faith Has Found
244	My Faith Looks Up to Thee
290	Only Trust Him
369	The Solid Rock

ROMANS 4:7–8

16	All That Thrills My Soul
129	Heaven Came Down
266	O Happy Day that Fixed My Choice
326	Since I Have Been Redeemed
340	Sunshine in My Soul

ROMANS 4:14–16

91	Free From the Law

ROMANS 4:16

21	Amazing Grace
153–St. 2	I Know That My Redeemer Liveth
428	Wonderful Grace of Jesus

ROMANS 4:18–21

138	Hope of the World
338	Standing on the Promises

358	The God of Abraham Praise

ROMANS 4:21

154	I Know Whom I Have Believed
389–St. 1	'Tis So Sweet To Trust in Jesus

ROMANS 4:25

31	At Calvary
126	He Lives
162	I Stand Amazed in the Presence
195	Jesus Paid it All
289	One Day
351–St. 3	Tell Me the Story of Jesus

ROMANS 5:1

30	Ask Ye What Great Thing I Know
129	Heaven Came Down
154	I Know Whom I Have Believed
297	Peace, Perfect Peace
429	Wonderful Peace

ROMANS 5:1–2

21	Amazing Grace
42	Blessed Assurance
58	Christ Receiveth Sinful Men
67	Come, Thou Fount
112	Grace Greater Than Our Sin
195	Jesus Paid it All
244	My Faith Looks Up to Thee
265	O God, Our Help in Ages Past
290	Only Trust Him
385	Thou Art the Way: to Thee Alone
389	'Tis So Sweet To Trust in Jesus

ROMANS 5:1–5

141	How Firm a Foundation
369	The Solid Rock

ROMANS 5:1–11

243	My Faith Has Found
246	My Tribute
252	Now I Belong to Jesus
390	To God Be the Glory
396–St. 3	We Are God's People

ROMANS 5:3

177	In the Hour of Trial
180	It Is Well with My Soul

ROMANS 5:5

63	Come, Holy Ghost
65	Come, Holy Spirit

152	I Know That My Redeemer Lives
169	I'll Live for Him
177–St. 2	In the Hour of Trial
230–St. 4	Love Divine, All Loves Excelling
238	Moment by Moment
263–St. 3	O For a Thousand Tongues to Sing
267–St. 2	O, How I Love Jesus
272–St. 4	O Love, That Will Not Let Me Go
327	Since Jesus Came Into My Heart
367	The Old Rugged Cross
431	Ye Must Be Born Again

ROMANS 6:8–11

16	All That Thrills My Soul
39	Because He Lives
43–St. 3	Blessed Be the Name
54	Christ Arose
71	Come, Ye Faithful, Raise
75	Crown Him with Many Crowns
91	Free From the Law
123–St. 4	He Hideth My Soul
152	I Know That My Redeemer Lives
153	I Know That My Redeemer Liveth
164	I Will Sing of My Redeemer
186	Jesus Christ Is Risen Today
252	Now I Belong to Jesus
277	O Sons and Daughters
308	Rejoice, the Lord Is King
372	The Strife Is O'er
384	This Is the Day
385–St. 3	Thou Art the Way: to Thee Alone

ROMANS 6:11

124	He Keeps Me Singing
204	Jesus, What a Friend for Sinners
390	To God Be the Glory
392–St. 2	Turn Your Eyes Upon Jesus
394	Victory in Jesus

ROMANS 6:13–18

10	All for Jesus
21	Amazing Grace
26	"Are Ye Able," Said the Master
58–St. 3	Christ Receiveth Sinful Men
91	Free From the Law
112	Grace Greater Than Our Sin
122	Have Thine Own Way, Lord
155–St. 1	I Lay My Sins on Jesus
163	I Surrender All
164	I Will Sing of My Redeemer
222	Living for Jesus

229	Lord, Speak to Me
262	O For a Heart to Praise My God
319–St. 3	Savior, Like a Shepherd Lead Us
345	Take My Life and Let It Be
424–St. 2	Whiter Than Snow
428	Wonderful Grace of Jesus

ROMANS 6:14

263	O For a Thousand Tongues to Sing
301	Praise the Lord! Ye Heavens

ROMANS 6:19

10	All for Jesus
163	I Surrender All
345	Take My Life and Let It Be
347	Take Time to Be Holy
424–St. 2	Whiter Than Snow

ROMANS 6:22–23

30	Ask Ye What Great Thing I Know
31	At Calvary
75–St. 6	Crown Him with Many Crowns
91	Free From the Law
138–St. 2	Hope of the World
153–St. 1	I Know That My Redeemer Liveth
164–St. 4	I Will Sing of My Redeemer
183	Jerusalem, My Happy Home
184	Jerusalem, the Golden
279	O That Will Be Glory For Me
298–St. 2	Praise Him! Praise Him!
317	Saved! Saved! Saved!
326	Since I Have Been Redeemed
368	The Savior Is Waiting
374	The Way of the Cross Leads Home
390	To God Be the Glory

ROMANS 7:4–6

145–St. 2	I Am Thine, O Lord
294	Out of My Bondage

ROMANS 7:14

202	Jesus, Thy Blood and Righteousness

ROMANS 7:18–25

145–St. 2	I Am Thine, O Lord
192–St. 3	Jesus, Lover of My Soul
294	Out of My Bondage

ROMANS 8:1–3

23	And Can It Be That I Should Gain
43–St. 3	Blessed Be the Name
58–St. 3	Christ Receiveth Sinful Men

91	Free From the Law
142–St. 3	How Great Thou Art
155–St. 1	I Lay My Sins on Jesus
164	I Will Sing of My Redeemer
174	In Loving Kindness Jesus Came
202	Jesus, Thy Blood and Righteousness
235	"Man of Sorrows," What a Name
252	Now I Belong to Jesus
263–St. 3	O For a Thousand Tongues to Sing
294	Out of My Bondage
307	Redeemed, How I Love to Proclaim
326	Since I Have Been Redeemed

ROMANS 8:1–5

49	Breathe on Me, Breath of God
135	Holy Spirit, Light Divine
136	Holy Spirit, Truth Divine
230	Love Divine, All Loves Excelling

ROMANS 8:6–11

49	Breathe on Me, Breath of God
63	Come, Holy Ghost
65	Come, Holy Spirit
67–St. 3	Come, Thou Fount
78	Dear Lord and Father of Mankind
122–St. 4	Have Thine Own Way, Lord
126	He Lives
129–St. 2	Heaven Came Down
135	Holy Spirit, Light Divine
136	Holy Spirit, Truth Divine
147–St. 1	I Gave My Life for Thee
163	I Surrender All
222–St. 1	Living for Jesus
238	Moment by Moment
297	Peace, Perfect Peace
319–St. 4	Savior, Like a Shepherd Lead Us
333	Spirit Divine, Attend Our Prayer
334	Spirit of God, Descend
335	Spirit of the Living God
429	Wonderful Peace

ROMANS 8:14–17

2	A Child of the King
38–St. 2	Be Thou My Vision
42	Blessed Assurance
49	Breathe on Me, Breath of God
53	Children of the Heavenly Father
66–St. 3	Come, Thou Almighty King
91–St. 3	Free From the Law
122–St. 4	Have Thine Own Way, Lord
141–St. 2	How Firm a Foundation

154–St. 3	I Know Whom I Have Believed
172	In Christ There Is No East
307–St. 1	Redeemed, How I Love to Proclaim
334	Spirit of God, Descend
347–St. 4	Take Time to Be Holy

ROMANS 8:17–18

177	In the Hour of Trial
180	It Is Well with My Soul
199	Jesus, Still Lead On
279	O That Will Be Glory For Me
417	When We All Get to Heaven
420–St. 4	Where He Leads Me

ROMANS 8:21

294	Out of My Bondage

ROMANS 8:23–25

2	A Child of the King
129–St. 3	Heaven Came Down
138	Hope of the World
167–St. 2	If Thou But Suffer God to Guide
265	O God, Our Help in Ages Past
273–St. 4	O Master, Let Me Walk with Thee
307	Redeemed, How I Love to Proclaim
369	The Solid Rock

ROMANS 8:26

63	Come, Holy Ghost
140	Hover O'er Me, Holy Spirit
305	Prayer Is the Soul's Sincere
333	Spirit Divine, Attend Our Prayer
336–St. 3	Stand Up and Bless the Lord
343	Sweet Hour of Prayer
407	What a Friend We Have in Jesus

ROMANS 8:28–30

12–St. 2	All Hail the Power of Jesus' Name
17	All the Way My Savior Leads Me
177–St. 3	In the Hour of Trial
180	It Is Well with My Soul
281	O to Be Like Thee!
394	Victory in Jesus

ROMANS 8:31

3	A Mighty Fortress Is Our God
53	Children of the Heavenly Father
81	Eternal Father, Strong to Save
84	Faith Is the Victory
123	He Hideth My Soul
180	It Is Well with My Soul
393	Under His Wings

394	Victory in Jesus
397	We Gather Together
426	Who Is on the Lord's Side?

ROMANS 8:32

17	All the Way My Savior Leads Me
74	Count Your Blessings
123	He Hideth My Soul
142–St. 3	How Great Thou Art
381	There's a Wideness

ROMANS 8:34

117–St. 3	Hail, Thou Once Despised Jesus
152	I Know That My Redeemer Lives
153	I Know That My Redeemer Liveth
177–St. 1	In the Hour of Trial
235	"Man of Sorrows," What a Name
324–St. 3	Shepherd of Tender Youth

ROMANS 8:35–39

20	Am I a Soldier of the Cross?
84	Faith Is the Victory
141	How Firm a Foundation
182	I've Found a Friend
192	Jesus, Lover of My Soul
193	Jesus Loves Even Me
194	Jesus Loves Me
200–St. 4	Jesus, the Very Thought of Thee
203	Jesus, Thy Boundless Love to Me
204	Jesus, What a Friend for Sinners
252	Now I Belong to Jesus
272	O Love, That Will Not Let Me Go
280	O the Deep, Deep Love of Jesus
365	The Lily of the Valley

ROMANS 8:37

86	Fight the Good Fight
212	Lead On, O King Eternal
231	Love Lifted Me
237	Mine Eyes Have Seen the Glory
291	Onward, Christian Soldiers
332	Soldiers of Christ, Arise
337	Stand Up, Stand Up for Jesus
382–St. 3	Thine Is the Glory
392–St. 2	Turn Your Eyes Upon Jesus
394	Victory in Jesus

ROMANS 8:37–39

53–St. 3	Children of the Heavenly Father
144	I Am His and He Is Mine
171	Immortal Love, Forever Full
196	Jesus, Priceless Treasure

302–St. 3	Praise the Savior, Ye Who Know

ROMANS 9:1

49	Breathe on Me, Breath of God
135	Holy Spirit, Light Divine
136	Holy Spirit, Truth Divine
292–St. 3	Open My Eyes

ROMANS 9:4–8

91	Free From the Law
338	Standing on the Promises

ROMANS 9:5

43	Blessed Be the Name
198	Jesus Shall Reign
232	Majestic Sweetness
298	Praise Him! Praise Him!
308	Rejoice, the Lord Is King
358	The God of Abraham Praise

ROMANS 9:8

129	Heaven Came Down
137	Holy, Holy, Holy
428	Wonderful Grace of Jesus

ROMANS 9:14–18

107–St. 3	God the Almighty One
230–St. 1	Love Divine, All Loves Excelling
381	There's a Wideness

ROMANS 9:21

122–St. 1	Have Thine Own Way, Lord

ROMANS 9:26

2	A Child of the King
53	Children of the Heavenly Father
129	Heaven Came Down
307	Redeemed, How I Love to Proclaim
396	We Are God's People

ROMANS 9:27

202–St. 4	Jesus, Thy Blood and Righteousness

ROMANS 9:33

389	'Tis So Sweet To Trust in Jesus

ROMANS 10:3–13

58–St. 3	Christ Receiveth Sinful Men
86–St. 4	Fight the Good Fight
91	Free From the Law
107–St. 3	God the Almighty One
129	Heaven Came Down

149	I Hear Thy Welcome Voice
163	I Surrender All
171	Immortal Love, Forever Full
195	Jesus Paid it All
201	Jesus, Thou Joy of Loving Hearts
208	Just As I Am, Without One Plea
216	Let Jesus Come Into Your Heart
231–St. 2	Love Lifted Me
262	O For a Heart to Praise My God
290	Only Trust Him
321–St. 3	Savior, Thy Dying Love
327	Since Jesus Came Into My Heart
359–St. 3	The Great Physician
368	The Savior Is Waiting
369	The Solid Rock
389	'Tis So Sweet To Trust in Jesus
427	Whosoever Will

ROMANS 10:12–15

43	Blessed Be the Name
55	Christ for the World We Sing
143	How Sweet the Name
284	O Zion, Haste
310	Rescue the Perishing
373	The Vision of a Dying World
399	We Have Heard the Joyful Sound
404	We've a Story to Tell

ROMANS 10:17

141–St. 1	How Firm a Foundation
154–St. 2	I Know Whom I Have Believed
282	O Word of God Incarnate
430	Wonderful Words of Life

ROMANS 10:21

185	Jesus Calls Us
269	O Jesus, Thou Art Standing
331	Softly and Tenderly
368	The Savior Is Waiting

ROMANS 11:2

12–St. 2	All Hail the Power of Jesus' Name

ROMANS 11:5–6

21	Amazing Grace
104	God of Grace and God of Glory
112	Grace Greater Than Our Sin
381	There's a Wideness
396	We Are God's People
428	Wonderful Grace of Jesus

ROMANS 11:22

218	Let Us with a Gladsome Mind
341	Surely Goodness and Mercy
412	When All Thy Mercies, O My God

ROMANS 11:29

12	All Hail the Power of Jesus' Name
114	Great Is Thy Faithfulness

ROMANS 11:33–36

9	All Creatures of Our God
103	God Moves in a Mysterious Way
104	God of Grace and God of Glory
170	Immortal, Invisible
328	Sing Praise to God Who Reigns
390	To God Be the Glory
432–St. 4	Ye Servants of God

ROMANS 12:1

222	Living for Jesus
321	Savior, Thy Dying Love
345	Take My Life and Let It Be
347	Take Time to Be Holy

ROMANS 12:1–2

10	All for Jesus
26	"Are Ye Able," Said the Master
49	Breathe on Me, Breath of God
90	Forth in Thy Name, O Lord
122	Have Thine Own Way, Lord
145	I Am Thine, O Lord
163	I Surrender All
169	I'll Live for Him
187	Jesus, I My Cross Have Taken
229	Lord, Speak to Me
268	O Jesus, I Have Promised
418	When We Walk with the Lord
424–St. 2	Whiter Than Snow

ROMANS 12:2

38	Be Thou My Vision
78–St. 1	Dear Lord and Father of Mankind
90	Forth in Thy Name, O Lord
292	Open My Eyes
311	Revive Us Again
349	Teach Me Thy Way, O Lord
421–St. 2	Wherever He Leads, I'll Go

ROMANS 12:3

249	Nearer, Still Nearer
262	O For a Heart to Praise My God

ROMANS 12:4–5

46	Blest Be the Tie
172	In Christ There Is No East
291	Onward, Christian Soldiers
353–St. 2	The Church's One Foundation

ROMANS 12:9

| 104–St. 2 | God of Grace and God of Glory |
| 288 | Once to Every Man and Nation |

ROMANS 12:10–13

46	Blest Be the Tie
206–St. 3	Joyful, Joyful, We Adore Thee
273	O Master, Let Me Walk with Thee
313	Rise Up, O Men of God
419	Where Cross the Crowded Ways

ROMANS 12:11–13

| 145–St. 2 | I Am Thine, O Lord |
| 268 | O Jesus, I Have Promised |

ROMANS 12:12

305	Prayer Is the Soul's Sincere
343	Sweet Hour of Prayer
369	The Solid Rock
407	What a Friend We Have in Jesus

ROMANS 12:15

| 419 | Where Cross the Crowded Ways |

ROMANS 12:21

104–St. 2	God of Grace and God of Glory
288	Once to Every Man and Nation
383	This Is My Father's World

ROMANS 13:1

| 383–St. 3 | This Is My Father's World |

ROMANS 13:11–14

| 34 | Awake, My Soul, and With the Sun |

ROMANS 13:12

106	God, That Madest Earth
130	Heavenly Sunlight
332	Soldiers of Christ, Arise
337–St. 3	Stand Up, Stand Up for Jesus
387	Thou Whose Almighty Word
395	Watchman, Tell Us of the Night

ROMANS 13:14

| 177–St. 2 | In the Hour of Trial |
| 240–St. 2 | More Love to Thee, O Christ |

ROMANS 14:6

| 253 | Now Thank We All Our God |

ROMANS 14:7–9

43	Blessed Be the Name
54	Christ Arose
75	Crown Him with Many Crowns
144	I Am His and He Is Mine
145	I Am Thine, O Lord
165–St. 5	I Will Sing the Wondrous Story
195	Jesus Paid it All
196	Jesus, Priceless Treasure
204	Jesus, What a Friend for Sinners
229	Lord, Speak to Me
232	Majestic Sweetness
233	Make Me a Blessing
238	Moment by Moment
252	Now I Belong to Jesus
298–St. 2	Praise Him! Praise Him!
362–St. 4	The King of Love My Shepherd Is
408	What a Wonderful Savior
425–St. 5	Who Is He in Yonder Stall?

ROMANS 14:11

14	All People That On Earth
66	Come, Thou Almighty King
190–St. 3	Jesus Is Tenderly Calling
263	O For a Thousand Tongues to Sing
283	O Worship the King

ROMANS 14:12

| 1–St. 3 | A Charge to Keep I Have |

ROMANS 14:17

49	Breathe on Me, Breath of God
63	Come, Holy Ghost
135	Holy Spirit, Light Divine
136	Holy Spirit, Truth Divine
252	Now I Belong to Jesus

ROMANS 14:17–18

90	Forth in Thy Name, O Lord
145	I Am Thine, O Lord
418	When We Walk with the Lord

ROMANS 14:22–23

| 84 | Faith Is the Victory |
| 243 | My Faith Has Found |

ROMANS 15:1–7

| 46 | Blest Be the Tie |

171–St. 2	Immortal Love, Forever Full
172	In Christ There Is No East
347–St. 1	Take Time to Be Holy
419	Where Cross the Crowded Ways

ROMANS 15:4

48	Break Thou the Bread
133	Holy Bible, Book Divine
138	Hope of the World
141–St. 1	How Firm a Foundation
154–St. 2	I Know Whom I Have Believed
239–St. 3	More About Jesus
282	O Word of God Incarnate
361	The Heavens Declare Thy Glory
430	Wonderful Words of Life

ROMANS 15:6

206	Joyful, Joyful, We Adore Thee
246	My Tribute
390	To God Be the Glory

ROMANS 15:8

153–St. 2	I Know That My Redeemer Liveth
338	Standing on the Promises

ROMANS 15:9–11

12	All Hail the Power of Jesus' Name
43	Blessed Be the Name
164	I Will Sing of My Redeemer
165	I Will Sing the Wondrous Story
198	Jesus Shall Reign
263	O For a Thousand Tongues to Sing
300	Praise the Lord Who Reigns Above
326	Since I Have Been Redeemed
381	There's a Wideness
404	We've a Story to Tell
414	When in Our Music
432	Ye Servants of God

ROMANS 15:12–13

17	All the Way My Savior Leads Me
42	Blessed Assurance
60–St. 3	Christ Whose Glory Fills
66–St. 3	Come, Thou Almighty King
132	Higher Ground
138	Hope of the World
154	I Know Whom I Have Believed
180	It Is Well with My Soul
200	Jesus, the Very Thought of Thee
226	Lord, Dismiss Us
247	Near to the Heart of God
265	O God, Our Help in Ages Past

272–St. 3	O Love, That Will Not Let Me Go
273–St. 4	O Master, Let Me Walk with Thee
290	Only Trust Him
297	Peace, Perfect Peace
318	Savior, Again to Thy Dear Name
369	The Solid Rock
389	'Tis So Sweet To Trust in Jesus
391	Trusting Jesus
429	Wonderful Peace

ROMANS 15:33

5	Abide with Me
75–St. 4	Crown Him with Many Crowns
100	God Be with You
159–St. 1	I Need Thee Every Hour
226	Lord, Dismiss Us
247	Near to the Heart of God
318	Savior, Again to Thy Dear Name

ROMANS 16:20

3	A Mighty Fortress Is Our God
75–St. 4	Crown Him with Many Crowns
226	Lord, Dismiss Us
337	Stand Up, Stand Up for Jesus
383–St. 3	This Is My Father's World
410–St. 2	What If It Were Today?

ROMANS 16:26

48	Break Thou the Bread
133	Holy Bible, Book Divine

ROMANS 16:27

206	Joyful, Joyful, We Adore Thee
237	Mine Eyes Have Seen the Glory
246	My Tribute
390	To God Be the Glory

1 CORINTHIANS 1:2

156	I Love Thy Kingdom, Lord

1 CORINTHIANS 1:3

318	Savior, Again to Thy Dear Name

1 CORINTHIANS 1:5

188	Jesus Is All the World to Me

1 CORINTHIANS 1:7

410	What If It Were Today?

1 CORINTHIANS 1:8–9

35	Awake, My Soul, Stretch
37	Be Still, My Soul

53	Children of the Heavenly Father
114	Great Is Thy Faithfulness
141	How Firm a Foundation
190	Jesus Is Tenderly Calling
204	Jesus, What a Friend for Sinners
208	Just As I Am, Without One Plea
213	Leaning on the Everlasting Arms
218	Let Us with a Gladsome Mind
221	Like a River Glorious
242	Must Jesus Bear the Cross Alone
250	No, Not One
299	Praise, My Soul, The King
337	Stand Up, Stand Up for Jesus

1 CORINTHIANS 1:10

46	Blest Be the Tie
172	In Christ There Is No East
353–St. 2	The Church's One Foundation

1 CORINTHIANS 1:17–18

31	At Calvary
32	At the Cross
41	Beneath the Cross of Jesus
80	Down at the Cross
175	In the Cross of Christ I Glory
191	Jesus, Keep Me Near the Cross
219	Lift High the Cross
272–St. 4	O Love, That Will Not Let Me Go
291	Onward, Christian Soldiers
315	Room at the Cross for You
360	The Head That Once Was Crowned
367	The Old Rugged Cross
374	The Way of the Cross Leads Home
413	When I Survey the Wondrous Cross

1 CORINTHIANS 1:20–31

104	God of Grace and God of Glory

1 CORINTHIANS 1:23–24

30	Ask Ye What Great Thing I Know
31	At Calvary
164–St. 3	I Will Sing of My Redeemer
298	Praise Him! Praise Him!

1 CORINTHIANS 1:27–31

195–St. 1	Jesus Paid it All
207	Just a Closer Walk with Thee

1 CORINTHIANS 1:30–31

30	Ask Ye What Great Thing I Know
31	At Calvary
43	Blessed Be the Name

83	Fairest Lord Jesus
164	I Will Sing of My Redeemer
246	My Tribute
252	Now I Belong to Jesus
263	O For a Thousand Tongues to Sing
266	O Happy Day that Fixed My Choice
307	Redeemed, How I Love to Proclaim
311	Revive Us Again
326	Since I Have Been Redeemed
369	The Solid Rock
390	To God Be the Glory
408	What a Wonderful Savior
413–St. 2	When I Survey

1 CORINTHIANS 2:2

10–St. 3	All for Jesus
30	Ask Ye What Great Thing I Know
32	At the Cross
41	Beneath the Cross of Jesus
157	I Love to Tell the Story
175	In the Cross of Christ I Glory
211	Lead Me to Calvary
219	Lift High the Cross
367	The Old Rugged Cross
374	The Way of the Cross Leads Home
413	When I Survey the Wondrous Cross

1 CORINTHIANS 2:5

84	Faith Is the Victory
141	How Firm a Foundation
243	My Faith Has Found
265	O God, Our Help in Ages Past
369	The Solid Rock

1 CORINTHIANS 2:7

103	God Moves in a Mysterious Way

1 CORINTHIANS 2:9

56–St. 3	Christ Is Made the Sure
184–St. 1	Jerusalem, the Golden
279	O That Will Be Glory For Me
286	On Jordan's Stormy Banks I Stand

1 CORINTHIANS 2:10

44–St. 2	Blessed Jesus, at Thy Word
154–St. 3	I Know Whom I Have Believed
292	Open My Eyes

1 CORINTHIANS 2:10–16

48	Break Thou the Bread
122–St. 4	Have Thine Own Way, Lord
135	Holy Spirit, Light Divine

1 CORINTHIANS 6:19

49	Breathe on Me, Breath of God
52	Built on the Rock
63	Come, Holy Ghost
66–St. 3	Come, Thou Almighty King
135	Holy Spirit, Light Divine
140	Hover O'er Me, Holy Spirit
230–St. 3	Love Divine, All Loves Excelling
334	Spirit of God, Descend
396–St. 4	We Are God's People

1 CORINTHIANS 6:19–20

1	A Charge to Keep I Have
163	I Surrender All
252	Now I Belong to Jesus
335	Spirit of the Living God
345	Take My Life and Let It Be

1 CORINTHIANS 6:20

10	All for Jesus
18	All Things Are Thine
26	"Are Ye Able," Said the Master
42	Blessed Assurance
122–St. 4	Have Thine Own Way, Lord
147	I Gave My Life for Thee
169	I'll Live for Him
187	Jesus, I My Cross Have Taken
222	Living for Jesus
246	My Tribute
319–St. 1	Savior, Like a Shepherd Lead Us
390	To God Be the Glory
394–Refrain	Victory in Jesus
408–St. 1	What a Wonderful Savior

1 CORINTHIANS 7:15

| 297 | Peace, Perfect Peace |

1 CORINTHIANS 7:19

| 418 | When We Walk with the Lord |

1 CORINTHIANS 7:22–23

145	I Am Thine, O Lord
147	I Gave My Life for Thee
169	I'll Live for Him
187	Jesus, I My Cross Have Taken
222	Living for Jesus
263–St. 3	O For a Thousand Tongues
292–St. 1	Open My Eyes
294	Out of My Bondage
319–St. 1	Savior, Like a Shepherd Lead Us
394–Refrain	Victory in Jesus

| 408–St. 1 | What a Wonderful Savior |

1 CORINTHIANS 7:31

| 5–St. 2 | Abide with Me |

1 CORINTHIANS 8:3

| 240 | More Love to Thee, O Christ |

1 CORINTHIANS 8:4

65	Come, Holy Spirit
320	Savior, Teach Me Day by Day
334	Spirit of God, Descend

1 CORINTHIANS 8:4–6

| 137–St. 3 | Holy, Holy, Holy |

1 CORINTHIANS 8:6

9	All Creatures of Our God
38	Be Thou My Vision
57	Christ Is the World's
66	Come, Thou Almighty King
170	Immortal, Invisible
206–St. 3	Joyful, Joyful, We Adore Thee

1 CORINTHIANS 8:11

| 347–St. 1 | Take Time to Be Holy |

1 CORINTHIANS 9:10

| 400 | We Plow the Fields |

1 CORINTHIANS 9:21

| 91 | Free From the Law |

1 CORINTHIANS 9:24–27

20	Am I a Soldier of the Cross?
35	Awake, My Soul, Stretch
86	Fight the Good Fight
132	Higher Ground
212	Lead On, O King Eternal
291	Onward, Christian Soldiers
332	Soldiers of Christ, Arise
337	Stand Up, Stand Up for Jesus
370	The Son of God Goes Forth to War
417–St. 4	When We All Get to Heaven

1 CORINTHIANS 10:1–4

| 115 | Guide Me, O Thou Great Jehovah |
| 362–St. 2 | The King of Love My Shepherd Is |

1 CORINTHIANS 10:4

| 4 | A Shelter in the Time of Storm |
| 17–St. 2 | All the Way My Savior Leads Me |

52	Built on the Rock
56	Christ Is Made the Sure
97	Glorious Things of Thee
123	He Hideth My Soul
298–St. 2	Praise Him! Praise Him!
314	Rock of Ages

1 CORINTHIANS 10:6

104–St. 2	God of Grace and God of Glory
261	O For a Closer Walk with God
262	O For a Heart to Praise My God
288	Once to Every Man and Nation

1 CORINTHIANS 10:12–13

114	Great Is Thy Faithfulness
138–St. 1	Hope of the World
141	How Firm a Foundation
158–St. 3	I Must Tell Jesus
159–St. 2	I Need Thee Every Hour
177	In the Hour of Trial
207	Just a Closer Walk with Thee
310–St. 3	Rescue the Perishing
343–St. 1	Sweet Hour of Prayer
365–St. 2	The Lily of the Valley

1 CORINTHIANS 10:14

135–St. 4	Holy Spirit, Light Divine
261	O For a Closer Walk with God

1 CORINTHIANS 10:16–22

6	According to Thy Gracious Word
47	Bread of the World
131	Here, O My Lord, I See Thee
217	Let Us Break Bread Together

1 CORINTHIANS 10:17

46	Blest Be the Tie
172	In Christ There Is No East
353–St. 2	The Church's One Foundation

1 CORINTHIANS 10:31

397	We Gather Together

1 CORINTHIANS 11:1

38	Be Thou My Vision
78–St. 2	Dear Lord and Father of Mankind
229	Lord, Speak to Me
287	Once in Royal David's City
320	Savior, Teach Me Day by Day
334	Spirit of God, Descend

1 CORINTHIANS 11:23–26

6	According to Thy Gracious Word
47	Bread of the World
131	Here, O My Lord, I See Thee
217	Let Us Break Bread Together
353–St. 2	The Church's One Foundation

1 CORINTHIANS 12:3

33	At the Name of Jesus
75	Crown Him with Many Crowns
136–St. 4	Holy Spirit, Truth Divine
154–St. 3	I Know Whom I Have Believed

1 CORINTHIANS 12:4–13

63	Come, Holy Ghost

1 CORINTHIANS 12:7

49	Breathe on Me, Breath of God
135	Holy Spirit, Light Divine
136	Holy Spirit, Truth Divine
292	Open My Eyes
333	Spirit Divine, Attend Our Prayer
334	Spirit of God, Descend

1 CORINTHIANS 12:9

154–St. 3	I Know Whom I Have Believed

1 CORINTHIANS 12:12–14

46	Blest Be the Tie
172	In Christ There Is No East
353–St. 2	The Church's One Foundation

1 CORINTHIANS 12:13

57	Christ Is the World's
64	Come, Holy Spirit, Dove Divine
335	Spirit of the Living God

1 CORINTHIANS 12:26–27

46	Blest Be the Tie
353–St. 2	The Church's One Foundation
396–St. 3	We Are God's People

1 CORINTHIANS 12:29

134–St. 3	Holy God, We Praise Thy Name

1 CORINTHIANS 13:1–13

65	Come, Holy Spirit
274	O Perfect Love
320	Savior, Teach Me Day by Day
334	Spirit of God, Descend

1 CORINTHIANS 13:12

82	Face to Face
162–St. 5	I Stand Amazed in the Presence
183	Jerusalem, My Happy Home
200–St. 1	Jesus, the Very Thought of Thee
258–St. 3	O Could I Speak the Matchless
279	O That Will Be Glory For Me
417	When We All Get to Heaven

1 CORINTHIANS 14:15

42–Refrain	Blessed Assurance
62	Come, Christians, Join to Sing
165	I Will Sing the Wondrous Story
167–St. 3	If Thou But Suffer God to Guide
263	O For a Thousand Tongues to Sing
305	Prayer Is the Soul's Sincere
321–St. 2	Savior, Thy Dying Love
343	Sweet Hour of Prayer
391–St. 3	Trusting Jesus
407	What a Friend We Have in Jesus
414	When in Our Music

1 CORINTHIANS 14:33

264	O God of Love, O King of Peace
297	Peace, Perfect Peace

1 CORINTHIANS 15:3

7	Ah, Holy Jesus
8	Alas! And Did My Savior Bleed?
30	Ask Ye What Great Thing I Know
31	At Calvary
32	At the Cross
45	Blessed Redeemer
117	Hail, Thou Once Despised Jesus
174	In Loving Kindness Jesus Came
180	It Is Well with My Soul
195	Jesus Paid it All
202	Jesus, Thy Blood and Righteousness
211	Lead Me to Calvary
235	"Man of Sorrows," What a Name
267–St. 2	O, How I Love Jesus
275	O Sacred Head, Now Wounded
321–St. 1	Savior, Thy Dying Love
394–St. 1	Victory in Jesus

1 CORINTHIANS 15:3–4

54	Christ Arose
59	Christ the Lord Is Risen Today
186	Jesus Christ Is Risen Today
243	My Faith Has Found
289	One Day

351–St. 3	Tell Me the Story of Jesus
355	The Day of Resurrection
372–St. 3	The Strife Is O'er

1 CORINTHIANS 15:10

21	Amazing Grace
67	Come, Thou Fount
112	Grace Greater Than Our Sin
192–St. 4	Jesus, Lover of My Soul
310–St. 4	Rescue the Perishing
428	Wonderful Grace of Jesus

1 CORINTHIANS 15:12–14

126	He Lives
152	I Know That My Redeemer Lives
153	I Know That My Redeemer Liveth
186	Jesus Christ Is Risen Today
243	My Faith Has Found

1 CORINTHIANS 15:19

138	Hope of the World
265	O God, Our Help in Ages Past
369	The Solid Rock

1 CORINTHIANS 15:20–28

16	All That Thrills My Soul
23	And Can It Be That I Should Gain
30–St. 3	Ask Ye What Great Thing I Know
31	At Calvary
43	Blessed Be the Name
54	Christ Arose
59	Christ the Lord Is Risen Today
71	Come, Ye Faithful, Raise
75–St. 6	Crown Him with Many Crowns
88	For All the Saints
126	He Lives
152	I Know That My Redeemer Lives
153	I Know That My Redeemer Liveth
198	Jesus Shall Reign
204	Jesus, What a Friend for Sinners
225	Look, Ye Saints!
232	Majestic Sweetness
252	Now I Belong to Jesus
289–St. 4	One Day
298–St. 3	Praise Him! Praise Him!
308	Rejoice, the Lord Is King
337	Stand Up, Stand Up for Jesus
355	The Day of Resurrection
385–St. 3	Thou Art the Way: to Thee Alone
392–St. 2	Turn Your Eyes Upon Jesus
394	Victory in Jesus

2 CORINTHIANS 1:6

222–St. 3   Living for Jesus

2 CORINTHIANS 1:7

381   There's a Wideness

2 CORINTHIANS 1:9–10

3   A Mighty Fortress Is Our God
67   Come, Thou Fount
115   Guide Me, O Thou Great Jehovah
389   'Tis So Sweet To Trust in Jesus
391   Trusting Jesus

2 CORINTHIANS 1:12

104   God of Grace and God of Glory

2 CORINTHIANS 1:20

114   Great Is Thy Faithfulness
153–St. 2   I Know That My Redeemer Liveth
167   If Thou But Suffer God to Guide
389   'Tis So Sweet To Trust in Jesus
390   To God Be the Glory

2 CORINTHIANS 1:20–22

67–St. 3   Come, Thou Fount
144   I Am His and He Is Mine
252   Now I Belong to Jesus
336   Stand Up and Bless the Lord
338   Standing on the Promises
396   We Are God's People

2 CORINTHIANS 1:24

84   Faith Is the Victory
180   It Is Well with My Soul
337   Stand Up, Stand Up for Jesus
391   Trusting Jesus

2 CORINTHIANS 2:11

180–St. 2   It Is Well with My Soul

2 CORINTHIANS 2:14

84   Faith Is the Victory
164   I Will Sing of My Redeemer
212   Lead On, O King Eternal
246   My Tribute
291   Onward, Christian Soldiers
298   Praise Him! Praise Him!
309   Rejoice, Ye Pure in Heart
310   Rescue the Perishing
332   Soldiers of Christ, Arise
337   Stand Up, Stand Up for Jesus
390   To God Be the Glory

394   Victory in Jesus
399   We Have Heard the Joyful Sound
404   We've a Story to Tell
426   Who Is on the Lord's Side?

2 CORINTHIANS 3:3

334   Spirit of God, Descend

2 CORINTHIANS 3:4–5

1–St. 4   A Charge to Keep I Have
17   All the Way My Savior Leads Me
146   I Am Trusting Thee, Lord Jesus
195–St. 1   Jesus Paid it All
389   'Tis So Sweet To Trust in Jesus
391   Trusting Jesus

2 CORINTHIANS 3:6

49   Breathe on Me, Breath of God
65   Come, Holy Spirit

2 CORINTHIANS 3:17–18

49   Breathe on Me, Breath of God
82   Face to Face
135   Holy Spirit, Light Divine
136–St. 4   Holy Spirit, Truth Divine
184–St. 1   Jerusalem, the Golden
222   Living for Jesus
230–St. 4   Love Divine, All Loves Excelling
279   O That Will Be Glory For Me
335   Spirit of the Living God

2 CORINTHIANS 4:6

44   Blessed Jesus, at Thy Word
57   Christ Is the World's
60   Christ Whose Glory Fills
82   Face to Face
83   Fairest Lord Jesus
86–St. 2   Fight the Good Fight
124–St. 3   He Keeps Me Singing
129   Heaven Came Down
130   Heavenly Sunlight
151–St. 3   I Heard the Voice of Jesus Say
170   Immortal, Invisible
200   Jesus, the Very Thought of Thee
220   Lift Up Your Heads
258   O Could I Speak the Matchless
272–St. 2   O Love, That Will Not Let Me Go
278   O Splendor of God's Glory
294–St. 4   Out of My Bondage
311–St. 2   Revive Us Again
322   Send the Light!
327   Since Jesus Came Into My Heart

340	Sunshine in My Soul		374	The Way of the Cross Leads Home
364	The Light of the World Is Jesus		417	When We All Get to Heaven
387	Thou Whose Almighty Word			
390	To God Be the Glory			

2 CORINTHIANS 5:7

84	Faith Is the Victory
141	How Firm a Foundation
180	It Is Well with My Soul
207	Just a Closer Walk with Thee
243	My Faith Has Found
244	My Faith Looks Up to Thee
261	O For a Closer Walk with God
265	O God, Our Help in Ages Past
338	Standing on the Promises
349–St. 1	Teach Me Thy Way, O Lord
389	'Tis So Sweet To Trust in Jesus
391	Trusting Jesus
418	When We Walk with the Lord

2 CORINTHIANS 4:7

122	Have Thine Own Way, Lord

2 CORINTHIANS 4:8–11

70	Come, Ye Disconsolate
177	In the Hour of Trial
222–St. 3	Living for Jesus

2 CORINTHIANS 4:10–11

75–St. 6	Crown Him with Many Crowns
144	I Am His and He Is Mine
281	O to Be Like Thee!
321	Savior, Thy Dying Love

2 CORINTHIANS 5:8

82	Face to Face
183	Jerusalem, My Happy Home
200–St. 1	Jesus, the Very Thought of Thee
279	O That Will Be Glory For Me
286	On Jordan's Stormy Banks I Stand
352	Ten Thousand Times Ten Thousand
417	When We All Get to Heaven

2 CORINTHIANS 4:13

157	I Love to Tell the Story
292	Open My Eyes

2 CORINTHIANS 4:14

59–St. 4	Christ the Lord Is Risen Today
416	When the Roll Is Called

2 CORINTHIANS 5:9–10

1	A Charge to Keep I Have
90	Forth in Thy Name, O Lord
268	O Jesus, I Have Promised
273	O Master, Let Me Walk with Thee
308–St. 4	Rejoice, the Lord Is King

2 CORINTHIANS 4:16–18

5–St. 2	Abide with Me
76	Day by Day
86–St. 4	Fight the Good Fight
165–St. 3	I Will Sing the Wondrous Story
177	In the Hour of Trial
180	It Is Well with My Soul
192	Jesus, Lover of My Soul
199	Jesus, Still Lead On
244–St. 2	My Faith Looks Up to Thee
311	Revive Us Again

2 CORINTHIANS 5:14

272	O Love, That Will Not Let Me Go

2 CORINTHIANS 5:14–15

8	Alas! And Did My Savior Bleed?
10	All for Jesus
32	At the Cross
67	Come, Thou Fount
147	I Gave My Life for Thee
169	I'll Live for Him
174	In Loving Kindness Jesus Came
186	Jesus Christ Is Risen Today
193	Jesus Loves Even Me
194	Jesus Loves Me
195	Jesus Paid it All
202	Jesus, Thy Blood and Righteousness
203	Jesus, Thy Boundless Love to Me
222	Living for Jesus

2 CORINTHIANS 4:18

131	Here, O My Lord, I See Thee
157	I Love to Tell the Story
170	Immortal, Invisible

2 CORINTHIANS 5:1

2–St. 4	A Child of the King
129–St. 3	Heaven Came Down
286	On Jordan's Stormy Banks I Stand
326–St. 4	Since I Have Been Redeemed

154	I Know Whom I Have Believed
174	In Loving Kindness Jesus Came
187–St. 1	Jesus, I My Cross Have Taken
271	O Love How Deep, How Broad
287	Once in Royal David's City
386	Thou Didst Leave Thy Throne
428	Wonderful Grace of Jesus

2 CORINTHIANS 8:13–14

| 419 | Where Cross the Crowded Ways |

2 CORINTHIANS 9:7–8

147	I Gave My Life for Thee
321	Savior, Thy Dying Love
345	Take My Life and Let It Be
398	We Give Thee but Thine Own

2 CORINTHIANS 9:8

17	All the Way My Savior Leads Me
21	Amazing Grace
112	Grace Greater Than Our Sin
154	I Know Whom I Have Believed
155	I Lay My Sins on Jesus
381	There's a Wideness

2 CORINTHIANS 9:11

| 89 | For the Beauty of the Earth |

2 CORINTHIANS 9:15

67	Come, Thou Fount
89	For the Beauty of the Earth
138–St. 2	Hope of the World
142	How Great Thou Art
147–St. 4	I Gave My Life for Thee
246	My Tribute
250–St. 5	No, Not One
289	One Day
311	Revive Us Again
317	Saved! Saved! Saved!
390	To God Be the Glory

2 CORINTHIANS 10:3–5

20	Am I a Soldier of the Cross?
84	Faith Is the Victory
86	Fight the Good Fight
102	God Is My Strong Salvation
104	God of Grace and God of Glory
128	He Who Would Valiant Be
212	Lead On, O King Eternal
268	O Jesus, I Have Promised
291	Onward, Christian Soldiers
332	Soldiers of Christ, Arise

| 337 | Stand Up, Stand Up for Jesus |

2 CORINTHIANS 10:5

122	Have Thine Own Way, Lord
200	Jesus, the Very Thought of Thee
229	Lord, Speak to Me
418	When We Walk with the Lord

2 CORINTHIANS 10:12

| 171–Last St. | Immortal Love, Forever Full |

2 CORINTHIANS 10:17

| 413–St. 2 | When I Survey |

2 CORINTHIANS 11:2–3

261	O For a Closer Walk with God
262	O For a Heart to Praise My God
391	Trusting Jesus
424	Whiter Than Snow
428–St. 3	Wonderful Grace of Jesus

2 CORINTHIANS 12:9–10

17	All the Way My Savior Leads Me
21	Amazing Grace
70	Come, Ye Disconsolate
76	Day by Day
112	Grace Greater Than Our Sin
115–St. 1	Guide Me, O Thou Great Jehovah
123–St. 2	He Hideth My Soul
141	How Firm a Foundation
177–St. 3	In the Hour of Trial
180	It Is Well with My Soul
188	Jesus Is All the World to Me
192	Jesus, Lover of My Soul
195–St. 1	Jesus Paid it All
204	Jesus, What a Friend for Sinners
207	Just a Closer Walk with Thee
212–St. 1	Lead On, O King Eternal
238	Moment by Moment
244	My Faith Looks Up to Thee
319–St. 3	Savior, Like a Shepherd Lead Us
330	So Send I You
332	Soldiers of Christ, Arise
334	Spirit of God, Descend
337	Stand Up, Stand Up for Jesus
348	"Take Up Thy Cross"
365	The Lily of the Valley
381	There's a Wideness
428	Wonderful Grace of Jesus

2 CORINTHIANS 12:10

| 234 | Make Me a Captive, Lord |

341–St. 2	Surely Goodness and Mercy
349	Teach Me Thy Way, O Lord

2 CORINTHIANS 13:4

8	Alas! And Did My Savior Bleed?
32	At the Cross
169	I'll Live for Him
195	Jesus Paid it All
207	Just a Closer Walk with Thee
390	To God Be the Glory

2 CORINTHIANS 13:5

33–St. 4	At the Name of Jesus
38	Be Thou My Vision
42	Blessed Assurance
122	Have Thine Own Way, Lord
154	I Know Whom I Have Believed

2 CORINTHIANS 13:7–8

48–St. 2	Break Thou the Bread
288	Once to Every Man and Nation
292	Open My Eyes

2 CORINTHIANS 13:11

75–St. 4	Crown Him with Many Crowns
230	Love Divine, All Loves Excelling
297	Peace, Perfect Peace
344	Sweet, Sweet Spirit
429	Wonderful Peace

2 CORINTHIANS 13:14

63	Come, Holy Ghost
66	Come, Thou Almighty King
100	God Be with You
137–St. 3	Holy, Holy, Holy
226	Lord, Dismiss Us
236	May the Grace of Christ
318	Savior, Again to Thy Dear Name

GALATIANS 1:3–5

30	Ask Ye What Great Thing I Know
117	Hail, Thou Once Despised Jesus
162	I Stand Amazed in the Presence
164	I Will Sing of My Redeemer
165	I Will Sing the Wondrous Story
174	In Loving Kindness Jesus Came
195	Jesus Paid it All
235	"Man of Sorrows," What a Name
246	My Tribute
252	Now I Belong to Jesus
258	O Could I Speak the Matchless
294	Out of My Bondage

298–St. 2	Praise Him! Praise Him!
307	Redeemed, How I Love to Proclaim
326	Since I Have Been Redeemed
390	To God Be the Glory
408	What a Wonderful Savior

GALATIANS 1:15

1	A Charge to Keep I Have
21	Amazing Grace

GALATIANS 1:23

85	Faith of Our Fathers

GALATIANS 2:10

419	Where Cross the Crowded Ways

GALATIANS 2:16–20

84	Faith Is the Victory
91	Free From the Law
154–St. 2	I Know Whom I Have Believed
234	Make Me a Captive, Lord
238	Moment by Moment
290	Only Trust Him
294	Out of My Bondage
353	The Church's One Foundation
385–St. 3	Thou Art the Way: to Thee Alone
389	'Tis So Sweet To Trust in Jesus

GALATIANS 2:20

16	All That Thrills My Soul
26	"Are Ye Able," Said the Master
30	Ask Ye What Great Thing I Know
32	At the Cross
33–St. 4	At the Name of Jesus
122	Have Thine Own Way, Lord
124	He Keeps Me Singing
126	He Lives
144	I Am His and He Is Mine
146	I Am Trusting Thee, Lord Jesus
147	I Gave My Life for Thee
162	I Stand Amazed in the Presence
164	I Will Sing of My Redeemer
169	I'll Live for Him
174	In Loving Kindness Jesus Came
180	It Is Well with My Soul
182	I've Found a Friend
187	Jesus, I My Cross Have Taken
192	Jesus, Lover of My Soul
193	Jesus Loves Even Me
194	Jesus Loves Me
203	Jesus, Thy Boundless Love to Me
211	Lead Me to Calvary

222	Living for Jesus
231	Love Lifted Me
252	Now I Belong to Jesus
266	O Happy Day that Fixed My Choice
272	O Love, That Will Not Let Me Go
280	O the Deep, Deep Love of Jesus
307	Redeemed, How I Love to Proclaim
317	Saved! Saved! Saved!
327	Since Jesus Came Into My Heart

GALATIANS 3:1–14

91	Free From the Law
135	Holy Spirit, Light Divine
154–St. 3	I Know Whom I Have Believed

GALATIANS 3:13–14

8	Alas! And Did My Savior Bleed?
32	At the Cross
33–St. 3	At the Name of Jesus
45	Blessed Redeemer
117	Hail, Thou Once Despised Jesus
162–St. 4	I Stand Amazed in the Presence
164–St. 1	I Will Sing of My Redeemer
174	In Loving Kindness Jesus Came
195	Jesus Paid it All
235	"Man of Sorrows," What a Name
289–St. 2	One Day
307	Redeemed, How I Love to Proclaim
324–St. 2	Shepherd of Tender Youth
326	Since I Have Been Redeemed
367	The Old Rugged Cross
377	There Is a Green Hill Far Away
390	To God Be the Glory
391–St. 2	Trusting Jesus
411	What Wondrous Love Is This?

GALATIANS 3:14–22

141	How Firm a Foundation
338	Standing on the Promises
389	'Tis So Sweet To Trust in Jesus

GALATIANS 3:16

153–St. 2	I Know That My Redeemer Liveth

GALATIANS 3:22

154–St. 2	I Know Whom I Have Believed

GALATIANS 3:24

91	Free From the Law
129	Heaven Came Down

GALATIANS 3:26–29

2	A Child of the King
38–St. 2	Be Thou My Vision
46	Blest Be the Tie
53	Children of the Heavenly Father
57	Christ Is the World's
64	Come, Holy Spirit, Dove Divine
154–St. 2	I Know Whom I Have Believed
172	In Christ There Is No East
213	Leaning on the Everlasting Arms
238	Moment by Moment
252	Now I Belong to Jesus
291	Onward, Christian Soldiers
338	Standing on the Promises

GALATIANS 4:1–7

2	A Child of the King
53	Children of the Heavenly Father

GALATIANS 4:4–7

38–St. 2	Be Thou My Vision
42	Blessed Assurance
91–St. 3	Free From the Law
95	Gentle Mary Laid Her Child
120	Hark! The Herald Angels Sing
138–St. 2	Hope of the World
142	How Great Thou Art
154	I Know Whom I Have Believed
174	In Loving Kindness Jesus Came
205	Joy to the World
289	One Day
307–St. 1	Redeemed, How I Love to Proclaim
353	The Church's One Foundation
357	The First Noel
390	To God Be the Glory

GALATIANS 4:8–9

67–St. 3	Come, Thou Fount
135–St. 4	Holy Spirit, Light Divine
261	O For a Closer Walk with God

GALATIANS 4:23

338	Standing on the Promises

GALATIANS 4:28

338	Standing on the Promises
389	'Tis So Sweet To Trust in Jesus

GALATIANS 4:31

91	Free From the Law

GALATIANS 5:1

31	At Calvary
91	Free From the Law
164–St. 1	I Will Sing of My Redeemer
230–St. 2	Love Divine, All Loves Excelling
263–St. 3	O For a Thousand Tongues to Sing
267–St. 2	O, How I Love Jesus
294	Out of My Bondage
428	Wonderful Grace of Jesus

GALATIANS 5:5

49	Breathe on Me, Breath of God
369	The Solid Rock

GALATIANS 5:6

240	More Love to Thee, O Christ
320	Savior, Teach Me Day by Day
321	Savior, Thy Dying Love
334	Spirit of God, Descend

GALATIANS 5:7

35	Awake, My Soul, Stretch
86	Fight the Good Fight

GALATIANS 5:13

1	A Charge to Keep I Have
91	Free From the Law
172	In Christ There Is No East
185	Jesus Calls Us
229	Lord, Speak to Me
230	Love Divine, All Loves Excelling
233	Make Me a Blessing
273	O Master, Let Me Walk with Thee
313	Rise Up, O Men of God

GALATIANS 5:13–14

320	Savior, Teach Me Day by Day
334	Spirit of God, Descend

GALATIANS 5:16–25

3–St. 4	A Mighty Fortress Is Our God
49	Breathe on Me, Breath of God
65	Come, Holy Spirit
66–St. 3	Come, Thou Almighty King
135	Holy Spirit, Light Divine
136	Holy Spirit, Truth Divine
177–St. 2	In the Hour of Trial
192–St. 3	Jesus, Lover of My Soul
222	Living for Jesus
230	Love Divine, All Loves Excelling
252	Now I Belong to Jesus

261	O For a Closer Walk with God
333	Spirit Divine, Attend Our Prayer
334	Spirit of God, Descend
335	Spirit of the Living God
344	Sweet, Sweet Spirit
392–St. 2	Turn Your Eyes Upon Jesus

GALATIANS 6:2

46	Blest Be the Tie

GALATIANS 6:3

3–St. 2	A Mighty Fortress Is Our God

GALATIANS 6:8–10

49–St. 4	Breathe on Me, Breath of God
86–St. 4	Fight the Good Fight
168	I'll Go Where You Want Me To Go
172	In Christ There Is No East
322–St. 4	Send the Light

GALATIANS 6:14

30	Ask Ye What Great Thing I Know
32	At the Cross
41	Beneath the Cross of Jesus
80	Down at the Cross
175	In the Cross of Christ I Glory
191	Jesus, Keep Me Near the Cross
212–St. 3	Lead On, O King Eternal
219	Lift High the Cross
272–St. 4	O Love, That Will Not Let Me Go
291	Onward, Christian Soldiers
313–St. 4	Rise Up, O Men of God
315	Room at the Cross for You
367	The Old Rugged Cross
374	The Way of the Cross Leads Home
377	There Is a Green Hill Far Away
413	When I Survey the Wondrous Cross

GALATIANS 6:15

230–St. 4	Love Divine, All Loves Excelling
431	Ye Must Be Born Again

EPHESIANS 1:2

318	Savior, Again to Thy Dear Name

EPHESIANS 1:3

67	Come, Thou Fount
123–St. 3	He Hideth My Soul
311	Revive Us Again

EPHESIANS 1:3–14

2	A Child of the King

8	Alas! And Did My Savior Bleed?
23	And Can It Be That I Should Gain
32	At the Cross
42	Blessed Assurance
129	Heaven Came Down
154	I Know Whom I Have Believed
164	I Will Sing of My Redeemer
174	In Loving Kindness Jesus Came
246	My Tribute
258	O Could I Speak the Matchless
302	Praise the Savior, Ye Who Know
307	Redeemed, How I Love to Proclaim
359–St. 2	The Great Physician
390	To God Be the Glory

EPHESIANS 1:4–6

2	A Child of the King
12–St. 2	All Hail the Power of Jesus' Name
167–St. 2	If Thou But Suffer God to Guide
396	We Are God's People

EPHESIANS 1:6–8

21	Amazing Grace
27	Are You Washed in the Blood
58	Christ Receiveth Sinful Men
67	Come, Thou Fount
112	Grace Greater Than Our Sin
208	Just As I Am, Without One Plea
298–St. 2	Praise Him! Praise Him!
307	Redeemed, How I Love to Proclaim
326	Since I Have Been Redeemed
381	There's a Wideness
428	Wonderful Grace of Jesus

EPHESIANS 1:7–8

80	Down at the Cross
117–St. 2	Hail, Thou Once Despised Jesus
155–St. 1	I Lay My Sins on Jesus
164	I Will Sing of My Redeemer
192–St. 4	Jesus, Lover of My Soul
195	Jesus Paid it All
202	Jesus, Thy Blood and Righteousness
216	Let Jesus Come Into Your Heart
235–St. 2	"Man of Sorrows," What a Name
251	Nothing But the Blood
252	Now I Belong to Jesus
263–St. 3	O For a Thousand Tongues to Sing
266	O Happy Day that Fixed My Choice
267–St. 2	O, How I Love Jesus
317	Saved! Saved! Saved!
376	There Is a Fountain

| 378 | There Is Power in the Blood |
| 408 | What a Wonderful Savior |

EPHESIANS 1:9

| 122 | Have Thine Own Way, Lord |
| 239 | More About Jesus |

EPHESIANS 1:13

135	Holy Spirit, Light Divine
136–St. 1	Holy Spirit, Truth Divine
146	I Am Trusting Thee, Lord Jesus
154	I Know Whom I Have Believed
180	It Is Well with My Soul
290	Only Trust Him
354	The Comforter Has Come
369	The Solid Rock
389	'Tis So Sweet To Trust in Jesus
391	Trusting Jesus

EPHESIANS 1:17

| 104 | God of Grace and God of Glory |

EPHESIANS 1:18

132	Higher Ground
154	I Know Whom I Have Believed
265	O God, Our Help in Ages Past
369	The Solid Rock

EPHESIANS 1:19–23

43–St. 2	Blessed Be the Name
75	Crown Him with Many Crowns
126	He Lives
142	How Great Thou Art
152	I Know That My Redeemer Lives
198	Jesus Shall Reign
232	Majestic Sweetness
289–St. 4	One Day
298–St. 3	Praise Him! Praise Him!
308	Rejoice, the Lord Is King
360	The Head That Once Was Crowned
432	Ye Servants of God

EPHESIANS 1:22–23

52	Built on the Rock
56	Christ Is Made the Sure Foundation
86–St. 4	Fight the Good Fight
156	I Love Thy Kingdom, Lord
353	The Church's One Foundation
396–St. 3	We Are God's People

EPHESIANS 2:1–10

| 23 | And Can It Be That I Should Gain? |

31	At Calvary
55–St. 2	Christ for the World We Sing
112	Grace Greater Than Our Sin
162	I Stand Amazed in the Presence
246	My Tribute
261	O For a Closer Walk with God
262	O For a Heart to Praise My God
331	Softly and Tenderly
381	There's a Wideness
431	Ye Must Be Born Again

EPHESIANS 2:4–5

71	Come, Ye Faithful, Raise
79	Depth of Mercy! Can There Be
144	I Am His and He Is Mine
191–St. 2	Jesus, Keep Me Near the Cross
203	Jesus, Thy Boundless Love to Me
231	Love Lifted Me
266	O Happy Day that Fixed My Choice
317	Saved! Saved! Saved!
319–St. 4	Savior, Like a Shepherd Lead Us
411	What Wondrous Love Is This?

EPHESIANS 2:4–10

21	Amazing Grace
59–St. 4	Christ the Lord Is Risen Today
164	I Will Sing of My Redeemer
174	In Loving Kindness Jesus Came
180	It Is Well with My Soul
232	Majestic Sweetness
243	My Faith Has Found
290	Only Trust Him
307	Redeemed, How I Love to Proclaim
317	Saved! Saved! Saved!
408	What a Wonderful Savior
428	Wonderful Grace of Jesus

EPHESIANS 2:8–9

91	Free From the Law
138–St. 2	Hope of the World
154	I Know Whom I Have Believed
192–St. 4	Jesus, Lover of My Soul
243	My Faith Has Found
244	My Faith Looks Up to Thee
314	Rock of Ages
389	'Tis So Sweet To Trust in Jesus

EPHESIANS 2:10

1	A Charge to Keep I Have
90	Forth in Thy Name, O Lord
222	Living for Jesus

233	Make Me a Blessing
273	O Master, Let Me Walk with Thee
313	Rise Up, O Men of God

EPHESIANS 2:13–16

7	Ah, Holy Jesus
8	Alas! And Did My Savior Bleed?
32	At the Cross
57	Christ Is the World's
80	Down at the Cross
117–St. 2	Hail, Thou Once Despised Jesus
138	Hope of the World
145	I Am Thine, O Lord
172	In Christ There Is No East
175	In the Cross of Christ I Glory
191	Jesus, Keep Me Near the Cross
208	Just As I Am, Without One Plea
228	Lord Jesus, Think on Me
235	"Man of Sorrows," What a Name
247	Near to the Heart of God
249	Nearer, Still Nearer
251	Nothing But the Blood
263–St. 3	O For a Thousand Tongues
267–St. 2	O, How I Love Jesus
298–St. 2	Praise Him! Praise Him!
314	Rock of Ages
369	The Solid Rock
374	The Way of the Cross Leads Home
376	There Is a Fountain
377	There Is a Green Hill Far Away
378	There Is Power in the Blood
408	What a Wonderful Savior

EPHESIANS 2:14–17

75–St. 4	Crown Him with Many Crowns
297	Peace, Perfect Peace
429	Wonderful Peace

EPHESIANS 2:16

41	Beneath the Cross of Jesus
219	Lift High the Cross
315	Room at the Cross for You
367	The Old Rugged Cross
413	When I Survey the Wondrous Cross

EPHESIANS 2:18

44	Blessed Jesus, at Thy Word
66	Come, Thou Almighty King
269	O Jesus, Thou Art Standing
385	Thou Art the Way: to Thee Alone
390	To God Be the Glory

EPHESIANS 2:19–22

2	A Child of the King
30	Ask Ye What Great Thing I Know
38–St. 2	Be Thou My Vision
52	Built on the Rock
56	Christ Is Made the Sure
88	For All the Saints
134–St. 3	Holy God, We Praise Thy Name
141	How Firm a Foundation
165	I Will Sing the Wondrous Story
172	In Christ There Is No East
353	The Church's One Foundation
396	We Are God's People

EPHESIANS 3:6

2	A Child of the King
42	Blessed Assurance
396	We Are God's People

EPHESIANS 3:6–8

21	Amazing Grace
55	Christ for the World We Sing
322	Send the Light!
399	We Have Heard the Joyful Sound
432	Ye Servants of God

EPHESIANS 3:9

75–St. 5	Crown Him with Many Crowns

EPHESIANS 3:10

104	God of Grace and God of Glory

EPHESIANS 3:12

146	I Am Trusting Thee, Lord Jesus
244	My Faith Looks Up to Thee
369	The Solid Rock
385	Thou Art the Way: to Thee Alone
407	What a Friend We Have in Jesus

EPHESIANS 3:14–15

33	At the Name of Jesus
101	God Himself Is with Us
134	Holy God, We Praise Thy Name
225	Look, Ye Saints!

EPHESIANS 3:16

3–St. 4	A Mighty Fortress Is Our God
63	Come, Holy Ghost
136–St. 3	Holy Spirit, Truth Divine
335	Spirit of the Living God
348	"Take Up Thy Cross"

EPHESIANS 3:16–19

163	I Surrender All
192	Jesus, Lover of My Soul
193	Jesus Loves Even Me
194	Jesus Loves Me
231	Love Lifted Me
334	Spirit of God, Descend

EPHESIANS 3:17

33–St. 4	At the Name of Jesus
126	He Lives
238	Moment by Moment

EPHESIANS 3:17–19

16–St. 2	All That Thrills My Soul
17	All the Way My Savior Leads Me
23	And Can It Be That I Should Gain?
162	I Stand Amazed in the Presence
171	Immortal Love, Forever Full
200	Jesus, the Very Thought of Thee
201	Jesus, Thou Joy of Loving Hearts
203	Jesus, Thy Boundless Love to Me
230	Love Divine, All Loves Excelling
271	O Love How Deep, How Broad
272	O Love, That Will Not Let Me Go
280	O the Deep, Deep Love of Jesus
320	Savior, Teach Me Day by Day
360	The Head That Once Was Crowned
381	There's a Wideness
411	What Wondrous Love Is This?

EPHESIANS 3:18

88	For All the Saints

EPHESIANS 3:19

65	Come, Holy Spirit
182	I've Found a Friend
204	Jesus, What a Friend for Sinners
229	Lord, Speak to Me
239	More About Jesus

EPHESIANS 3:20–21

136–St. 3	Holy Spirit, Truth Divine
156	I Love Thy Kingdom, Lord
246	My Tribute
291	Onward, Christian Soldiers
356	The Day Thou Gavest
390	To God Be the Glory
415	When Morning Gilds the Skies

EPHESIANS 4:1

1	A Charge to Keep I Have
185	Jesus Calls Us
261	O For a Closer Walk with God

EPHESIANS 4:1–7

166	I Would Be True
234	Make Me a Captive, Lord
236	May the Grace of Christ
291	Onward, Christian Soldiers

EPHESIANS 4:2–3

46	Blest Be the Tie
49	Breathe on Me, Breath of God
344	Sweet, Sweet Spirit

EPHESIANS 4:3–6

57	Christ Is the World's
137–St. 3	Holy, Holy, Holy
172	In Christ There Is No East
206–St. 3	Joyful, Joyful, We Adore Thee
253–St. 3	Now Thank We All Our God
353–St. 2	The Church's One Foundation

EPHESIANS 4:7

21	Amazing Grace
112	Grace Greater Than Our Sin
428	Wonderful Grace of Jesus

EPHESIANS 4:8–10

75	Crown Him with Many Crowns
116	Hail the Day That Sees Him Rise
232	Majestic Sweetness
235–St. 4	"Man of Sorrows," What a Name
289–St. 4	One Day
360	The Head That Once Was Crowned

EPHESIANS 4:11

1	A Charge to Keep I Have
134–St. 2	Holy God, We Praise Thy Name

EPHESIANS 4:13–16

17	All the Way My Savior Leads Me
56	Christ Is Made the Sure
93–Last st.	From Every Stormy Wind
239	More About Jesus
292–St. 3	Open My Eyes
347	Take Time to Be Holy
353	The Church's One Foundation

EPHESIANS 4:20–21

229	Lord, Speak to Me

292	Open My Eyes
385–St. 2	Thou Art the Way: to Thee Alone

EPHESIANS 4:22–24

78–St. 1	Dear Lord and Father of Mankind
108	God Who Touchest Earth
166	I Would Be True
262	O For a Heart to Praise My God
266	O Happy Day that Fixed My Choice
281	O to Be Like Thee!
311	Revive Us Again
347	Take Time to Be Holy
431	Ye Must Be Born Again

EPHESIANS 4:25

292–St. 3	Open My Eyes

EPHESIANS 4:27

132–St. 3	Higher Ground

EPHESIANS 4:28

419	Where Cross the Crowded Ways

EPHESIANS 4:30

45	Blessed Redeemer
261	O For a Closer Walk with God
302	Praise the Savior, Ye Who Know
326	Since I Have Been Redeemed

EPHESIANS 4:32

46	Blest Be the Tie
281	O to Be Like Thee!

EPHESIANS 5:1–2

26	"Are Ye Able," Said the Master
36	Away in a Manger
38	Be Thou My Vision
122	Have Thine Own Way, Lord
148	I Have Decided to Follow Jesus
193	Jesus Loves Even Me
194	Jesus Loves Me
273	O Master, Let Me Walk with Thee
281	O to Be Like Thee!
320	Savior, Teach Me Day by Day
418	When We Walk with the Lord

EPHESIANS 5:2

27–St. 2	Are You Washed in the Blood?
31	At Calvary
162	I Stand Amazed in the Presence
203	Jesus, Thy Boundless Love to Me
240	More Love to Thee, O Christ

199	Jesus, Still Lead On
200	Jesus, the Very Thought of Thee
222	Living for Jesus
238	Moment by Moment
249	Nearer, Still Nearer
250	No, Not One
252	Now I Belong to Jesus
298	Praise Him! Praise Him!
345	Take My Life and Let It Be
362–St. 4	The King of Love My Shepherd Is

PHILIPPIANS 1:27–30

20	Am I a Soldier of the Cross?
55	Christ for the World We Sing
86	Fight the Good Fight
212	Lead On, O King Eternal
291	Onward, Christian Soldiers
332	Soldiers of Christ, Arise
337	Stand Up, Stand Up for Jesus
370	The Son of God Goes Forth to War

PHILIPPIANS 1:28

102	God Is My Strong Salvation
104–St. 2	God of Grace and God of Glory
124–St. 1	He Keeps Me Singing

PHILIPPIANS 1:29

222	Living for Jesus

PHILIPPIANS 2:1–5

46	Blest Be the Tie
55–St. 3	Christ for the World We Sing
65	Come, Holy Spirit
70	Come, Ye Disconsolate
171–Last st.	Immortal Love, Forever Full
239	More About Jesus
281	O to Be Like Thee!
334	Spirit of God, Descend
347–St. 2	Take Time to Be Holy

PHILIPPIANS 2:5–11

2–St. 2	A Child of the King
33	At the Name of Jesus
117	Hail, Thou Once Despised Jesus
155–St. 3	I Lay My Sins on Jesus
235	"Man of Sorrows," What a Name
250	No, Not One
285	Of the Father's Love Begotten
289	One Day
360	The Head That Once Was Crowned
386	Thou Didst Leave Thy Throne

PHILIPPIANS 2:6–8

7	Ah, Holy Jesus
8	Alas! And Did My Savior Bleed?
32	At the Cross
33–St. 3	At the Name of Jesus
75–St. 2	Crown Him with Many Crowns
165–St. 1	I Will Sing the Wondrous Story
271	O Love How Deep, How Broad
284–St. 3	O Zion, Haste

PHILIPPIANS 2:8

41	Beneath the Cross of Jesus
80	Down at the Cross
211	Lead Me to Calvary
275	O Sacred Head, Now Wounded
351–St. 2	Tell Me the Story of Jesus
367	The Old Rugged Cross
413	When I Survey the Wondrous Cross

PHILIPPIANS 2:9–11

12	All Hail the Power of Jesus' Name
33	At the Name of Jesus
43	Blessed Be the Name
83	Fairest Lord Jesus
124–Refrain	He Keeps Me Singing
143	How Sweet the Name
190–St. 3	Jesus Is Tenderly Calling
198	Jesus Shall Reign
200–St. 2	Jesus, the Very Thought of Thee
225	Look, Ye Saints!
232	Majestic Sweetness
258	O Could I Speak the Matchless
263	O For a Thousand Tongues to Sing
267	O, How I Love Jesus
298–St. 3	Praise Him! Praise Him!
308	Rejoice, the Lord Is King
346	Take the Name of Jesus with You
359	The Great Physician
390	To God Be the Glory
415	When Morning Gilds the Skies
432	Ye Servants of God

PHILIPPIANS 2:13

49	Breathe on Me, Breath of God
90	Forth in Thy Name, O Lord
122	Have Thine Own Way, Lord
233	Make Me a Blessing
268	O Jesus, I Have Promised
273	O Master, Let Me Walk with Thee
292	Open My Eyes
326–St. 2	Since I Have Been Redeemed

| 349 | Teach Me Thy Way, O Lord |
| 418 | When We Walk with the Lord |

PHILIPPIANS 2:15–16

35	Awake, My Soul, Stretch
38–St. 2	Be Thou My Vision
91–St. 3	Free From the Law
130	Heavenly Sunlight
284	O Zion, Haste
295	Pass It On
310	Rescue the Perishing
404	We've a Story to Tell
430	Wonderful Words of Life

PHILIPPIANS 3:1

124	He Keeps Me Singing
126–St. 3	He Lives
340	Sunshine in My Soul

PHILIPPIANS 3:3

| 240–St. 2 | More Love to Thee, O Christ |

PHILIPPIANS 3:7–9

10	All for Jesus
30	Ask Ye What Great Thing I Know
38	Be Thou My Vision
258	O Could I Speak the Matchless
294–St. 2	Out of My Bondage
369	The Solid Rock
389	'Tis So Sweet To Trust in Jesus
392	Turn Your Eyes Upon Jesus
413	When I Survey the Wondrous Cross

PHILIPPIANS 3:8–11

99	Go to Dark Gethsemane
126	He Lives
211	Lead Me to Calvary
239	More About Jesus
242	Must Jesus Bear the Cross Alone

PHILIPPIANS 3:12–14

1–St. 4	A Charge to Keep I Have
35	Awake, My Soul, Stretch
38	Be Thou My Vision
86	Fight the Good Fight
132	Higher Ground
174–St. 4	In Loving Kindness Jesus Came
239	More About Jesus
417–St. 4	When We All Get to Heaven

PHILIPPIANS 3:15

| 166 | I Would Be True |

| 222 | Living for Jesus |

PHILIPPIANS 3:18

3	A Mighty Fortress Is Our God
41	Beneath the Cross of Jesus
191	Jesus, Keep Me Near the Cross
212	Lead On, O King Eternal
337	Stand Up, Stand Up for Jesus
367	The Old Rugged Cross

PHILIPPIANS 3:20–21

2	A Child of the King
163	I Surrender All
184–St. 4	Jerusalem, the Golden
307	Redeemed, How I Love to Proclaim

PHILIPPIANS 4:4

124	He Keeps Me Singing
201	Jesus, Thou Joy of Loving Hearts
206	Joyful, Joyful, We Adore Thee
266	O Happy Day that Fixed My Choice
272–St. 3	O Love, That Will Not Let Me Go
308	Rejoice, the Lord Is King
309	Rejoice, Ye Pure in Heart
340	Sunshine in My Soul
390	To God Be the Glory

PHILIPPIANS 4:6–7

75–St. 4	Crown Him with Many Crowns
124–St. 1	He Keeps Me Singing
145–St. 3	I Am Thine, O Lord
158	I Must Tell Jesus
209	Just When I Need Him
247	Near to the Heart of God
297	Peace, Perfect Peace
305	Prayer Is the Soul's Sincere
318	Savior, Again to Thy Dear Name
343	Sweet Hour of Prayer
407	What a Friend We Have in Jesus
429	Wonderful Peace

PHILIPPIANS 4:8

| 78–St. 1 | Dear Lord and Father of Mankind |
| 108 | God Who Touchest Earth |

PHILIPPIANS 4:9

| 75–St. 4 | Crown Him with Many Crowns |
| 264 | O God of Love, O King of Peace |

PHILIPPIANS 4:11–13

| 86 | Fight the Good Fight |
| 104 | God of Grace and God of Glory |

125	He Leadeth Me	279	O That Will Be Glory For Me
188	Jesus Is All the World to Me	292	Open My Eyes
204–St. 2	Jesus, What a Friend for Sinners	313	Rise Up, O Men of God
207	Just a Closer Walk with Thee	418	When We Walk with the Lord
332	Soldiers of Christ, Arise		

PHILIPPIANS 4:19

16	All That Thrills My Soul
74	Count Your Blessings
109	God Will Take Care of You
115	Guide Me, O Thou Great Jehovah
146	I Am Trusting Thee, Lord Jesus
159	I Need Thee Every Hour
167	If Thou But Suffer God to Guide
188	Jesus Is All the World to Me
208–St. 4	Just As I Am, Without One Plea
209	Just When I Need Him
297	Peace, Perfect Peace
362	The King of Love My Shepherd Is

PHILIPPIANS 4:20

206	Joyful, Joyful, We Adore Thee
390	To God Be the Glory

PHILIPPIANS 4:23

226	Lord, Dismiss Us

COLOSSIANS 1:3

253	Now Thank We All Our God

COLOSSIANS 1:5

129–St. 3	Heaven Came Down
282	O Word of God Incarnate
369	The Solid Rock
417	When We All Get to Heaven

COLOSSIANS 1:8

65	Come, Holy Spirit
66–St. 3	Come, Thou Almighty King
230	Love Divine, All Loves Excelling

COLOSSIANS 1:9–10

1	A Charge to Keep I Have
90	Forth in Thy Name, O Lord
104	God of Grace and God of Glory
145–St. 2	I Am Thine, O Lord
163	I Surrender All
222	Living for Jesus
233	Make Me a Blessing
239	More About Jesus
268	O Jesus, I Have Promised
273	O Master, Let Me Walk with Thee

COLOSSIANS 1:11

146	I Am Trusting Thee, Lord Jesus

COLOSSIANS 1:12–14

5	Abide with Me
8	Alas! And Did My Savior Bleed?
27	Are You Washed in the Blood?
30–St. 3	Ask Ye What Great Thing I Know
31	At Calvary
58	Christ Receiveth Sinful Men
60	Christ Whose Glory Fills
67	Come, Thou Fount
74–St. 3	Count Your Blessings
80	Down at the Cross
85	Faith of Our Fathers
86–St. 1	Fight the Good Fight
88	For All the Saints
151–St. 3	I Heard the Voice of Jesus Say
164	I Will Sing of My Redeemer
165	I Will Sing the Wondrous Story
174	In Loving Kindness Jesus Came
192–St. 4	Jesus, Lover of My Soul
201	Jesus, Thou Joy of Loving Hearts
204–St. 2	Jesus, What a Friend for Sinners
208	Just As I Am, Without One Plea
235	"Man of Sorrows," What a Name
251	Nothing But the Blood
263	O For a Thousand Tongues to Sing
266	O Happy Day that Fixed My Choice
267	O, How I Love Jesus
290–St. 2	Only Trust Him
298–St. 2	Praise Him! Praise Him!
307	Redeemed, How I Love to Proclaim
308	Rejoice, the Lord Is King
317	Saved! Saved! Saved!
326	Since I Have Been Redeemed
348	"Take Up Thy Cross"
376	There Is a Fountain
377	There Is a Green Hill Far Away
378	There Is Power in the Blood
390	To God Be the Glory
394	Victory in Jesus

COLOSSIANS 1:13–17

170	Immortal, Invisible

COLOSSIANS 1:15–19

12	All Hail the Power of Jesus' Name
33–St. 2	At the Name of Jesus
75–St. 5	Crown Him with Many Crowns
160	I Sing the Almighty Power of God
196	Jesus, Priceless Treasure
232	Majestic Sweetness
258	O Could I Speak the Matchless

COLOSSIANS 1:18

43	Blessed Be the Name
52	Built on the Rock
56	Christ Is Made the Sure
156	I Love Thy Kingdom, Lord
353	The Church's One Foundation

COLOSSIANS 1:19–22

7	Ah, Holy Jesus
8	Alas! And Did My Savior Bleed?
27	Are You Washed in the Blood?
31	At Calvary
32	At the Cross
41	Beneath the Cross of Jesus
80	Down at the Cross
117–St. 2	Hail, Thou Once Despised Jesus
174	In Loving Kindness Jesus Came
175	In the Cross of Christ I Glory
191	Jesus, Keep Me Near the Cross
202	Jesus, Thy Blood and Righteousness
219	Lift High the Cross
235	"Man of Sorrows," What a Name
251	Nothing But the Blood
266	O Happy Day that Fixed My Choice
297	Peace, Perfect Peace
298	Praise Him! Praise Him!
307	Redeemed, How I Love to Proclaim
314	Rock of Ages
315	Room at the Cross for You
326	Since I Have Been Redeemed
362–St. 3	The King of Love My Shepherd Is
367	The Old Rugged Cross
374	The Way of the Cross Leads Home
376	There Is a Fountain
377	There Is a Green Hill Far Away
378	There Is Power in the Blood
408	What a Wonderful Savior
413	When I Survey the Wondrous Cross

COLOSSIANS 1:19–23

129–St. 3	Heaven Came Down
154	I Know Whom I Have Believed

369	The Solid Rock

COLOSSIANS 1:24

222–St. 3	Living for Jesus
353	The Church's One Foundation

COLOSSIANS 1:27

23	And Can It Be That I Should Gain?
42	Blessed Assurance
104	God of Grace and God of Glory
122–St. 4	Have Thine Own Way, Lord
138	Hope of the World
200	Jesus, the Very Thought of Thee
238	Moment by Moment
298–St. 2	Praise Him! Praise Him!
369	The Solid Rock

COLOSSIANS 1:29

86	Fight the Good Fight
204	Jesus, What a Friend for Sinners

COLOSSIANS 2:2–3

104	God of Grace and God of Glory
206	Joyful, Joyful, We Adore Thee
432–St. 4	Ye Servants of God

COLOSSIANS 2:5

20	Am I a Soldier of the Cross?
391	Trusting Jesus

COLOSSIANS 2:6–7

128	He Who Would Valiant Be
145	I Am Thine, O Lord
229	Lord, Speak to Me
261	O For a Closer Walk with God
273	O Master, Let Me Walk with Thee
349	Teach Me Thy Way, O Lord
418	When We Walk with the Lord

COLOSSIANS 2:7

141	How Firm a Foundation
244	My Faith Looks Up to Thee

COLOSSIANS 2:9–10

66–St. 2	Come, Thou Almighty King
155	I Lay My Sins on Jesus
230	Love Divine, All Loves Excelling
258	O Could I Speak the Matchless
271	O Love How Deep, How Broad
365	The Lily of the Valley

COLOSSIANS 2:12

64	Come, Holy Spirit, Dove Divine

COLOSSIANS 2:13–15

3–St. 3	A Mighty Fortress Is Our God
41	Beneath the Cross of Jesus
54	Christ Arose
80	Down at the Cross
129	Heaven Came Down
138–Last st.	Hope of the World
155	I Lay My Sins on Jesus
174	In Loving Kindness Jesus Came
175	In the Cross of Christ I Glory
180–St. 3	It Is Well with My Soul
219	Lift High the Cross
307	Redeemed, How I Love to Proclaim
359–St. 2	The Great Physician
367	The Old Rugged Cross
372	The Strife Is O'er
374	The Way of the Cross Leads Home
383–St. 3	This Is My Father's World
394	Victory in Jesus
406	Were You There?
413	When I Survey the Wondrous Cross

COLOSSIANS 3:1–2

132	Higher Ground
145	I Am Thine, O Lord
163	I Surrender All
239	More About Jesus
308	Rejoice, the Lord Is King

COLOSSIANS 3:1–15

230	Love Divine, All Loves Excelling

COLOSSIANS 3:3–4

33–St. 5	At the Name of Jesus
80	Down at the Cross
82	Face to Face
88	For All the Saints
124–St. 5	He Keeps Me Singing
142–St. 4	How Great Thou Art
144	I Am His and He Is Mine
153–St. 3	I Know That My Redeemer Liveth
154–St. 4	I Know Whom I Have Believed
223	Lo, He Comes with Clouds
238	Moment by Moment
279	O That Will Be Glory For Me
410	What If It Were Today?
416	When the Roll Is Called
417	When We All Get to Heaven

COLOSSIANS 3:5–14

177–St. 2	In the Hour of Trial

COLOSSIANS 3:9–11

16	All That Thrills My Soul
46	Blest Be the Tie
57	Christ Is the World's
86–St. 4	Fight the Good Fight
172	In Christ There Is No East
262	O For a Heart to Praise My God
431	Ye Must Be Born Again

COLOSSIANS 3:12–13

171–Last st.	Immortal Love, Forever Full
281	O to Be Like Thee!
347	Take Time to Be Holy
396	We Are God's People

COLOSSIANS 3:14

65	Come, Holy Spirit
230	Love Divine, All Loves Excelling
320	Savior, Teach Me Day by Day
334	Spirit of God, Descend

COLOSSIANS 3:15

297	Peace, Perfect Peace
318	Savior, Again to Thy Dear Name

COLOSSIANS 3:16

48	Break Thou the Bread
62	Come, Christians, Join to Sing
67	Come, Thou Fount
83–St. 2	Fairest Lord Jesus
124	He Keeps Me Singing
164	I Will Sing of My Redeemer
165	I Will Sing the Wondrous Story
243–St. 3	My Faith Has Found
263	O For a Thousand Tongues to Sing
282	O Word of God Incarnate
309	Rejoice, Ye Pure in Heart
391–St. 2	Trusting Jesus
414	When in Our Music
430	Wonderful Words of Life

COLOSSIANS 3:16–17

253	Now Thank We All Our God
390	To God Be the Glory

COLOSSIANS 3:17

90	Forth in Thy Name, O Lord
222	Living for Jesus

| 321–St. 3 | Savior, Thy Dying Love |
| 346 | Take the Name of Jesus with You |

COLOSSIANS 3:18–21

| 119 | Happy the Home When God Is There |

COLOSSIANS 3:24

17	All the Way My Savior Leads Me
35	Awake, My Soul, Stretch
90	Forth in Thy Name, O Lord
121	Hark, the Voice of Jesus Calling
145	I Am Thine, O Lord
242	Must Jesus Bear the Cross Alone
268	O Jesus, I Have Promised

COLOSSIANS 4:1

| 268 | O Jesus, I Have Promised |
| 432 | Ye Servants of God |

COLOSSIANS 4:2

| 305 | Prayer Is the Soul's Sincere |
| 343 | Sweet Hour of Prayer |

COLOSSIANS 4:5

| 229 | Lord, Speak to Me |
| 295 | Pass It On |

COLOSSIANS 4:12

1	A Charge to Keep I Have
49	Breathe on Me, Breath of God
90	Forth in Thy Name, O Lord
122	Have Thine Own Way, Lord
145–St. 2	I Am Thine, O Lord
349	Teach Me Thy Way, O Lord
418	When We Walk with the Lord
421–St. 2	Wherever He Leads, I'll Go

1 THESSALONIANS 1:3

| 369 | The Solid Rock |

1 THESSALONIANS 1:6

66–St. 3	Come, Thou Almighty King
135–St. 3	Holy Spirit, Light Divine
136–St. 6	Holy Spirit, Truth Divine

1 THESSALONIANS 1:7

| 233 | Make Me a Blessing |

1 THESSALONIANS 1:8

| 322–St. 2 | Send the Light! |

1 THESSALONIANS 1:9

145–St. 2	I Am Thine, O Lord
261–St. 3	O For a Closer Walk with God
365–St. 2	The Lily of the Valley

1 THESSALONIANS 1:10

| 152 | I Know That My Redeemer Lives |

1 THESSALONIANS 1:12

| 166 | I Would Be True |
| 222 | Living for Jesus |

1 THESSALONIANS 2:2

20	Am I a Soldier of the Cross?
291	Onward, Christian Soldiers
337	Stand Up, Stand Up for Jesus

1 THESSALONIANS 2:12

| 1–St. 1 | A Charge to Keep I Have |
| 185 | Jesus Calls Us |

1 THESSALONIANS 2:13

133	Holy Bible, Book Divine
141–St. 1	How Firm a Foundation
154–St. 2	I Know Whom I Have Believed
430	Wonderful Words of Life

1 THESSALONIANS 2:19

42	Blessed Assurance
83	Fairest Lord Jesus
86–St. 1	Fight the Good Fight
124–St. 5	He Keeps Me Singing
181–St. 4	It May Be at Morn
298–St. 3	Praise Him! Praise Him!
308–St. 4	Rejoice, the Lord Is King
340	Sunshine in My Soul
360	The Head That Once Was Crowned
390	To God Be the Glory
410	What If It Were Today?

1 THESSALONIANS 3:5

| 180–St. 2 | It Is Well with My Soul |

1 THESSALONIANS 3:10

| 305 | Prayer Is the Soul's Sincere |

1 THESSALONIANS 3:12–13

65	Come, Holy Spirit
240	More Love to Thee, O Christ
320	Savior, Teach Me Day by Day
334	Spirit of God, Descend
347–St. 4	Take Time to Be Holy

1 THESSALONIANS 3:13

181	It May Be at Morn
223	Lo, He Comes with Clouds
262	O For a Heart to Praise My God

1 THESSALONIANS 4:1–7

49	Breathe on Me, Breath of God
166	I Would Be True
169	I'll Live for Him
222	Living for Jesus
347	Take Time to Be Holy

1 THESSALONIANS 4:9–10

46	Blest Be the Tie
206–St. 3, 4	Joyful, Joyful, We Adore Thee
230	Love Divine, All Loves Excelling
240	More Love to Thee, O Christ
320	Savior, Teach Me Day by Day
334	Spirit of God, Descend

1 THESSALONIANS 4:13–17

37–St. 3	Be Still, My Soul
39	Because He Lives
82	Face to Face
88	For All the Saints
124–St. 5	He Keeps Me Singing
127	He the Pearly Gates Will Open
142–St. 4	How Great Thou Art
152	I Know That My Redeemer Lives
153–St. 3	I Know That My Redeemer Liveth
154–St. 4	I Know Whom I Have Believed
155–St. 3	I Lay My Sins on Jesus
180–St. 4	It Is Well with My Soul
181	It May Be at Morn
223	Lo, He Comes with Clouds
235–St. 5	"Man of Sorrows," What a Name
242	Must Jesus Bear the Cross Alone
279	O That Will Be Glory For Me
286	On Jordan's Stormy Banks I Stand
289–St. 5	One Day
352	Ten Thousand Times Ten Thousand
365–St. 3	The Lily of the Valley
369–St. 4	The Solid Rock
410	What If It Were Today?
416	When the Roll Is Called
417	When We All Get to Heaven

1 THESSALONIANS 5:2

| 154–St. 4 | I Know Whom I Have Believed |
| 189 | Jesus Is Coming Again |

1 THESSALONIANS 5:4–8

34	Awake, My Soul, and With the Sun
60	Christ Whose Glory Fills
130	Heavenly Sunlight
151–St. 3	I Heard the Voice of Jesus Say
244–St. 3	My Faith Looks Up to Thee
267–St. 3	O, How I Love Jesus
327–St. 1	Since Jesus Came Into My Heart
395	Watchman, Tell Us of the Night

1 THESSALONIANS 5:8

84	Faith Is the Victory
332	Soldiers of Christ, Arise
337	Stand Up, Stand Up for Jesus

1 THESSALONIANS 5:9–10

31	At Calvary
106	God, That Madest Earth
144	I Am His and He Is Mine
147	I Gave My Life for Thee
222	Living for Jesus
252	Now I Belong to Jesus
290	Only Trust Him
311	Revive Us Again
314	Rock of Ages
317	Saved! Saved! Saved!
376	There Is a Fountain
377	There Is a Green Hill Far Away
394	Victory in Jesus
399	We Have Heard the Joyful Sound

1 THESSALONIANS 5:10

279	O That Will Be Glory For Me
286	On Jordan's Stormy Banks I Stand
352	Ten Thousand Times Ten Thousand
410–St. 2	What If It Were Today?
417	When We All Get to Heaven

1 THESSALONIANS 5:14

46	Blest Be the Tie
273	O Master, Let Me Walk with Thee
347–St. 1	Take Time to Be Holy

1 THESSALONIANS 5:16–18

124	He Keeps Me Singing
206	Joyful, Joyful, We Adore Thee
266	O Happy Day that Fixed My Choice
309	Rejoice, Ye Pure in Heart
327	Since Jesus Came Into My Heart
415	When Morning Gilds the Skies

1 THESSALONIANS 5:17

305	Prayer Is the Soul's Sincere
343	Sweet Hour of Prayer
407	What a Friend We Have in Jesus

1 THESSALONIANS 5:18

253	Now Thank We All Our God

1 THESSALONIANS 5:19

49	Breathe on Me, Breath of God
65	Come, Holy Spirit
334	Spirit of God, Descend
335	Spirit of the Living God

1 THESSALONIANS 5:21–22

104–St. 2	God of Grace and God of Glory
171–Last st.	Immortal Love, Forever Full
288	Once to Every Man and Nation
389–Refrain	'Tis So Sweet To Trust in Jesus

1 THESSALONIANS 5:23

26	"Are Ye Able," Said the Master
53–St. 4	Children of the Heavenly Father
163	I Surrender All
318–St. 4	Savior, Again to Thy Dear Name
345	Take My Life and Let It Be

1 THESSALONIANS 5:23–24

72	Come, Ye Sinners, Poor and Needy
114	Great Is Thy Faithfulness
121	Hark, the Voice of Jesus Calling
190	Jesus Is Tenderly Calling
208	Just As I Am, Without One Plea
222–St. 2	Living for Jesus
269	O Jesus, Thou Art Standing
294	Out of My Bondage
331	Softly and Tenderly
420	Where He Leads Me

1 THESSALONIANS 5:28

226	Lord, Dismiss Us

2 THESSALONIANS 1:7–10

181	It May Be at Morn
223	Lo, He Comes with Clouds

2 THESSALONIANS 1:11–12

1	A Charge to Keep I Have
21	Amazing Grace
168	I'll Go Where You Want Me To Go

2 THESSALONIANS 1:12

43	Blessed Be the Name
143	How Sweet the Name
267	O, How I Love Jesus
345	Take My Life and Let It Be

2 THESSALONIANS 2:8

363	The King Shall Come When Morning

2 THESSALONIANS 2:9

3	A Mighty Fortress Is Our God

2 THESSALONIANS 2:13

12–St. 2	All Hail the Power of Jesus' Name
161	I Sought the Lord

2 THESSALONIANS 2:14

185	Jesus Calls Us
190	Jesus Is Tenderly Calling
294	Out of My Bondage

2 THESSALONIANS 2:16

21	Amazing Grace
138	Hope of the World
369	The Solid Rock
428	Wonderful Grace of Jesus

2 THESSALONIANS 2:16–17

70	Come, Ye Disconsolate
247	Near to the Heart of God

2 THESSALONIANS 2:17

20–St. 4	Am I a Soldier of the Cross?
273	O Master, Let Me Walk with Thee

2 THESSALONIANS 3:3

53–St. 2	Children of the Heavenly Father
102	God Is My Strong Salvation
114	Great Is Thy Faithfulness
141	How Firm a Foundation
188	Jesus Is All the World to Me
238	Moment by Moment
265	O God, Our Help in Ages Past
319–St. 2	Savior, Like a Shepherd Lead Us
393	Under His Wings

2 THESSALONIANS 3:5

167	If Thou But Suffer God to Guide
173	In Heavenly Love Abiding
240	More Love to Thee, O Christ

2 THESSALONIANS 3:16

75–St. 4	Crown Him with Many Crowns
78–St. 4	Dear Lord and Father of Mankind
297	Peace, Perfect Peace
318	Savior, Again to Thy Dear Name
429	Wonderful Peace

2 THESSALONIANS 3:16–18

226	Lord, Dismiss Us

1 TIMOTHY 1:1

138	Hope of the World
369	The Solid Rock

1 TIMOTHY 1:5

65	Come, Holy Spirit
240	More Love to Thee, O Christ
320	Savior, Teach Me Day by Day
334	Spirit of God, Descend

1 TIMOTHY 1:12

86–St. 1	Fight the Good Fight
166	I Would Be True
268	O Jesus, I Have Promised
348	"Take Up Thy Cross"

1 TIMOTHY 1:14–15

8	Alas! And Did My Savior Bleed?
21	Amazing Grace
31	At Calvary
32	At the Cross
43–St. 3	Blessed Be the Name
58	Christ Receiveth Sinful Men
67	Come, Thou Fount
79	Depth of Mercy! Can There Be?
80	Down at the Cross
112	Grace Greater Than Our Sin
123	He Hideth My Soul
174	In Loving Kindness Jesus Came
195	Jesus Paid it All
204	Jesus, What a Friend for Sinners
243	My Faith Has Found
266	O Happy Day that Fixed My Choice
294	Out of My Bondage
307	Redeemed, How I Love to Proclaim
310	Rescue the Perishing
326	Since I Have Been Redeemed
399	We Have Heard the Joyful Sound
428	Wonderful Grace of Jesus

1 TIMOTHY 1:14–17

129	Heaven Came Down
162	I Stand Amazed in the Presence
246	My Tribute
289	One Day
299	Praise, My Soul, the King
309	Rejoice, Ye Pure in Heart
390	To God Be the Glory

1 TIMOTHY 1:16

229	Lord, Speak to Me

1 TIMOTHY 1:17

66–St. 1	Come, Thou Almighty King
137	Holy, Holy, Holy
170	Immortal, Invisible
215	Let All the World
308	Rejoice, the Lord Is King
328	Sing Praise to God Who Reigns
358	The God of Abraham Praise

1 TIMOTHY 1:18–19

20	Am I a Soldier of the Cross?
86	Fight the Good Fight
128	He Who Would Valiant Be
212	Lead On, O King Eternal
291	Onward, Christian Soldiers
332	Soldiers of Christ, Arise
337	Stand Up, Stand Up for Jesus

1 TIMOTHY 2:1–2

78–St. 4	Dear Lord and Father of Mankind
105	God of Our Fathers

1 TIMOTHY 2:3–6

310	Rescue the Perishing
315	Room at the Cross for You
331	Softly and Tenderly
399	We Have Heard the Joyful Sound
404	We've a Story to Tell
427	Whosoever Will

1 TIMOTHY 2:5–6

117	Hail, Thou Once Despised Jesus
147	I Gave My Life for Thee
155	I Lay My Sins on Jesus
164–St. 2	I Will Sing of My Redeemer
174	In Loving Kindness Jesus Came
202	Jesus, Thy Blood and Righteousness
266	O Happy Day that Fixed My Choice
307	Redeemed, How I Love to Proclaim

326   Since I Have Been Redeemed
351–St. 3   Tell Me the Story of Jesus
369   The Solid Rock
374   The Way of the Cross Leads Home
376   There Is a Fountain
377   There Is a Green Hill Far Away
385   Thou Art the Way: to Thee Alone
390   To God Be the Glory
408   What a Wonderful Savior

1 TIMOTHY 2:8

305   Prayer Is the Soul's Sincere
343   Sweet Hour of Prayer
407   What a Friend We Have in Jesus

1 TIMOTHY 3:15

52   Built on the Rock
156   I Love Thy Kingdom, Lord
353   The Church's One Foundation

1 TIMOTHY 3:16

66–St. 2   Come, Thou Almighty King
289   One Day
351   Tell Me the Story of Jesus
425   Who Is He in Yonder Stall?

1 TIMOTHY 4:1

177   In the Hour of Trial

1 TIMOTHY 4:6

282   O Word of God Incarnate

1 TIMOTHY 4:6–12

166   I Would Be True
233   Make Me a Blessing
347   Take Time to Be Holy

1 TIMOTHY 4:10

39   Because He Lives
102   God Is My Strong Salvation
146   I Am Trusting Thee, Lord Jesus
290   Only Trust Him
369   The Solid Rock
389   'Tis So Sweet To Trust in Jesus
391   Trusting Jesus

1 TIMOTHY 5:6

177–St. 2   In the Hour of Trial

1 TIMOTHY 5:8

119   Happy the Home When God Is There

1 TIMOTHY 6:3

389–St. 1   'Tis So Sweet To Trust in Jesus
430   Wonderful Words of Life

1 TIMOTHY 6:6

78   Dear Lord and Father of Mankind

1 TIMOTHY 6:9

177–St. 2   In the Hour of Trial

1 TIMOTHY 6:12

20   Am I a Soldier of the Cross?
84   Faith Is the Victory
86   Fight the Good Fight
88   For All the Saints
104   God of Grace and God of Glory
128   He Who Would Valiant Be
212   Lead On, O King Eternal
279   O That Will Be Glory For Me
291   Onward, Christian Soldiers
309   Rejoice, Ye Pure in Heart
332   Soldiers of Christ, Arise
337   Stand Up, Stand Up for Jesus
370   The Son of God Goes Forth to War
374   The Way of the Cross Leads Home
426   Who Is on the Lord's Side?

1 TIMOTHY 6:15–16

66   Come, Thou Almighty King
75   Crown Him with Many Crowns
83   Fairest Lord Jesus
117–St. 4   Hail, Thou Once Despised Jesus
170   Immortal, Invisible
212   Lead On, O King Eternal
225   Look, Ye Saints!
283   O Worship the King
299   Praise, My Soul, the King
304   Praise to the Lord, the Almighty
410-Refrain   What If It Were Today?
432   Ye Servants of God

1 TIMOTHY 6:17

74–St. 3   Count Your Blessings
89   For the Beauty of the Earth
362   The King of Love My Shepherd Is
389   'Tis So Sweet To Trust in Jesus
391   Trusting Jesus

1 TIMOTHY 6:19

88   For All the Saints
127   He the Pearly Gates Will Open

2 TIMOTHY 2:9

48–St. 2	Break Thou the Bread
153–St. 2	I Know That My Redeemer Liveth
282	O Word of God Incarnate

2 TIMOTHY 2:10–13

114	Great Is Thy Faithfulness
124–St. 5	He Keeps Me Singing
126	He Lives
144	I Am His and He Is Mine
177–St. 1	In the Hour of Trial
188	Jesus Is All the World to Me
238	Moment by Moment
279	O That Will Be Glory For Me
338	Standing on the Promises
360	The Head That Once Was Crowned

2 TIMOTHY 2:15

1	A Charge to Keep I Have
229	Lord, Speak to Me
321	Savior, Thy Dying Love

2 TIMOTHY 2:19

33–St. 4	At the Name of Jesus
56	Christ Is Made the Sure
114	Great Is Thy Faithfulness
141	How Firm a Foundation
346	Take the Name of Jesus with You

2 TIMOTHY 2:20–21

27	Are You Washed in the Blood?
35	Awake, My Soul, Stretch
222	Living for Jesus
229	Lord, Speak to Me
233	Make Me a Blessing
345	Take My Life and Let It Be
424	Whiter Than Snow

2 TIMOTHY 2:22

78	Dear Lord and Father of Mankind
108	God Who Touchest Earth

2 TIMOTHY 2:24–25

229	Lord, Speak to Me

2 TIMOTHY 2:26

3	A Mighty Fortress Is Our God
180–St. 2	It Is Well with My Soul
294	Out of My Bondage

2 TIMOTHY 3:4

177–St. 2	In the Hour of Trial

2 TIMOTHY 3:12

85	Faith of Our Fathers
222–St. 3	Living for Jesus

2 TIMOTHY 3:15–17

48	Break Thou the Bread
133	Holy Bible, Book Divine
154	I Know Whom I Have Believed
282	O Word of God Incarnate
361	The Heavens Declare Thy Glory
430	Wonderful Words of Life

2 TIMOTHY 4:5

222	Living for Jesus
229	Lord, Speak to Me
233	Make Me a Blessing

2 TIMOTHY 4:7–8

20	Am I a Soldier of the Cross?
35	Awake, My Soul, Stretch
74–St. 4	Count Your Blessings
84	Faith Is the Victory
85	Faith of Our Fathers
86	Fight the Good Fight
212	Lead On, O King Eternal
242	Must Jesus Bear the Cross Alone
245–St. 4	My Jesus, I Love Thee
291	Onward, Christian Soldiers
332	Soldiers of Christ, Arise
337	Stand Up, Stand Up for Jesus
349–St. 4	Teach Me Thy Way, O Lord
367–St. 4	The Old Rugged Cross
370	The Son of God Goes Forth to War

2 TIMOTHY 4:8

124–St. 5	He Keeps Me Singing
322–St. 4	Send the Light!
359–St. 2	The Great Physician
410	What If It Were Today?

2 TIMOTHY 4:18

53	Children of the Heavenly Father
252–St. 1	Now I Belong to Jesus

2 TIMOTHY 4:22

200	Jesus, the Very Thought of Thee
201–St. 5	Jesus, Thou Joy of Loving Hearts

TITUS 1:2

88	For All the Saints
183	Jerusalem, My Happy Home

184	Jerusalem, the Golden
279	O That Will Be Glory For Me
286	On Jordan's Stormy Banks I Stand
338	Standing on the Promises
342	Sweet By and By
417	When We All Get to Heaven

TITUS 1:9

| 430 | Wonderful Words of Life |

TITUS 1:15

78	Dear Lord and Father of Mankind
108	God Who Touchest Earth
230–St. 4	Love Divine, All Loves Excelling

TITUS 1:16

| 177–St. 1 | In the Hour of Trial |
| 188–St. 3 | Jesus Is All the World to Me |

TITUS 2:4–5

| 119 | Happy the Home When God Is There |

TITUS 2:7

| 35–St. 2 | Awake, My Soul, Stretch |
| 233 | Make Me a Blessing |

TITUS 2:9–14

163	I Surrender All
166	I Would Be True
169	I'll Live for Him
222	Living for Jesus

TITUS 2:11

21	Amazing Grace
31	At Calvary
58	Christ Receiveth Sinful Men
79	Depth of Mercy! Can There Be
91	Free From the Law
112	Grace Greater Than Our Sin
154	I Know Whom I Have Believed
192–St. 4	Jesus, Lover of My Soul
310–St. 3	Rescue the Perishing
381	There's a Wideness
399	We Have Heard the Joyful Sound
428	Wonderful Grace of Jesus

TITUS 2:13

42	Blessed Assurance
126–St. 2	He Lives
153–St. 3	I Know That My Redeemer Liveth
181	It May Be at Morn
189	Jesus Is Coming Again

200	Jesus, the Very Thought of Thee
223	Lo, He Comes with Clouds
289–St. 5	One Day
298–St. 3	Praise Him! Praise Him!
363	The King Shall Come When Morning
369	The Solid Rock
410	What If It Were Today?

TITUS 2:14

8	Alas! And Did My Savior Bleed?
32	At the Cross
45	Blessed Redeemer
80	Down at the Cross
117	Hail, Thou Once Despised Jesus
147	I Gave My Life for Thee
164	I Will Sing of My Redeemer
174	In Loving Kindness Jesus Came
195	Jesus Paid it All
204	Jesus, What a Friend for Sinners
244–St. 2	My Faith Looks Up to Thee
307	Redeemed, How I Love to Proclaim
326	Since I Have Been Redeemed
376	There Is a Fountain
377	There Is a Green Hill Far Away
390	To God Be the Glory
408	What a Wonderful Savior

TITUS 3:2

| 166–St. 2 | I Would Be True |

TITUS 3:3

| 177–St. 2 | In the Hour of Trial |

TITUS 3:3–6

| 43 | Blessed Be the Name |

TITUS 3:3–7

21	Amazing Grace
27	Are You Washed in the Blood?
31	At Calvary
42	Blessed Assurance
58	Christ Receiveth Sinful Men
79	Depth of Mercy! Can There Be?
80	Down at the Cross
112	Grace Greater Than Our Sin
162	I Stand Amazed in the Presence
174	In Loving Kindness Jesus Came
195	Jesus Paid it All
202	Jesus, Thy Blood and Righteousness
208	Just As I Am, Without One Plea
230	Love Divine, All Loves Excelling
246	My Tribute

251	Nothing But the Blood
252	Now I Belong to Jesus
266	O Happy Day that Fixed My Choice
298–St. 2	Praise Him! Praise Him!
307	Redeemed, How I Love to Proclaim
311	Revive Us Again
317	Saved! Saved! Saved!
319–St. 3	Savior, Like a Shepherd Lead Us
378	There Is Power in the Blood
381	There's a Wideness
390	To God Be the Glory
394	Victory in Jesus
408	What a Wonderful Savior
424	Whiter Than Snow

TITUS 3:5–6

63	Come, Holy Ghost
135–St. 2	Holy Spirit, Light Divine
290	Only Trust Him
314	Rock of Ages
431	Ye Must Be Born Again

TITUS 3:7

2	A Child of the King
138	Hope of the World
417	When We All Get to Heaven
428	Wonderful Grace of Jesus

PHILEMON 5

240	More Love to Thee, O Christ
320	Savior, Teach Me Day by Day
334	Spirit of God, Descend

PHILEMON 6

157	I Love to Tell the Story
233	Make Me a Blessing
295	Pass It On

PHILEMON 25

226	Lord, Dismiss Us
318	Savior, Again to Thy Dear Name

HEBREWS 1:2–8

43	Blessed Be the Name
75–St. 5	Crown Him with Many Crowns
80	Down at the Cross
83	Fairest Lord Jesus
198	Jesus Shall Reign
212	Lead On, O King Eternal
225	Look, Ye Saints!
232	Majestic Sweetness
235	"Man of Sorrows," What a Name

258	O Could I Speak the Matchless
278	O Splendor of God's Glory
285	Of the Father's Love Begotten
289–St. 4	One Day
299–St. 4	Praise, My Soul, the King
308–St. 2	Rejoice, the Lord Is King
386	Thou Didst Leave Thy Throne
432	Ye Servants of God

HEBREWS 1:4

124–Refrain	He Keeps Me Singing
143	How Sweet the Name
200–St. 2	Jesus, the Very Thought of Thee
263	O For a Thousand Tongues to Sing
267	O, How I Love Jesus
346	Take the Name of Jesus with You

HEBREWS 1:6

12	All Hail the Power of Jesus' Name
24	Angels from the Realms of Glory
43–St. 2	Blessed Be the Name
120	Hark! The Herald Angels Sing
179	It Came Upon a Midnight Clear
256	O Come, All Ye Faithful
423	While Shepherds Watched

HEBREWS 1:10

160	I Sing the Almighty Power of God
371	The Spacious Firmament

HEBREWS 2:4

63	Come, Holy Ghost
135	Holy Spirit, Light Divine

HEBREWS 2:7–10

12	All Hail the Power of Jesus' Name
75	Crown Him with Many Crowns
225	Look, Ye Saints!
298	Praise Him! Praise Him!
360	The Head That Once Was Crowned

HEBREWS 2:9–10

7	Ah, Holy Jesus
23	And Can It Be That I Should Gain?
57–St. 1	Christ Is the World's
117	Hail, Thou Once Despised Jesus
162–St. 4	I Stand Amazed in the Presence
164	I Will Sing of My Redeemer
195	Jesus Paid it All
202	Jesus, Thy Blood and Righteousness
232	Majestic Sweetness
275	O Sacred Head, Now Wounded

308	Rejoice, the Lord Is King
382	Thine Is the Glory
403	We Would See Jesus; Lo! His Star
408	What a Wonderful Savior

HEBREWS 2:9–12

43	Blessed Be the Name
165	I Will Sing the Wondrous Story
258	O Could I Speak the Matchless

HEBREWS 2:11

182	I've Found a Friend
204	Jesus, What a Friend for Sinners

HEBREWS 2:11–13

2	A Child of the King
53	Children of the Heavenly Father

HEBREWS 2:12

12	All Hail the Power of Jesus' Name
62	Come, Christians, Join to Sing
142	How Great Thou Art
156	I Love Thy Kingdom, Lord
164	I Will Sing of My Redeemer
215	Let All the World
263	O For a Thousand Tongues to Sing
414	When in Our Music

HEBREWS 2:14–15

33–St. 3	At the Name of Jesus
54	Christ Arose
57	Christ Is the World's
59–St. 2, 3	Christ the Lord Is Risen Today
75	Crown Him with Many Crowns
180	It Is Well with My Soul
362–St. 4	The King of Love My Shepherd Is
372	The Strife Is O'er
382	Thine Is the Glory

HEBREWS 2:14–17

3–St. 3	A Mighty Fortress Is Our God
33–St. 3	At the Name of Jesus
75–St. 2	Crown Him with Many Crowns
117	Hail, Thou Once Despised Jesus
202	Jesus, Thy Blood and Righteousness
324–St. 2, 3	Shepherd of Tender Youth
376	There Is a Fountain

HEBREWS 2:18

158	I Must Tell Jesus
159–St. 2	I Need Thee Every Hour
177	In the Hour of Trial

271–St. 2	O Love How Deep, How Broad
343–St. 1	Sweet Hour of Prayer
351–St. 2	Tell Me the Story of Jesus
365–St. 2	The Lily of the Valley

HEBREWS 3:1–6

43	Blessed Be the Name
83	Fairest Lord Jesus
171–Last st.	Immortal Love, Forever Full
196	Jesus, Priceless Treasure
258	O Could I Speak the Matchless
298	Praise Him! Praise Him!
353	The Church's One Foundation
415	When Morning Gilds the Skies
425	Who Is He in Yonder Stall?

HEBREWS 3:4

19	All Things Bright and Beautiful
371	The Spacious Firmament

HEBREWS 3:6

52	Built on the Rock
200	Jesus, the Very Thought of Thee
369	The Solid Rock

HEBREWS 3:7–8

190	Jesus Is Tenderly Calling
292–St. 2	Open My Eyes
368	The Savior Is Waiting

HEBREWS 3:12–13

262	O For a Heart to Praise My God

HEBREWS 3:14

242	Must Jesus Bear the Cross Alone
337	Stand Up, Stand Up for Jesus

HEBREWS 3:15

79	Depth of Mercy! Can There Be?
190	Jesus Is Tenderly Calling
331	Softly and Tenderly
368	The Savior Is Waiting

HEBREWS 4:1–11

17–St. 3	All the Way My Savior Leads Me
28	Are You (Art Thou) Weary?
58–St. 2	Christ Receiveth Sinful Men
109	God Will Take Care of You
154–St. 2	I Know Whom I Have Believed
190	Jesus Is Tenderly Calling
228	Lord Jesus, Think on Me
230–St. 2	Love Divine, All Loves Excelling

HEBREWS 7:2

264	O God of Love, O King of Peace

HEBREWS 7:19

61	Close to Thee
145	I Am Thine, O Lord
247	Near to the Heart of God
248	Nearer, My God, to Thee
249	Nearer, Still Nearer
364	The Light of the World Is Jesus

HEBREWS 7:19–22

369	The Solid Rock

HEBREWS 7:24–25

39	Because He Lives
86–St. 4	Fight the Good Fight
114	Great Is Thy Faithfulness
152	I Know That My Redeemer Lives
154	I Know Whom I Have Believed
266	O Happy Day that Fixed My Choice
267	O, How I Love Jesus
271	O Love How Deep, How Broad
290	Only Trust Him
294	Out of My Bondage
307	Redeemed, How I Love to Proclaim
310	Rescue the Perishing

HEBREWS 7:25–28

117–St. 3	Hail, Thou Once Despised Jesus
196	Jesus, Priceless Treasure
258	O Could I Speak the Matchless
308	Rejoice, the Lord Is King
324–St. 3	Shepherd of Tender Youth
390	To God Be the Glory

HEBREWS 7:27

23	And Can It Be That I Should Gain?
80	Down at the Cross
91	Free From the Law
117	Hail, Thou Once Despised Jesus
235	"Man of Sorrows," What a Name
367	The Old Rugged Cross
376	There Is a Fountain
377	There Is a Green Hill Far Away
408	What a Wonderful Savior
413	When I Survey the Wondrous Cross

HEBREWS 8:1–2

225	Look, Ye Saints!
232	Majestic Sweetness

298–St. 3	Praise Him! Praise Him!
324–St. 3	Shepherd of Tender Youth
360	The Head That Once Was Crowned

HEBREWS 8:6

43–St. 3	Blessed Be the Name
369	The Solid Rock
385	Thou Art the Way: to Thee Alone
389	'Tis So Sweet To Trust in Jesus
390	To God Be the Glory

HEBREWS 8:6–13

338	Standing on the Promises
369	The Solid Rock

HEBREWS 8:12

155–St. 1	I Lay My Sins on Jesus
331–St. 4	Softly and Tenderly

HEBREWS 9:7

27	Are You Washed in the Blood?
251	Nothing But the Blood
267–St. 2	O, How I Love Jesus
378	There Is Power in the Blood

HEBREWS 9:11–28

7	Ah, Holy Jesus
8	Alas! And Did My Savior Bleed?
32	At the Cross
42	Blessed Assurance
45	Blessed Redeemer
80	Down at the Cross
91	Free From the Law
112	Grace Greater Than Our Sin
117–St. 2	Hail, Thou Once Despised Jesus
164	I Will Sing of My Redeemer
195	Jesus Paid it All
202	Jesus, Thy Blood and Righteousness
235–St. 2	"Man of Sorrows," What a Name
263–St. 3	O For a Thousand Tongues to Sing
298–St. 2	Praise Him! Praise Him!
307	Redeemed, How I Love to Proclaim
314	Rock of Ages
367	The Old Rugged Cross
376	There Is a Fountain
378	There Is Power in the Blood
390	To God Be the Glory
408	What a Wonderful Savior
413	When I Survey the Wondrous Cross

HEBREWS 9:14

27	Are You Washed in the Blood?

42	Blessed Assurance
58–St. 3	Christ Receiveth Sinful Men
145–St. 2	I Am Thine, O Lord
155–St. 1	I Lay My Sins on Jesus
195	Jesus Paid it All
202	Jesus, Thy Blood and Righteousness
208	Just As I Am, Without One Plea
251	Nothing But the Blood
290–St. 2	Only Trust Him
314	Rock of Ages
389–St. 2	'Tis So Sweet To Trust in Jesus
394	Victory in Jesus
424	Whiter Than Snow

HEBREWS 9:15

88	For All the Saints
252	Now I Belong to Jesus
266	O Happy Day that Fixed My Choice
294	Out of My Bondage
326	Since I Have Been Redeemed
338	Standing on the Promises
374	The Way of the Cross Leads Home
385	Thou Art the Way: to Thee Alone
417	When We All Get to Heaven

HEBREWS 9:22

23	And Can It Be That I Should Gain?
27	Are You Washed in the Blood?
42	Blessed Assurance
251	Nothing But the Blood
275	O Sacred Head, Now Wounded
378	There Is Power in the Blood

HEBREWS 9:24

116	Hail the Day That Sees Him Rise
117	Hail, Thou Once Despised Jesus
321–St. 2	Savior, Thy Dying Love

HEBREWS 9:28

123–St. 4	He Hideth My Soul
155	I Lay My Sins on Jesus
162	I Stand Amazed in the Presence
189	Jesus Is Coming Again
223	Lo, He Comes with Clouds
235	"Man of Sorrows," What a Name
289	One Day
353	The Church's One Foundation
363	The King Shall Come When Morning
410	What If It Were Today?

HEBREWS 10:10–14

23	And Can It Be That I Should Gain?

43–St. 3	Blessed Be the Name
91	Free From the Law
275	O Sacred Head, Now Wounded
367	The Old Rugged Cross
378	There Is Power in the Blood
390	To God Be the Glory
408	What a Wonderful Savior
413	When I Survey the Wondrous Cross

HEBREWS 10:12

93	From Every Stormy Wind
225	Look, Ye Saints!
232	Majestic Sweetness
321–St. 2	Savior, Thy Dying Love
360	The Head That Once Was Crowned

HEBREWS 10:12–14

235–St. 4	"Man of Sorrows," What a Name
311–St. 1	Revive Us Again

HEBREWS 10:15

63	Come, Holy Ghost

HEBREWS 10:17–18

91	Free From the Law
112	Grace Greater Than Our Sin
155	I Lay My Sins on Jesus
195	Jesus Paid it All
252	Now I Belong to Jesus
331–St. 4	Softly and Tenderly
376	There Is a Fountain

HEBREWS 10:19–23

149	I Hear Thy Welcome Voice
251	Nothing But the Blood
269	O Jesus, Thou Art Standing
298–St. 2	Praise Him! Praise Him!
378	There Is Power in the Blood
385	Thou Art the Way: to Thee Alone

HEBREWS 10:22

27	Are You Washed in the Blood?
42	Blessed Assurance
58–St. 3	Christ Receiveth Sinful Men
112	Grace Greater Than Our Sin
145	I Am Thine, O Lord
155–St. 1	I Lay My Sins on Jesus
180	It Is Well with My Soul
216	Let Jesus Come Into Your Heart
230	Love Divine, All Loves Excelling
231–St. 2	Love Lifted Me
244	My Faith Looks Up to Thee

247	Near to the Heart of God
249	Nearer, Still Nearer
262	O For a Heart to Praise My God
321–St. 3	Savior, Thy Dying Love
327–St. 2	Since Jesus Came Into My Heart
394–St. 2	Victory in Jesus
424	Whiter Than Snow

HEBREWS 10:23

20	Am I a Soldier of the Cross?
53	Children of the Heavenly Father
84	Faith Is the Victory
86	Fight the Good Fight
114	Great Is Thy Faithfulness
141	How Firm a Foundation
153–St. 2	I Know That My Redeemer Liveth
188–St. 3	Jesus Is All the World to Me
212	Lead On, O King Eternal
332	Soldiers of Christ, Arise
337	Stand Up, Stand Up for Jesus
338	Standing on the Promises
369	The Solid Rock

HEBREWS 10:34

183	Jerusalem, My Happy Home
184	Jerusalem, the Golden

HEBREWS 10:34–38

37	Be Still, My Soul
338	Standing on the Promises

HEBREWS 10:35–38

1	A Charge to Keep I Have
273–St. 3	O Master, Let Me Walk with Thee

HEBREWS 10:37

33–St. 5	At the Name of Jesus
126–St. 2	He Lives
181	It May Be at Morn
189	Jesus Is Coming Again
223	Lo, He Comes with Clouds
313–St. 2	Rise Up, O Men of God
410	What If It Were Today?

HEBREWS 10:38

67–St. 3	Come, Thou Fount
146	I Am Trusting Thee, Lord Jesus
180	It Is Well with My Soul
244	My Faith Looks Up to Thee
290	Only Trust Him
369	The Solid Rock
389	'Tis So Sweet To Trust in Jesus

391	Trusting Jesus
418	When We Walk with the Lord

HEBREWS 11:1

42	Blessed Assurance
154	I Know Whom I Have Believed
180	It Is Well with My Soul
273–St. 4	O Master, Let Me Walk with Thee

HEBREWS 11:1–40

84	Faith Is the Victory
85	Faith of Our Fathers
88	For All the Saints
338	Standing on the Promises

HEBREWS 11:3

19	All Things Bright and Beautiful
160	I Sing the Almighty Power of God
371	The Spacious Firmament
383	This Is My Father's World

HEBREWS 11:6

76	Day by Day
146	I Am Trusting Thee, Lord Jesus
243	My Faith Has Found
290	Only Trust Him
389	'Tis So Sweet To Trust in Jesus
391	Trusting Jesus

HEBREWS 11:10

97	Glorious Things of Thee
129–St. 3	Heaven Came Down
183	Jerusalem, My Happy Home
184	Jerusalem, the Golden

HEBREWS 11:12

202–St. 4	Jesus, Thy Blood and Righteousness

HEBREWS 11:13–16

37–St. 3	Be Still, My Soul
88	For All the Saints
115–St. 1	Guide Me, O Thou Great Jehovah
128	He Who Would Valiant Be
183	Jerusalem, My Happy Home
184	Jerusalem, the Golden
279	O That Will Be Glory For Me
286	On Jordan's Stormy Banks I Stand
323	Shall We Gather at the River
342	Sweet By and By
352	Ten Thousand Times Ten Thousand

HEBREWS 11:25

177–St. 2	In the Hour of Trial
288	Once to Every Man and Nation

HEBREWS 11:26

74–St. 3	Count Your Blessings
242	Must Jesus Bear the Cross Alone?
330	So Send I You

HEBREWS 11:34

115–St. 1	Guide Me, O Thou Great Jehovah
128	He Who Would Valiant Be
291	Onward, Christian Soldiers
341–St. 2	Surely Goodness and Mercy

HEBREWS 11:36–37

20	Am I a Soldier of the Cross?
85	Faith of Our Fathers

HEBREWS 12:1

86–St. 2	Fight the Good Fight
88	For All the Saints
330	So Send I You

HEBREWS 12:1–2

35	Awake, My Soul, Stretch
132	Higher Ground
268	O Jesus, I Have Promised
273	O Master, Let Me Walk with Thee
321	Savior, Thy Dying Love
347	Take Time to Be Holy
349–St. 4	Teach Me Thy Way, O Lord

HEBREWS 12:2

32	At the Cross
33	At the Name of Jesus
41	Beneath the Cross of Jesus
75	Crown Him with Many Crowns
117	Hail, Thou Once Despised Jesus
186	Jesus Christ Is Risen Today
219	Lift High the Cross
225	Look, Ye Saints!
232	Majestic Sweetness
235	"Man of Sorrows," What a Name
243	My Faith Has Found
244	My Faith Looks Up to Thee
289	One Day
360	The Head That Once Was Crowned
367	The Old Rugged Cross
432–St. 3	Ye Servants of God

HEBREWS 12:2–4

7	Ah, Holy Jesus
200	Jesus, the Very Thought of Thee
211	Lead Me to Calvary

HEBREWS 12:5–7

397–St. 1	We Gather Together

HEBREWS 12:14

262	O For a Heart to Praise My God
347	Take Time to Be Holy
424	Whiter Than Snow

HEBREWS 12:22

69	Come, We That Love the Lord
97	Glorious Things of Thee
134–St. 2	Holy God, We Praise Thy Name
155–St. 3	I Lay My Sins on Jesus
183	Jerusalem, My Happy Home
184	Jerusalem, the Golden
293	Open Now Thy Gates of Beauty
352	Ten Thousand Times Ten Thousand

HEBREWS 12:24

27	Are You Washed in the Blood?
117	Hail, Thou Once Despised Jesus
202	Jesus, Thy Blood and Righteousness
235	"Man of Sorrows," What a Name
251	Nothing But the Blood
263–St. 3	O For a Thousand Tongues to Sing
369	The Solid Rock
376	There Is a Fountain
378	There Is Power in the Blood
385	Thou Art the Way: to Thee Alone
408	What a Wonderful Savior

HEBREWS 12:28

101	God Himself Is with Us
145–St. 2	I Am Thine, O Lord
336	Stand Up and Bless the Lord

HEBREWS 13:1

46	Blest Be the Tie
65	Come, Holy Spirit
320	Savior, Teach Me Day by Day
334	Spirit of God, Descend

HEBREWS 13:4

119	Happy the Home When God Is There
274	O Perfect Love

HEBREWS 13:5–6

3	A Mighty Fortress Is Our God
96	Give to the Winds
104	God of Grace and God of Glory
109	God Will Take Care of You
114	Great Is Thy Faithfulness
124–St. 1	He Keeps Me Singing
141	How Firm a Foundation
158	I Must Tell Jesus
167	If Thou But Suffer God to Guide
204	Jesus, What a Friend for Sinners
209	Just When I Need Him
213	Leaning on the Everlasting Arms
230–St. 3	Love Divine, All Loves Excelling
265	O God, Our Help in Ages Past
365	The Lily of the Valley
401	We Praise Thee, O God

HEBREWS 13:8

83	Fairest Lord Jesus
86–St. 4	Fight the Good Fight
113	Great God, We Sing That Mighty Hand
201–St. 2	Jesus, Thou Joy of Loving Hearts
253–St. 3	Now Thank We All Our God
285	Of the Father's Love Begotten
298	Praise Him! Praise Him!
302–St. 3	Praise the Savior, Ye Who Know
358	The God of Abraham Praise

HEBREWS 13:9

| 67–St. 3 | Come, Thou Fount |

HEBREWS 13:12

117	Hail, Thou Once Despised Jesus
147–St. 3	I Gave My Life for Thee
235–St. 2	"Man of Sorrows," What a Name
251	Nothing But the Blood
275	O Sacred Head, Now Wounded
298–St. 2	Praise Him! Praise Him!
376	There Is a Fountain
377	There Is a Green Hill Far Away
378	There Is Power in the Blood
408	What a Wonderful Savior

HEBREWS 13:14

127	He the Pearly Gates Will Open
183	Jerusalem, My Happy Home
184	Jerusalem, the Golden
279	O That Will Be Glory For Me
342	Sweet By and By

HEBREWS 13:15

30	Ask Ye What Great Thing I Know
42	Blessed Assurance
43	Blessed Be the Name
62	Come, Christians, Join to Sing
73	Come, Ye Thankful People, Come
80	Down at the Cross
89	For the Beauty of the Earth
92	From All That Dwell Below
157	I Love to Tell the Story
215	Let All the World
253	Now Thank We All Our God
303	Praise to God, Immortal Praise
328	Sing Praise to God Who Reigns
336	Stand Up and Bless the Lord
346	Take the Name of Jesus with You
401	We Praise Thee, O God
415	When Morning Gilds the Skies
432	Ye Servants of God

HEBREWS 13:16

44	Blessed Jesus, at Thy Word
233	Make Me a Blessing
345	Take My Life and Let It Be
419	Where Cross the Crowded Ways

HEBREWS 13:20–21

49	Breathe on Me, Breath of God
122	Have Thine Own Way, Lord
125	He Leadeth Me
145–St. 2	I Am Thine, O Lord
222	Living for Jesus
226	Lord, Dismiss Us
229	Lord, Speak to Me
246	My Tribute
319–St. 4	Savior, Like a Shepherd Lead Us
345	Take My Life and Let It Be
390	To God Be the Glory

JAMES 1:2–3

| 159 | I Need Thee Every Hour |
| 177 | In the Hour of Trial |

JAMES 1:4

| 273–St. 3 | O Master, Let Me Walk with Thee |

JAMES 1:5

| 104 | God of Grace and God of Glory |

JAMES 1:6

| 197 | Jesus Savior, Pilot Me |

349–St. 3	Teach Me Thy Way, O Lord
391	Trusting Jesus

JAMES 1:12

33–St. 4	At the Name of Jesus
159–St. 2	I Need Thee Every Hour
199	Jesus, Still Lead On
242	Must Jesus Bear the Cross Alone?
245–St. 4	My Jesus, I Love Thee
322–St. 4	Send the Light!
337	Stand Up, Stand Up for Jesus
338	Standing on the Promises
349–St. 4	Teach Me Thy Way, O Lord
359–St. 2	The Great Physician

JAMES 1:13–14

158	I Must Tell Jesus
228	Lord Jesus, Think on Me
268–St. 2	O Jesus, I Have Promised

JAMES 1:17

67	Come, Thou Fount
74	Count Your Blessings
89	For the Beauty of the Earth
114	Great Is Thy Faithfulness
170	Immortal, Invisible
206	Joyful, Joyful, We Adore Thee
218	Let Us with a Gladsome Mind
253	Now Thank We All Our God
400	We Plow the Fields

JAMES 1:21–25

48–St. 3	Break Thou the Bread
107–St. 2	God the Almighty One
133	Holy Bible, Book Divine
273–St. 3	O Master, Let Me Walk with Thee
321–St. 3	Savior, Thy Dying Love
430	Wonderful Words of Life

JAMES 1:27

1	A Charge to Keep I Have
78	Dear Lord and Father of Mankind
230–St. 4	Love Divine, All Loves Excelling

JAMES 2:5

2	A Child of the King
129–St. 3	Heaven Came Down
187–St. 1	Jesus, I My Cross Have Taken
338	Standing on the Promises

JAMES 2:10

235–St. 3	"Man of Sorrows," What a Name

JAMES 2:14–26

233	Make Me a Blessing
330	So Send I You
345	Take My Life and Let It Be
418	When We Walk with the Lord

JAMES 2:23

358	The God of Abraham Praise

JAMES 3:13–17

104	God of Grace and God of Glory

JAMES 3:18

297	Peace, Perfect Peace

JAMES 4:4

177–St. 2	In the Hour of Trial

JAMES 4:6

21	Amazing Grace
57–St. 3	Christ Is the World's
378–St. 2	There Is Power in the Blood
428	Wonderful Grace of Jesus

JAMES 4:7

42	Blessed Assurance
122	Have Thine Own Way, Lord
163	I Surrender All
180–St. 2	It Is Well with My Soul
187	Jesus, I My Cross Have Taken
345	Take My Life and Let It Be

JAMES 4:8–10

27	Are You Washed in the Blood?
58	Christ Receiveth Sinful Men
61	Close to Thee
145	I Am Thine, O Lord
165–St. 4	I Will Sing the Wondrous Story
182	I've Found a Friend
228	Lord Jesus, Think on Me
247	Near to the Heart of God
248	Nearer, My God, to Thee
249	Nearer, Still Nearer
262	O For a Heart to Praise My God
368	The Savior Is Waiting

JAMES 4:15

49	Breathe on Me, Breath of God
90–St. 2	Forth in Thy Name, O Lord
122	Have Thine Own Way, Lord
319–St. 4	Savior, Like a Shepherd Lead Us
418	When We Walk with the Lord

421–St. 2	Wherever He Leads, I'll Go

JAMES 5:7–9

124–St. 5	He Keeps Me Singing
126–St. 2	He Lives
181	It May Be at Morn
189	Jesus Is Coming Again
220	Lift Up Your Heads
223	Lo, He Comes with Clouds
410	What If It Were Today?

JAMES 5:7–11

273–St. 4	O Master, Let Me Walk with Thee

JAMES 5:10–11

20–St. 4	Am I a Soldier of the Cross?
222–St. 3	Living for Jesus

JAMES 5:13

42	Blessed Assurance
62	Come, Christians, Join to Sing
67–St. 1	Come, Thou Fount
263	O For a Thousand Tongues to Sing
326–St. 1	Since I Have Been Redeemed
414	When in Our Music

JAMES 5:13–16

46	Blest Be the Tie
158	I Must Tell Jesus
167–St. 3	If Thou But Suffer God to Guide
305	Prayer Is the Soul's Sincere
391–St. 3	Trusting Jesus
407	What a Friend We Have in Jesus

1 PETER 1:2

23	And Can It Be That I Should Gain?
49	Breathe on Me, Breath of God
251	Nothing But the Blood
353–St. 2	The Church's One Foundation
378	There Is Power in the Blood
396	We Are God's People

1 PETER 1:3

59–St. 4	Christ the Lord Is Risen Today
71	Come, Ye Faithful, Raise
126	He Lives
277	O Sons and Daughters
355	The Day of Resurrection

1 PETER 1:3–5

88	For All the Saints
152	I Know That My Redeemer Lives

153	I Know That My Redeemer Liveth
246	My Tribute
279	O That Will Be Glory For Me
286	On Jordan's Stormy Banks I Stand
311	Revive Us Again
390	To God Be the Glory
417	When We All Get to Heaven

1 PETER 1:3–9

30	Ask Ye What Great Thing I Know
129	Heaven Came Down
138	Hope of the World
164	I Will Sing of My Redeemer
244–St. 4	My Faith Looks Up to Thee
273–St. 4	O Master, Let Me Walk with Thee
369	The Solid Rock

1 PETER 1:5

53–St. 4	Children of the Heavenly Father
154	I Know Whom I Have Believed
238	Moment by Moment
319–St. 2	Savior, Like a Shepherd Lead Us

1 PETER 1:7

177	In the Hour of Trial
222–St. 3	Living for Jesus

1 PETER 1:7–9

42	Blessed Assurance
307–St. 2	Redeemed, How I Love to Proclaim
308	Rejoice, the Lord Is King
340	Sunshine in My Soul

1 PETER 1:8–9

157–St. 1	I Love to Tell the Story
200	Jesus, the Very Thought of Thee
201	Jesus, Thou Joy of Loving Hearts
240	More Love to Thee, O Christ
245	My Jesus, I Love Thee
266	O Happy Day that Fixed My Choice
267	O, How I Love Jesus

1 PETER 1:13

21	Amazing Grace
138	Hope of the World
153–St. 3	I Know That My Redeemer Liveth
369	The Solid Rock
410	What If It Were Today?
428	Wonderful Grace of Jesus

1 PETER 1:14

320–St. 2	Savior, Teach Me Day by Day

1 PETER 1:15–16

134	Holy God, We Praise Thy Name
137	Holy, Holy, Holy
347	Take Time to Be Holy

1 PETER 1:17

170–St. 2	Immortal, Invisible

1 PETER 1:18–19

27	Are You Washed in the Blood?
45	Blessed Redeemer
80	Down at the Cross
112	Grace Greater Than Our Sin
117–St. 2	Hail, Thou Once Despised Jesus
155–St. 1	I Lay My Sins on Jesus
164	I Will Sing of My Redeemer
202	Jesus, Thy Blood and Righteousness
208	Just As I Am, Without One Plea
235	"Man of Sorrows," What a Name
243	My Faith Has Found
244	My Faith Looks Up to Thee
251	Nothing But the Blood
266	O Happy Day that Fixed My Choice
267–St. 2	O, How I Love Jesus
290–St. 2	Only Trust Him
298–St. 2	Praise Him! Praise Him!
307	Redeemed, How I Love to Proclaim
311–St. 3	Revive Us Again
314	Rock of Ages
326	Since I Have Been Redeemed
359	The Great Physician
376	There Is a Fountain
378	There Is Power in the Blood
394	Victory in Jesus
408	What a Wonderful Savior

1 PETER 1:21

63	Come, Holy Ghost
138	Hope of the World
369	The Solid Rock

1 PETER 1:22

320	Savior, Teach Me Day by Day
334	Spirit of God, Descend

1 PETER 1:23

431	Ye Must Be Born Again

1 PETER 1:23–25

3–St. 2	A Mighty Fortress Is Our God
31–St. 2	At Calvary

48	Break Thou the Bread
141–St. 1	How Firm a Foundation
282	O Word of God Incarnate
361	The Heavens Declare Thy Glory
430	Wonderful Words of Life

1 PETER 2:2

48	Break Thou the Bread
133	Holy Bible, Book Divine
239	More About Jesus
282	O Word of God Incarnate
347–St. 1	Take Time to Be Holy
430	Wonderful Words of Life

1 PETER 2:3

42	Blessed Assurance
159–St. 1	I Need Thee Every Hour
218	Let Us with a Gladsome Mind
412	When All Thy Mercies, O My God

1 PETER 2:4–7

44	Blessed Jesus, at Thy Word
52	Built on the Rock
56	Christ Is Made the Sure
83	Fairest Lord Jesus
141	How Firm a Foundation
143	How Sweet the Name
201	Jesus, Thou Joy of Loving Hearts
258	O Could I Speak the Matchless
298–St. 2	Praise Him! Praise Him!
307	Redeemed, How I Love to Proclaim
321	Savior, Thy Dying Love
353	The Church's One Foundation
396	We Are God's People

1 PETER 2:9–10

12–St. 2	All Hail the Power of Jesus' Name
55	Christ for the World We Sing
62	Come, Christians, Join to Sing
92	From All That Dwell Below
134–St. 3	Holy God, We Praise Thy Name
151–St. 3	I Heard the Voice of Jesus Say
222–St. 2	Living for Jesus
229	Lord, Speak to Me
252	Now I Belong to Jesus
327	Since Jesus Came Into My Heart
328	Sing Praise to God Who Reigns
336–St. 1	Stand Up and Bless the Lord
353–St. 2	The Church's One Foundation
364	The Light of the World Is Jesus
396	We Are God's People

1 PETER 2:11

115–St. 1	Guide Me, O Thou Great Jehovah
128	He Who Would Valiant Be
177–St. 2	In the Hour of Trial
187	Jesus, I My Cross Have Taken
288	Once to Every Man and Nation

1 PETER 2:12

233	Make Me a Blessing

1 PETER 2:17

46	Blest Be the Tie
172	In Christ There Is No East
206–St. 3, 4	Joyful, Joyful, We Adore Thee
313	Rise Up, O Men of God
320	Savior, Teach Me Day by Day
334	Spirit of God, Descend

1 PETER 2:21

26	"Are Ye Able," Said the Master
38	Be Thou My Vision
87	Footsteps of Jesus
99	Go to Dark Gethsemane
148	I Have Decided to Follow Jesus
171–Last St.	Immortal Love, Forever Full
185	Jesus Calls Us
188–St. 3	Jesus Is All the World to Me
222	Living for Jesus
229	Lord, Speak to Me
268	O Jesus, I Have Promised
273	O Master, Let Me Walk with Thee
281	O to Be Like Thee!
321–St. 3	Savior, Thy Dying Love

1 PETER 2:21–25

147	I Gave My Life for Thee
155	I Lay My Sins on Jesus
187	Jesus, I My Cross Have Taken
289	One Day
348	"Take Up Thy Cross"
421	Wherever He Leads, I'll Go

1 PETER 2:22–25

195	Jesus Paid it All

1 PETER 2:24–25

30	Ask Ye What Great Thing I Know
80	Down at the Cross
117	Hail, Thou Once Despised Jesus
155–St. 1	I Lay My Sins on Jesus
162–St. 4	I Stand Amazed in the Presence

164	I Will Sing of My Redeemer
165	I Will Sing the Wondrous Story
169	I'll Live for Him
174	In Loving Kindness Jesus Came
175	In the Cross of Christ I Glory
191	Jesus, Keep Me Near the Cross
195	Jesus Paid it All
235	"Man of Sorrows," What a Name
243	My Faith Has Found
266	O Happy Day that Fixed My Choice
267–St. 2	O, How I Love Jesus
275	O Sacred Head, Now Wounded
307	Redeemed, How I Love to Proclaim
314	Rock of Ages
324	Shepherd of Tender Youth
367	The Old Rugged Cross
377	There Is a Green Hill Far Away
392	Turn Your Eyes Upon Jesus
394	Victory in Jesus
408	What a Wonderful Savior
413	When I Survey the Wondrous Cross

1 PETER 2:25

67–St. 3	Come, Thou Fount
298	Praise Him! Praise Him!
319–St. 2	Savior, Like a Shepherd Lead Us
327–St. 2	Since Jesus Came Into My Heart
341	Surely Goodness and Mercy
362–St. 3	The King of Love My Shepherd Is
366	The Lord's My Shepherd

1 PETER 3:1

119	Happy the Home When God Is There

1 PETER 3:4

167–St. 2	If Thou But Suffer God to Guide
347	Take Time to Be Holy

1 PETER 3:7

119	Happy the Home When God Is There
274	O Perfect Love

1 PETER 3:8

46	Blest Be the Tie
166	I Would Be True
206–St. 3, 4	Joyful, Joyful, We Adore Thee
334	Spirit of God, Descend
419	Where Cross the Crowded Ways

1 PETER 3:8–12

288	Once to Every Man and Nation

1 PETER 3:12

56–St. 2	Christ Is Made the Sure
305	Prayer Is the Soul's Sincere
343	Sweet Hour of Prayer
407	What a Friend We Have in Jesus

1 PETER 3:14–15

96	Give to the Winds
124	He Keeps Me Singing

1 PETER 3:15

30	Ask Ye What Great Thing I Know
233	Make Me a Blessing
262	O For a Heart to Praise My God
284	O Zion, Haste
326–St. 3	Since I Have Been Redeemed
369	The Solid Rock
404	We've a Story to Tell

1 PETER 3:18

7	Ah, Holy Jesus
8	Alas! And Did My Savior Bleed?
45	Blessed Redeemer
65	Come, Holy Spirit
117	Hail, Thou Once Despised Jesus
147–St. 3	I Gave My Life for Thee
162–St. 4	I Stand Amazed in the Presence
195	Jesus Paid it All
266	O Happy Day that Fixed My Choice
275	O Sacred Head, Now Wounded
289–St. 2	One Day
298–St. 2	Praise Him! Praise Him!
307	Redeemed, How I Love to Proclaim
314	Rock of Ages
377	There Is a Green Hill Far Away
390	To God Be the Glory
408	What a Wonderful Savior

1 PETER 3:22

43–St. 2	Blessed Be the Name
75	Crown Him with Many Crowns
116	Hail the Day That Sees Him Rise
225	Look, Ye Saints!
232	Majestic Sweetness
289–St. 4	One Day
298–St. 3	Praise Him! Praise Him!
308–St. 2	Rejoice, the Lord Is King
425–St. 5	Who Is He in Yonder Stall?
432–St. 3	Ye Servants of God

1 PETER 4:2–3

177–St. 2	In the Hour of Trial
261	O For a Closer Walk with God

1 PETER 4:7

305	Prayer Is the Soul's Sincere

1 PETER 4:8

320	Savior, Teach Me Day by Day
334	Spirit of God, Descend

1 PETER 4:10–11

1	A Charge to Keep I Have
55	Christ for the World We Sing
147–St. 4	I Gave My Life for Thee
229	Lord, Speak to Me
268	O Jesus, I Have Promised
292–St. 3	Open My Eyes
298	Praise Him! Praise Him!
321	Savior, Thy Dying Love
330	So Send I You
398	We Give Thee but Thine Own
418	When We Walk with the Lord

1 PETER 4:12–13

70	Come, Ye Disconsolate
124–St. 4	He Keeps Me Singing
141–St. 4	How Firm a Foundation
177	In the Hour of Trial
180	It Is Well with My Soul
222–St. 3	Living for Jesus
238	Moment by Moment
407	What a Friend We Have in Jesus

1 PETER 4:13

74–St. 2	Count Your Blessings
82	Face to Face
145–St. 4	I Am Thine, O Lord
181–St. 4	It May Be at Morn
211–St. 4	Lead Me to Calvary
235	"Man of Sorrows," What a Name
272	O Love, That Will Not Let Me Go
298	Praise Him! Praise Him!
410	What If It Were Today?
417–St. 3	When We All Get to Heaven

1 PETER 4:19

124–St. 4	He Keeps Me Singing
141–St. 2, 3	How Firm a Foundation
180	It Is Well with My Soul
238	Moment by Moment

365	The Lily of the Valley

1 PETER 5:4

33–St. 5	At the Name of Jesus
124–St. 5	He Keeps Me Singing
212–St. 3	Lead On, O King Eternal
223	Lo, He Comes with Clouds
245–St. 4	My Jesus, I Love Thee
279	O That Will Be Glory For Me
298	Praise Him! Praise Him!
349–St. 4	Teach Me Thy Way, O Lord
359–St. 2	The Great Physician
410	What If It Were Today?

1 PETER 5:5–6

113	Great God, We Sing That Mighty Hand
115–St. 1	Guide Me, O Thou Great Jehovah
141–St. 2	How Firm a Foundation
166–St. 2	I Would Be True
262	O For a Heart to Praise My God

1 PETER 5:6–7

74–St. 2	Count Your Blessings
76	Day by Day
86–St. 3	Fight the Good Fight
96	Give to the Winds
109	God Will Take Care of You
146	I Am Trusting Thee, Lord Jesus
155–St. 2	I Lay My Sins on Jesus
158	I Must Tell Jesus
165–St. 4	I Will Sing the Wondrous Story
167	If Thou But Suffer God to Guide
177	In the Hour of Trial
209	Just When I Need Him
238	Moment by Moment
267–St. 4	O, How I Love Jesus
283–St. 3	O Worship the King
343	Sweet Hour of Prayer
362	The King of Love My Shepherd Is
366	The Lord's My Shepherd
407	What a Friend We Have in Jesus

1 PETER 5:8–11

3	A Mighty Fortress Is Our God
20	Am I a Soldier of the Cross?
104–St. 2	God of Grace and God of Glory
132–St. 3	Higher Ground
212	Lead On, O King Eternal
222–St. 3	Living for Jesus
291	Onward, Christian Soldiers
332	Soldiers of Christ, Arise

337	Stand Up, Stand Up for Jesus
370	The Son of God Goes Forth to War

1 PETER 5:10–11

53	Children of the Heavenly Father
96	Give to the Winds
185	Jesus Calls Us
298	Praise Him! Praise Him!
328	Sing Praise to God Who Reigns
390	To God Be the Glory

1 PETER 5:14

226	Lord, Dismiss Us

2 PETER 1:2

226	Lord, Dismiss Us
429	Wonderful Peace

2 PETER 1:3–4

3	A Mighty Fortress Is Our God
16	All That Thrills My Soul
122	Have Thine Own Way, Lord
153–St. 2	I Know That My Redeemer Liveth
201	Jesus, Thou Joy of Loving Hearts
222–St. 2	Living for Jesus
294	Out of My Bondage
338	Standing on the Promises
347	Take Time to Be Holy
389–St. 1	'Tis So Sweet To Trust in Jesus

2 PETER 1:5

239	More About Jesus

2 PETER 1:6

273–St. 3	O Master, Let Me Walk with Thee

2 PETER 1:7

206–St. 3	Joyful, Joyful, We Adore Thee
320	Savior, Teach Me Day by Day
334	Spirit of God, Descend

2 PETER 1:9

21	Amazing Grace
27	Are You Washed in the Blood?

2 PETER 1:10

1	A Charge to Keep I Have
12–St. 2	All Hail the Power of Jesus' Name

2 PETER 1:11

127	He the Pearly Gates Will Open
129–St. 3	Heaven Came Down

279	O That Will Be Glory For Me
286	On Jordan's Stormy Banks I Stand
308	Rejoice, the Lord Is King
352	Ten Thousand Times Ten Thousand

2 PETER 1:16–17

83	Fairest Lord Jesus
198	Jesus Shall Reign
223	Lo, He Comes with Clouds
232	Majestic Sweetness
308	Rejoice, the Lord Is King
432	Ye Servants of God

2 PETER 1:19

57–St. 1	Christ Is the World's
60	Christ Whose Glory Fills
103	God Moves in a Mysterious Way
130	Heavenly Sunlight
151–St. 3	I Heard the Voice of Jesus Say
206–St. 4	Joyful, Joyful, We Adore Thee
395	Watchman, Tell Us of the Night

2 PETER 1:20–21

48	Break Thou the Bread
133	Holy Bible, Book Divine
282	O Word of God Incarnate
288	Once to Every Man and Nation

2 PETER 2:9

159–St. 2	I Need Thee Every Hour
177	In the Hour of Trial
230–St. 3	Love Divine, All Loves Excelling
343–St. 1	Sweet Hour of Prayer
383–St. 3	This Is My Father's World

2 PETER 2:20–21

222	Living for Jesus

2 PETER 3:3–14

181	It May Be at Morn
223	Lo, He Comes with Clouds
308	Rejoice, the Lord Is King
363	The King Shall Come When Morning
410	What If It Were Today?

2 PETER 3:4

33–St. 5	At the Name of Jesus
189	Jesus Is Coming Again

2 PETER 3:8

265–St. 4	O God, Our Help in Ages Past

2 PETER 3:9

284–St. 1	O Zion, Haste
296	Pass Me Not, O Gentle Savior
310	Rescue the Perishing
315	Room at the Cross for You
338	Standing on the Promises
381	There's a Wideness

2 PETER 3:11

222	Living for Jesus
347	Take Time to Be Holy

2 PETER 3:13–14

127	He the Pearly Gates Will Open
183	Jerusalem, My Happy Home
184	Jerusalem, the Golden
230–St. 4	Love Divine, All Loves Excelling
374	The Way of the Cross Leads Home
417	When We All Get to Heaven

2 PETER 3:17

132	Higher Ground

2 PETER 3:18

21	Amazing Grace
124	He Keeps Me Singing
239	More About Jesus
258	O Could I Speak the Matchless
298	Praise Him! Praise Him!
350	Tell Me the Old, Old Story
390	To God Be the Glory

1 JOHN 1:1

292	Open My Eyes

1 JOHN 1:2

385–St. 3	Thou Art the Way: to Thee Alone

1 JOHN 1:3–4

46	Blest Be the Tie
201	Jesus, Thou Joy of Loving Hearts
213	Leaning on the Everlasting Arms

1 JOHN 1:5–7

44–St. 3	Blessed Jesus, at Thy Word
151–St. 3	I Heard the Voice of Jesus Say
170–St. 2	Immortal, Invisible
206	Joyful, Joyful, We Adore Thee
272–St. 2	O Love, That Will Not Let Me Go
278	O Splendor of God's Glory
284–St. 1	O Zion, Haste
340	Sunshine in My Soul

364   The Light of the World Is Jesus
387   Thou Whose Almighty Word

1 JOHN 1:5–9

129   Heaven Came Down
261   O For a Closer Walk with God

1 JOHN 1:7

46   Blest Be the Tie
130   Heavenly Sunlight
202   Jesus, Thy Blood and Righteousness
263–St. 3 O For a Thousand Tongues to Sing
267   O, How I Love Jesus
307   Redeemed, How I Love to Proclaim
327   Since Jesus Came Into My Heart
376   There Is a Fountain
389–St. 2 'Tis So Sweet To Trust in Jesus

1 JOHN 1:7–9

8   Alas! And Did My Savior Bleed?
27   Are You Washed in the Blood?
31   At Calvary
32   At the Cross
58   Christ Receiveth Sinful Men
80   Down at the Cross
112   Grace Greater Than Our Sin
155–St. 1 I Lay My Sins on Jesus
192–St. 3 Jesus, Lover of My Soul
208   Just As I Am, Without One Plea
251   Nothing But the Blood
290   Only Trust Him
359–St. 2 The Great Physician
378   There Is Power in the Blood
381   There's a Wideness
408   What a Wonderful Savior
418   When We Walk with the Lord
424   Whiter Than Snow

1 JOHN 1:9

70   Come, Ye Disconsolate
72   Come, Ye Sinners, Poor and Needy
78   Dear Lord and Father of Mankind
114–St. 3 Great Is Thy Faithfulness
216   Let Jesus Come Into Your Heart
266   O Happy Day that Fixed My Choice
311   Revive Us Again
319–St. 3 Savior, Like a Shepherd Lead Us
331   Softly and Tenderly
365–St. 1 The Lily of the Valley
394–St. 2 Victory in Jesus

1 JOHN 2:1–2

16   All That Thrills My Soul
27   Are You Washed in the Blood?
43–St. 3   Blessed Be the Name
58   Christ Receiveth Sinful Men
117   Hail, Thou Once Despised Jesus
155   I Lay My Sins on Jesus
162   I Stand Amazed in the Presence
164   I Will Sing of My Redeemer
202   Jesus, Thy Blood and Righteousness
244   My Faith Looks Up to Thee
252   Now I Belong to Jesus
369   The Solid Rock
385   Thou Art the Way: to Thee Alone
392–St. 2 Turn Your Eyes Upon Jesus
394   Victory in Jesus
408   What a Wonderful Savior
424   Whiter Than Snow

1 JOHN 2:3–6

163   I Surrender All
261   O For a Closer Walk with God
273   O Master, Let Me Walk with Thee
289–St. 1 One Day
418   When We Walk with the Lord

1 JOHN 2:8

57   Christ Is the World's
60   Christ Whose Glory Fills
130   Heavenly Sunlight
151–St. 3 I Heard the Voice of Jesus Say
201–St. 5 Jesus, Thou Joy of Loving Hearts
206   Joyful, Joyful, We Adore Thee
272–St. 2 O Love, That Will Not Let Me Go
278   O Splendor of God's Glory
311–St. 2 Revive Us Again
340   Sunshine in My Soul
364   The Light of the World Is Jesus
404   We've a Story to Tell

1 JOHN 2:10

136   Holy Spirit, Truth Divine
320   Savior, Teach Me Day by Day
334   Spirit of God, Descend

1 JOHN 2:11

21–St. 1   Amazing Grace

1 JOHN 2:12

112   Grace Greater Than Our Sin
162   I Stand Amazed in the Presence

1 JOHN 3:9

2	A Child of the King
431	Ye Must Be Born Again

1 JOHN 3:11–18

46	Blest Be the Tie
50–Last st.	Brethren, We Have Met
65	Come, Holy Spirit
206–St. 3	Joyful, Joyful, We Adore Thee
230	Love Divine, All Loves Excelling
240	More Love to Thee, O Christ
320	Savior, Teach Me Day by Day
334	Spirit of God, Descend
419	Where Cross the Crowded Ways

1 JOHN 3:16

23	And Can It Be That I Should Gain?
45	Blessed Redeemer
75–St. 3	Crown Him with Many Crowns
142–St. 3	How Great Thou Art
147	I Gave My Life for Thee
169	I'll Live for Him
171	Immortal Love, Forever Full
174	In Loving Kindness Jesus Came
182	I've Found a Friend
194	Jesus Loves Me
200–St. 4	Jesus, the Very Thought of Thee
203	Jesus, Thy Boundless Love to Me
222	Living for Jesus
230	Love Divine, All Loves Excelling
267	O, How I Love Jesus
320	Savior, Teach Me Day by Day
321	Savior, Thy Dying Love
348	"Take Up Thy Cross"
351–St. 3	Tell Me the Story of Jesus
411	What Wondrous Love Is This?

1 JOHN 3:19–21

216	Let Jesus Come Into Your Heart
262	O For a Heart to Praise My God

1 JOHN 3:22

319–St. 4	Savior, Like a Shepherd Lead Us

1 JOHN 3:23

143	How Sweet the Name
154	I Know Whom I Have Believed
290	Only Trust Him
320	Savior, Teach Me Day by Day

1 JOHN 3:23–24

65	Come, Holy Spirit
334	Spirit of God, Descend

1 JOHN 3:24

5	Abide with Me
49	Breathe on Me, Breath of God
63	Come, Holy Ghost
135	Holy Spirit, Light Divine
136	Holy Spirit, Truth Divine
163	I Surrender All
333	Spirit Divine, Attend Our Prayer
335	Spirit of the Living God

1 JOHN 4:4

38	Be Thou My Vision
332	Soldiers of Christ, Arise
391	Trusting Jesus

1 JOHN 4:7

431	Ye Must Be Born Again

1 JOHN 4:7–21

65	Come, Holy Spirit
108–St. 4	God Who Touchest Earth
136–St. 2	Holy Spirit, Truth Divine
230	Love Divine, All Loves Excelling
240	More Love to Thee, O Christ
295	Pass It On
320	Savior, Teach Me Day by Day
334	Spirit of God, Descend

1 JOHN 4:8–10

23	And Can It Be That I Should Gain?
169	I'll Live for Him
222	Living for Jesus
267	O, How I Love Jesus
280	O the Deep, Deep Love of Jesus
285	Of the Father's Love Begotten

1 JOHN 4:9–10

157	I Love to Tell the Story
162	I Stand Amazed in the Presence
164	I Will Sing of My Redeemer
165	I Will Sing the Wondrous Story
231	Love Lifted Me
284–St. 3	O Zion, Haste
298	Praise Him! Praise Him!
307	Redeemed, How I Love to Proclaim
408	What a Wonderful Savior

1 JOHN 4:10

31	At Calvary
271	O Love How Deep, How Broad
320	Savior, Teach Me Day by Day
404–St. 3	We've a Story to Tell

1 JOHN 4:11

295	Pass It On

1 JOHN 4:12

137–St. 3	Holy, Holy, Holy

1 JOHN 4:13

38	Be Thou My Vision
42	Blessed Assurance
49	Breathe on Me, Breath of God
66–St. 3	Come, Thou Almighty King
126	He Lives
135	Holy Spirit, Light Divine
136	Holy Spirit, Truth Divine
140	Hover O'er Me, Holy Spirit
144	I Am His and He Is Mine
145	I Am Thine, O Lord
204	Jesus, What a Friend for Sinners
206–St. 3	Joyful, Joyful, We Adore Thee
238	Moment by Moment
252	Now I Belong to Jesus
333	Spirit Divine, Attend Our Prayer
334	Spirit of God, Descend
335	Spirit of the Living God
347	Take Time to Be Holy

1 JOHN 4:14

43	Blessed Be the Name
123	He Hideth My Soul
164	I Will Sing of My Redeemer
235	"Man of Sorrows," What a Name
326	Since I Have Been Redeemed
390	To God Be the Glory
408	What a Wonderful Savior

1 JOHN 4:15

75–St. 2	Crown Him with Many Crowns
83–St. 1	Fairest Lord Jesus

1 JOHN 4:16

230	Love Divine, All Loves Excelling
271	O Love How Deep, How Broad
280	O the Deep, Deep Love of Jesus
284–St. 3	O Zion, Haste

1 JOHN 4:18

96	Give to the Winds
326–St. 3	Since I Have Been Redeemed

1 JOHN 4:19

8	Alas! And Did My Savior Bleed?
23	And Can It Be That I Should Gain?
32	At the Cross
182	I've Found a Friend
203	Jesus, Thy Boundless Love to Me
204	Jesus, What a Friend for Sinners
240	More Love to Thee, O Christ
244–St. 2	My Faith Looks Up to Thee
245	My Jesus, I Love Thee
252	Now I Belong to Jesus
267	O, How I Love Jesus
272–St. 1	O Love, That Will Not Let Me Go
280	O the Deep, Deep Love of Jesus
319–St. 4	Savior, Like a Shepherd Lead Us
320	Savior, Teach Me Day by Day
321	Savior, Thy Dying Love
350	Tell Me the Old, Old Story
377	There Is a Green Hill Far Away
396–St. 2	We Are God's People
411	What Wondrous Love Is This?

1 JOHN 4:20–21

46	Blest Be the Tie
172	In Christ There Is No East
206–St. 3	Joyful, Joyful, We Adore Thee
419	Where Cross the Crowded Ways

1 JOHN 5:1

172	In Christ There Is No East
290	Only Trust Him
427	Whosoever Will
431	Ye Must Be Born Again

1 JOHN 5:3

1	A Charge to Keep I Have
418	When We Walk with the Lord

1 JOHN 5:4–5

42	Blessed Assurance
55	Christ for the World We Sing
84	Faith Is the Victory
128	He Who Would Valiant Be
180	It Is Well with My Soul
291	Onward, Christian Soldiers
332	Soldiers of Christ, Arise
337	Stand Up, Stand Up for Jesus

JUDE 21

173	In Heavenly Love Abiding
191	Jesus, Keep Me Near the Cross
199	Jesus, Still Lead On
381	There's a Wideness

JUDE 22–23

310	Rescue the Perishing

JUDE 24

53–St. 4	Children of the Heavenly Father
91–St. 3	Free From the Law
146	I Am Trusting Thee, Lord Jesus
154	I Know Whom I Have Believed
304	Praise to the Lord, the Almighty
319–St. 2	Savior, Like a Shepherd Lead Us

JUDE 24–25

11	All Glory, Laud and Honor
170	Immortal, Invisible
206	Joyful, Joyful, We Adore Thee
230	Love Divine, All Loves Excelling
232	Majestic Sweetness
235	"Man of Sorrows," What a Name
258	O Could I Speak the Matchless
298	Praise Him! Praise Him!
308	Rejoice, the Lord Is King
328	Sing Praise to God Who Reigns
432	Ye Servants of God

REVELATION 1:3

282	O Word of God Incarnate
430	Wonderful Words of Life

REVELATION 1:5–6

27	Are You Washed in the Blood?
31	At Calvary
42	Blessed Assurance
43	Blessed Be the Name
66	Come, Thou Almighty King
75	Crown Him with Many Crowns
80	Down at the Cross
117	Hail, Thou Once Despised Jesus
162	I Stand Amazed in the Presence
174	In Loving Kindness Jesus Came
195	Jesus Paid it All
225	Look, Ye Saints!
246	My Tribute
251	Nothing But the Blood
258	O Could I Speak the Matchless
266	O Happy Day that Fixed My Choice

267–St. 2	O, How I Love Jesus
298	Praise Him! Praise Him!
308	Rejoice, the Lord Is King
311	Revive Us Again
376	There Is a Fountain
389–St. 2	'Tis So Sweet To Trust in Jesus
390	To God Be the Glory
392–St. 2	Turn Your Eyes Upon Jesus
408	What a Wonderful Savior
411	What Wondrous Love Is This?

REVELATION 1:7–8

33–St. 5	At the Name of Jesus
189	Jesus Is Coming Again
223	Lo, He Comes with Clouds
289–St. 5	One Day
298–St. 3	Praise Him! Praise Him!
410	What If It Were Today?

REVELATION 1:8

114	Great Is Thy Faithfulness
170	Immortal, Invisible
230–St. 2	Love Divine, All Loves Excelling
285	Of the Father's Love Begotten
299	Praise, My Soul, the King
358	The God of Abraham Praise

REVELATION 1:13–16

60	Christ Whose Glory Fills
83–St. 2	Fairest Lord Jesus

REVELATION 1:17–18

39	Because He Lives
75–St. 6	Crown Him with Many Crowns
115–St. 3	Guide Me, O Thou Great Jehovah
126	He Lives
127	He the Pearly Gates Will Open
141–St. 2	How Firm a Foundation
152	I Know That My Redeemer Lives
153	I Know That My Redeemer Liveth
164–St. 3	I Will Sing of My Redeemer
232	Majestic Sweetness
285	Of the Father's Love Begotten
308–St. 3	Rejoice, the Lord Is King
405	Welcome, Happy Morning
417	When We All Get to Heaven

REVELATION 2:2–3

86–St. 4	Fight the Good Fight
273	O Master, Let Me Walk with Thee

REVELATION 2:4

67–St. 3	Come, Thou Fount

REVELATION 2:7

279	O That Will Be Glory For Me
286	On Jordan's Stormy Banks I Stand
292–St. 2	Open My Eyes
342	Sweet By and By

REVELATION 2:8

39	Because He Lives
126	He Lives
152	I Know That My Redeemer Lives
153	I Know That My Redeemer Liveth
382	Thine Is the Glory

REVELATION 2:10

85	Faith of Our Fathers
86	Fight the Good Fight
166	I Would Be True
212–St. 3	Lead On, O King Eternal
242	Must Jesus Bear the Cross Alone
322–St. 4	Send the Light
337	Stand Up, Stand Up for Jesus
349–St. 4	Teach Me Thy Way, O Lord
359–St. 2	The Great Physician

REVELATION 2:10–11

75–St. 6	Crown Him with Many Crowns

REVELATION 2:11

292–St. 2	Open My Eyes

REVELATION 2:17

50	Brethren, We Have Met to Worship
292–St. 2	Open My Eyes
365–St. 3	The Lily of the Valley

REVELATION 2:19

273	O Master, Let Me Walk with Thee

REVELATION 2:23

122–St. 2	Have Thine Own Way, Lord
262	O For a Heart to Praise My God

REVELATION 2:28

191–St. 2	Jesus, Keep Me Near the Cross
206–St. 4	Joyful, Joyful, We Adore Thee
365–Refrain	The Lily of the Valley

REVELATION 2:29

292–St. 2	Open My Eyes

REVELATION 3:3

181	It May Be at Morn
189	Jesus Is Coming Again

REVELATION 3:5

123–St. 4	He Hideth My Soul
184–St. 3	Jerusalem, the Golden

REVELATION 3:6

292–St. 2	Open My Eyes

REVELATION 3:7–8

257–St. 4	O Come, O Come, Emmanuel
308–St. 3	Rejoice, the Lord Is King

REVELATION 3:8

250	No, Not One
269	O Jesus, Thou Art Standing
385	Thou Art the Way: to Thee Alone

REVELATION 3:10

154	I Know Whom I Have Believed
159–St. 2	I Need Thee Every Hour
177	In the Hour of Trial
180–St. 2	It Is Well with My Soul

REVELATION 3:11

242–St. 3	Must Jesus Bear the Cross Alone

REVELATION 3:12

43	Blessed Be the Name
183	Jerusalem, My Happy Home
184	Jerusalem, the Golden

REVELATION 3:13

292–St. 2	Open My Eyes

REVELATION 3:17

3–St. 2	A Mighty Fortress Is Our God

REVELATION 3:19

397–St. 1	We Gather Together

REVELATION 3:20

149	I Hear Thy Welcome Voice
151	I Heard the Voice of Jesus Say
185	Jesus Calls Us
190	Jesus Is Tenderly Calling
208	Just As I Am, Without One Plea
216	Let Jesus Come Into Your Heart
269	O Jesus, Thou Art Standing
294	Out of My Bondage

310	Rescue the Perishing
315	Room at the Cross for You
331	Softly and Tenderly
359	The Great Physician
368	The Savior Is Waiting
427	Whosoever Will

REVELATION 3:21

20–St. 4	Am I a Soldier of the Cross?
30	Ask Ye What Great Thing I Know
337–St. 4	Stand Up, Stand Up for Jesus
432–St. 3	Ye Servants of God

REVELATION 3:22

292–St. 2	Open My Eyes

REVELATION 4:5

107–St. 1	God the Almighty One

REVELATION 4:6

165–Refrain	I Will Sing the Wondrous Story
394–St. 3	Victory in Jesus

REVELATION 4:8–11

12	All Hail the Power of Jesus' Name
77–Refrain	Day Is Dying in the West
134	Holy God, We Praise Thy Name
137	Holy, Holy, Holy
165	I Will Sing the Wondrous Story
260–St. 4	O Day of Rest and Gladness
358	The God of Abraham Praise
415	When Morning Gilds the Skies
432	Ye Servants of God

REVELATION 4:10

230–St. 4	Love Divine, All Loves Excelling

REVELATION 4:11

9	All Creatures of Our God
19	All Things Bright and Beautiful
75	Crown Him with Many Crowns
160	I Sing the Almighty Power of God
301	Praise the Lord! Ye Heavens
304	Praise to the Lord, the Almighty
383	This Is My Father's World

REVELATION 5:8

305	Prayer Is the Soul's Sincere

REVELATION 5:9

27	Are You Washed in the Blood?
55–St. 4	Christ for the World We Sing

164	I Will Sing of My Redeemer
235–St. 5	"Man of Sorrows," What a Name
307	Redeemed, How I Love to Proclaim
326	Since I Have Been Redeemed
408	What a Wonderful Savior

REVELATION 5:9–14

16–St. 5	All That Thrills My Soul
43	Blessed Be the Name
62	Come, Christians, Join to Sing
117–St. 4	Hail, Thou Once Despised Jesus
198	Jesus Shall Reign
219	Lift High the Cross
258	O Could I Speak the Matchless
298	Praise Him! Praise Him!
311	Revive Us Again
390	To God Be the Glory
394–St. 3	Victory in Jesus
432–St. 3, 4	Ye Servants of God

REVELATION 5:11–14

12	All Hail the Power of Jesus Name
21–Last st.	Amazing Grace
75	Crown Him with Many Crowns
83	Fairest Lord Jesus
134–St. 2	Holy God, We Praise Thy Name
137	Holy, Holy, Holy
170–St. 4	Immortal, Invisible
183	Jerusalem, My Happy Home
225	Look, Ye Saints!
232	Majestic Sweetness
283	O Worship the King
285	Of the Father's Love Begotten
301	Praise the Lord! Ye Heavens
352	Ten Thousand Times Ten Thousand
358	The God of Abraham Praise
415	When Morning Gilds the Skies

REVELATION 6:9–11

85	Faith of Our Fathers
88	For All the Saints
134–St. 3	Holy God, We Praise Thy Name
370	The Son of God Goes Forth to War

REVELATION 6:14

180–St. 4	It Is Well with My Soul

REVELATION 7:9–17

55–St. 4	Christ for the World We Sing
75	Crown Him with Many Crowns
88	For All the Saints
115–St. 3	Guide Me, O Thou Great Jehovah

117–St. 4	Hail, Thou Once Despised Jesus
183	Jerusalem, My Happy Home
184	Jerusalem, the Golden
352	Ten Thousand Times Ten Thousand
370	The Son of God Goes Forth to War
411	What Wondrous Love Is This?
417	When We All Get to Heaven
432	Ye Servants of God

REVELATION 7:10–12

12	All Hail the Power of Jesus' Name
21–Last st.	Amazing Grace
62	Come, Christians, Join to Sing
134–St. 2	Holy God, We Praise Thy Name
137–St. 2	Holy, Holy, Holy
170–St. 4	Immortal, Invisible
225	Look, Ye Saints!
253	Now Thank We All Our God
285–St. 4	Of the Father's Love Begotten
298	Praise Him! Praise Him!
301	Praise the Lord! Ye Heavens
394–St. 3	Victory in Jesus

REVELATION 7:14–15

27	Are You Washed in the Blood?
80	Down at the Cross
112	Grace Greater Than Our Sin
195–St. 4	Jesus Paid it All
202	Jesus, Thy Blood and Righteousness
230–St. 3	Love Divine, All Loves Excelling
251	Nothing But the Blood
307	Redeemed, How I Love to Proclaim
378	There Is Power in the Blood
389–St. 2	'Tis So Sweet To Trust in Jesus
408	What a Wonderful Savior
424	Whiter Than Snow

REVELATION 7:16–17

17	All the Way My Savior Leads Me
37–St. 3	Be Still, My Soul
69	Come, We That Love the Lord
70	Come, Ye Disconsolate
82	Face to Face
87–St. 4	Footsteps of Jesus
97–St. 2	Glorious Things of Thee
125	He Leadeth Me
151–St. 2	I Heard the Voice of Jesus Say
181–St. 4	It May Be at Morn
192	Jesus, Lover of My Soul
199	Jesus, Still Lead On
201	Jesus, Thou Joy of Loving Hearts

286	On Jordan's Stormy Banks I Stand
316	Satisfied
341	Surely Goodness and Mercy
362	The King of Love My Shepherd Is
366	The Lord's My Shepherd

REVELATION 8:3

| 305 | Prayer Is the Soul's Sincere |

REVELATION 10:6

| 160 | I Sing the Almighty Power of God |

REVELATION 10:11

| 404 | We've a Story to Tell |

REVELATION 11:15–17

12	All Hail the Power of Jesus' Name
43	Blessed Be the Name
57–St. 3	Christ Is the World's
75	Crown Him with Many Crowns
137	Holy, Holy, Holy
142	How Great Thou Art
170	Immortal, Invisible
198	Jesus Shall Reign
205	Joy to the World
225	Look, Ye Saints!
253	Now Thank We All Our God
298–St. 3	Praise Him! Praise Him!
299	Praise, My Soul, the King
308	Rejoice, the Lord Is King
358	The God of Abraham Praise
432–St. 3	Ye Servants of God

REVELATION 12:10–11

20	Am I a Soldier of the Cross?
27	Are You Washed in the Blood
80	Down at the Cross
251	Nothing But the Blood
337–St. 4	Stand Up, Stand Up for Jesus
370	The Son of God Goes Forth to War
376	There Is a Fountain
378	There Is Power in the Blood
383–St. 3	This Is My Father's World

REVELATION 13:8

117–St. 2	Hail, Thou Once Despised Jesus
311–St. 3	Revive Us Again
359–St. 3	The Great Physician

REVELATION 13:9

| 292 | Open My Eyes |

REVELATION 13:10

273–St. 3	O Master, Let Me Walk with Thee

REVELATION 14:1–4

12–St. 4	All Hail the Power of Jesus' Name
62	Come, Christians, Join to Sing
69	Come, We That Love the Lord
107–St. 1	God the Almighty One
117–St. 2	Hail, Thou Once Despised Jesus
134–St. 2	Holy God, We Praise Thy Name
142–St. 1	How Great Thou Art
235–St. 5	"Man of Sorrows," What a Name
358	The God of Abraham Praise
417	When We All Get to Heaven
432	Ye Servants of God

REVELATION 14:6

55	Christ for the World We Sing
284	O Zion, Haste
310	Rescue the Perishing
399	We Have Heard the Joyful Sound
404	We've a Story to Tell

REVELATION 14:7

9	All Creatures of Our God
14	All People That On Earth
89	For the Beauty of the Earth
160	I Sing the Almighty Power of God
328	Sing Praise to God Who Reigns

REVELATION 14:12–13

5	Abide with Me
17–St. 3	All the Way My Savior Leads Me
28	Are You (Art Thou) Weary?
58–St. 2	Christ Receiveth Sinful Men
88	For All the Saints
145	I Am Thine, O Lord
166	I Would Be True
183	Jerusalem, My Happy Home
199	Jesus, Still Lead On
242	Must Jesus Bear the Cross Alone?
260–St. 4	O Day of Rest and Gladness
268	O Jesus, I Have Promised
273–St. 3	O Master, Let Me Walk with Thee
279	O That Will Be Glory For Me
286	On Jordan's Stormy Banks I Stand
417	When We All Get to Heaven

REVELATION 14:13–15

73	Come, Ye Thankful People, Come
121	Hark, the Voice of Jesus Calling

REVELATION 15:2–4

14	All People That On Earth
134	Holy God, We Praise Thy Name
137	Holy, Holy, Holy
165–Refrain	I Will Sing the Wondrous Story
394–St. 3	Victory in Jesus

REVELATION 15:3–4

62	Come, Christians, Join to Sing
66	Come, Thou Almighty King
92	From All That Dwell Below
235–St. 5	"Man of Sorrows," What a Name
299	Praise, My Soul, the King
411-Last St.	What Wondrous Love Is This?
432	Ye Servants of God

REVELATION 16:7

170–St. 2	Immortal, Invisible

REVELATION 16:15

410	What If It Were Today?

REVELATION 16:18

78–St. 5	Dear Lord and Father of Mankind
107–St. 1	God the Almighty One

REVELATION 17:14

12	All Hail the Power of Jesus' Name
20	Am I a Soldier of the Cross?
66	Come, Thou Almighty King
75	Crown Him with Many Crowns
212	Lead On, O King Eternal
225	Look, Ye Saints!
283	O Worship the King
291	Onward, Christian Soldiers
360	The Head That Once Was Crowned
370	The Son of God Goes Forth to War
425–St. 4	Who Is He in Yonder Stall?
426	Who Is on the Lord's Side?

REVELATION 19:1–10

75–St. 1	Crown Him with Many Crowns
298	Praise Him! Praise Him!
308	Rejoice, the Lord Is King
372	The Strife Is O'er
432	Ye Servants of God

REVELATION 19:5–7

62	Come, Christians, Join to Sing
66	Come, Thou Almighty King
107–St. 1	God the Almighty One

283	O Worship the King		75–St. 6	Crown Him with Many Crowns
301	Praise the Lord! Ye Heavens		82	Face to Face
304	Praise to the Lord, the Almighty		97	Glorious Things of Thee
328	Sing Praise to God Who Reigns		181–St. 4	It May Be at Morn
352–St. 2	Ten Thousand Times Ten Thousand		183	Jerusalem, My Happy Home

REVELATION 19:7

410–St. 1	What If It Were Today?

REVELATION 19:12

75	Crown Him with Many Crowns

REVELATION 19:13

33	At the Name of Jesus
66–St. 2	Come, Thou Almighty King
243–St. 3	My Faith Has Found

REVELATION 19:15

237	Mine Eyes Have Seen the Glory

REVELATION 19:16

12	All Hail the Power of Jesus' Name
198	Jesus Shall Reign
225	Look, Ye Saints!
298–St. 3	Praise Him! Praise Him!

REVELATION 20:4–6

88	For All the Saints
134–St. 2	Holy God, We Praise Thy Name
370	The Son of God Goes Forth to War

REVELATION 20:6

124–St. 5	He Keeps Me Singing

REVELATION 20:10

3–St. 3	A Mighty Fortress Is Our God
383–St. 3	This Is My Father's World

REVELATION 20:14

308–St. 3	Rejoice, the Lord Is King
405	Welcome, Happy Morning

REVELATION 21:1–27

156–St. 5	I Love Thy Kingdom, Lord
183	Jerusalem, My Happy Home
184	Jerusalem, the Golden
352	Ten Thousand Times Ten Thousand

REVELATION 21:2–4

37–St. 3	Be Still, My Soul
69	Come, We That Love the Lord
70	Come, Ye Disconsolate

184	Jerusalem, the Golden
230–St. 1	Love Divine, All Loves Excelling
286	On Jordan's Stormy Banks I Stand
353	The Church's One Foundation
410–St. 2	What If It Were Today?
417	When We All Get to Heaven
419–St. 5	Where Cross the Crowded Ways

REVELATION 21:6

151–St. 2	I Heard the Voice of Jesus Say
191–St. 1	Jesus, Keep Me Near the Cross
201	Jesus, Thou Joy of Loving Hearts
230–St. 2	Love Divine, All Loves Excelling
285	Of the Father's Love Begotten
316	Satisfied
376	There Is a Fountain

REVELATION 21:7

332	Soldiers of Christ, Arise

REVELATION 21:9

353	The Church's One Foundation
410–St. 1	What If It Were Today?

REVELATION 21:10

69	Come, We That Love the Lord
183	Jerusalem, My Happy Home
184	Jerusalem, the Golden

REVELATION 21:18

391–St. 4	Trusting Jesus

REVELATION 21:21

127	He the Pearly Gates Will Open
394–St. 3	Victory in Jesus
417–St. 4	When We All Get to Heaven

REVELATION 21:23–25

60	Christ Whose Glory Fills
83–St. 3	Fairest Lord Jesus
130	Heavenly Sunlight
151–St. 3	I Heard the Voice of Jesus Say
278	O Splendor of God's Glory
311–St. 2	Revive Us Again
340	Sunshine in My Soul
364	The Light of the World Is Jesus

REVELATION 21:27

286   On Jordan's Stormy Banks I Stand

REVELATION 22:1–5

16–St. 5	All That Thrills My Soul
67	Come, Thou Fount
70–St. 3	Come, Ye Disconsolate
75	Crown Him with Many Crowns
82	Face to Face
97–St. 2	Glorious Things of Thee
115–St. 2	Guide Me, O Thou Great Jehovah
151–St. 2, 3	I Heard the Voice of Jesus
162–St. 5	I Stand Amazed in the Presence
165–Refrain	I Will Sing the Wondrous Story
183	Jerusalem, My Happy Home
191	Jesus, Keep Me Near the Cross
200–St. 1	Jesus, the Very Thought of Thee
223–Last st.	Lo, He Comes with Clouds
225	Look, Ye Saints!
242	Must Jesus Bear the Cross Alone
258–St. 3	O Could I Speak the Matchless
279	O That Will Be Glory For Me
286	On Jordan's Stormy Banks I Stand
323	Shall We Gather at the River
342	Sweet By and By
346	Take the Name of Jesus with You
352	Ten Thousand Times Ten Thousand
358	The God of Abraham Praise
359	The Great Physician
364	The Light of the World Is Jesus
365–St. 3	The Lily of the Valley
394–St. 3	Victory in Jesus
432	Ye Servants of God

REVELATION 22:12

35	Awake, My Soul, Stretch
242–St. 3	Must Jesus Bear the Cross Alone?
410	What If It Were Today?

REVELATION 22:13

230–St. 2	Love Divine, All Loves Excelling
285	Of the Father's Love Begotten
358	The God of Abraham Praise

REVELATION 22:14

127   He the Pearly Gates Will Open

327–St. 3, 4	Since Jesus Came Into
417–St. 4	When We All Get to Heaven

REVELATION 22:16

51	Brightest and Best
83	Fairest Lord Jesus
191–St. 2	Jesus, Keep Me Near the Cross
365	The Lily of the Valley

REVELATION 22:17

72	Come, Ye Sinners, Poor and Needy
97–St. 2	Glorious Things of Thee
149	I Hear Thy Welcome Voice
151–St. 2	I Heard the Voice of Jesus Say
190	Jesus Is Tenderly Calling
208	Just As I Am, Without One Plea
216	Let Jesus Come Into Your Heart
269	O Jesus, Thou Art Standing
294	Out of My Bondage
296	Pass Me Not, O Gentle Savior
307	Redeemed, How I Love to Proclaim
309	Rejoice, Ye Pure in Heart
315	Room at the Cross for You
316	Satisfied
331	Softly and Tenderly
368	The Savior Is Waiting
392	Turn Your Eyes Upon Jesus
427	Whosoever Will

REVELATION 22:20

33–St. 5	At the Name of Jesus
68	Come, Thou Long-Expected Jesus
142–St. 4	How Great Thou Art
153	I Know That My Redeemer Liveth
181	It May Be at Morn
189	Jesus Is Coming Again
223	Lo, He Comes with Clouds
289–St. 5	One Day
363	The King Shall Come When Morning
410	What If It Were Today?

REVELATION 22:21

100	God Be with You
226	Lord, Dismiss Us
236	May the Grace of Christ

Part
THREE

Topical Index

BRIDE OF CHRIST, CHURCH

396	We Are God's People

BROTHERHOOD

46	Blest Be the Tie That Binds
57	Christ Is the World's True Light
172	In Christ There Is No East or West
206–St. 4	Joyful, Joyful, We Adore Thee
313	Rise Up, O Men of God

BURDENS

28	Art Thou Weary, Art Thou Languid?
74	Count Your Blessings
96	Give to the Winds
158	I Must Tell Jesus
207	Just a Closer Walk with Thee
209	Just When I Need Him
228	Lord Jesus, Think on Me
238	Moment by Moment
428	Wonderful Grace of Jesus

CALL OF CHRIST

28	Art Thou Weary, Art Thou Languid
58	Christ Receiveth Sinful Men
72	Come, Ye Sinners, Poor and Needy
149	I Hear Thy Welcome Voice
151	I Heard the Voice of Jesus Say
185	Jesus Calls Us
190	Jesus Is Tenderly Calling
216	Let Jesus Come Into Your Heart
222	Living for Jesus
269	O Jesus, Thou Art Standing
294	Out of My Bondage, Sorrow and Night
315	Room at the Cross for You
331	Softly and Tenderly
368	The Savior Is Waiting
392	Turn Your Eyes Upon Jesus
420	Where He Leads Me

CALL OF GOD

35	Awake, My Soul, Stretch Every Nerve
168	I'll Go Where You Want Me To Go

CALL TO MINISTRY

1	A Charge to Keep I Have
121	Hark, the Voice of Jesus Calling
330	So Send I You

CALLING

1	A Charge to Keep I Have

CALMNESS

37	Be Still, My Soul
93	From Every Stormy Wind that Blows
347	Take Time to Be Holy

CALVARY

31	At Calvary
99	Go to Dark Gethsemane
211	Lead Me to Calvary

CARE, DIVINE

37	Be Still, My Soul
53	Children of the Heavenly Father
74	Count Your Blessings
100	God Be with You
103	God Moves in a Mysterious Way
109	God Will Take Care of You
115	Guide Me, O Thou Great Jehovah
123	He Hideth My Soul
173	In Heavenly Love Abiding
238	Moment by Moment
283	O Worship the King
319	Savior, Like a Shepherd Lead Us
359	The Great Physician
362	The King of Love My Shepherd Is
366	The Lord's My Shepherd
393	Under His Wings

CARES

96	Give to the Winds
158	I Must Tell Jesus
343	Sweet Hour of Prayer

CERTAINTY OF GOD

114	Great Is Thy Faithfulness

CHALLENGE

35	Awake, My Soul, Stretch Every Nerve
212	Lead On, O King Eternal
288	Once to Every Man and Nation
370	The Son of God Goes Forth to War
426	Who Is on the Lord's Side?

CHERUBIM

137	Holy, Holy, Holy

CHILDHOOD OF JESUS

287	Once in Royal David's City

CHILDREN OF GOD

2	A Child of the King
36	Away in a Manger

COME TO JESUS   See Invitation

COMFORT

5	Abide with Me
17	All the Way My Savior Leads Me
53	Children of the Heavenly Father
70	Come, Ye Disconsolate
96	Give to the Winds
158	I Must Tell Jesus
173	In Heavenly Love Abiding
180	It Is Well with My Soul
199	Jesus, Still Lead On
204	Jesus, What a Friend for Sinners
207	Just a Closer Walk with Thee
209	Just When I Need Him
210	Lead, Kindly Light
213	Leaning on the Everlasting Arms
247	Near to the Heart of God
318	Savior, Again to Thy Dear Name
362	The King of Love My Shepherd Is
365	The Lily of the Valley
366	The Lord's My Shepherd
375	There Is a Balm in Gilead
393	Under His Wings
407	What a Friend We Have in Jesus
412	When All Thy Mercies, O My God
429	Wonderful Peace

COMFORTER, HOLY SPIRIT

354	The Comforter Has Come

COMMITMENT

1	A Charge to Keep I Have
10	All for Jesus
20	Am I a Soldier of the Cross?
26	"Are Ye Able," Said the Master
41	Beneath the Cross of Jesus
61	Close to Thee
87	Footsteps of Jesus
121	Hark, the Voice of Jesus Calling
122	Have Thine Own Way, Lord
132	Higher Ground
145	I Am Thine, O Lord
147	I Gave My Life for Thee
148	I Have Decided to Follow Jesus
154	I Know Whom I Have Believed
163	I Surrender All
168	I'll Go Where You Want Me To Go
169	I'll Live for Him
185	Jesus Calls Us
187	Jesus, I My Cross Have Taken

203	Jesus, Thy Boundless Love to Me
204	Jesus, What a Friend for Sinners
208	Just As I Am, Without One Plea
222	Living for Jesus
229	Lord, Speak to Me
234	Make Me a Captive, Lord
252	Now I Belong to Jesus
268	O Jesus, I Have Promised
288	Once to Every Man and Nation
294	Out of My Bondage, Sorrow and Night
313	Rise Up, O Men of God
321	Savior, Thy Dying Love
345	Take My Life and Let It Be
418	When We Walk with the Lord
421	Wherever He Leads, I'll Go
426	Who Is on the Lord's Side?

COMMUNION

6	According to Thy Gracious Word
47	Bread of the World in Mercy Broken
131	Here, O My Lord, I See Thee
217	Let Us Break Bread Together

COMMUNION WITH GOD

5	Abide with Me
77	Day Is Dying in the West
78	Dear Lord and Father of Mankind
125	He Leadeth Me
145	I Am Thine, O Lord
247	Near to the Heart of God
248	Nearer, My God, to Thee
249	Nearer, Still Nearer

COMMUNION WITH NATURE

77	Day Is Dying in the West

COMPASSION

281	O to Be Like Thee!

COMPASSION OF GOD

230	Love Divine, All Loves Excelling

COMPASSION OF JESUS

155	I Lay My Sins on Jesus
359	The Great Physician

CONDEMNATION, NO

91	Free From the Law

CONFESSION OF SIN

7	Ah, Holy Jesus
41	Beneath the Cross of Jesus

417	When We All Get to Heaven

ETERNAL PRAISE

92	From All That Dwell Below the Skies
336	Stand Up and Bless the Lord
415–St. 4	When Morning Gilds the Skies
432	Ye Servants of God

ETERNAL REIGN OF JESUS

116	Hail the Day That Sees Him Rise

EUCHARIST

6	According to Thy Gracious Word
47	Bread of the World in Mercy Broken
131	Here, O My Lord, I See Thee
217	Let Us Break Bread Together

EVANGELISM

55	Christ for the World We Sing
121	Hark, the Voice of Jesus Calling
157	I Love to Tell the Story
284	O Zion, Haste
295	Pass It On
310	Rescue the Perishing
320	Savior, Teach Me Day by Day
322	Send the Light
373	The Vision of a Dying World
399	We Have Heard the Joyful Sound
404	We've a Story to Tell to the Nations

EVENING

5	Abide with Me
15	All Praise to Thee, My God, This Night
77	Day Is Dying in the West
106	God, That Madest Earth and Heaven
254	Now the Day Is Over
318	Savior, Again to Thy Dear Name
339	Sun of My Soul, Thou Savior Dear
356	The Day Thou Gavest

EVIL, FACING

288	Once to Every Man and Nation
383–St. 3	This Is My Father's World

EXALTATION OF JESUS
See Jesus, Exaltation

EXAMPLE OF JESUS

38	Be Thou My Vision
155	I Lay My Sins on Jesus
229	Lord, Speak to Me
262	O For a Heart to Praise My God

287	Once in Royal David's City
320	Savior, Teach Me Day by Day
334	Spirit of God, Descend Upon My Heart

EXAMPLE, CHRISTIAN

233	Make Me a Blessing

FACE OF CHRIST

82	Face to Face

FAITH

4	A Shelter in the Time of Storm
17	All the Way My Savior Leads Me
30	Ask Ye What Great Thing I Know
37	Be Still, My Soul
42	Blessed Assurance
76	Day by Day
78	Dear Lord and Father of Mankind
84	Faith Is the Victory
85	Faith of Our Fathers
141	How Firm a Foundation
146	I Am Trusting Thee, Lord Jesus
151	I Heard the Voice of Jesus Say
154	I Know Whom I Have Believed
159	I Need Thee Every Hour
173	In Heavenly Love Abiding
180	It Is Well with My Soul
238	Moment by Moment
243	My Faith Has Found a Resting Place
244	My Faith Looks Up to Thee
265	O God, Our Help in Ages Past
290	Only Trust Him
297	Peace, Perfect Peace
319	Savior, Like a Shepherd Lead Us
338	Standing on the Promises
369	The Solid Rock
389	'Tis So Sweet To Trust in Jesus
391	Trusting Jesus
393	Under His Wings
418	When We Walk with the Lord

FAITH IN JESUS   See Trust in Jesus

FAITHFULNESS

1	A Charge to Keep I Have
90	Forth in Thy Name, O Lord
166	I Would Be True

FAITHFULNESS OF GOD
See God, Faithfulness of

FOURTH OF JULY

22	America the Beautiful

FREEDOM FROM SIN

23	And Can It Be That I Should Gain?
91	Free From the Law
263	O For a Thousand Tongues to Sing
294	Out of My Bondage, Sorrow and Night
428	Wonderful Grace of Jesus

FRIEND, JESUS   See Jesus, Friend

FUNERAL   See Death

FUTURE

113	Great God, We Sing Thy Mighty Hand

FUTURE LIFE

115	Guide Me, O Thou Great Jehovah
286	On Jordan's Stormy Banks I Stand
342	Sweet By and By
417	When We All Get to Heaven

GATES OF HEAVEN

417	When We All Get to Heaven

GETHSEMANE

99	Go to Dark Gethsemane
162	I Stand Amazed in the Presence
211	Lead Me to Calvary
388	'Tis Midnight and on Olive's Brow

GIFTS

18	All Things Are Thine
89	For the Beauty of the Earth
400	We Plow the Fields

GLORY GIVEN TO GOD

1	A Charge to Keep I Have
170	Immortal, Invisible
237	Mine Eyes Have Seen the Glory
246	My Tribute
390	To God Be the Glory

GLORIFIED CHRIST See Jesus, Glorified

GOD, ALMIGHTY

107	God the Almighty One
170	Immortal, Invisible
304	Praise to the Lord, the Almighty
336	Stand Up and Bless the Lord

GOD, CALL OF   See Call of God

GOD, CONSTANCY OF

114	Great Is Thy Faithfulness
218	Let Us with a Gladsome Mind

GOD, CREATOR

9	All Creatures of Our God and King
14	All People That On Earth Do Dwell
19	All Things Bright and Beautiful
40	Begin, My Tongue, Some
92	From All That Dwell Below the Skies
142	How Great Thou Art
160	I Sing the Almighty Power of God
301	Praise the Lord! Ye Heavens Adore Him
304	Praise to the Lord, the Almighty
328	Sing Praise to God Who Reigns Above
371	The Spacious Firmament
383	This Is My Father's World

GOD, DEFENDER

102	God Is My Strong Salvation
283	O Worship the King
304	Praise to the Lord, the Almighty
397	We Gather Together

GOD, DELIVERER

109	God Will Take Care of You
115	Guide Me, O Thou Great Jehovah
167	If Thou But Suffer God to Guide Thee

GOD, DEPENDENCE ON
                           See Dependence on God

GOD, ETERNAL

66	Come, Thou Almighty King
265	O God, Our Help in Ages Past
299	Praise, My Soul, the King of Heaven
358	The God of Abraham Praise

GOD, FAITHFULNESS OF

37	Be Still, My Soul
114	Great Is Thy Faithfulness
141	How Firm a Foundation
218	Let Us with a Gladsome Mind
299	Praise, My Soul, the King of Heaven

GOD, FATHER

53	Children of the Heavenly Father
66	Come, Thou Almighty King
358	The God of Abraham Praise
383	This Is My Father's World

JESUS, CRUCIFIXION

8	Alas! And Did My Savior Bleed?
30	Ask Ye What Great Thing I Know
31	At Calvary
32	At the Cross
45	Blessed Redeemer
377	There Is a Green Hill Far Away
406	Were You There?

JESUS, DAYSPRING/DAYSTAR

60	Christ Whose Glory Fills the Sky

JESUS, DEATH OF

7	Ah, Holy Jesus
8	Alas! And Did My Savior Bleed?
23	And Can It Be That I Should Gain
30	Ask Ye What Great Things I Know
31	At Calvary
32	At the Cross
41	Beneath the Cross of Jesus
45	Blessed Redeemer
99	Go to Dark Gethsemane
117	Hail, Thou Once Despised Jesus
165	I Will Sing the Wondrous Story
195	Jesus Paid it All
211	Lead Me to Calvary
235	"Man of Sorrows," What a Name
275	O Sacred Head, Now Wounded
289	One Day
351	Tell Me the Story of Jesus
367	The Old Rugged Cross
377	There Is a Green Hill Far Away
406	Were You There?
413	When I Survey the Wondrous Cross

JESUS, ENTHRONED

232	Majestic Sweetness Sits Enthroned

JESUS, ETERNAL

39	Because He Lives
75	Crown Him with Many Crowns
111	Good Christian Men, Rejoice and Sing
126	He Lives
152	I Know That My Redeemer Lives
153	I Know That My Redeemer Liveth
225	Look, Ye Saints! The Sight Is Glorious
285	Of the Father's Love Begotten
308	Rejoice, the Lord Is King
382	Thine Is the Glory

JESUS, EXALTATION   See Jesus, Reign

JESUS, EXAMPLE OF

38	Be Thou My Vision
155	I Lay My Sins on Jesus
229	Lord, Speak to Me
281	O to Be Like Thee!
287	Once in Royal David's City
320	Savior, Teach Me Day by Day

JESUS, FAITH IN   See Trust in Jesus

JESUS, FOUNDATION

56	Christ Is Made the Sure Foundation
141	How Firm a Foundation

JESUS, FRIEND

62	Come, Christians, Join to Sing
129	Heaven Came Down
182	I've Found a Friend
188	Jesus Is All the World to Me
204	Jesus, What a Friend for Sinners
250	No, Not One
258	O Could I Speak the Matchless Worth
365	The Lily of the Valley
407	What a Friend We Have in Jesus

JESUS, GLORIFIED

12	All Hail the Power of Jesus' Name
33	At the Name of Jesus
60	Christ Whose Glory Fills the Sky
75	Crown Him with Many Crowns
223	Lo, He Comes with Clouds Descending

JESUS, GUIDE

17	All the Way My Savior Leads Me
28	Art Thou Weary, Art Thou Languid
86	Fight the Good Fight
108	God Who Touchest Earth with Beauty
146	I Am Trusting Thee, Lord Jesus
228	Lord Jesus, Think on Me
324	Shepherd of Tender (Eager) Youth
341	Surely Goodness and Mercy
391	Trusting Jesus

JESUS, HELPER

158	I Must Tell Jesus
209	Just When I Need Him

LOVE

65	Come, Holy Spirit, Heavenly Dove
240	More Love to Thee, O Christ
295	Pass it On
320	Savior, Teach Me Day by Day
334	Spirit of God, Descend Upon My Heart

LOVE FOR JESUS

83	Fairest Lord Jesus
240	More Love to Thee, O Christ
245	My Jesus, I Love Thee
258	O Could I Speak the Matchless Worth
267	O, How I Love Jesus
320	Savior, Teach Me Day by Day
359	The Great Physician
377	There Is a Green Hill Far Away

LOVE OF GOD   See God, Love of

LOVE OF JESUS   See Jesus, Love of

LOVE, PERFECT

203	Jesus, Thy Boundless Love to Me

LOYALTY

148	I Have Decided to Follow Jesus
166	I Would Be True
291	Onward, Christian Soldiers

MACEDONIAN CALL

322	Send the Light!

MAJESTY OF GOD
See God, Majesty and Power of

MANNA

50	Brethren, We Have Met to Worship

MANSION IN HEAVEN

394	Victory in Jesus
152–St.4	I Know That My Redeemer Lives

MARCHING

291	Onward, Christian Soldiers

MARRIAGE

274	O Perfect Love

MARTYRS

85	Faith of Our Fathers
134	Holy God, We Praise Thy Name
370	The Son of God Goes Forth to War

MASTER   See Jesus, Master

MATURITY, SPIRITUAL

230	Love Divine, All Loves Excelling
234	Make Me a Captive, Lord
347	Take Time to Be Holy
349	Teach Me Thy Way, O Lord

MAUNDY THURSDAY

388	'Tis Midnight and on Olive's Brow

MERCY

16	All That Thrills My Soul Is Jesus
21	Amazing Grace
31	At Calvary
58	Christ Receiveth Sinful Men
290	Only Trust Him
331	Softly and Tenderly
428	Wonderful Grace of Jesus

MERCY SEAT

70	Come, Ye Disconsolate
93	From Every Stormy Wind that Blows

MESSIAH

68	Come, Thou Long-Expected Jesus
118	Hail to the Lord's Anointed

MINISTRY

1	A Charge to Keep I Have

MINISTRY OF JESUS   See Jesus, Life of

MISSIONS

1	A Charge to Keep I Have
55	Christ for the World We Sing
57	Christ Is the World's True Light
121	Hark, the Voice of Jesus Calling
138	Hope of the World
157	I Love to Tell the Story
168	I'll Go Where You Want Me To Go
198	Jesus Shall Reign
229	Lord, Speak to Me
284	O Zion, Haste
295	Pass It On
310	Rescue the Perishing
320	Savior, Teach Me Day by Day
322	Send the Light!
330	So Send I You
373	The Vision of a Dying World
399	We Have Heard the Joyful Sound
404	We've a Story to Tell to the Nations

366	The Lord's My Shepherd
400	We Plow the Fields

PURIFICATION
See Sins Cleansed and Forgiven

PURITY

78	Dear Lord and Father of Mankind
108	God Who Touchest Earth with Beauty
216	Let Jesus Come Into Your Heart
262	O For a Heart to Praise My God
347	Take Time to Be Holy
424	Whiter Than Snow

QUIETNESS

78	Dear Lord and Father of Mankind
167–St. 2	If Thou But Suffer God to Guide

RACE RELATIONS

57	Christ Is the World's True Light

RACE, RUN

35	Awake, My Soul, Stretch Every Nerve
86	Fight the Good Fight

RECONCILIATION

117	Hail, Thou Once Despised Jesus
172	In Christ There Is No East or West
408	What a Wonderful Savior

REDEMPTION

31	At Calvary
42	Blessed Assurance
43	Blessed Be the Name
67	Come, Thou Fount of Every Blessing
123	He Hideth My Soul
164	I Will Sing of My Redeemer
165	I Will Sing the Wondrous Story
174	In Loving Kindness Jesus Came
208	Just As I Am, Without One Plea
246	My Tribute
252	Now I Belong to Jesus
258	O Could I Speak the Matchless Worth
266	O Happy Day That Fixed My Choice
307	Redeemed, How I Love to Proclaim It
317	Saved! Saved! Saved!
326	Since I Have Been Redeemed
331	Softly and Tenderly
377	There Is a Green Hill Far Away
390	To God Be the Glory
401	We Praise Thee, O God, Our Redeemer
408	What a Wonderful Savior

REFUGE, DIVINE

3	A Mighty Fortress Is Our God
4	A Shelter in the Time of Storm
53	Children of the Heavenly Father
192	Jesus, Lover of My Soul
197	Jesus Savior, Pilot Me
213	Leaning on the Everlasting Arms
265	O God, Our Help in Ages Past
393	Under His Wings

REGENERATION

431	Ye Must Be Born Again

REIGN OF JESUS   See Jesus, Reign of

REJOICING   See Joy

RELIANCE ON GOD
See Dependence on God

RENEWAL

108	God Who Touchest Earth with Beauty
145	I Am Thine, O Lord
255	O Breath of Life
261	O For a Closer Walk with God
262	O For a Heart to Praise My God
311	Revive Us Again
334	Spirit of God, Descend Upon My Heart
344	Sweet, Sweet Spirit
345	Take My Life and Let It Be
379	There Shall Be Showers of Blessing

REPENTANCE

72	Come, Ye Sinners, Poor and Needy
79	Depth of Mercy! Can There Be?
149	I Hear Thy Welcome Voice
155	I Lay My Sins on Jesus
200	Jesus, the Very Thought of Thee
227	Lord, I'm Coming Home
231	Love Lifted Me
261	O For a Closer Walk with God
262	O For a Heart to Praise My God
294	Out of My Bondage, Sorrow and Night
296	Pass Me Not, O Gentle Savior
331	Softly and Tenderly
394	Victory in Jesus
424	Whiter Than Snow
431	Ye Must Be Born Again

REST

15	All Praise to Thee, My God, This Night
28	Art Thou Weary, Art Thou Languid?

292	Open My Eyes

WALK, CHRISTIAN

1	A Charge to Keep I Have
61	Close to Thee
130	Heavenly Sunlight
176	In the Garden
207	Just a Closer Walk with Thee
261	O For a Closer Walk with God
273	O Master, Let Me Walk with Thee
418	When We Walk with the Lord

WANDERER

341	Surely Goodness and Mercy

WARFARE, SPIRITUAL

3	A Mighty Fortress Is Our God
20	Am I a Soldier of the Cross?
84	Faith Is the Victory
86	Fight the Good Fight
212	Lead On, O King Eternal
291	Onward, Christian Soldiers
332	Soldiers of Christ, Arise
337	Stand Up, Stand Up for Jesus
370	The Son of God Goes Forth to War
426	Who Is on the Lord's Side?

WATER OF LIFE

151	I Heard the Voice of Jesus Say
316	Satisfied

WAY TO GOD

86	Fight the Good Fight
349	Teach Me Thy Way, O Lord
374	The Way of the Cross Leads Home
385	Thou Art the Way: to Thee Alone
390	To God Be the Glory

WEAKNESS

207	Just a Closer Walk with Thee
306	Precious Lord, Take My Hand

WEALTH, SPIRITUAL

74–St. 3	Count Your Blessings
316	Satisfied

WEDDING

274	O Perfect Love

WELL OF WATER

316	Satisfied

WHEAT AND TARES

73	Come, Ye Thankful People, Come

WILL OF GOD   See God, Will of

WISDOM

38–St. 2	Be Thou My Vision
104	God of Grace and God of Glory

WISE MEN

29	As with Gladness Men of Old
51	Brightest and Best
357	The First Noel
402	We Three Kings

WITNESSING

157	I Love to Tell the Story
229	Lord, Speak to Me
233	Make Me a Blessing
273	O Master, Let Me Walk with Thee
284	O Zion, Haste
292	Open My Eyes
295	Pass It On
310	Rescue the Perishing
326	Since I Have Been Redeemed
345	Take My Life and Let It Be
375	There Is a Balm in Gilead
399	We Have Heard the Joyful Sound
404	We've a Story to Tell to the Nations

WORD OF GOD

48	Break Thou the Bread of Life
133	Holy Bible, Book Divine
239	More About Jesus
282	O Word of God Incarnate
361	The Heavens Declare Thy Glory
430	Wonderful Words of Life

WORD OF JESUS

146–St. 3	I Am Trusting Thee, Lord Jesus
153–St. 2	I Know That My Redeemer Liveth
243	My Faith Has Found a Resting Place
290	Only Trust Him

WORDS OF LIFE

430	Wonderful Words of Life

WORK

1	A Charge to Keep I Have
415	When Morning Gilds the Skies

Part
FOUR

Index of Hymns

78 Dear Lord and Father of Mankind
79 Depth of Mercy! Can There Be?
80 Down at the Cross
81 Eternal Father, Strong to Save
82 Face to Face
83 Fairest Lord Jesus
84 Faith Is the Victory
85 Faith of Our Fathers
86 Fight the Good Fight
87 Footsteps of Jesus
88 For All the Saints
89 For the Beauty of the Earth
90 Forth in Thy Name, O Lord
91 Free From the Law
92 From All That Dwell Below the Skies
93 From Every Stormy Wind that Blows
94 From Heaven Above to Earth I Come
95 Gentle Mary Laid Her Child
96 Give to the Winds
97 Glorious Things of Thee Are Spoken
98 Go, Tell It on the Mountain
99 Go to Dark Gethsemane
100 God Be with You
101 God Himself Is with Us
102 God Is My Strong Salvation
103 God Moves in a Mysterious Way
104 God of Grace and God of Glory
105 God of Our Fathers
106 God, That Madest Earth and Heaven
107 God the Almighty One
108 God Who Touchest Earth with Beauty
109 God Will Take Care of You
110 Good Christian Men, Rejoice
111 Good Christian Men, Rejoice and Sing
112 Grace Greater Than Our Sin
113 Great God, We Sing That Mighty Hand
114 Great Is Thy Faithfulness
115 Guide Me, O Thou Great Jehovah
116 Hail the Day That Sees Him Rise
117 Hail, Thou Once Despised Jesus
118 Hail to the Lord's Anointed
119 Happy the Home When God Is There
120 Hark! The Herald Angels Sing
121 Hark, the Voice of Jesus Calling
122 Have Thine Own Way, Lord
123 He Hideth My Soul
124 He Keeps Me Singing
125 He Leadeth Me
126 He Lives
127 He the Pearly Gates Will Open
128 He Who Would Valiant Be

129 Heaven Came Down and Glory Filled
      My Soul
130 Heavenly Sunlight
131 Here, O My Lord, I See Thee
132 Higher Ground
133 Holy Bible, Book Divine
134 Holy God, We Praise Thy Name
135 Holy Spirit, Light Divine
136 Holy Spirit, Truth Divine
137 Holy, Holy, Holy
138 Hope of the World
139 Hosanna, Loud Hosanna
140 Hover O'er Me, Holy Spirit
141 How Firm a Foundation
142 How Great Thou Art
143 How Sweet the Name of Jesus Sounds
144 I Am His and He Is Mine
145 I Am Thine, O Lord
146 I Am Trusting Thee, Lord Jesus
147 I Gave My Life for Thee
148 I Have Decided to Follow Jesus
149 I Hear Thy Welcome Voice
150 I Heard the Bells on Christmas Day
151 I Heard the Voice of Jesus Say
152 I Know That My Redeemer Lives
153 I Know That My Redeemer Liveth
154 I Know Whom I Have Believed
155 I Lay My Sins on Jesus
156 I Love Thy Kingdom, Lord
157 I Love to Tell the Story
158 I Must Tell Jesus
159 I Need Thee Every Hour
160 I Sing the Almighty Power of God
161 I Sought the Lord
162 I Stand Amazed in the Presence
163 I Surrender All
164 I Will Sing of My Redeemer
165 I Will Sing the Wondrous Story
166 I Would Be True
167 If Thou But Suffer God to Guide Thee
168 I'll Go Where You Want Me To Go
169 I'll Live for Him
170 Immortal, Invisible
171 Immortal Love, Forever Full
172 In Christ There Is No East or West
173 In Heavenly Love Abiding
174 In Loving Kindness Jesus Came
175 In the Cross of Christ I Glory
176 In the Garden
177 In the Hour of Trial
178 Infant Holy, Infant Lowly

280 O the Deep, Deep Love of Jesus
281 O to Be Like Thee!
282 O Word of God Incarnate
283 O Worship the King
284 O Zion, Haste
285 Of the Father's Love Begotten
286 On Jordan's Stormy Banks I Stand
287 Once in Royal David's City
288 Once to Every Man and Nation
289 One Day
290 Only Trust Him
291 Onward, Christian Soldiers
292 Open My Eyes
293 Open Now Thy Gates of Beauty
294 Out of My Bondage, Sorrow and Night
295 Pass It On
296 Pass Me Not, O Gentle Savior
297 Peace, Perfect Peace
298 Praise Him! Praise Him!
299 Praise, My Soul, the King of Heaven
300 Praise the Lord Who Reigns Above
301 Praise the Lord! Ye Heavens Adore Him
302 Praise the Savior, Ye Who Know Him
303 Praise to God, Immortal Praise
304 Praise to the Lord, the Almighty
305 Prayer Is the Soul's Sincere Desire
306 Precious Lord, Take My Hand
307 Redeemed, How I Love to Proclaim It
308 Rejoice, the Lord Is King
309 Rejoice, Ye Pure in Heart
310 Rescue the Perishing
311 Revive Us Again
312 Ride On, Ride On in Majesty!
313 Rise Up, O Men of God
314 Rock of Ages
315 Room at the Cross for You
316 Satisfied
317 Saved! Saved! Saved!
318 Savior, Again to Thy Dear Name
319 Savior, Like A Shepherd Lead Us
320 Savior, Teach Me Day by Day
321 Savior, Thy Dying Love
322 Send the Light!
323 Shall We Gather at the River?
324 Shepherd of Tender (Eager) Youth
325 Silent Night! Holy Night
326 Since I Have Been Redeemed
327 Since Jesus Came Into My Heart
328 Sing Praise to God Who Reigns Above
329 Sing to the Lord of Harvest
330 So Send I You

331 Softly and Tenderly
332 Soldiers of Christ, Arise
333 Spirit Divine, Attend Our Prayer
334 Spirit of God, Descend Upon My Heart
335 Spirit of the Living God
336 Stand Up and Bless the Lord
337 Stand Up, Stand Up for Jesus
338 Standing on the Promises
339 Sun of My Soul, Thou Savior Dear
340 Sunshine in My Soul
341 Surely Goodness and Mercy
342 Sweet By and By
343 Sweet Hour of Prayer
344 Sweet, Sweet Spirit
345 Take My Life and Let It Be
346 Take the Name of Jesus with You
347 Take Time to Be Holy
348 "Take Up Thy Cross," the Savior Said
349 Teach Me Thy Way, O Lord
350 Tell Me the Old, Old Story
351 Tell Me the Story of Jesus
352 Ten Thousand Times Ten Thousand
353 The Church's One Foundation
354 The Comforter Has Come
355 The Day of Resurrection
356 The Day Thou Gavest
357 The First Noel
358 The God of Abraham Praise
359 The Great Physician
360 The Head That Once Was Crowned
361 The Heavens Declare Thy Glory
362 The King of Love My Shepherd Is
363 The King Shall Come When Morning
      Dawns
364 The Light of the World Is Jesus
365 The Lily of the Valley
366 The Lord's My Shepherd
367 The Old Rugged Cross
368 The Savior Is Waiting
369 The Solid Rock
370 The Son of God Goes Forth to War
371 The Spacious Firmament
372 The Strife Is O'er
373 The Vision of a Dying World
374 The Way of the Cross Leads Home
375 There Is a Balm in Gilead
376 There Is a Fountain
377 There Is a Green Hill Far Away
378 There Is Power in the Blood
379 There Shall Be Showers of Blessing
380 There's a Song in the Air

Number of References
by Books of the Bible

Genesis	109	Jeremiah	223	2 Corinthians	356
Exodus	141	Lamentations	42	Galatians	198
Leviticus	55	Ezekiel	111	Ephesians	442
Numbers	51	Daniel	68	Philippians	202
Deuteronomy	250	Hosea	41	Colossians	242
Joshua	39	Joel	15	1 Thessalonians	147
Judges	12	Amos	14	2 Thessalonians	42
Ruth	5	Obadiah	1	1 Timothy	146
1 Samuel	37	Jonah	14	2 Timothy	150
2 Samuel	53	Micah	51	Titus	103
1 Kings	34	Nahum	24	Philemon	8
2 Kings	28	Habakkuk	31	Hebrews	582
1 Chronicles	97	Zephaniah	24	James	101
2 Chronicles	66	Haggai	12	1 Peter	339
Ezra	22	Zechariah	88	2 Peter	80
Nehemiah	67	Malachi	61	1 John	357
Esther	1	Matthew	806	2 John	5
Job	109	Mark	375	3 John	6
Psalms	2,442	Luke	754	Jude	43
Proverbs	168	John	1,033	Revelation	492
Ecclesiastes	23	Acts	587		
Song of Songs	11	Romans	689	Old Testament	5,406
Isaiah	766	1 Corinthians	446	New Testament	8,731

Total	14,137